# Producers on Producing

# McFarland Classics

Anderson. *Science Fiction Films of the Seventies*
Archer. *Willis O'Brien*
Benson. *Vintage Science Fiction Films, 1896–1949*
Bernardoni. *The New Hollywood*
Broughton. *Producers on Producing*
Byrge & Miller. *The Screwball Comedy Films*
Chesher. *"The End": Closing Lines...*
Cline. *In the Nick of Time*
Cline. *Serials-ly Speaking*
Darby & Du Bois. *American Film Music*
Derry. *The Suspense Thriller*
Douglas. *The Early Days of Radio Broadcasting*
Drew. *D.W. Griffith's* Intolerance
Ellrod. *Hollywood Greats of the Golden Years*
Erickson. *Religious Radio and Television in the U.S., 1921–1991*
Erickson. *Syndicated Television*
Frasier. *Russ Meyer—The Life and Films*
Fury. *Kings of the Jungle*
Galbraith. *Motor City Marquees*
Harris. *Children's Live-Action Musical Films*
Harris. *Film and Television Composers*
Hayes. *The Republic Chapterplays*
Hayes. *3-D Movies*
Hayes. *Trick Cinematography*
Hill. *Raymond Burr*
Hogan. *Dark Romance*
Holland. *B Western Actors Encyclopedia*
Horner. *Bad at the Bijou*
Jarlett. *Robert Ryan*
Kinnard. *Horror in Silent Films*

Langman & Gold. *Comedy Quotes from the Movies*
Levine. *The 247 Best Movie Scenes in Film History*
McGee. *Beyond Ballyhoo*
McGee. *The Rock & Roll Movie Encyclopedia of the 1950s*
McGee. *Roger Corman*
McGhee. *John Wayne*
Mank. *Hollywood Cauldron: Thirteen Horror Films*
Martin. *The Allied Artists Checklist*
Nollen. *The Boys: ...Laurel and Hardy*
Nowlan. *Cinema Sequels and Remakes, 1903–1987*
Okuda. *The Monogram Checklist*
Okuda & Watz. *The Columbia Comedy Shorts*
Parish. *Prison Pictures from Hollywood*
Pitts. *Western Movies*
Quarles. *Down and Dirty: Hollywood's Exploitation Filmmakers*
Selby. *Dark City: The Film Noir*
Sigoloff. *The Films of the Seventies*
Slide. *Nitrate Won't Wait*
Smith. *Famous Hollywood Locations*
Sturcken. *Live Television*
Tropp. *Images of Fear*
Tuska. *The Vanishing Legion: ...Mascot Pictures*
Von Gunden. *Alec Guinness*
Von Gunden. *Flights of Fancy*
Warren. *Keep Watching the Skies!*
Watson. *Television Horror Movie Hosts*
Watz. *Wheeler & Woolsey*
Weaver. *Poverty Row HORRORS!*
Weaver. *Return of the B Science Fiction and Horror Heroes*
West. *Television Westerns*

# Producers on Producing
## The Making of Film and Television

*Edited by*
Irv Broughton

McFarland Classics

McFarland & Company, Inc., Publishers
*Jefferson, North Carolina, and London*

PN
1992.75
.B77
2001

Grateful acknowledgment is made to the University of Washington Press, which has granted permission to reprint herein copyrighted selections from David Wagoner (ed.), *Straw from the Fire: From the Notebooks of Theodore Roethke.*

All photographs courtesy of the interview subjects except page 1 (Max Liebman) and page 203 (Pat Weaver) courtesy of National Broadcasting Company, Inc.; page 60 (Mark Goodson) courtesy of Goodson-Todman Productions; page 100 (Perry Wolff) courtesy of CBS News; page 249 (Pam Hill) courtesy of ABC News; page 261 (Edwin Vane) courtesy of Group W. Productions; page 289 (Al Masini) courtesy of Tele-Rep Photos; pages 161 (Roy Huggins) and 273 (Jon Epstein) © Universal City Studios; and page 179 (Agnes Nixon) by Warman, N.Y.

*The present work is a reprint of the library bound edition of* Producers on Producing: The Making of Film and Television, *first published in 1986. McFarland Classics is an imprint of McFarland & Company, Inc., Publishers, Jefferson, North Carolina, who also published the original edition.*

**Library of Congress Cataloguing-in-Publication Data**

Broughton, Irv.
    Producers on producers : the making of film and television /
Irv Broughton
        p.      cm.
    Includes index.
    ISBN-13: 978-0-7864-1207-5 (softcover : 50# alkaline paper) ∞
    1. Television—Production and direction.   2. Television
producers and directors—United States—Interviews.   I. Title.
PN1992.75.B77   2001        791.45'0232'0973          85-43572

British Library cataloguing data are available

On the cover: Max Liebman *(Photofest)*

Manufactured in the United States of America

*McFarland & Company, Inc., Publishers*
  *Box 611, Jefferson, North Carolina 28640*
  *www.mcfarlandpub.com*

for Connie
and for
McKenzie and Sayer —
with love

# Contents

*Introduction*    ix
*Acknowledgments*    viii
Max Liebman    1
Frederic W. Ziv    16
Bob Stabler    23
Chuck Jones    37
Fred Rogers    48
Mark Goodson    60
Imre Horvath    74
Michael Wiese    87
Perry Wolff    100
David Wolper    116
Bill Burrud    129
Jay McMullen    141
Roy Huggins    161
Agnes Nixon    179
Earl Hamner, Jr.    191
Pat Weaver    203
Steve Allen    222
Len Levy    237
Pamela Hill    249
Edwin T. Vane    261
Jon Epstein    273
Al Masini    289
*Index*    301

# Acknowledgments

A book of interviews is a complicated logistical undertaking that is not possible without the fullest cooperation and assistance of its subjects. I want to thank all of those persons interviewed herein for allowing me access to their lives. I am grateful, too, to the staff assistants and others who made the task easier. I also would like to thank NBC and the interview subjects for providing me with photographs.

My thanks to Connie Broughton for her editing, Fredda Summers and Vince McShan for their dedication and assistance in preparing the manuscript, and my friends in the business: Gerry Cook, Bill Jensen, Art Summers, Connie Collins, Harry Dawson, Mike McLeod and Rich Blakeslee, who continue to believe as producers do — in all the possibilities. Finally, I want to thank George P. Garrett, who knows as much about possibilities as anyone.

# Introduction

This collection of interviews is intended as a practical, unfiltered look at the problems and decision-making, the philosophies and day-to-day workings of producers, writers, creators and program executives from practically every television program genre — documentary, network series, animation, game show, soap opera, cable segment, commercials, news, network public affairs and children's programming. The individuals featured here clearly have had a profound impact on American television and film in our century. In numerical terms, over six hundred years of producing experience is included in these pages.

In a sense, every person who works in a field such as television stands a possibility of being a pioneer because of the infinite variety of techniques and ideas that the mass medium makes possible. But the persons in this book have had a significant impact — not only in the "firsts" that many of them have contributed, but also in the subtlety that may be found in good taste or clarity of vision.

These pioneers are also important for reasons beyond their own pioneering, for these are persons whose opinions count. As respected and successful producers in their fields, their philosophies and dreams, trials and tribulations, and lessons learned serve as a quiet apprenticeship to all of us in television and film production.

There are, of course, other producers I wish I had space to highlight. I would hope the sheer impossibility of chronicling a field of endeavor so broad and varied does not diminish my attempt to color in part of television's history.

IB

*To have happy Novembers, you must
have great Septembers.*

Coach Jim Walden

*I had just gone out to the icebox
to replenish my intuitions.*

Theodore Roethke

*There are a lot of hyphens in this industry.*

Fred Ziv

*Max Liebman*

MAX LIEBMAN, PRODUCER of many of television's "finest hours,"
has been called the "Ziegfeld of TV." In his early television shows —
"The Admiral Broadway Revue," "Max Liebman Presents," and the
well-known "Your Show of Shows" — Liebman, perhaps more than
anyone else, helped show us the possibilities that this fledgling
medium of television could have.

Liebman was a producer's producer, and his contributions are
many. Not only did he bring many of the established techniques
of Broadway and vaudeville to the rectangular screen, he was a
remarkable discoverer of talent. Names like Mel Brooks, Neil
Simon, Lucille Kallen, Sid Caesar, Imogene Coca, Marge and
Gower Champion, Danny Kaye, and Jerome Robbins — one of his
proudest discoveries — were discovered and nurtured by him.

As do all producers worth their salt, Liebman selected and
brought the different talents and elements together. He found working with talent to be difficult, as he points out in the interview, but
somehow, by direct intervention or even non-intervention, made it
all happen.

Max Liebman died in New York in 1981, at the age of 78.

*Could you tell me a little about programming in early-day television?*
Well, it all ties in with the basic approach. In my time there was no
such thing as programming, because there wasn't the ambulance-chasing
for the ratings. Ratings were a product of the productive approach of
those who were doing the producing. But then things turned around completely. Producing was more or less a product of the approach of those
who were doing the programming. This was producing and programming. In other words, the numbers became the factor and we didn't even
know there was such a thing when we first started. The very first
months — we knew there were ratings, but we never were privy to the
results, or curious about what they even were. And now everything is
determined by the ratings.

*Did you like the live thing? Did you really enjoy that?*
I had an organization that was more or less operating on the same
plateau. It filtered through a period of getting started and then settled
down to a group of people who were more or less compatible as to their
approach to what we were doing. Also, I had been doing television at a
summer theater for fifteen years — I had been doing television without
cameras. I was doing a revue every single week that was new, original,
and it had to be done week after week, for a highly critical audience.

*Where was this?*
A place called Tamiment in Pennsylvania, a summer resort.

*So you felt that there was a lot of relationship between directing and
producing for television and producing for the stage?*

In producing for motion pictures or producing for nightclubs or producing even for radio in its time, there is a relationship in the basic fundamentals that apply to the entire world of entertainment. Except, I will admit that television (and in its time, radio) has criteria that are quite different from those of any other form of entertainment, in that nobody pays to see what they're looking at, and paid television has not developed sufficiently to affect commercial television much yet.

*Was there any one hard transition coming from theater to television?*
In general, yes, there were a number of things. The theater is what I call a class form of entertainment, whereas television is one of the biggest mass entertainments, like motion pictures used to be. Mechanically, too, the approach is different in television from what it is in the theater. I was in the theater, mostly a product of the revue form of entertainment, and I had to adjust. My very first show in television was with the orchestra in the pit in an attempt to reproduce a night at the theater, and the spill from the sound into each other's microphones became impossible. By the second show, I had already abandoned that concept.

*So what did you do — spread the musicians out, or . . . ?*
I put the musicians over on the side, and we experimented with microphone placement and speaker placement, etc., in order to get the best balance so that we could distinguish between the people who were performing and the men who were creating the music.

*So there were a lot of things nobody seemed to know much about at that time?*
There were things that were evident to me right from the beginning. When I came into television — when Milton Berle was "Mr. Television" and "The Milton Berle Show" was Number One in the minds and hearts of men and in the lineup of popularity — one thing not yet evident was the fact that, as well as an oral medium, television was a visual medium.

*So how did you try to accentuate the visual in your show?*
Merely by being cognizant of the fact that it existed, that it was something to *look at* — differentiating it from radio, something to *listen to*.

*So do you feel like you pioneered in some visual aspects?*
A lot of visual aspects. When I came into television, my scenic designer, Freddie Fox, who came from the theater, was also a lighting man. The engineers believed in a general strip lighting, which was large bulbs in big reflectors, but their object was to get it clear; when the characters close to the camera were being photographed, they wanted the bookcase twenty feet behind them to reveal what the titles of the books

were. We wanted an element of depth, an element of mood, and we put gelatines into the lighting of a scene, instead of making it just the glaring white light, and created some moods and depths to the visual aspect of what was being shown.

*What year was this?*
1949 was the first show I did, and then 1950 was "Your Show of Shows." '49 was "The Admiral Broadway Revue." The title itself indicates how I was affiliated with the theater.

*What was the hardest thing about doing "The Admiral Broadway Revue"?*
Personality conflicts between my theater people, whom I brought with me, and the, well, I would call them the electronic people—the engineers—who were still experimenting, both at the time when we were doing black and white and then when we got to do color. I was the first one really to emerge with a series in color, and our problems were to reconcile our differences.

*How did you do that?*
By the time we got the color we had already established ourselves as knowing what we were doing, and the color men at NBC came to see our operation and to come in contact with the practical problems in early color broadcasting.

*When were you doing color? When was your first . . . ?*
When I started to do what was known as "spectaculars." Now we call them "specials," a title which they gave to the very first series that I did. I did thirty-two spectaculars in two years, one and one-half hours long. But "spectacular" was a word that was a little too boastful for me. I called them "specials."

*And were these called "Max Liebman Presents"?*
Right.

*What was the toughest thing about doing that series? That's a lot of shows.*
Nothing was really tough, and everything was. It was simply a matter of doing them. The chief activity that we were involved with, that I was involved with, was trying in every department to get the best there was—people—the writers, the scenic designers, the costumers, the musicians, and the performers; and the best there was, of course, had to be judged by whatever my own chemistry consisted of.

*What did that consist of?*
Well, I could write a book about it.

*Give me an example of what you considered when you were choosing a performer or talent?*

The important thing, I was a specialist in comedy, and my approach to comedy was based upon a credo that great comedy – "great" is in huge letters, engraved on the biggest piece of granite you could find – that *great* comedy can only be projected by great comedians. That was my approach to comedy. It didn't omit the possibility that good comedy and successful comedy could also be projected by people who weren't great comedians, but I was talking of *great* comedians, and my god of comedy in my time, in my lifetime, is Charlie Chaplin.

*So what did you learn from Chaplin?*

Great comedy is closely linked to the elements of genius, and genius is very difficult to define. I would say that originality, which is another hard ingredient to define, is something that's unique, something that is the comedian's own thing, and when he can take something that everybody else is doing and make it his own, he has become someone to be reckoned with. At least, one of the important practitioners in the field of comedy.

*You had some great writers, like Mel Brooks and Neil Simon.*
Yes.

*Do you consider them great in retrospect?*

I started out in the world of entertainment as a writer, too; I always was a writer. Two people, Mel Tolken and Lucille Kallen, who I brought to television with me, were, I would say, the linchpins of the whole writing staff. If I believe that great comedians make great comedy, my approach was the fact that a comedian, to fit my criteria, would have to have it in him. The task was for the director or the mastermind, the impressario, the producer, or whoever was in charge of developing the comedian, to bring it out, but if he hasn't got it in him he'll never be great. You can make good comedians better, but you can't make them great.

*Is Sid Caesar great?*
Yes.

*Imogene Coca?*
Yes.

*Did you feel like a history maker when you were doing this? When you were doing "Your Show of Shows," did you feel like you were making history?*

Yes, I did. I felt that we were not in competition with anyone else, but by the time I started counting the awards that we won (we won sixty-five awards), I felt apart from what everybody else was doing.

*Can you explain that? You felt apart.*

They were all in competition, and I felt that what we were doing was different. I suppose anybody feels that way about what they're doing, but that was the way I felt. We were different from what everybody else was. I don't want to say that we were above, below or in between, or anything else, but I think that we all had the same objective and that was to be successful. My objective was to be successful. I had to reach the audience that I was being beamed to, and in order to do that I had my own standards, my own criteria.

*Did the network ever bother you at all?*

I have never found, outside of minor things, that I was ever interfered with by the networks or the sponsors. We were lucky in that we were a big hit right away, and being a big hit meant that we were getting good ratings, and as long as that went on we had no communication even with the networks or sponsors.

*What was your youth like? Were you interested in comedy?*

When I went to high school – Boys High School in Brooklyn – I was a writer. I won a short story contest when I was a freshman, and then I became a staff member of the magazine. And I became a comedy writer. I had a humor column. I was also in the drama when dramatics were being performed in high school. I didn't go to college. When I got out of high school, instead of going to Columbia, where my parents thought I would be going, I headed for a talent agency and got involved in vaudeville and began to write for and put on what were known as "flash" acts for places like the Paramount Theater, a big moving picture house, and vaudeville. I began to write for comedians, on the road mostly – those that weren't advanced enough to come into New York, even on the Loew Circuit, as differentiated from the Keith-Albee Circuit. So that's where I started.

*What was a "flash" act?*

A "flash" act had a live show behind the picture. They had a couple of dancers and comedians.

*It was really a variety show, wasn't it?*

That's right. It was a kind of revue.

*Why did they call it a "flash" act?*

The word "flash" was, I think, to give it an adjective. It isn't my term. I ran smack into it when it already existed. The "flash" act was one that was just inside of an hour duration and the kind they put on at the Roxy, the Capital, the Paramount and other big houses in big cities.

*You brought a lot of talents into the biz.*

I was known as a discoverer of talent. Danny Kaye was supposed to have been one of my big discoveries, among others. But I would say that the greatest talent developed during that period was a fellow who I never brought to television at all because he had already become a genius beyond the reach of television – one of the world's greatest choreographers of all times, Jerome Robbins.

*How did you discover him?*　'

I was working up at Tamiment and somebody in New York, some choreographer, called me up and said, "I have a young boy here. He's fifteen years old. Can I send him up?" And I said, "Send him up," because Tamiment was known as the home of ballet dancers or anybody who had a problem in developing themselves in the field of dancing. They sent this young boy up, fifteen years old, and he stayed with me for seven years, from fifteen to twenty-two. Practically everything he did he was doing for the first time. Today he's really the world's greatest choreographer.

*What were facilities like in the early days?*

I didn't even have an office at the beginning. My office was the rehearsal hall or the men's room.

*The men's room?*

Yes, we did a lot of rehearsing in the men's room. Writing. Wherever we could find a seat.

*There was just no space?*

Well, there wasn't enough space, at first, but that was only at the very beginning, during the Admiral show.

*You must have had some long days.*

Long days seven days a week, but I believed in a day's work and a day's time from the others.

*Was there any particular thing on "Your Show of Shows" that you wanted to have extra control over?*

I had control over everything. I think one might say that what I brought to the medium at that time was my introduction to people in tights doing ballet and people in costumes singing opera. I had been involved in a number of Broadway shows, submitting and having sketches done in revues, and also directing and writing for the Revue Theatre on Broadway. When I had the summer theater I also introduced the element of grand opera and ballet over there in Pennsylvania. But I would say that today, if I were to do a show, the last thing in the world I would attempt is opera or ballet. What I was doing was being distilled through the sieve of popular entertainment, reaching an audience that had never seen it before. In the early days our mail from the sticks or from the country, where they traveled fifty miles to see a television set, used to be from people who had heard opera for the first time, seen ballet for the first time. There was a lot of fan mail from that. Today I wouldn't attempt it because the real thing is being done so well on public broadcasting. Channel 13 here in New York does classical music, symphony orchestras, ballet productions, opera productions, and it's just magnificent.

*Did you ever get criticized by television establishment as being snobby or too culturally oriented back then?*
   Yes. Some of my friends, when they heard I was going to do it, said, "The people are going to go to the bathroom while you've got opera singers on," and I said, "No." It was my job as a showman to make it palatable, and I think I did. I had done it before in a summer resort there at Tamiment, and I had brought a revue from Tamiment to Broadway in 1939, when Jerome Robbins was a chorus boy. I brought him right from Tamiment to Broadway. He was in the ballet. That was called *Straw Hat Revue*, and the dancing consisted of a mixture of jazz and whatever else was current, and ballet, even at that time.

*What sorts of things did you do to the production to make opera and some of these things palatable, as you say?*
   By trying only to present the great. My first opera singer was Robert Merrill, right from the Metropolitan Opera. I was always looking for the top personality in that field.

*Did Merrill have any misgivings about TV?*
   No.

*How did some of those people who had never been on TV look at it?*
   There were a few people who were scared of it. Besides, by the time I had done nineteen shows on the Admiral show and come to the third show of "Your Show of Shows" — the Admiral show was an hour show and "Your Show of Shows" was an hour and a half — I had reached certain conclusions. I had the first stock company, a company of players that were the same people every week, in television, and that's because really everything we were doing was the first, more or less, chronologically. My first master of ceremonies was Burgess Meredith, my next one was Rex Harrison. The first guest star that I had, outside of my own company, was Gertrude Lawrence. In other words, I was reaching the people who were, I would say, part of the legitimate theater rather than those who came from nightclubs.

*When you say "stock" company, what do you mean?*
   I had a group of dancers, I had a group of singers, I had solo dancers

and solo singers; I had Sid Caesar, Imogene Coca, comedians; I had Carl Reiner and Howard Morris, second comedians; I had a team of dancers; I had all the elements that are usually employed in a Broadway revue. I had a scenic designer, I had a choreographer, and when I was doing "Your Show of Shows," John Crosby of the *Herald Tribune*, who was the broadcasting critic, said, "It looks as though something is going to happen in television. Liebman has brought a group of players and practitioners who are permanently ensconced, and it looks as though they will get some movement in the medium itself."

*Did the legitimate theater feel any threat from you?*
No, I think the one who felt the threats, not from me but from the medium of television itself, was the motion picture business.

*Of the big stars that you tried to get on your programs, which was maybe the most frightened of television?*
We had a different guest star every week, and they were usually from motion pictures. There were a few who were scared. One broke down in a dress rehearsal and said, "I can't go on," but she did.

*Who was that?*
I would rather not say her name.

*Are you an analytical person?*
No, I think my leaning toward show business — I put on the class show in high school — was instinctive. I was a big, big follower of vaudeville. I used to go all over the city to see vaudeville acts.

*Did you ever bring any of those old vaudeville acts over to TV?*
Sure. Quite a number. Every once in a while we would put up a sign on an easel which said it was from some music hall, and presented a vaudeville act, a juggler, a new dance team. I never brought any comedians or comediennes because I didn't want them to compete with my own, or singers, ballet dancers, opera singers, though they weren't from vaudeville, but vaudeville acts, yes.

*Did you ever steal any actual lines? Were there any kinds of gags that you brought over to TV?*
Everything I ever did was remembered from years ago in one way or another. I mean I was influenced. I was a great theatergoer, so everything in the theater and everything or anybody who sang, danced or told jokes somehow or other crossed my path at sometime or another. Essentially, however, we never appropriated material.

*What did vaudeville mean to you?*

I once wrote a play with Allen Boretz that was done on Broadway, called *Off to Buffalo*, which was about vaudeville. One of the characters in the play, a press agent, more or less gives the essence that would provide the answer to your question. He says, "A vaudevillian is a person who has developed fifteen minutes of patter or tricks to such a point of its entertainment values that it became the mainstay of his livelihood, or, as they call it, his act."

*What were those writing sessions like on "Your Show of Shows"? Were they ever uncontrollable?*
You're confusing that with some other show that some of them were on. No, quite the opposite. We were not, as seems to be the myth or the legend, a barrel of inebriated monkeys, screaming and yelling. In fact, Fred Allen used to come Saturday morning to the theater when we were blocking the show for the evening's performance, and he would sit in the back and said it was like a church. If anybody raised his voice, he was stopped, and if he did it too often he didn't last very long.

*Tell me about working with your writers.*
I had a great deal of respect for any writer who worked for me for any period of time, and I would say that any one of them would tell you that my forte, more than anything else I did, was the element of being a stalwart editor, a knowledgeable one.

*Stalwart editor?*
Yes, of material. Not only the writers, but it was also true of acting talent. When I saw Danny Kaye step out on the stage in a little revue upstairs from a Chinese restaurant on 52nd Street I turned to whoever was with me at the time and said, "That's it."

*"That's it?"*
I would take him to Tamiment with me. He passed my test.

*How long did you rehearse for each show on "Your Show of Shows"?*
We started each week practically with nothing. Every show had to be prepared and delivered in a week.

*Did you ever worry about not making the hour and a half?*
I had no qualms about that. Once I was set, I had no qualms about ever being in real trouble. I have changed schedules after a dress rehearsal, I have fired an emcee after a dress rehearsal, and we had to go on an hour after that. I had absolutely no qualms.

*Did you ever have extra material in case you ran short?*
Once we began to build up a kinescope library of stuff, we could

always fall back on something if we got into trouble, because I would rather repeat something old that I was sure of than try something new that I was uncertain about (in my mind, of course).

*Marital sketches were big, weren't they, on the show?*
We had a whole series based upon two characters called "The Hickenlopers," a couple who were married. They were the forerunners, I guess, of situation comedies of domesticity.

*What was . . . is there one sketch that sort of stands out in your mind?*
I don't know. I mean, I would have to bring up at least a half dozen memorable ones. One would be a domestic sketch, and I'd have to choose from a hundred of those; the other would be a thing that Sid Caesar did with Howard Morris where Sid Caesar was a general and Howard Morris was his corporal, who was dressing him. Sid Caesar was a German general with a German dialect. Then it proved that he was really the doorman of a hotel when he went out and called a taxi with a whistle.

*Was '50s TV really the "Golden Age"?*
Yes, it was. I'm going to reveal something that is the key to the article that I just finished, and this is a very special sort of appraisal, the difference between what took place then and what is happening now.
My whole theme is based on, "They swept out the clowns." I'll mention some names to you; some people call them "Liebman's Double Dozen." Twenty-four names. Lucille Ball, Carol Burnett, Imogene Coca, Nancy Walker, Milton Berle, Sid Caesar, Jerry Lewis, Red Skelton, Red Buttons, names like that. What have they got in common? They're all comedians, correct? What else have they got in common? The fact that each one of them had his or her own television show. What else have they got in common? None of them, not one, has a show of his own now. So who's taking their place? These people are from vaudeville, from nightclubs, from the theater, except a few, but most of them are entertainers. They are the clowns who were born to make us laugh. That's the cue phrase. And they've been swept out in the ratings race. So who's left? Not what I would call professional comedians. Not what I would call our clowns. Some of them aren't even professional actors. They don't know how to do a "take," a reaction to a joke. They don't know any of the mechanics of being a comedian. So the ones that are taking their place can't handle the same kind of material, and what we're getting now is really something that begins to resemble soap opera with a laugh track.

*You really feel the loss of these people, these clowns.*
Of course, I feel it. And I could think of twenty-four names without going to research, but if you'll look it up, you'll find twenty-four who have had their own shows, who were comedians or comics.

*Is comedy akin to tragedy?*

Oh, that's an old premise — that laughter is just a moment away from tears and vice versa. I suppose they're related. The two masks of the entertainment world are the comic mask and the tragic mask, and they are closely related. There are things about tragedy and comedy that are common to both, but, essentially, there's all kinds of comedy. All the people that are my "double dozen" represent nearly every form of comedy. Not everyone is an audience's preference, cup of tea, but they're all professionals, and they know their craft, and some of them are artists. You ask me do I feel that loss. I, personally, don't, but as a showman, I do.

*How long did it take to move the heavy TV equipment around? Was that ever a problem when you were doing live shows?*

No. That was no problem because the problem was so basic that it was like saying, "If you're going to have a show you've got to pull up the curtain." Everything was done to alleviate it. Now, I was once in California on a visit and I came into a small television studio and there was a guy called Sanner. (This was while I was doing the Admiral show, before I went into the second season.) He was mounting a dolly on which the camera was mounted, and he was seated. It was very easy to handle and was called the "Sanner dolly" after his own name. I wired Pat Weaver, who was vice-president in charge of production, and I said, "I'm going to, with your permission, order one of these dollies for my show," and he said, "Go ahead and do it." The dolly was a thing that was pushed from behind by a pusher while a cameraman sat — it was standard equipment in the motion picture industry — but there it was done electrically, and it gradually got to be done that way in television. It was mobile enough to move in all directions, up and down and sideways, to take in a lot of the territory in which the action on the stage or the playing area would occur, and it made camera movement on live television that much easier. From that they developed all kinds of lenses and dollies and camera movement that they had in motion pictures.

*Did you do many taped shows?*

I really only did a few taped shows. I did live shows — about two hundred live shows — sixteen of them on "Your Show of Shows."

*Did you ever have Plan B, a backup plan in case something went wrong? Maybe backup equipment?*

There was enough equipment. I was the first one to come into television (which was then operating with three cameras) with five cameras, and occasionally, a camera would conk out and we would have to do it with four. But one time something went wrong and we were off the air when the show was half-done — this was the Admiral show — and we just kept doing it but it wasn't going over the air.

*You knew you weren't going out on the air. You just decided to finish it?*
The actors didn't know. And the next week we had half a show all ready to perform that hadn't gone over the air. We had a kinescope of the show.

*Was there any other occupational hazard?*
We had many — we had quick changes to do in the theater itself. Operating from the International Theater in Columbus Circle, we were not allowed to set any scenery or really perform in front of the asbestos curtain, as proclaimed and demanded by the fire department. That curtain had to be down or ready to come down, with nothing in front of it, in case anything happened on the stage. A person could step in front, but no props. So we had our problems. We had an opera singer called Marguerite Piazza, and Bill Hayes, who was a gondolier, singing some Neopolitan songs while she was in the gondola. We wanted to do that down front while we were setting the stage behind the curtain for the next thing. So we had the gondolier just with a pole, standing behind her; but we had nothing for her to sit on, so we built a seat into her costume. The seat was a tin can, a five-gallon can of peach preserves, tied around under her costume, and she sat on that. We had some lights coming down and up, playing on what might have been rippling waters, in order to foil the fire department.

*Did they used to come in and inspect you very often?*
Oh, they were always there — every show. Finally, I gave them an ultimatum. I said, "Unless we get out of this straitjacket, I'm going to move the show to California."

*What did they say to that?*
They made some compromises, and we straightened it out. Finally, they said, "Oh, well, all right, just be sure to send us what you want to do, and do it, and then send us a memorandum of what you did." That seemed to be against the rules. So we tried to adjust the whole thing and make it applicable to both the safety of the audience that was in the theater, and the flexibility that you want in the operation.

*Was there ever anything risqué that happened — somebody was undressing, or anything?*
Well, we had a department, called "script approval," or something like that, which was really the watchdog of the moral attitude that was being preserved by the networks. They came to the run-through of the day's performance to see if there was anything objectionable. Now, Imogene Coca brought from the theater into our early show a striptease that she did, and the striptease consisted of removing the belt from her overcoat — that's the extent to which she stripped. And they objected to it.

I said, "Why? She's absolutely decent. She's just kidding the whole thing," and they said, "Yes, but the music is so dirty." I said, "Well, that's what makes it funny. It's not risqué or objectionable, it's what enhances the humor." They finally saw the light of day and let us do it. After that we had no problem. We had our own sense of what I would say was proper. We never attempted anything that would raise the eyebrows of the censors. We weren't inclined that way.

*What was the hardest thing about doing live TV? We touched on a little bit of it. Is there anything else that strikes you as being complicated?*

After the Saturday night curtain came down, there was a great deal of celebrating, but it was very sad at times. Maybe because I had to say, "What are we going to do next week?" The idea of getting into the next show, although Mel Tolken and Lucille Kallen were already thinking about the domestic sketch for the next week, which we talked about the day before, was always a new challenge. Looking back on it, it was, as people said at times, a weekly miracle.

*How would Max Liebman be remembered?*

As a pioneer who had very high standards. There's a magazine, *TV Facts*, something like that. It's sent out to the trade. It had a poll taken of 1500 people who were executives in the film business, to cast their votes for fifty of the greatest films ever made of all time, and they did. Then they had another one to vote on fifty of the greatest TV programs of all times, and they did, and we came out second. That was about four years ago. That included every TV variety show that was on at that time — "All in the Family," "Carol Burnett," "Mary Tyler Moore," and so on. We came out second. The one that came out first was "Perry Mason," and the third was "Star Trek," which I had never heard of. And I was remembered; when *Billboard* magazine reviewed the first "Your Show of Shows," the headline was, "NBC should build a statue to Max Liebman."

*Did producers work a lot between networks then? Was it fairly free-flowing?*

No. No. I went to CBS after I left NBC and didn't come back afterwards. There was a flow of talent of all kinds, technical and performing talent. There wasn't a free flow, but there were revolving doors in both the networks, and there are now in the three networks.

*In your mind, what personality trait is the most important to the successful producer?*

The most important trait for the producer who is involved with a series on television, because of the closely knit contact of the members of the series in all departments, is that he has to be some kind of amateur psychiatrist.

*"Amateur psychiatrist?"*

I never was in any kind of psychiatric treatment, and it's only in retrospect that I look upon myself as having the experience to recognize some of the problems of those who are in the entertainment field.

*What sorts of problems, generally speaking?*

Like, let's say, I had a dance team in my company who did a different dance number, which they created themselves, every week. They would show it to me on Sunday before I put it on the schedule for that week to go on Saturday, and they were very good and usually succeeded in everything they did. Occasionally, they would show me one that didn't work, for me. I would let them do it. The last thing I would want to do is to put something in a show that I didn't like, but I let them do it.

*You would let them do it?*

Yes, their record was so high and their enthusiasm was so great for that particular thing that I couldn't break their spirit. I would break their spirit if I had said, "I don't think this is going to work." Now I wouldn't do that with the writers. With the writers, very often, I would say, "I don't think this will work"; but even then, I would say, "Well, okay, do it," and then someone would say, "Uh-huh, Max is handing us the rope."

*Max is what?*

"Handing us the rope – to hang ourselves with."

*Did you really ever fret after you had let them do something you really didn't want?*

Oh, I didn't fret. My scorecard was pretty high on having some kind of premonition about how it would work out, and that was mainly because I was the senior member of the group. I had respect for their abilities. I admired them very much or I wouldn't have them. It was my experience that gave me the edge in guessing what would and what wouldn't work.

*Frederic W. Ziv*

FREDERIC W. ZIV is a radio and television pioneer, having founded the Frederic W. Ziv Company in 1931 and Ziv Television Programs in 1947. His contributions are many. He anticipated color, producing some of his programs in color in the 1950s. He admits to being "particularly effective in 'the chase,' " moving his heroes from horses ("Cisco Kid") to highways ("Highway Patrol") to underwater ("Sea Hunt").

The Ziv Company also produced "I Led Three Lives," "Bat Masterson," and many more for television. On radio he produced, among others, "The Guy Lombardo Show," "Easy Aces," and "The Red Skelton Show." He is known as "the father of syndication."

Ziv Television Programs was sold to United Artists Corporation, where years later Mr. Ziv retired as chairman. He remains president of the Frederic W. Ziv Company.

Mr. Ziv serves on the faculty of the University of Cincinnati as distinguished Professor of Radio-Television and Theater Crafts, and is a graduate of the University of Michigan with a juris doctor degree. He also holds a Litt. D. from the College of Mt. St. Joseph. He is author of two books: *The Business of Writing*, and *The Valiant Muse*, published by G. P. Putnam. Mr. Ziv is prominent in civic activities in Cincinnati.

*How long did it take to produce a thirty-minute TV show in the late 1950s?*

It would take thirty hours to produce. That could be three ten-hour days; it could be four eight-hour days.

*Would that thirty hours be shooting and editing?*

It would be thirty hours of principal photography.

*How many shows did you produce a year?*

Thirty-nine half hours, and repeated thirteen in each series. As you know, we did several series each year.

*What generally was the hardest thing about putting together a TV show in those days?*

Well, you have to start with the concept — one that's not wobbly. If you have a wobbly concept, you're going to have a wobbly series. If you start with a sound concept, sound treatment, then you're on firm ground. After all, if you have a pilot that is a prototype that can be followed, and that prototype is successful, you're going to have a successful series.

*Did a network ever censor or reject a show in those early days?*

Most of our shows were not offered to the network. A program like "Sea Hunt," for example, was turned down by the network. We showed it to each of the networks, showed them the pilot. They liked the pilot, but they figured—and each one seemed to be of the same opinion—"Well, what do you do the second week and what do you do the third week—you've done it all the first week." Well, of course, they were wrong; we produced it year after year.

The program scored very high ratings, too. Then, all the networks were after it. Of course, we were already in syndication and had satisfied sponsors and we would not take the program away from any of our sponsors to put it on the network.

*Did you do any programs for the network?*
"Bat Masterson" was on the network; "Tombstone Territory" was on the network; "West Point" was on the network—those occur to me at the moment.

*Did they work with you very closely, or did you have a free hand?*
Well, you know what the network's attitude is today. It was the same then. The networks knew everything, and assigned someone as a supervisor. They dominated the production of any show we put on the network, and that is one of the reasons why I, personally, preferred to put shows in syndication.

*Yours was a pioneering technique: to send sales people out into the field to sell the shows to local stations.*
If you read the trade papers, you will find that I'm usually referred to as the "father of syndication." That's the tag that followed me and is still being used. I developed the technique; I didn't originate it. I'm not sure if anyone preceded me. I did expand on it and brought it to what was probably its highest level.

*What did people in Hollywood think about that idea when you first came up with it? Was it looked upon as outrageous?*
No, I don't think so. After all, I'm a pioneer as far as television production is concerned. "The Cisco Kid" might have been one of the very first, if not the first program filmed for television, and everyone was delighted to be employed.

*What other production techniques did you pioneer?*
Well, we did "The Cisco Kid," for example, when there was no such thing as color television—everything was black and white. We shot "Cisco Kid" in color. The people—the engineers, the laboratory—felt that the color film would never be usable—if color ever came. It turned out they were all wrong. Color television did come, and as you know, the programs we shot in color in the very early days are still being used.

*How closely did you work with camerapersons and directors?*

I came to television as a writer. I had two books published and many articles. So my major contribution was in the writing, rather than the technical end of it. I depended mostly on the experienced film personnel – the pool of technicians in Hollywood – for all the technical work.

*But you had a fair amount of artistic control, didn't you?*
Well, I would say complete artistic control.

*I read in one magazine that you are supposed to have a very soft heart – that you are a very kind and compassionate person. Did the soft heart ever get in the way?*
(Laughs) Well, I'm delighted. I know the article – it was my former employees who felt that I had a soft heart. Many of them were with me throughout my career, and in many cases, their careers started with me; so it was a very nice thing for them to say. But as far as competitiveness was concerned, I was very competitive. I don't think I had a soft heart for my competitors – I merely had a soft heart for my associates.

*What film format did you shoot in – 35 or 16?*
Originally "The Cisco Kid" was filmed in 16mm color. The network-owned-and-operated stations preferred 35mm, and so we subsequently went to 35. I believe Cisco was the only show shot in 16mm.

*How did you come up with your innovative sales techniques? Had you done some selling yourself?*
Prior to television, our company syndicated radio programs. We syndicated radio programs starring Humphrey Bogart, Lauren Bacall, Ronald Coleman, Adolph Menjou, Tyrone Power, Fred MacMurray – you can go down the list of some of our radio programs – and they were syndicated the very same way. So we had a sales organization.

*What did you look for in the people that were selling for you?*
Simply, the ability to make the sale – to make a clean, lasting sale where both the sponsor and the seller, which was our company, would be happy with the situation.

*I understand there was antagonism at first on the part of the local stations.*
We were not competitive to the stations, and in many cases I would say, most cases, the stations welcomed us because we not only furnished programming, but we furnished substantial sponsors, sometimes local, sometimes regional, and sometimes national. On rare occasions there would be a station that would object to the fact that we called on their

customers. That was mostly in a city where there was a single station, and that station would feel that all customers in that area were theirs so we should not go around them. But it was never our intention to work against them; we had to work *with* the stations in order to "clear" time and in order to promote and make the program a success.

*Was it fairly easy to "clear" time in those days?*
In the early days it was; but as the networks began to gobble up more and more time, fewer and fewer prime-time slots became available. So it was very difficult to clear time for programming like ours.

*You supplied the advertising?*
Our company did not supply the advertising. We supplied the advertiser. The advertiser's agency supplied the advertising. But we did pay advertising agency commissions.

*Did you work mostly with the New York agencies?*
All over the country, wherever there were agencies—every city. Occasionally, in a very small town, there might not be an agency.

*Who were some of your big advertisers?*
The top names in the country: Proctor and Gamble and Phillips Petroleum, for example.

*How did you have time to do everything?*
Well, I loved my work; but I don't want to create the impression that this was a one-man operation. I had a wonderful group of men and women whose contribution was gigantic. Whenever I'm interviewed, I make sure that the interviewer understands that I'm not claiming that I did this thing single-handed. People were with me twenty to twenty-five years, and we developed an excellent team.

*How many hours did you work a day?*
I would have to say that the hours had nothing to do with it. I enjoyed the work. I started early each morning. After dinner in the evening, if I was so inspired, I would be at my desk. But I really can't account for a specific number of hours.

*Did you help to cast the shows you did? How did you come up with Broderick Crawford ("Highway Patrol") and Lloyd Bridges ("Sea Hunt"), for example?*
We had a man named Herb Gordon, who was in charge of artists, and it would be his job to sound out artists who might be available. He would come up with a list. For example, you mentioned Broderick Crawford and Lloyd Bridges. They both were available at the same time.

I knew about Crawford's work. I knew that he was just perfect for "Highway Patrol," which was a command role, and I immediately said, "Let's go with Brod Crawford." A few of my associates didn't agree with me, but it turned out that I was right. As far as Lloyd Bridges was concerned, Herb Gordon walked Lloyd Bridges around our studio so I could look at him, since that was a very physical role and I wanted somebody who would look well in swim trunks and a wet suit, who could swim, who had the physical attributes, and Lloyd Bridges certainly had them. In addition, I had looked at footage of what he had done in other pictures. So I selected Lloyd Bridges. I selected Brod Crawford. But I didn't select every actor in every case. That would have been impossible.

*It's been said that you put "heroes onto wheels" and took them off horses. Is that a safe assessment?*

We did both; in other words, the chase is a technique that was particularly desired at the time. "Cisco Kid" was a chase on horseback; "Highway Patrol" was a chase on the highway; "Sea Hunt" was a chase underwater. We were particularly effective in "the chase."

*You put so many people in the business—that must give you a good feeling.*

Well, I'm particularly happy when I learn that someone that spent a long period of time with me became a great success. Quinn Martin, (producer of "The Fugitive") for example, started on our lot. His earliest screen credit I remember was on "I Led Three Lives," where Quinn Martin was listed as "Audio Supervisor." That's the bottom listing—about as far down the line as you list on the screen. Now, Quinn Martin has become one of Hollywood's top producers. I can go down the line that way one after another.

*How did you come up with rates for these programs? Were there rates for different markets?*

Yes, according to population. We established those rates. It was very high in a city like New York and very low in a city like Paducah. I don't have the specific information in front of me, but it did change through the years—as more homes had sets. We started with relatively low prices. Only about 10 percent of the homes had television sets, but when we got up where 90 percent of the homes had television sets, well, of course, the rates were much higher.

*Many programs in the '50s were actually produced by ad agencies.*

Yes, many of the network programs were produced by advertising agencies. It wasn't until Sylvester "Pat" Weaver of NBC came along with his magazine concept that the networks took away from the national advertising agencies their opportunity to produce.

*Did you ever have any great competition with the ad agencies? You were producing programs, they were producing programs — that didn't present a problem?*

No, it did not. You see, for the most part, it was only the very largest agencies that were producing programs, and they wanted their clients to have the best program available. If the one we offered was more desirable than the one they might have had in mind, I think they took the broad view; I think they took the best interest of their clients.

*You were turning out three series a year. That's an incredible amount.*

Sometimes more. I would have to look at each individual year.

*How did you manage to do that?*

We had a substantial Hollywood lot with seven soundstages, ample cutting rooms, projection rooms — we had quite a staff.

*What was the most you employed at one time?*

The FCC once asked for a list, and we listed full- and part-time and it came to 3,000, but many of those may have been part-time. I don't know what the full-time employees totaled.

*What was the hardest program to produce?*

I would say "Sea Hunt" because of the underwater shooting. We had to find clear water — that was the biggest problem. We shot at Tarpon Springs; we shot at Marineland; we went wherever we could get fresh locales and clear water.

*You were one of the first producers to really get away from the studio.*

Most of our shows were done at least half of the time at practical locations and half on the lot. But each script called for a different number of days in and a different number of days out.

*Did you have a favorite show?*

Well, I look back with fondness on "Highway Patrol," "Sea Hunt," "Bat Masterson" — those were, I guess, my personal favorites.

*A final question: Are producers misunderstood?*

As you know, I have been teaching for fifteen years. My rank is Distinguished Professor, University of Cincinnati. I find that most of my students as well as many of the faculty think that the producer's job is to raise the money — that the director makes the picture. That may be true of Broadway theater in some cases, but in creating and making the television program the producer does not raise the money; he produces the program, from idea to finished product. The producer's decision is in every step of the process.

*Bob Stabler*

"I've got a reputation for being a tough son-of-a-bitch," Bob Stabler says. "But I don't think that's fair." He is simply not one to tolerate amateurs. While there is a certain tough-mindedness to this gravelly-voiced veteran of over 850 television episodes, there is also an earnestness, even a freshness to hearing him lambast network operations or the term "filmmaker," which he says he can't stand.

His independent company competes with the big ones. As example, his feature film "The Incredible Rocky Mountain Race" got a 36 share when it was shown nationally on NBC.

Stabler brought "Hopalong Cassidy" (William Boyd) out of retirement in 1948 and went on to produce many of the best-loved television Westerns — "Gunsmoke," "Have Gun Will Travel," and "Death Valley Days." He has produced several feature films, including "The Resurrection of Zachary Wheeler," the first feature produced entirely on videotape.

Currently Stabler lives in California and British Columbia, supervising his two companies — Madison Pacific, Inc., and Dorrab Productions. He is a graduate of UCLA and is married to the former actress Dorothy Schuyler. They have one daughter.


*How did you get into the business?*

I was involved with "Hopalong Cassidy" back then, beginning in 1948. I joined Hoppy because I felt there was a great television thing coming up, which hadn't really materialized at that point. We got the rights to the old Hoppy features and got them on television, and he became a tremendous economic force. It was a magnificent thing. These were the original old features that had been made in the 30s and early 40s.

*Did you edit them down?*

No, we put in spots for commercials and that's all. They played and played and played, and then in the latter part of '51, NBC and General Foods wanted half-hour shows, so we had to make some half-hour Hoppies. Hoppy himself was a very unique guy. He had been in the business a long, long time and had built up a general distrust for Hollywood producers *per se.* He had his own organization, which he trusted, but which was not tuned to making pictures — it was everything else. So we went ahead and did this series "in house," so to speak, and it fell to my lot to, in effect, become producer, which I had never done before. I had worked at the studios a little bit in labor jobs, you know, Class B grip, etc., so I had to learn it that quick, but I did, and I liked it. When that was done, Hoppy wanted to, in effect, retire, and did, and so I took that crew and got a contract from CBS to do "Gunsmoke." That worked, and from that we went to "Have Gun Will Travel."

*Any anecdotes about problems about trying to cut those early movies of Hoppy into television form?*

Well, there was nothing about content because they were what we would now call family pictures, and television didn't have any no-no's at that point in time, for shooting or violence or anything else. It was just entertainment. At the end of an act or scene, we would make a cut in the fade-out for a commercial break. Now, in a few cases we trimmed them; in some cases they were a little too long and we would trim out little unnecessary things like over-long rides and chases. We would cut them down as much as we needed, but it was no big problem.

The "Gunsmoke" show is considered to be the first adult Western. I became aware of "Gunsmoke" while I was still involved with the Hoppy show because "Gunsmoke" followed the "Hopalong Cassidy" radio show on CBS and I liked it. I liked the guy who produced it, Norman MacDonnell. The writer was John Meston, and Bill Conrad was Matt Dillon. I was interested in adult Westerns for television because they worked in theaters—they worked very well. First I went to CBS, to friends of mine; they were running the newly formed CBS-TV. I tried to get the rights to "Gunsmoke" and they laughed me out of the shop. First, they said, "We don't get rid of rights, anyway, but on top of that you're an ass to try to make an adult Western. It won't fit for television. The audience won't like it, the costs are too high, blah, blah, blah." And remember, at that time there was very little location exterior shooting done. Television shows were live shows, live cameras, mostly.

I couldn't get that property, so then I tried to sell another adult Western anthology. I went to William Morris Agency in New York. One guy there thought it was the greatest idea in the world. The rest of them thought I was out of my head. But this one guy felt so strongly about it he quit William Morris and we did some things together. Then a year or two later, when I was with Hoppy down in Australia on a tour, the CBS guys called up and said, "Are you still interested in the show?" I said, "Sure," so they said they thought they might give it a go and make a pilot. When I came back we did that. It was the first thing my newly formed company did. We made the pilot and it sold almost instantly.

*Why was it called an "adult" Western?*
Because it dealt with very adult, realistic problems of that time. Most Westerns, even the Hoppies, were called "formula" Westerns. You start out with the problem, the good guys meet the hero, you meet some other people who have a hell of a problem, hero then says, "Well, forget what I had to do. I'm going to solve your problem." He proceeds in that area, gets in trouble himself, but does overcome whatever the situation is and then the problem is happily resolved. That's a "formula" Western. "Gunsmoke" wasn't that at all. "Gunsmoke" took on the state of mind of a frontier city and the principals and lived with them, whatever they did. They had bad moods and good moods and they weren't all cut in black and white. They were lots of shades of gray, which was an adult type of thing. The resolutions were sometimes happy and sometimes they weren't, again as real life would be at that time.

*How did the concept evolve over the years? Was there any major therapy or changes in approach?*

Well, I only did four years, the first four years — the most successful four years, I must add. Then CBS took over the show and produced it themselves. The first major change, of course, was in that fifth year when Dennis Weaver stepped out and the part of Chester was removed. Later on they added new people. They tried Burt Reynolds and that didn't work. Then they got Ken Curtiss and that worked tremendously well, but the other people stayed pretty much the same — Doc and Matt and Kitty.

*What was "Gunsmoke's" main contribution, other than being the first adult Western?*

Well, it was the first television show that attempted to achieve a highly professional stature. It was made just as we would have made a movie. Charles Marquis Warren, who directed the first thirty-nine, had very high standards and a remarkable feel for quality and perfection and reality. Through his talent, the overall "feel" of the show and its honesty was established. It was done, during those times, expensively, but by today's standards, peanuts. It was done seriously, on a very highly professional basis, and I think that that was later mirrored in other shows that came down the pike in all areas, not only Westerns.

*Fred Ziv said that he took his people on location as much as he could. Were you a pioneer at doing that, too?*

More so than Fred was. Interestingly enough, on "Gunsmoke" I tried to do that. We did do a couple of pictures on location, but CBS was not in favor of it. In a sense they had a right to feel that way, because basically "Gunsmoke" was Dodge City. You had the street and you had the interior, and the countryside was not that important. On the other hand, in "Have Gun Will Travel" the countryside changed in every episode, and it was important to that show to go on location. We wound up doing about 50 percent of those on location, which made it a better show. I believe in it, and I had a hell of a time proving it, but I did.

*About what year was this?*

In "Have Gun" we went on location starting in '58 and '59. Then we took over the "Death Valley Days" show. The people who owned that — the sponsors, U.S. Borax — they owned it for years in the radio show, too.

*How did that work? They owned it and they just hired you to produce it?*

Yes. They owned the radio show, they owned the copyrights, the whole works, and they hired my company to make them. I made a deal with them, to start with, that not less than 35% of the overall product of the year would be shot on distant location; we wound up doing 50% the first year and increased it so during the last seven years of it we were doing 100 percent on location.

*How many television shows do you estimate you've done over the years?*
It's something over 850 television shows.

*What's your most traumatic moment in all those?*
I don't think anything really is traumatic, but we did a "Playhouse 90," written and directed by David Swift, which was called "No Time at All," and it was the story of an airliner which left Miami and flew to LaGuardia in New York. It took off in a rainstorm, and shortly after they were off the ground, the radios went out and they flew on, not knowing what was in New York, and it was raining when they landed. We shot that down at the Long Beach airport, and we took an extraordinary number of lights, for a television show — in those days you tried to stay away from night shooting. This whole damned thing took place at night. We took lights, arcs, the whole works; wind machines, rain machines. We made extensive arrangements with the airport, the fire department and the Long Beach fire department to wet down the runways and get us pumps and all that. We were to start shooting at 6:00 at night, and about 5:00 it started raining, and by 5:30 it was pouring. The wind was blowing, the arcs and everything were flattened out and knocked down, the reflectors were all over the field. A real gale, just as in the story, developed; airplanes tied down nearby were flipping over. And we did that whole thing for real. All of our rain equipment was a total waste. It just poured and it looked great, it looked wonderful. But it was a little bit hairy to decide whether to go on with this or . . . the actors were supposed to run out to the plane and run back, and they had to fight it; I mean, they really got drenched, but it looked great. It was a very successful trauma, if it was a trauma.

*Were the lights shorting out and everything?*
They didn't so much, because they were pretty well insulated, but we lost some of them because things blew over and we lost a lot of expensive bulbs. The arcs worked and they were the most important, but it was a hell of a rough night of shooting. We shot all night, but we got great stuff, so it was worth it.

*How important were the unions at that time? Were they tough?*
Yeah, they were tough. They were the same unions that have been around for years in motion pictures, but they go right along with it. In this instance we paid additional premiums for night shooting and all that, so it was expensive, but it was well worth it. The film looked great!

*Why did you like making Westerns?*

I liked making Westerns most of all because you got out in good country. That's what I liked about it.

*What made doing Westerns difficult?*
Well, you've got built-in wardrobe problems, props, livestock. All of those things you don't have to worry about if you've got interior comedies, for example. And you're out where you're in weather a lot. If you use judgment as to when you're going to do these things and go when the weather is probably going to be good, you can minimize that, but you're outside and anything can happen. I had a company stranded on "Death Valley Days" on the other side of a river, which, when we went over in the morning, was three inches deep, and by that evening it was seven or eight feet, and rushing, and everybody had to wait until it went down. It took several hours, but that's part of the game.

*What was the early-days equipment like? What kind of cameras? Give us some names.*
Well, we used Mitchell cameras. On interior stuff we used a BNC. Usually on location we would use an NC Mitchell on a tripod. We used Western dollies. We did a lot of valley track stuff, but on a board track. Mikes were much the same as now. The recording equipment was much bulkier and not as good. There were a number of different makes that we used — RCA, etc. On stage we would use a Fisher boom, but exteriors we fishpoled.

*What was the most outrageous piece of makeshift equipment you used?*
Well, it wasn't necessarily equipment, but we were caught one time — I don't recall what the show was — but a cloud cover came over, and we had to finish the show that night, and we couldn't beat the sun. In those days a good production manager, when he looked at a location, would figure the sun; and of course, with a lot of hills involved, the higher up the hill you went, the longer you had sun. If you were down in a valley, you lost the sun. We would always keep moving uphill. We had gotten the masters, but we had a lot of individuals, singles and close-ups, to do, and we were out of sunshine. But we did have some vehicles; so we lined them up, jacked them up, put them on logs and everything else, and we would point them in and do the stuff pretty close. We used car lights in a lot of them to shoot the last five minutes of the story in which there were a lot of close-ups. There again, to minimize that effort, we would move the people in to where the lights were and frame them in such a way that they could have been where they were, so everybody was standing on the same marks, facing a different direction. It worked fine, and we've used it a lot since then, as a matter of fact. But that time there was no way out of it — and it worked amazingly well. I think a lot of time in this business, people get "equipment happy" — you've got to have this for this, and this

for that — and actually, for light you need light, that's all. If it comes from a flashlight, it will work just as well as an arc, within a limited area. You're forced sometimes into improvising and using some realistic imagination.

*Any other type of makeshift equipment that you ended up using a lot?*
Oh, we've got into situations where the dolly track wouldn't work — couldn't get in — and we've put a cameraman with a hand-held camera literally on horseback. We would look and find the horse that was the most stable and we shot the damn thing that way. The sound and the camera, in those days, were synchronized through an interlocked cable. Today, of course, it's all microcrystal. Then it was a pain in the neck. Yeah, it generally worked, and it worked as well as you do today.

*That opener for "Gunsmoke" is a classic. The shot through the legs. Did you come up with that?*
It was not any particular invention of mine; actually, it was a very brilliant lady who was with Dancer, Fitzgerald & Sample on the West Coast, Betty O'Hara. She was a hell of an advertising woman and a real dynamic lady, and to the best of my knowledge it was her thought to do it that way. I remember the extra that we hired as the guy who got hit. I won't mention his name, but he was just delighted to have that spot and the fact that it appeared every week, you know, he was as pleased as hell. Then somebody told him he should be getting residuals for it. The extras didn't get residuals and still don't. I argued with him, "Hell, you're an extra, you don't get residuals," and he went through the role, several years of it. Finally, three or four years later, CBS agreed to pay him something; I don't know what it was, but he finally got paid a thousand dollars, or something like that.

*What was the toughest thing about working with ad agencies back then? They were superintendents of the account.*
Yes, they were, because in the case of "Gunsmoke" they bought the whole show — all the spots in it — and that gave them the right to interject themselves. Frankly, I didn't have any trouble at all. We kept them pretty well posted on what we were doing. They got copies of the scripts and they were very, very few exceptions. The only real bump I think we ever had on "Gunsmoke" was with the same Betty O'Hara, and it was on a shot of Amanda Blake in the Long Branch Saloon. Now Amanda is a very well endowed young lady. We watched that pretty closely so that we didn't get the cleavage in, but in this shot, we were shooting down a bit, which made a hell of a shot. It was beautiful — beautiful breasts — and everybody liked it, but the agency got a little bit traumatic about it and we had to reshoot it. Two years later you could have gone three times that far and they wouldn't have mentioned it.

*What year did that happen?*
Oh, that was probably in '59, somewhere in there.

*What made you a good producer?*
Well, I think that my background overall has always been in the creative area — music, records. I was a kid radio actor when I was about thirteen. I didn't like acting as a career. I enjoyed fussing around with it, but on top of that, I did know and understand the creative side of it. I also was a graduate in business administration, so I knew the business side of it; and I think, if I have been successful, it's because I combine the business and the creative sides.

*How primitive was the sound process in those days? Any stories about that?*
No, we really didn't have a hell of a lot of trouble. The main thing we had to watch on location, the biggest sound problem, was wind, and we had a couple of mixers who were excellent, who developed their own concept of wind screens that worked very well. The only problem we bumped into — and stayed away from — was getting under trees. In a little wind they started rattling, and the sound of leaves doesn't sound like the sound of leaves, if you know what I mean; so we just had to move away from that. If you watch yourself and plan in the beginning and become aware of sound, then you can always arrange to shoot so you're not affected very much.

*In the early days of TV everything was new to everybody, wasn't it?*
There were no rules.

*Yeah, was that tough?*
No. Basically, the technicians were from the motion picture business, and there's nothing really different in shooting television or feature films. For features you can go on a wider scope basis, bigger shots, and in television you tend to go in for more close-ups, but there's nothing really different in any of that. There's no problem with it. The only problems that existed, which weren't particularly problems, were in the beginning, establishing how long is a television show. I recall arguments we had about whether shows would be twelve minutes, five minutes, twenty minutes, and they made them in all forms, but it didn't take long before it got into the same pattern as radio — then thirty minutes — and later an hour.

*What year were they saying it was twelve minutes?*
'52 to '53. There were a lot of eight-minute shows made. I know one friend of mine who got on a musical jag, signed up a bunch of pretty good artists and vocalists, and he made . . . he must have made 200 eight-

minute musicals, which consisted of two musical numbers and some interview, blah, blah, blah. He finally recovered part of it by, first of all, going to fifteen minutes, which meant adding another number; then he had to vamp a little bit because he only had two numbers from that star, so he brought in her friend so-and-so, who did a number, which was stretching a little bit. Then he got a fifteen-minute show and that worked, and then later they were out, and he finally wound up putting together three groups — two songs from three different artists. That was "Hollywood Showcase," or something.

*Did you ever have to totally rewrite a script on location?*
Not really. We made a big effort at CBS and at NBC, also, working together and getting the script locked down as far as you could, way up front, so there was never any debate on the subject. You've got to know what it's going to be, where you're going, and when you start you shoot it the way it's written, so we didn't have any real problems like that. We had to improvise once in a while when physical things changed, but, no, basically, no trouble with scripts.

*What was the toughest lesson you had to learn when you first came on board? You said you had to learn the business fast.*
The hardest thing for me to learn was patience. The motion picture technique of a single camera and a master shot and over-the-shoulder and two-shots and all this. The repetition of it. I know it has to be, but it drives me out of my mind, and I've even tried shooting multiple cameras. That didn't work well either. But the hardest thing for me to learn was patience. You can look at a scene and you know damn well that you're going to have to cover it, let's say six different ways. It's going to take four hours to maybe eight, all doing the same thing over and over, and that tends to drive me up the wall, but I can't do anything about it. We can beat it when we go into tape, and we'll soon be into tape.

*Did you use two or three cameras — multiple cameras — in the early days?*
I did do it on a couple of occasions but I found it didn't work and it didn't save anything. That was probably, I don't know, '58, or somewhere in there. There had been multiple camera shows done inside, like the Groucho Marx show "You Bet Your Life." That was done on film with up to five cameras, each from established angles, hard lenses, and acres of film.

*Hard lenses? You mean fixed lens?*
Yeah, fixed lenses. We used to call them hard lenses and I still do. But I found that multiple cameras didn't work very well because you're using exterior light as your key, basically, and to get the best angles on actors you can't light both of them at the same time. It just doesn't work. And

actors are pretty smart, too. They want their singles, they want to insure, and they'll blow a line or flub it a little bit, and, of course, you have to go in and pick it up to get their close-up.

*Did that happen very much in any of your shows?*
Oh, yes, to get close-ups. That happened a hell of a lot. With all experienced actors it will happen. The neophytes, no. They don't know enough yet.

*How did you keep the tone of "Have Gun Will Travel"? That's obviously a thing you have to maintain.*
Well, first of all, the stories have to be proper for that tone, and then when you've got the star — in the case of a Richard Boone, he has very definite opinions of what his role is and he doesn't forget them. He's going to do them that way regardless of what you may think. I think the writing has to fit, but, basically, it's the actor that establishes the tone and carries it in any series. Directors come and go, mostly. On some of these interior shows — the greatest of which, I think, is "Barney Miller" — the same guy will direct any number of shows, the actors are so into their roles, they're so established in them, that he doesn't have to worry about that. They know who they are and they do whatever — stage directions aren't particularly important at that time, because they know how they move, how they do everything, so the tone will stay that way.

*What was your production schedule on the average one of those '50s programs?*
Well, our schedule was three days of shooting, and that was true with "Gunsmoke" and "Have Gun." We did one show a week of each of those shows, so we had a day of so-called rehearsal, which we didn't rehearse. It was a good thing for the actors because they had two days off, in effect, every week.

*Two days off a week?*
Well, we would shoot one show a week, so we would generally shoot Tuesday, Wednesday, and Thursday, and they were off Friday and Monday. Now theoretically, Monday we would rehearse, but that was theory; they would come in and say, "How are you," and maybe if there were some wardrobe changes they would fit for those, but that's about all. They were very reasonably done shows. We went on to "Death Valley Days" and did those in three days right straight through. We would start a show on Monday and a second one on Thursday and just go right on until we finished. About a ten-hour day would be normal and average.

*How long in post-production?*
The post-production time applied to these shows was about a week

and a half, overall; that is, if you did twenty-six shows, you would finish them in thirty-nine weeks.

*But you were doing thirty-nine shows back then, weren't you?*
Yeah, but we were doing the thirty-nine shows in thirty-nine weeks and we would just about finish a show out every time we started another one – close to it.

*What's your greatest television moment – your greatest thrill in directing or producing?*
If you could pin it down with "Gunsmoke" – George Gobel on NBC had been the number one show the year before and that year, '55, he was number one. It took us just eleven weeks for "Gunsmoke" to knock him out of number one, and that was a tremendous kick to me. It never got out of that spot for the next four years, but that time I really did get a boot out of.

*Did you use color film at any point in the early days, or was it all black and white?*
It was all black and white. The first color film I got into on television was in 1962 on "Death Valley Days." We started out shooting ten out of twenty-six shows that year in color. I believe we did thirteen out of twenty-six the next year, and then I thought it imperative that we go to all color. We couldn't get any more money from the sponsor, but we worked out a pretty comprehensive study of costs and I found that the cost of 16 [mm] color was the exact equivalent of 35 [mm] black and white, so we did it without any budget increase. It came out within a few dollars, so we went to 16 [mm] and it worked fine.

*Any Ronald Reagan anecdotes from "Death Valley Days"?*
Well, no, the only thing I think of was in one of the early shows he did for us. Ronald is a hell of a horseman, you know. People don't know that, but he's an authority on horses – he raises them – and he knows what he's talking about. He's a great rider. We had a show in which he played William Bent. It was a story about Susan McLoughlin, the first woman that moved West in style. Bill Bent was at Bent's Fort in Colorado, and he rode out to meet the McLoughlin party coming in from the East and – the story is true – he rode a white mule. So we got a white mule, but the only one we could find had a backbone that stuck up about two inches above the meat. I told Ronald when he landed, "We got a white mule," and he said, "A white mule?" I said, "Yes," and he said, "Well, what the hell." Then he went on and got on this thing, and it was a ball-breaker. It really hurt, you know, but he rode it and he rode it pretty well. He refused to react as I had hoped. I thought he would get mad and raise hell and we could substitute a horse.

*How did you get the film to the lab from Death Valley? Did you ever have logistical problems?*

Sure. For example, Kanab, Utah — we made a number of pictures up there, a lot of them. It's been a great motion picture location for thirty-five years, but it's very isolated. Certainly it was then. It was four hours by car to Las Vegas. We got so we would store up about two days of shooting at a time. We had our own company planes, and we would fly it down to L.A. and put it in the lab. But we had to use our own planes to do it.

*What do you think you pioneered in television series production?*

Well, I think that "Gunsmoke" established, as I mentioned earlier, a new and much higher form of dramatic storytelling than had been existent before. And I think in pioneering, the real work was on the "Hopalong Cassidy." We were making a twenty-five-minute show in three days, and we — as a group — kind of established, in doing it, that it could be done. It worked and it became a standard. I think we've done it now in Canada. They run a six-day schedule for a half-hour show. It's ludicrous. We went to four days and never went our full hours. We would finish off in four nine-hour days, which is still very, very generous, and next year, say, we'll go to three.

*Tell me about producing "Huckleberry Finn."*

It wasn't hard because we told a story everybody knows. We took the two books, *Tom Sawyer* and *Huckleberry Finn.* The first eleven episodes of the twenty-six are from the book *Tom Sawyer.* The last fifteen are from *Huckleberry Finn.* We told it as a serial — each story in itself, but as it ends it moved on to the next one, in just the exact progression as it does in the books. It was really quite simple. We had to eliminate some material. There was more in the books than you could tell in twenty-six half-hours. We just lifted whole sequences and didn't put them in. But basically, it's a very faithful recreation of the two novels.

*Any other feelings you have about the old days of TV?*

I would say in the old days — the '50s I'm talking about now — it was more fun than it is today. There wasn't this tremendous network pressure, which is, for the most part, crap, very self-serving crap, and there was always time to fool around. There were a lot of funny gags that the crew would work on themselves and on others and on me.

*For example?*

Oh, I'll give you an example. I had to go out one day to the location at the old Autry ranch, which has since burned down, and get some papers signed by Boyd. I zipped out and parked the car on a Western street. It had overhang roofs up on posts. I parked the car by one of the buildings, out of the camera angles, and got the stuff signed. I came back and got in the car and took off, and I tore down the whole front of the building because these characters, the grips, had put a chain from my front bumper around the supporting post. I pulled away and the whole thing came down. Well, it was fun. It probably held things up five minutes, because these guys were very clever and they had the roof back up again. We had a good laugh, and I miss those things today. They were great.

*What else did they do?*
Well, there were a lot of practical jokes. They had one gag which worked particularly well on visitors to the set. They would get a cardboard box and two of them would get off and look in it, and put a stick in, and jump back and react. Gradually people would wonder what's in that box, so they would go over. But the guys would get the box lower and lower so to see in it a person would have to lean over pretty good, and at that point they would haul off and hit them in the ass with a stick. You know, silly gags. But there was a much better, relaxed attitude than there is any more. It's just push, push, now — which is all right, I guess, it's part of the game, but it isn't as pleasant as it used to be.

*What were Hoppy and "Gunsmoke" costing in the early days?*
The Hoppy shows — we made fifty-two of them, in '52 and '53 — were $21,000 a show, and made a profit on that. Today that would be $130,000–$140,000, maybe more. "Gunsmoke" I don't want to give the figures out on because it's a CBS property, but it was about 50 percent more than the Hoppies, and before they were finished they went into hour shows; before they were finished they were costing $600,000 or $700,000 an episode.

*So, is the '50s the Golden Age of TV?*
It was the most interesting time, yeah. I think it was the Golden Age. I think that we're making much better pictures now, we're spending a lot more money, more scope; in fact, I think that a great many television pictures today, series pictures and movies, are as well done or better than feature motion pictures — theatricals. I have no illusions about that. I bitch like the public does about the quality of the stories and the subject matters, but not how they're done. Technically, they're excellent, terrific.

*What about explosives in the old days? Did you have trouble rigging explosives or gunshots?*
No. It wasn't that primitive. Powder men have been shooting explosives off in films since 1920 and they're very good at it. The guys then were better than the ones today. Now they're into some electronic fusing and all that, which is probably safer, but, hell, the squibs for

gunshots and all worked just as well then as they do now. It's a small explosive charge and it still is, so there was nothing primitive about it.

Basically, today we use lighter cameras, better lenses, more maneuverable lenses, lighting equipment that's a hell of a lot easier to move and to use than the old iron lights; but they do the same thing, and that's the name of the game. Nothing has really changed. The one thing that's changed a hell of a lot is film. It's much better — much more versatile and much more forgiving, and that's good. It's also much more expensive, but the improvement in film in the last few years, last twelve years, has been very remarkable and very noticeable. Exposure levels are lower and color is better, the whole overall aspect of laboratory and processing is better and that's very helpful. As I say, it's more forgiving. Some of these guys today, some of these cameramen, would have fallen right on their ass twenty years ago.

*How's that?*

Because then you had damn small latitude. You had to be right or you were wrong. Now you can go up and down the scale and you've got to be really bad to be wrong. Today if you underexpose the lab will correct it, and they can do it. Then, they couldn't; if you were under, you were under, so it was far more demanding of the cameraman. But, by and large, most of the guys today are excellent — good technicians, and in Hollywood more than any other areas, good techniques. They have done it so many times they know what works and what doesn't. There is no need of experimenting, they've been through it, and that's what saves time and money and gets better effects.

*Chuck Jones*

Beep-beep zoom!!
Who has not felt like Wile E. Coyote in a world full of Road
Runners? Who has not felt as forlorn as the poor fellow betrayed by
his singing frog in "One Froggy Evening?" These are the characters of
art – the ones we think we know, or the ones we think we are.

Chuck Jones, the animator who created the Road Runner, is an
intellectual and a gentleman in manner and person, and an artist
clear through. A tall, slim man with a retiring quality to his voice,
he has a magic ability to laugh at life and yet be absolutely serious
about his art.

Jones is known principally as a director, having directed more
than 200 Bugs Bunny cartoons and more than two dozen Road Runners during his twenty-four years (1938–1962) in the "Termite Ter-
race" at Warner Bros. There, he and other animator geniuses turned
out frame after frame of drawings and brought to life characters
who are more real than most people: Daffy Duck, Porky Pig, Sylvester and Tweetie Bird, Pepe Le Pew.

Recognized as one of the best animators in the world, Jones has
won three Oscars and numerous other awards for his work. He now
has his own production company, which has produced several
animated television specials.

*You believe that movement and acting are really the most important
things in animation?*
I don't think that acting is the only thing that counts, but what we
call character animation is just like any other kind of acting: The
character is identified not primarily by the way he looks, but by the way
he moves. This is true of anything that's alive; all living things are defined
as individuals by their movements, not by what they look like. If a turtle
moved fast we would not recognize him as a turtle. The slow action of his
head and the way his feet struggle are what make him a turtle, not
because he looks like a turtle. Also, if you are animating a turtle, you
must ask yourself, "Okay, we're doing a turtle, but *which* turtle?" – just as
we would with a particular person. Each turtle, each person is different
because they think, act, and move differently. This is what's wrong with
Saturday morning cartoons. The audience, children particularly, are left
with the idea that personality is determined by what people look like and
not how they move. Edmund Gwenn demonstrates how false this idea is.
He can play Santa Claus in *Miracle on 34th Street* and in *Foreign
Correspondent* he can be a psychopathic killer. That's because he *acted*
differently with the same body – he changed his whole attitude to fit each
part. This is as true with actors like [Peter] Sellers or [Laurence] Olivier or
[Alec] Guinness as it was with all the Disney characters, who were *always*
identified by the way they moved.

*What is some of the most remarkable character animation you've seen in
your pictures?*

Great animators are lovely people to work with. I had a crew of great animators for nearly twenty-five years. In "What's Opera, Doc?" the ballet sequence was animated by Ken Harris, who did a remarkable piece of animation. It is remarkable because it is very funny; it is also remarkable because it is art, and the ballet is honestly done even though Bugs and Elmer are the principals. Ed Wynn said that a comedian is not a man who opens a funny door; he is a man who opens a door funny. I don't think anything more profound has ever been said about animation or humor.

A curious thing about character animation has been overlooked by nearly everybody: Character animation is unique to America. No foreign country has developed a Mickey Mouse or Bugs Bunny; not *one* of their characters has gained international acceptance. I know of only a few characters that have even gone from one country to another, such as "Asterisk," who does very well in France and Italy, but doesn't do well in England and the United States. There are some characters that are popular *within* countries, but the United States has created a communication form with character animation—just as jazz is an American innovation. I'm sure it never occurred to great jazz musicians that they had created a form of art unique to the world. Nor did we. True character animation, which can survive without any background or color or dialogue, originated in Southern California and New York. Even Canada and Yugoslavia, who have done remarkable things in film graphics, have not stabilized characters that can move across international borders.

We were very fortunate to be part of this birth and growth of a communication form. It is a unique phenomenon that has been largely ignored by critics, particularly in America. Animators work with such simple tools: a flurry of pieces of paper and pencil—that's really all that is needed. You don't even need a camera. You can hold this bundle of drawings in your hands and flip it. Just like children do when they make those little stick figures on the corners of tablets and books and by flipping, make them dance. That's all there is to animation. But when you want them to come to a more complicated life, you need more education. Grim Natwick, one of the great animators, said that a journeyman animator needs approximately 2,000 basic tools. One of those tools, he said, is knowledge of how a horse gallops. That's just *one* tool. Another tool is how a dog runs, which is very different from a horse galloping or an elephant running or a kangaroo hopping. They are all wonderfully different. These are some of the tools an animator must learn. It takes as long to become a journeyman character animator as it does to become a doctor—seven or eight years.

*What are the principal art skills needed? You touched on that, but . . . ?*
It's very simple. The same basic tool you'll find underlying every

graphic form: line control. The ability to make a line and live with that
line. Take Degas, for example, and look at the line that runs down the leg
of the ballerina. If you look at it closely you will see that it's a very, very
simple straight line with an opposing curved line. That defines the shape
of the leg. This line control holds just as true with the early Picassos as it
does with Leonardo. It also holds true with cartoonists like Herblock,
Lowe, the *New Yorker* cartoonists, Andy Warhol, and Claës Oldenberg.
All these people have that ability, and that's one of the hardest things, the
most demanding tool to achieve. It's easy to draw by doing a lot of
shading and diffuse lines, etc., but if you are to succeed at drawing, you
must cut away all the fat until you are left with that single line, the line
that has to tell the story. It's a very subtle matter. Bugs Bunny has a tiny
nose resting on a stubby form. If your rabbit, say, has a three-inch-high
head, in this scale, then 3/16 of the mouth on either side of the nose
defines the mouth. The cheek overlaps the mouth. We noticed that
cheekiness was true of babies and an actress named Sonia Heine: she just
had too chubby cheeks to make a broad smile. So, incorporating that
unlikely idea into Bugs, you must be able to express his reactions with
those little tiny 3/16ths. When he's sad, it turns down; when happy, up. If
he's disgusted, then we must know what to do. Bugs's upper teeth are
anchored to his skull, just like all upper teeth are. If the animator lets the
upper teeth move, then the face appears rubbery and you lose
believability. And believability is the name of the game in humor.

*What kind of animation moves do the "Saturday morning" producers do?*
    What they're doing on Saturday morning is what I call "Illustrated
Radio." They build a full dialogue and use as *few* drawings as they can.
They anchor the heads on one cell; the lips move and the eyes blink,
maybe. Occasionally, the heads will turn, but everyone moves the same.
They're getting to the point now where the so-called animator can punch
a button and bring up an already animated run applicable to that
character. When they run, they all run lockstep, which is very much like
early English hunting prints, which had all the horses' legs spread out and
running in step. Horses don't run that way, but it is much cheaper to
animate that way. The main thing is that they are really not expressing
character by movement. If a teacher got up in front of a class and held her
body still and only moved her lips, and maybe blinked occasionally, the
child would very soon lose interest in what she was saying. But if she
demonstrates what she is talking about by her hand movements or body
movements, the children catch the essence of her personality and her
interest in what she is saying. In order to find out whether we were telling
our stories with animation and not dialogue, we ran all of our pictures
without dialogue, music, or sound effects, just the line test or pencil
test—just like Marcel Marceau working on a bare stage. The whole story
is there. Does it explain itself? With the line test you will not get all the

subtleties of the speech patterns, but you should be able to tell in a line test what's happening, without the dialogue.

*So you used that as a test to see whether or not it really worked?*
 Yes, that's right. You do make little changes after the test running, but all the editing was done by the director before going into animation. The astonishing thing to most live-action directors is that the animation film, at least at Warner Bros., was always completely timed and there was practically *no* editing at the end. The editing was always completely timed by the director before it went to animation, every frame accounted for on exposure sheets: Where the director wants the characters to land, to stop, each move of a dance sequence is carefully plotted out musically for the animator. This doesn't mean the animator isn't a brilliant contributor—like great actors, he is vital and necessary. As I say, for something like this marvelous dance sequence, Ken Harris studied the actions of ballet so he would have all the movements right in "What's Opera, Doc?" There was also a great dance sequence in a picture called "A Bear for Punishment"—it's one of the funniest pieces of action ever done and is considered by animators to be one of the greatest pieces of animation ever done. This middle-aged, slatternly old lady bear doing a dance, a tribute to her husband for Father's Day, is overwhelmingly, enormously funny and it took a great animator to bring it off. Often the difference between 1/32 of an inch and ¼ of an inch can make the difference between good animation and great animation. It's about the same relationship of an eighth note and a sixteenth note in a Chopin etude. That tiny little hesitation is just as vital as any full note. The same thing is true in animation. If you don't have respect for 1/24 of a second, you had better go into another trade.

*What's the main difference between producing animation for theaters and animation for television?*
 There is no difference as far as I am concerned. When I did "How the Grinch Stole Christmas" or "The Cricket in Times Square," I never made them for a particular audience. We always try to make them for ourselves, with the utmost skill we have available. I believe that is what an audience has a right to expect. Pauline Kaël said it as well as anybody: "The very least that an artist owes an audience is his very best." Also, you must never talk down to an audience. If you are talking to children, you must never suppose you know better than they do, because they're very quick to recognize the false and falseness immediately turns a child off. I don't know who the audience is, and I don't pay any attention to what the size of the screen is, but I believe any film should be able to play in a theater. In order to see something thin, pick any one of the Saturday morning shows and run it on a full-size screen. These shows are so thin they only have one side. As Abraham Lincoln said, "This is as thin as

chicken soup made by boiling the shadow of a chicken that died of starvation."

*That's great. Are you a patient person?*
Oh, that's hard to say. People think that you must be because of the seeming slowness of animation. It took us five weeks in each department to make a single six-minute animated cartoon, and I would direct ten a year. I don't know whether I'm patient or not. I've never worked with live action, but friends of mine who direct live action who finish a picture and then spend fourteen months editing . . . I don't think I could take that. They shoot a 9,000-foot film in maybe ten or twelve or fourteen weeks, and it takes me a lot longer from start to finish to do the same amount of footage. We do the same kind of editing, but ours is pre-editing; theirs is post-editing.

People often ask where the characters come from. In my experience, they can come only from within. Robert Benchley said the greatest danger to human beings is that we tend to become the kind of person we despise most. So if, for instance, you're doing a Daffy Duck, you fish down into the area of yourself, into the area of the despicable where the character like Daffy resides; all of us, like Daffy, are somewhat parsimonious, miserly . . . I simply bring this to the surface and exaggerate it . . . and Voila! Daffy. Daffy would agree with Mark Twain that it isn't enough that I succeed but also my best friend must fail—pure Daffy. Daffy is what I am. Bugs is what I would like to be. He is a heroic figure, and there aren't many of those among comedians. Most of our characters are failures: The Coyote is a failure, just as Chaplin is a failure. He simply isn't very lucky in life. Buster Keaton and Woody Allen are losers, comedians after very simple things. I think that the difference between tragedy and comedy is that the goals, the comedian's needs, are very simple; his failures are easy to understand.

*How do you sell an idea to the network? What was the most difficult idea to sell to the network?*
The first TV special I worked on was "How the Grinch Stole Christmas." The networks put up the money for the storyboard, and then I had to go out and sell a sponsor on this idea. It was very difficult. I think I made twenty-five presentations to various clients before we got one to buy. Today it is different. Even a presold show won't do you any good anymore with the network. Apparently enough people are begging to buy into good shows. So the network makes its own decisions about what shows it will buy.

*What year was that—when "The Grinch" was first on?*
1983 was the seventeenth year that "The Grinch" has been on.

*What makes Chuck Jones run?—and don't say "the Road Runner."*

No, I wouldn't say that. I have a friend in New York, one of the best heart transplant surgeons in the world. His interests are very, very catholic—very broad—nothing channelized. The fact that he has the incredibly difficult knowledge to perform these fantastic heart operations doesn't keep him from being a man of wide interests. That's what we like about each other: Each of us is a specialist, but he said one time what a fantastic thing it is to be paid well for doing what you would do for nothing. Being paid well for what you love to do is so astonishing; but money is not an excuse for putting down your pencil and picking up a golf club, which is a ridiculous trade. I have been lucky enough to fall into a craft that I love and enjoy. I've had to fight, sure, but I suppose if you don't fight for something, you aren't really able to find your way—there must be opposition. I'm seventy-one years old, and from the time I was nineteen I've been doing things that I enjoy. So what better luck can you have than that?

*Do you like to be around during the sound mix? And what's the hardest thing about recordings?*
Yes, I insist upon being there during the sound mix because you've usually got a battle going on between your musicians and your sound editor. The mixers are perfectly happy to do whatever you want them to do, but if there's a musician there and a sound effects man, and sometimes a speech man, too, each with his own ideas, you're in trouble. Basically, they really don't seem to realize that we're making a motion picture. They are often seemingly unaware of the visual side of motion pictures.

*Any generality about the importance of character in animation?*
Bugs is forty-four years old, forty-five years old. Mickey Mouse will never see fifty again. We had no idea of making pictures for following generations. It is startling to find out that the Bugs Bunnies that we made, and the Road Runners, and all the others—many, many others of all different kinds—are being viewed by succeeding generations as contemporary. Our cartoons are not treated by today's audiences as if they were looking at artifacts. That's staggering because we certainly didn't have any idea that we were making films that would become history. Bugs and his friends and his relatives survive. That's pretty damn surprising and pretty damn neat, too. It sure wasn't planned that way. But I can still enjoy the pleasure, even though we didn't plan to produce films with lasting qualities—nor did Chaplin or Keaton or Laurel and Hardy.

*Any generalities on the personality types of animators?*
No, I don't think it makes any difference. It is like working with an actor—I don't care what his personality is. A great puppeteer I once knew was so shy that he actually couldn't talk in public. He could barely talk in

private without blushing, and yet he could do astonishing things with marionettes. As long as he couldn't be seen, he was expressing himself through the marionettes. They were outgoing, they were crazy, they were sexy, I mean, brilliantly sexy, and could dance beautifully, too, although the puppeteer could not. One of our greatest animators, Ken Harris, on the outside seemed to be a very simple person and not one that could be a great artist, but he was a great artist.

*Obviously you're versed in many arts. It's very hard to communicate the importance of this to students and to other people who want to go into the field. They sometimes just want to learn the technical stuff.*

You just never know in animation or comedy when you're going to be called upon to have knowledge of some obscure something. I have always been interested in how the human body works, and so I was ready when I was asked to direct a film on the human senses. I directed the animation sequences for the Bell Telephone science series and although I had to do a lot of background work, I had something to start with just because it interested me. I knew, generally, how the senses worked, but I was startled when I found that a good case could be made that there is only one sense. I had always assumed there were five, but there may be seventeen more. There are several that are very puzzling; one set of senses I wasn't aware of responds to cold, one set responds to heat and one sense responds to pressure, so you have three right there I'd never heard of in the area that you would normally think of having as only one: touch. Okay. But then how do we know where our arms are when we're moving them in a dark room? If I lift my arm over my head and wave it around, how do I know where it is? I can't see it. Something new! A sense called "feedback," one of the most intricate set of neural responses in the world. You need curiosity working for you all the time, because if somebody comes along and says, "Do a picture on the senses," chances are pretty good that without any background or any knowledge, without curiosity you won't know where to start. Reading *everything* is very important. If someone asks "How about producing *Alice in Wonderland* or *Through the Looking Glass*," if you haven't read it, you're dead right now. You can't say, "I'll produce *Alice in Wonderland* but I don't know what it's all about." So it seems to me that you have to have a thread of knowledge that extends all the way through an entire culture of our times. The main thing is that reading is in itself provocative. I enjoy opening the dictionary and finding a word, any word. I've never been able to stop there because one word in the dictionary will eventually lead you to every other word in the dictionary. So people who read the dictionary for fun are always interesting people. I could never have produced the Dickens or Kipling if I had never read them. I have a very deep feeling about "Rikki Tikki Tavi" — my mother read the story to me when I was four years old. It enchanted me then, and over the years it has stuck in my mind. I never knew that I was going to do it as a film, but when I did, I knew what to do and what to look for, the kinds of action needed. How does a cobra move? How does a mongoose move? It must be believable. Like the animators who brought the dinosaurs to life in *Fantasia*. What an incredible accomplishment! Here are animals who have been extinct for 50 million years, and by studying the bone structure they were able to figure out what kind of muscles were needed to operate those bones and how such an animal *had* to move. Animals always move the way they *have* to move. A kangaroo is structured so it can *only* jump — it cannot do anything else. Oddly enough, when it's born the kangaroo doesn't have any hind legs to speak of. The newborn kangaroo, whose mother is six feet tall, is only about the size of a clothespin. The front legs are well developed because they must climb from the womb up to the pouch by themselves, and the hind legs would be such a hindrance that they probably would never make it. Inside the pouch the reverse happens: They develop huge hind legs and the front legs become proportionately small. The hands and arms are used only to help him to eat, not for locomotion. Even if you are never called upon to animate a kangaroo, the knowledge is stimulating. One vertebrate is all you need to study because from then on you can study all vertebrates with comparative anatomy, from shrews to whales. Whales even have legs buried deep within their bodies, and snakes *do* have hips. It's all interesting not because I'm an animator; it's interesting because I'm me.

*You mentioned your childhood. Was your childhood a kind of enchanted childhood?*

No, it was quite normal, I think. The only thing was that my father was great on reading. He told us at the breakfast table, "The breakfast table is no place for conversation. You should read, and if you don't have anything else to read, read the cereal box. You never know where you're going to find something." I was pretty good on Post Toasties and Shredded Wheat. I had them pretty well memorized. Reading anything will stimulate your interest in reading; Shredded Wheat led to study of Niagara Falls, which led to waterfalls in general and thus to mountains and things that live on mountains. I know of no way to get knowledge so quickly as by reading. Because your chances of meeting someone like Mark Twain in life are extremely remote. Even getting to meet Woody Allen, very much a person of our time, is not likely. But you can read Woody Allen as well as enjoy him as the great comedian he is.

*Can we inspire creativity in children?*

There are several good rules, I think. First of all, many teachers, and most parents, consider themselves to be art critics, which is a staggering assumption when you consider that they would never consider themselves to be music critics. Art to many people is considered a gift;

music must be learned. So when a child comes in with his drawing on which his child is bigger than his house, parent says, "Oh, come on now, you know better than that. People aren't bigger than houses." Maybe the flowers too are bigger than the child and the smile that goes across the child's face is bigger than the face. All those things are pertinent to childhood and the discovery and exploration of this brave new world. A drawing of a child dancing may have seven elbows and the very first thing the parent says, flatly and foolishly, is, "You don't have seven elbows." But when a child first learns to dance, freely and happily, you do seem to have seven elbows and seven knees, too, and a happy smile is always bigger than the face.

My parents never overcriticized or overpraised, and when any of us would come in with a drawing they wouldn't say, "That's wonderful." Most parents either criticize or say "wonderful." By the time they've said "wonderful" five or six times, the child will lose any faith, any belief in his parents' opinion. To the child, the parent is not interested. If you look at a child's drawing carefully, there is always something that may be said that doesn't have anything to do with the quality of the drawing. If there's a lot of blue in it, you can safely say, "Hey, you sure used a lot of blue," or if it's a wild scribble you could say, "That must have been fun! You scribbled all over the place, didn't you?" Well, right now, the kid did scribble, he saw that he scribbled, and he can say to himself, "Hey, man, we can share this." You try to observe intelligently what he has done. If he makes little drawings way down in the corner of the page, which he may do if he's not feeling very well or feeling put upon, you might say, "Look at all that white space around there; I've seldom seen a drawing way down in the corner that way." Such a response may stimulate exploration and indicates interest. "Hey, that's a good idea! Next time I'll try it on the other corner, maybe, or maybe I'll make just a big loose drawing." Often a child will present a drawing of a black sun — just a black spot in the sky — and the parent will say, "What's that?" "It's the sun," and the parent with lofty and erroneous response says, "Yeah, but the sun is yellow, it's not black," which is absolute nonsense. The sun isn't yellow. Nobody knows what color it is. Our eyes will not receive such brilliance. But one thing is absolutely certain: When a child glances at the sun and looks away very quickly because it hurts, he'll see an afterimage of the sun that *is* black, and that afterimage is just as real as the sun itself. Also, it's much easier for anybody to draw a black sun on a blue sky than it is to make a yellow sun, if you like, and put blue all over the sky. So, first of all, it isn't a question of helping the children to draw — children will draw anyway if they're encouraged to draw and given proper tools. The proper tools are very simple . . . they're just a lot of paper and a lot of pencils. They don't have to be color. Just anything to draw with. My father used to tell us never to draw on both sides of the paper. When you think about it, that's very important, because it gives dignity to a drawing not to work on both sides, and dignity is the kind of encouragement a child needs when he starts to draw. Picasso said he spent all his life trying to draw like child. Children can make astonishing drawings. The best giraffe I ever saw was made by a child who drew a cerise giraffe with purple spots. It looked more like a giraffe than most giraffes because a giraffe is such an astonishing creature. This six-year-old girl was so interested in the astonishing quality of the giraffe that it wasn't nearly good enough to make it yellow and brownish black, so she drew a cerise giraffe with purple spots and it really worked beautifully. Then she put a pale pink background and the whole conception just came zinging out of the frame. I traded her out of it. I gave her a Bugs Bunny for it, and she was the loser although she didn't seem to think so.

The important thing, I think, is to give dignity to our children's efforts. To realize the basic difference between adult drawing and child drawing. The genius of the child drawing is infinite, but the one thing a child cannot do is to repeat what he has just done, and that is exactly what the adult artist in his lifetime strives to do. If the adult artist does something well, he wants to repeat it. If you ask a child to make another one like the one he has just drawn, he can't do it. If he tries, it will look like an awkward imitation. Drawing is so much fun, and children do it so beautifully, but criticism is the death of the whole matter. Any child can draw, and all children could draw for all their lives if they were not stamped on so early.

*Fred Rogers*

YES, FRED ROGERS is as calm and deliberate in real life as he is in "Mister Rogers' Neighborhood." He says, "I have to take time to think about what I've been asked, and if that doesn't go along with television technology, then that's too bad. I am not just a prepackaged man."

After graduating from Rollins College in Winter Park, Florida, with a degree in music composition, Fred Rogers headed to New York to work as assistant producer of "The Voice of Firestone," "The NBC Television Opera Theater," "The Kate Smith Hour," and "Your Lucky Strike Parade."

In 1953 he joined WQED-TV in Pittsburgh and was assigned development of a program schedule. "Children's Corner" grew out of that. "Children's Corner," which Rogers helped to write, produce and perform, won the Sylvania Award in 1955 as the best locally produced children's show in the country. It ran for seven years.

In 1963 Rogers was ordained a minister of the United Presbyterian Church, dedicating his ministry to working with young people and their parents by using the television medium. That year he introduced "Mister Rogers" on the Canadian Broadcasting Corporation as a fifteen-minute program. In 1964 he incorporated his programs into thirty-minute productions, and the show made its appearance over the ABC-TV affiliate in Pittsburgh. By 1966, "Mister Rogers" was seen for the first time in Chicago, New York, Philadelphia, Boston, San Francisco, and over the Maine and Eastern Educational Networks.

Today the show is carried by over 250 public television stations, and Fred Rogers has received a George Foster Peabody Award, five Emmy nominations, a Saturday Review Television Award, and numerous honorary doctoral degrees from leading universities. Rogers was chairman of the panel on mass media at the 1970 White House Conference on Children.

Rogers was born in Latrobe, Pennsylvania. He is the father of two sons, James and John; his wife, Joanne, is a concert pianist.

*You began in television with Firestone as a producer. What sort of things did you do as assistant producer?*

Well, I carried coffee and Coca-Cola and, generally, what was known as a "gopher." Do you know what that means? Well, I would "go for" things so that's what they would call it — "gopher" — in the early days, and an assistant to the producer did most of that and took notes. Then I became a network floor manager.

*What were the lessons that you learned for your subsequent producing efforts?*

Well, when I was floor managing, I was assistant to the producer to begin with, and afterwards I got to be a network floor manager. On the other side of the camera I really learned a lot. I remember floor managing "The Gabby Hayes Show." Once, I said to him, "Mr. Hayes, when you see the camera and know that there are millions of people watching you, what do you think?" And he said, "Freddy, I just think of one little bucka-roo." It was very important to me to be able to remember that later on and think, "My, that's exactly what I do." I look at the camera and think of one person. It could be a conglomerate of all the children that I've worked with or have ever known or read about, but still it's just one person, and I think that has to do with my being very personal as far as the camera is concerned. But I also learned that you can't separate your work from your living. I have seen people walk into a studio—floor managers, that is—who knew it all, and they would say to the stagehands, "Get this for me," and, "Do this and do that," and sometimes the productions just didn't go very smoothly at all. I remember the first day I walked into the studio after I was made a floor manager. I said to the head stagehand, who had been there since practically the beginning of NBC, "You know, I'm new on the job. This is the first floor-managing job I've ever had and I really need your help," and he patted me on the back and said, "You'll do fine, buddy." And he and the rest of the crew could not have been more helpful to me. If there were things I didn't know I would go and ask them, and they did so much for me. It was very different from the floor manager that I observed who walked in on his first day and knew it all.

*Was there any major "boo-boo" that you made back then?*
    Oh yes. When I was floor manager for "The Kate Smith Hour," I gave a cue too soon to fly one of the sets. Miss Smith was singing in front of this farmhouse, and I thought that she had finished the song and we were going on to the next episode. I gave the cue, and the farmhouse started to go up in the air, which on camera, of course, looked like she was going down. I saw it on the monitor quick enough to be able to stop it, but I'll never forget that. Everybody was so particular on that program, naturally. They did it every day, five days a week, and it was all live, of course. I remember the big contact lenses that she used. They covered her whole eyeball and they must have been so painful. Whenever there was a commercial she had them taken out and they put new liquid in. You know, these were the days before all of the very flimsy contact lenses—tiny things. Hers were just enormous.

*You worked on "The Hit Parade" show. That was an old radio redo for TV. Were there any great changes they had to make for TV?*
    Well, I remember how difficult it was. Each week, for instance, when a song was very, very popular and it might be on "The Hit Parade" fifteen or sixteen weeks on a row, to be able to do that song in different locations, even just slightly different vignettes, you know, was very demanding creatively. I remember "Shrimp Boats" was on for a long, long time and they would have different people sing it. They used to have a mini-drama around each song. There were five floor managers for that

program. It went just like clockwork. We began at 7:00 in the morning, and I'll never forget it — in fact, I'm sure it influenced me a lot as far as being on time for things — but I remember: 7:00, Dorothy Collins rehearses "Shrimp Boats"; 7:09, so-and-so does something else; 7:16, Snooky Lansen — he was there and in fact, he used to play craps behind the set with the stagehands and there were times when I would have to go back and I'd say, "Mr. Lansen, you're on in three minutes," because, of course, it was all live. All day long it was that closely scheduled up until the time we went on — I think it was 10:00 at night — but that entire day was that heavily scheduled. It was a wonderfully well-produced program.

*How do you look back on that experience in terms of today's production standards and the kinds of sophistications that we now have? Do you have any thoughts on that?*

Well, there was a lot of rear screen projection. You know what I mean by that. And I think there was an awful lot of imagination. Of course, it was all live and people didn't have the chance to do it over because there was no videotape. We didn't even show kinescopes. We might have a kinescope recording just to have a record of the program, but kine quality wasn't that good in those days. I think there was a certain excitement about it, just as there is in live theater — an excitement that taped programs sometimes don't have. It was different. You can't knock the technological advances because there are lots of things that add to the color, certainly add to the craft itself. The editors have an awful lot to do with today's productions. In fact, they can make or break them at times.

*How did "Mister Rogers' Neighborhood" get started? I know you had a "Children's Corner" show. Was that more or less the format that you had later with "Mister Rogers"?*

Not really. When I went to Canada in '62, after I graduated from the seminary, I went to CBC in Canada; I had never been on camera before that. We started "The Children's Corner" in '54. Josie Carey was the person who talked to the puppets, and there just wasn't any difference between reality and fantasy in that program. She would just go to her backdrop, and there would be a clock or a castle or something like that. But in Canada, the head of children's programming — his name was Dr. Frederick Rainsberry — insisted that I be on camera talking to kids. So we had to divide the program into parts because I would have to run from my piano over to the set that had the puppets, and then we would have different guests come and talk to the puppets. But that's the first time that I really addressed myself to children on camera, and it was Fred Rainsberry's idea to call it "Mister Rogers." It was a fifteen-minute program, and we did it every day. My assistant puppeteer was Ernie Coombs, who came with me from Pittsburgh, and when I decided to come back to Pittsburgh (I just felt that I wanted to raise our kids in

America), Ernie stayed on at my suggestion and they built a program around him which is still going on CBC, called "Mr. Dress-Up." So that was the beginning of Ernie's association with them, and he's just been all over Canada. He's a wonderful person.

*How did your show evolve in terms of appealing to children — meeting children's needs and so forth?*

Gee, I think all of that just came from inside. The original "Children's Corner" was meant to be Josie introducing free films, which I would get from all over the country. The program was an hour in length, and Josie would introduce the film, and five or ten minutes into the film it would break, because free films are often poor quality. So when it would break, I would dip into my bag of puppets and pull out a different one, and that's how I had to learn to be a puppeteer. I mean, I did that when I was a child, but all I thought I would ever do on the "Children's Corner" would be to play the organ for Josie to sing, and be the producer. So, little by little, those films forced us into something that we never expected we would have to do, and, of course, that was the making of it.

*What were the subjects of the films?*

Oh, how to grow grass in Connecticut, I mean, I would get anything that I could. When you're on for an hour a day you do whatever you can. It was all appropriate stuff, but certainly not stuff that one would think that a preschool child would eat up with relish. For instance, there was one series called, "Ein, Zwei, Drei," which was a series that taught German to children. Well, obviously, there were people who wanted to listen to what we were giving. In those days there was practically nothing for children to see, and we were on at 5:00 in the afternoon and we had no idea that anybody was watching, none at all. Then one day, Daniel Tiger said, "It's my birthday on Friday," and Josie said, "Well, why don't we invite everybody to come?" Well, there were people standing around the block on Friday, waiting to get into the station, and it was then that we got scared, because we realized that people *were* watching. We thought we were just going into the studio and talking to each other every day. I mean, this was the first community television station in the United States. The first station that was supported by the community. We did that "Children's Corner" for eight years.

*How did that affect you? Did you end up doing anything in response to your fright?*

Oh, no, we started things like the Tame Tiger Torganization and encouraged kids to write to us. We had little contests so the kids could send in drawings and things. When I brought King Friday out as a puppet who said he was a king without a country, he asked the kids if they would send their suggestions for his country. One child said since his name was

King Friday the Thirteenth he should be king of Calendarland, and so we did that, and we had that child come in and we crowned him Prince. You know, there's a lot you can do with local television that you can't do with national television. We could be timely. We talked about the weather. These were all the very early days of "The Children's Corner." But then, of course, we grew in different directions. Josie went to commercial television and I went and started this thing in Canada, which I never realized would turn into what it is now — "Mister Rogers' Neighborhood."

*You have children of your own. Do you ever end up testing your ideas on them?*
    Well, I used to. I used to ask them what they thought about it. I've also worked with children all of my professional life and so I've always had a community of kids that could give me responses to what we were doing. I've worked with them one-to-one, as well as in groups, and that's the way I learned about what their inner needs are.

*Kids are pretty honest. They'll sort of give you what they feel, won't they?*
    Oh, I had a wonderful conversation with a six-year-old girl this morning. She was telling me about the different friends that she had. Her mother and father were divorced and so she was here with her dad and her mother lives in New York. She said, "Yes, I have about thirty friends in New York and I have five friends here in Pittsburgh," and I said, "Well, I imagine that you make friends wherever you go, because you are a really good player," and do you know what her response was? "Yeah, I don't cheat." And I thought, "What a fascinating response." She knows that that makes for good relationships.

*Your concern is making children feel good about themselves. That seems to be one of the major thrusts of your program.*
    That's right, because I feel that if you can feel good about who you are, then you're able to feel good about your neighbor, whoever you happen to be with at the moment. But, of course, the corollary is also true: If you don't feel good about who you are, you do not have the basis within you of being able to look on someone else with compassion and care and value. So I think it's important to start with self.

*You compliment people a lot. Is that to teach appreciation? "Mr. McFeely is an excellent delivery person" — that type of thing.*
    I don't think that it's helpful to compliment someone if you don't mean it. If, in fact, Mr. McFeely did make a delivery one day that was very unsatisfactory, I think it would be important *not* to say, "Oh, well, you're a wonderful delivery man." I think that it's important to let him know, or to let anybody know, when you have differences of opinion with them. It's like being in touch with someone who has an obvious

physical handicap. It's important right from the beginning to acknowledge that the person does have that handicap, because if you don't, that person might think that you are not accepting all of him. I met a man with braces on his leg at a gym one time and after a few pleasantries, I said, "What is the need for your braces?" And he went into a long tale about how he was in an automobile accident and all the rest of it. But, you know, if I had avoided that, he might have thought, "Well, that man accepts me for everything except this thing, which is very important to me."

*You have studied child psychology, have you not, at the graduate level?*
Yes.

*Do you ever find in your studies that your own first instincts about children and what makes them tick are really remarkably right?*
Well, this is what our chief consultant always says to me, and she was my chief teacher as far as the Child Development Department was concerned. She was the head of the whole thing when I studied at Pitt, and she will invariably remind me of the days before I had any work in psychology. She says, "Fred, you know, you were in tune with kids when you first came here." She says, "Sure, hopefully, we've been able to help in your development, but don't ever forget that the ground of your being was already there." I have wonderful people to help us — wonderful people. I don't know — have you been in touch with David Newell, who plays Mr. McFeely?

*Yes, I have.*
Well, David is just a supreme human being. This morning in a meeting, for instance, he gave me an idea, which will, most certainly, carry through to an entire week of "Neighborhood" programs next year — an idea about competition. It was beautifully thought out. Last season it was his idea to do the whole week on superheroes, too. You know, we have a real community here of people who feel exceedingly invested in what we do.

*How does Mister Rogers keep from becoming pedantic? How do you keep the balance between the real social needs of children and entertainment, or do you see any dichotomy there?*
Well, Irv, I think what I try to do is keep in touch with the Fred Rogers of my youth, as much as I can, and realize that I can't be a "star" to that child; I have to be a compassionate, caring person to the child within, and in so doing, I would hope that I would be that to the children who are on the outside of me. It's a relationship, this work that I do; it's a television relationship. It is not a show. It's a sharing of a person. And those puppets are all part of me. They are all facets of what I am, and

when I write and when I compose music, sing songs, and actually appear on the camera—I consider all that a gift. I'm giving a person, I'm giving an adult who has a care for children. That's what I'm doing. I'm not putting on a show, and I think that's what comes through. You know, people are just astounded that kids, even hyperactive kids, will sit for half a hour and be in touch with what we do on the air. Many adults are just agog at the reaction of children. Well, I think that people long for honesty and they are looking for it anywhere they can find it.

*What was your youth like? Was it a kind of magical time?*
    I think that my early youth was a fairly lonely time. I was an only child until my sister came when I was eleven, and I was fairly heavily protected. So I was forced to make up a lot of my own play—my own friends even—and so I'm sure that's why I played with puppets and at five started to play the piano. I had to do an awful lot of entertainment of myself, and I was around adults a great deal.

*What did you learn from adults? Did they relate to you? I mean, did it seem to them like you were older?*
    I think so, yes, and I think that their expectations were fairly high. Happily, I had a grandfather—incidentally, his name was Mr. McFeely—who would say to my mother and grandmother, whenever they would tell me I wasn't allowed to walk on his walls, or something—he would say, "Hell's fire, let the kid walk on the wall. He's got to learn to do things for himself." So, happily, that is part of me, too.

*What's the hardest thing about producing a children's show?*
    Understanding children, and caring enough to use your understanding, to put it in the program, rather than expecting that it will be adults who determine what is seen and that consequently, the show must have a lot of adult gimmickry and values and humor.

*Humor?*
    Adult humor. There is a great deal of adult humor, double entendre things, in children's programming.

*Are you saying that's good or bad?*
    I'm saying that that's easy. You asked what was difficult and I'm telling you that children's programming needs to be concerned with children.

*What makes a good children's host or hostess? Could you audition somebody, for example, and talk to them for a few minutes and say, "Well, that person might make a good children's host," or, "That person would probably not"?*

Yes, if you leave those few words out, "in a few minutes." I mean, I would need longer than a few minutes.

*What would you look for if you were looking for such a person?*
I would look for empathy. I would look for how that person feels about children and about parents. I would certainly look for talent, as far as being able to put something across, you know, there are lots of things. You can feel it in your fingers, you can see a person's ears wiggle, figuratively. In fact, I think that's a very good question. A friend of mine wants to start a children's center at a college nearby and he would like to have part of that center have workshops in television for children. I think it would be great to be able to work with aspiring people, and I have done it in a few instances — worked with people who really are serious about communicating with children through the mass media.

*What about the idea of ritual in children's shows? You change your shoes, put your coat on and so forth, that seems to me to be kind of ritual.*
Yes, it is, and I think that children are comfortable with things that are repeated. It's just like children like to know where they're going to sit at the dining room table and when they're going to go to bed and who's going to tuck them in. You know, we all like to know what's in store for us.

*You usually have a theme on your show. What makes a good theme?*
Well, I talk over those things with our consultant before I ever write the script, and so the things are always built on general growth tasks in childhood, and so if you find a universal growth task, such as the concern about separation and return, you can't go wrong as far as themes are concerned. For instance, the fear of going down the bathtub drain, that is a universal concern of kids between two and four years old. To deal with that in a creative way is a challenge, but it's worth doing. You may have seen cartoons where a diver goes down to the bottom of the sea and pulls the plug and all the water and all the boats and all the people and all the houses go down the drain of the sea. I don't think that that is anyone who has set out to be malicious, but it's someone who definitely had an unresolved childhood fantasy, and what that person is doing is just spewing that fantasy out on the screen for all the other kids to worry about.

*Mister Rogers is concerned with the physical world, as well as the spiritual world. You often carry something with you on the show.*
As children get closer and closer to school age, they get more and more interested in their physical world. I would like to help them to enlarge that to feel that the things that are around them are things to be curious about, things to learn about and things to play about, because, in

playing, children are able to manipulate their environment to an extent that they can then understand it. Now with little toy cars, for instance, they can play about how cars move. Play is essential. As far as creation is concerned, we would never invent anything if we hadn't thought of it and played with it first.

*Can you explain that?*
   Well, if someone had never thought of going to the moon we would never have gone to the moon. I like to encourage kids to play about their feelings.

*Can we inspire creativity in children?*
   Yes. By helping them to feel that there is a chance to bridge the gap between what *is* and what they would *like* it to be, because I believe that is what the definition of creativity is: the attempt to bridge that gap.

*How do you keep from defeating the creative instinct in children? It seems that children are extremely receptive and creative when let alone, or at least not stymied.*
   Yes. I think it depends. I think that we have to give enough limits so that the child is comfortable and yet enough freedom so that child can play out his or her own curiosity. It's a difficult question.

*How much control do you believe that a host like yourself should take over the final show? In other words, what do you delegate and what do you try to handle yourself?*
   That's unique in our situation, because I write the scripts and I do all the puppets' voices and am actually the executive producer of the program. We don't have a writer that tells me what to say, so it's a unique situation with us. I do think that it's important to entertain the ideas of those around you, and certainly this morning was a good indication of how helpful the entire staff can be; but when it comes right down to it, to make a whole out of the communication, it really does have to have an integrity.

*In a children's show, must you really be conscious of getting the facts right?*
   Oh my, yes, as well as we can possibly do it. In our last series, for instance, we went to a weather station, and while we weren't terribly specific about things — there is only just so much information that small children can assimilate — at least we edited the program in a way that showed the steps in order. Oh, I feel very committed to telling the truth in any way we can.

*The song, "Everybody's Fancy," that you wrote — how did that originate?*

Children around the age of five are often very curious about the parts of the body and how little girls and little boys differ, and the song was written because I wanted little girls and little boys to feel that they were both unique, that some people are fancy on the inside and some on the outside, and, of course, that goes in many directions. There are some kids with obvious physical handicaps, for instance, who have all kinds of equipment on their outside, but they may be also very fancy on the inside as far as thoughts are concerned. It's a complicated song and can be read in many different ways, but we have heard that it's been well used in many settings: the home, the church, the school.

*Did you feel that that was quite a daring song for you to do at first?*

I think maybe I did, and I think it was probably Margaret's idea that I go ahead and do it. That's Dr. Margaret McFarland, who was our chief psychological consultant. And I'm glad that I did. I think it's a helpful song, just like the Mad song, which I think is very helpful. You know, "What do you do with the mad that you feel when you feel so mad you could bite?" Now that is a direct quote from a little boy. The whole thing. He once said that to a friend of mine, and I just took it word for word.

*How long does it take for you to write a song? Is it a long process or does it evolve quickly on an inspiration basis?*

It depends. I do the words first and then the music usually comes very quickly, but sometimes it takes a long time for the words to come. A friend of mind from a hospital in Boston called me in Nantucket one day and said, "Fred, I wish you would do something on permissible regression," and that was enough just to trigger my creative inspiration; I had a song by that night, which is one of my favorites. I don't use it all that often because it's fairly long, but it goes, "Please don't think it's funny when you want an extra kiss. There are lots and lots of people who sometimes feel like this. Please don't think it's funny when you want the ones you miss. There are lots and lots of people who sometimes feel like this." The verse goes something like this: "Sometimes you feel like holding your pillow all night long. Sometimes you hug your teddy bear tightly; he's old but he's still strong. Sometimes you want to cuddle up closely with your own mom and dad at night. You even need the light sometimes but that's not bad," and then it goes into, "Please don't think it's funny when you want an extra kiss." His saying to me, "permissible regression," was all I needed.

*You did a live national phone-in for parents of children who were starting school, and you've also done them on violence, monsters, and so forth. What was the hardest thing about doing these phone-in specials?*

We had some excellent producers and they worked with the satellite pick-ups, etc., and they took care of all that. No, it was the actual doing it live and not knowing what people were going to ask; and the toughest thing for me in any phone-in program is knowing that I will not give a pat answer, and yet knowing that people expect it. I refuse to do it. I have to take time to think about what I've been asked, and if that doesn't go along with television technology, then that's too bad. I am not just a prepackaged man. Life is much more than a question and answer time. It has to do with relationships, and if you can't have somewhat of a major in relationships, well, you've really lost out. I have some very, very good friends, and they're the treasures of my life.

*You are a sort of program sage, and you write about talking with children about death and other important issues. Can you talk about the pressure you feel from that responsibility?*

I just don't dwell on that too much. When I travel I'm able to see the extent of our work. When you travel with this face that I've got, there are people who come up to you all the time, and it happens in Anchorage and it happens in Honolulu and it happens wherever I go that there is a lively public television state. I was on a train in Connecticut two weeks ago, and I was going from this town in Connecticut to Grand Central Station, and it so happened there were about 200 high school girls got on at the same time. Well, I was mobbed, and yet I was interested to talk with these kids. It's different. It's not—I told you before—I don't have this sense of "stardom." I'll meet a kid and the first thing that kid might say to me is, "My grandmother's in the hospital," without even saying "hello." That says something to me about the quality of the communication on the screen. I've had kids who have told me about their dog dying, right off the bat. Now what greater gift can you have than to be in touch with people at such a deep level. I mean, we don't have to go through the whole business about the weather. That's taken care of. There's evidently some kind of trust that people feel when they approach me, and it has come from the television. We got a letter last week from a woman who has a five-year-old son, and lives in Corvallis, Oregon, and it's one of the most moving letters you can imagine. She told us that they have an autistic five-year-old, and that child spoke his first words to Mister Rogers on television. The very first word that he ever spoke was "Rog." And that child has gone on now to use "yes" and "no" in appropriate ways, will put on a sweater, try on sneakers. You know, I would love to do a research project that involves autistic kids, because I think that we could be so helpful. Autistic kids can manipulate machines a lot better than they can have relationships with people. Well, here's a machine that we can make personal. Now what would it mean, for instance, if we could get an autistic child's mother and/or father on the screen with me on a little video cassette? How could that help to make the transition into "real" life? There are ways of using these new technologies in very human terms, and that's what we must constantly try to discover.

*Mark Goodson*

NOBODY HAS CONTRIBUTED MORE to the television game show than Mark Goodson. As the creative half of Goodson-Todman Productions, he has been responsible for more successful game shows than any other person.

Goodson started his game show career in radio and then moved to television in 1950 with "What's My Line," which ran for seventeen years.

A list of Goodson-Todman shows produced during the last thirty years includes some very familiar names: "I've Got a Secret," "To Tell the Truth," "Password," "The Price Is Right," "Match Game," "Tattletales," "Family Feud," "Concentration," and about thirty more.

None of the Goodson-Todman shows were involved in the quiz show scandals of the '50s. In fact, Goodson has never offered large cash prizes, believing that contestants don't play so much for the money as for the fun.

Game shows are often scorned, but while most other television programming offers little mental exercise, game shows let the audience participate, let the folks at home play along. One of Goodson's prime considerations has been to produce game shows in which the viewing audience will participate.

Goodson is responsible for many of the features that we associate with the game show today—the buzzers, the bells, the champion contestant who plays until defeated, and the opponent who has a chance to steal the plot.

Although Goodson admits there is no status in game shows, he has not stinted his energies. He is a perfectionist who refines each game show idea until it is impeccable.

*How did you happen to get into the game show business?*
I began my broadcast career in radio as an announcer, newscaster, and sometime actor. I then turned to the direction of dramatic shows. I directed some soap operas, and several shows for the Treasury Department during the war. I wrote and directed the dramatic spots on the original "Kate Smith Variety Hour." Game shows were not my field until the late 1940s. Then I developed and sold (with Bill Todman) a show called "Winner Take All," and discovered I had quite a knack for games.

When television came along in the early 1950s, the timing was right for me. Networks were looking for inexpensive shows, and in 1950 I developed the program "What's My Line?" which at that time cost practically zip to put on. From then on I began to specialize in the game show field—however, I must note that in the middle '50s, Goodson-Todman did have quite an extensive film department in California, doing such shows as "The Rebel," "Branded," and "The Richard Boone Repertory Theatre."

Nonetheless, games were my primary thing, and I became a specialist in that kind of programming.

*You have been in game shows almost all of your life. How do you feel about that kind of concentration on one aspect of show business?*

Well, it is strange in a way to have dedicated most of your adult career to such a special corner of the show business world. I made my start in television games in early 1950, and because I stayed with that specialty, and concentrated on it with single purpose, I suppose I ended up knowing more about this unique fragment of our business than most.

Now, whether that's a great thing or not I can't say, but television over the years has become increasingly specialized, just as have other fields, such as law and medicine. So, in one sense, I admit it feels good to know that I have more knowledge about TV games than the competition.

On the other hand, there are many times when I regret not having taken the gamble of spreading out into the rest of show business. Sure, I might not have been that successful, but it would have been more challenging to have been involved in a more diversified way.

*Someone has observed that you might have been more interested in the players than the game.*

No, I don't think that's true. I think both are important. It is almost like asking what is more important to the body – the skin or the bones. They are equal essentially, and intertwined. Or, what's more important in a play – the plot or the dialogue, or the acting. Or in a song – the lyrics or the music. All these are inexorably intertwined.

If I had to weigh the importance of the elements that make up a game show, I would say (1) the underlying idea, (2) the structure or format, and (3) the players.

By the way, *ideas* and *formats* are often confused. They are not the same thing. An idea is an unformulated glimmer only. Hopefully, ideas will inspire formats. So often someone approaches you with a general idea for a game show based on, say, "gossip." Fine and good. But what counts is the format – the structure, the spine – and the ultimate working out of the show itself.

In spite of the very simple look of audience participation shows, games are highly intricate forms to develop, and the simpler the game seems, like "What's My Line?" "To Tell the Truth" or "Password," it usually indicates that more work has gone in to bring that concept to fruition.

I don't want to denigrate the "players" – celebrities, hosts, etc. – in game shows, but they do come second. We cast these stars *after* we've sold the show, certainly long after we've created the idea and developed the format.

This is in sharp contrast to the motion picture business. Most often there you must cast in advance in order to get studio and financial backing. The right actor insures the biggest bank loan. In our end of show business, bankability is not a problem.

When we begin thinking about a new game show we generally haven't the vaguest idea of who is going to be in front of the cameras. First, we do our best to come up with an idea—is the idea new and fresh? Does it seem to offer the possibility of intriguing the public? Then we go on to the second part. How can we make it work? What sort of format can we develop?

When these two are put together (and that takes months, and sometimes years) we then make our first "presentation" to the networks.

In that presentation—a rough form of the show put on in our offices—I generally host the run-through. We usually illustrate the show with Goodson-Todman people who play the role of celebrities. Only when the program is bought and we are about to go on the air do we concentrate on "casting the players."

As the show begins to run, the players become increasingly important. And we remain flexible for quite a period of time. On certain panel shows, for example, we have not settled on the final group of participants for months while that program is being played on the air.

We also adjust and fine-tune the format somewhat during these early weeks. A new game show is similar to soft wax. We keep molding and pressing and manipulating and rubbing off little edges here and there until in about its thirteenth week (if the show is not cancelled!) we allow the wax to harden. After that, fundamental changes become very difficult to make.

By the way, I do *not* intend, in any way, to denigrate the role of our players. They are very, very important. John Daly was of critical importance to "What's My Line?" as is Richard Dawson to "The Family Feud," and Bob Barker to "The Price Is Right," etc. On the other hand, "To Tell the Truth" was hosted for many years by Bud Collyer—a fine emcee. When Bud passed away, the show survived for ten additional years with a different host, Garry Moore. "The Price Is Right" was very successful in its original 1956 form with Bill Cullen. When we changed the format and put it back on in 1972, Bill Cullen was not available, so we recast the show with Bob Barker in the lead role, and he has guided the show brilliantly.

*What qualities does the host of a game show need?*
The host of a game show needs many skills. Obviously, he should have charisma and humor, and the other attributes of a good entertainer. He must also be highly *organized*, be able to think on his feet. He should really have the mindset of a *producer*. Remember, in most cases, the host of a game show is working without lines. He is thinking on his feet and ad-libbing his way through the show. He should be verbally dextrous—with the capacity to respond instantly to all types of contestants and celebrities he must deal with. Then, of course, there are those ineffable extras. He should be attractive, sexy, likable, and so on.

However, the most *important* attribute of all is that he be a great technician. I emphasize this because what a game show host does *looks* so easy. Take my word for it, it is not. In other words, it is not hard to find performers who offer charm, but it *is* difficult to find people who are charming and *also* technically adept.

By the way, this should not strike anyone as being that unusual. If you're casting for a charismatic opera singer, you don't start out looking for charisma. You look for a great singer. Then comes charisma. I emphasize this because most people discount the technical ability of game show hosts.

*The announcer was key-noted on some of your shows — Johnny Olson, for example. How did that come about?*

The announcer? Well, Johnny and Gene Wood and the others we use have two jobs. They read the lines of the opening and closing, they introduce contestants, and so on. But one of their most important functions in game shows is the "warm-up," in which they get the studio audience involved, and keep them involved throughout the program. An audience *participation* show is really exactly that. The audience in the studio should feel like it is participating, and their reaction, in turn, makes the audience at home feel involved. They identify with the audience in the studio.

Theoretically, you could do a game show *without* a real live audience there. In the early days of radio broadcasting there were a few little games done without an audience. There are such game shows produced in Europe without an audience, and contestants are simply pitted against a problem, with the only viewers being those in front of their television sets. Such programs seem flat and, in my opinion, would not work in America.

Anyway, the pressure of a live audience is essential to a good game show.

*Was that in any way related to radio? Did you go on radio when you first began?*

Absolutely. Game shows are definitely derived from radio. Most "reality" programs such as "Meet the Press," or talk shows in general, came out of radio — and games fit in this "reality" family.

As TV came along and cameras became available, changes were made to accommodate the fact that you could do more with cameras than you could with microphones alone, but there is no question about the fact that audience participation is indigenous to radio broadcasting.

*What is the biggest philosophical change that you've experienced over the years, or say, since you first began, in regard to game shows — the idea, the concept, or what would work?*

The biggest philosophical change in games was probably introduced by us in the 1950s, at the very beginning of television. Up until our show "What's My Line," game shows were essentially the equivalent of classroom quizzes. The teacher (or, in this case, the emcee) would ask you a question. If you had the answer, he would reward you with some money as opposed to giving you a good grade. The ultimate extension of this was "The $64,000 Question" (not one of our shows), where if you were really a good "student," instead of making you a Phi Beta Kappa, they made you rich.

The twist that *we* put into games — our contribution — was to introduce *human* puzzles and *human* games, as opposed to simple question-and-answer schoolroom quizzes. Thus, "What's My Line" was a game where the puzzle to be solved was a *human being* with a job, and our panel of celebrities was challenged to uncover what that average person did for a living. It was quite a revolutionary turn for games.

"To Tell the Truth," in a similar way, played with a human puzzle. Three contestants were placed in front of a panel. One would be the truth-teller; the other two would be impostors, i.e., "liars." The task of the panel (and the audience) was to find out which of these three human beings was telling the truth.

Take another example: "Password," another game that was not a straight question-and-answer show. In "Password," the player's challenge was to make his partner come up with the "password" — by giving him the synonym or shadings of other words to induce him to make the appropriate response.

These complexities in game shows helped revolutionize the medium and were the imaginative twists we were always looking for. The various forms of question-and-answer quizzes which are still around, and keep coming back, are, as I say, dressed up versions of schoolroom quizzes.

*You mentioned "The $64,000 Question." You people were not involved in that, but did the quiz scandals affect the game show business — the other producers?*

Yes, it affected it in a couple of ways. First of all, because of the sensitivity of the networks to the scandals, there was considerable talk at the time of the cancellation of "$64,000 Question," and the program "21," about getting rid of *all* game shows across the board. Some network executives reasoned that if one show could be in trouble, perhaps all could be, so why take on the headache of getting involved in a possibly scandalous area — let's get rid of them all. Luckily that outcome did not eventuate.

Another way the scandal affected all game show producers was that it brought about changes in the Federal Communications Act, and shows had to be carefully policed. When one does a game show now, one is surrounded by a virtual army of FBI-types who are there to make sure that no cheating is going on.

*Is that right? How did you respond to that?*
We accommodated to it. As a matter of fact, we had, as a matter of policy, introduced our own forms of protection against cheating long before the quiz scandals broke. So we were not very much affected.

*Did you know Lou Cowan?*
Yes, Lou Cowan produced "The $64,000 Question" and was a friend of mine.

*What do you remember about him?*
He was a lovely man — and a good friend. We were partners in a show called "Stop the Music," a radio game show which I created and which went on the air in 1947 and swept the country. It was the first big radio show which allowed people *at home* to play. Lou Cowan was also the original producer of "The Quiz Kids," and had been in the game business in Chicago. He was a very good friend of mine. However, I declined his very generous offer to participate in "The $64,000 Question" because I felt, after I looked over the format, that the show had no way of being made truly effective without excessive "controls." It turned out that the excessive use of these controls was what got "The $64,000 Question" in trouble and ultimately forced it off the air.

*What have you learned about daytime television audiences?*
Well, the daytime audience, of course, is made up mainly of women. There are some young children and a minority representation of men — unemployed, retired, or night workers. One of the major problems in the game show business is demographics. Soap operas tend to attract younger women, and networks and advertisers consider these younger people more valuable. We are, therefore, constantly fighting the battle of demographics and attempting to attract younger viewers for our shows.

*What was the division of labor between you and Bill Todman?*
He was in the managerial and business division of our company — I was in the creative and production side.

*Did he ever get into creating?*
Rarely.

*When you sell a game show to the networks you talked about doing a pilot — what is the standard procedure for selling a network a show?*
There are two ways to go about getting a game show sold. First, you can go the network route. Second, you can try syndication. Most people try the networks first. If we want to present a game to a network, we invite the network brass to our office and put on a demonstration of the concept in fairly rough form. It is likely that before the actual

presentation we would have discussed the general idea with them to give them a sense of participating. Also, some of the network programming people may have suggestions we consider valuable. We are always willing to listen.

I should say parenthetically, at Goodson-Todman "selling" *per se* is not our problem. Our problem lies in the creativity — how do we get enough new shows?

Anyway, getting back to the network, we do a demonstration for them. If they like what they see, they usually agree to make a pilot, which is in essence an audition of the show. After the pilot is done (for which the network pays most of the costs) they look at the tape, "test it" — and then decide whether to put it on for a certain period of time, usually thirteen weeks, with the right to extend those weeks at the sole option.

If they don't like the pilot, they have a certain holding period, after which we can take the show somewhere else.

In certain situations, if the show seems very impressive and we are in a good enough bargaining position, we will get a direct order to go on the air without a pilot. That is what happened, for example, in the case of "The Price Is Right."

Syndication is handled somewhat differently. You can also take a program which is already on the network and, presuming that you have a contractual right to syndicate it separately, you can hire a syndicating organization, or put salesmen on the road and offer the program station by station. If the program is a new one that has not yet been exposed on the network, it is generally necessary to make pilot which the producer finances, and sell it across country market by market.

*You mentioned "bargaining power." Does it come with experience?*

Yes, that's true. Producers with long and effective track records can make better deals. On the other hand, the networks have the greater bargaining power by far — because they control the exposure of the programs. There are basically three networks, i.e., *three store windows* available, and unless you can get into one of these windows you can't get your program shown. That's where the networks have their clout.

Once you are on the air and have a hit, the packager develops more leverage.

*Can you give me an example of the bargaining power you have once the show is on the air?*

If a program is a hit and runs the duration of the contract, say five or seven years, then you are contractually free to offer that program to other networks, who will pay much more for an established hit; or you can put it into syndication at going market rates.

*Do you have a favorite game show?*

That's like asking a father which is his favorite child! However, I would say that "To Tell the Truth" is probably my all-time favorite. It's the most classically perfect of all formats. "Family Feud" is another favorite of mine, and is one of the most successful of our current shows.

*Please explain why "To Tell the Truth" is classically perfect.*

I'll try. "To Tell the Truth" is based on a *real life challenge* to the viewer. We present three candidates. One is the "central character," who claims to be, and is, the real person. For example, he claims to be a Secret Service man in charge of protecting the President. The other two candidates are "impostors"—in effect, "liars." The viewers at home get to *play along* and must solve the problem at exactly the *same time* that the panel is doing its best. The viewer must make the *same decision* as the panel as to which of the three contestants is the "real" person. Also, the problem is one "from real life"—an actual pair of people, not actors, is trying to fool you, and you are trying not to be fooled.

There's also a "moment of truth"—a climactic revelation when the emcee pronounces that now-classic line: "Will the real so-and-so please stand up!"

Frankly, each "spot" scheduled on "To Tell the Truth" tells a *separate story*, and the show, therefore, contains not only elements of game, but elements of drama as well.

*Can you tell me if there are any shows where a slight format change made all the difference? Where you almost had it, but not quite, so you changed it?*

Yes, "Password" fits that. In the beginning we tested the show with one contestant trying to give verbal clues to his partner, but somehow it didn't hold up. Then we came up with the simple concept that made the difference. One celebrity gives a clue to his partner, and then an *opposing* celebrity picks up that clue, *adds on his own clue*, and passes it to *his partner*, in effect enabling him to steal the point from the other side. That format change made "Password" come to life.

In "Family Feud" we also had a change of format that helped. We introduced the concept of "stealing" on that show as well. One family must commit to play by uncovering as many unrevealed answers as possible. If that teams fails to uncover the entire board, the other team has the right to take over—and if they can reveal just one more answer, they steal all the money in the bank. That little change, small as it sounds, helps make "Family Feud" a dynamite format.

*Have you ever had programs going on all three networks—did that ever present a problem to you?*

We have often been on all three at the same time. We have programs on opposite each other.

*Do the networks feel jealous as to who's offered the show?*
Sure they do.

*How do you resolve that?*
By deciding where we think we will get the best deal, where we think we will get the best treatment.

*Your shows often emphasize guessing. Do you think that's a safe assumption?*
Guessing?

*Yeah.*
No, I wouldn't say we emphasize guessing, although certainly "educated hunch" plays a role on our programs. Thus, on "To Tell the Truth," the audience watches the three individuals who answer the panel's questions, and at the end of the questioning period attempts to decide who the real person is. I suppose one could label this process as "guessing." I would say it is clever use of analytical judgment.

Similarly, on "Price Is Right," the attempt to come closest to the price of an item without going over requires common sense and judgment.

What we try to do, in many of our programs, is test capacities that are other than purely informational or eruditional. When a program asks, "who discovered America?", the contestant either knows or doesn't. But if, as the case of our program "Card Sharks," we polled 100 secretaries and asked them, "Do you think you could do your boss's job as well as he can?" then asked the contestant, "How many of these 100 women do you think said yes?" We are asking for *more than a guess* – we are demanding that the contestant display a kind of sociological insight.

*The prime time access rule really resulted in some strong lines being drawn between game show producers, very often, and series producers. Has the dust settled on that?*
I don't know if the dust has settled or not. The dust never settles totally on any controversial regulation. The networks opposed the rule because it required that they forgo network programming from 7:30–8:00 p.m. Many dramatic show producers went along with the networks because they felt this prime time access rule was depriving them of a potential outlet for their products. Most local stations, and many nonnetwork groups of stations, such as Westinghouse and Metromedia, and certain independent producers who could turn out product for syndication, were in favor of the rule because it gave them an outlet for programs other than the three networks. 7:30 was always a marginal time period and while there were, prior to the prime time access rule, some good shows on at 7:30, there was a plethora of bad ones, such as "My Mother the Car," and so on.

Several local stations have used the prime time access period to put on programs of their own origin. Also, if a local station wants to buy a syndicated show, it can do so, and make higher profits than if it were taking that show directly from the network.

*What do you think about canned effects and sound in game shows?*
I am not thrilled with artifice of any kind, but we do occasionally "sweeten" certain programs. In general, I would say that I do not object to canned *applause.* I do have some objection to synthetic laughter – not on moralistic grounds but because such laughter tends to sound phony.

*Did the networks have any control over your efforts in the early '50s, or were the controls fairly lax then?*
I would say that until the quiz scandals came along in the 1950s, the networks had a basic hands-off policy, except when it came to censorship. You couldn't televise a girl in a bikini, or show her navel – things of that sort. You were afraid to say "damn" on television in those early days, and there are still more restrictions on our kind of shows, for example, than on soap operas, which are much looser. In terms of program controls over what we did, it was pretty much left in our hands as producer. The total absence of network supervision was partly responsible for the quiz scandals of the 1950s.

*Why are game shows so popular?*
Game shows are popular because they represent that form of "theater" or drama which uses real people "playing the roles," instead of actors.

Games are "reality" programs. Shakespeare said, "All the world's a stage and all the men and women merely players," and that is certainly true in a game show. The participants (with the exception of celebrity guests) are nonprofessionals – just folks. The audience knows that the participant on screen is *really* John Jones, a medical student who is working his way through college and whose wife is a teacher and pregnant. So, first, every game is based on reality. Secondly, there is *no ending that is written or prepared* so no one, including the producers, knows how it's going to come out. Like in a sporting event – the outcome is uncertain. The medical student who needs the money may or may not get it. It's a real life drama. There's also comedy, but it's the comedy of "reality" – not crafted by comedy writers. There is also for the viewer a great element of voyeurism – the joy of people watching. You sit in front of your TV set and watch real people doing their thing – and you'll say, "Look at that guy. Isn't his shirt ridiculous? Or that young girl – isn't she too tall for her husband?" On the opposite side of that coin, those *who go on* these shows are going on overwhelmingly with the desire to *expose themselves,* to show off. They *want* to be seen. If you cut the prizes down, if you made a universal agreement between all producers that the most you could ever give away was $500, it would not reduce the number of people who would want to go on game shows, because these participants really go on with the desire to be seen and have their day in the sun.

*What's the biggest mistake that beginning producers of game shows make?*
Thinking that they can get large audiences by giving away large amounts of money. Or, that they can make a show interesting by complicating it with rules and by synthesizing a lot of old-hat ideas and piling them all together and coming up with a show. Or, that you can necessarily translate a nontelevision game like Backgammon or Scrabble or Gin Rummy into television simply because the original parlor game is popular. There is a vast difference between a "player's" game and a "viewer's" game, and that is commonly misunderstood. You and I can enjoy playing a game but no one else will want to *watch* us play it.

*Where is the game show going?*
I don't know. If I knew that I would be the richest man in the world.

*You mean you're not?*
(laughs) Hardly.

*One thing I wanted to ask you about. Because of what he considered unfair criticism from columnist Dorothy Kilgallen, Jack Paar routinely attacked Ms. Kilgallen on the air. Did this feud actually hurt or help the show?*
I don't know whether it hurt us or helped us, but it undoubtedly hurt Dorothy's feelings, although she tried not to let the public know. Dorothy was quite unhappy about the attacks – but then Dorothy was a gossip columnist, and while you would think that people who dish it out should be able to take it, quite the contrary is true.
If you recall, Jack Paar almost single-handedly destroyed Walter Winchell, and if you ever knew Walter during his heyday, he was an enormous power and he was not used to having anyone hit back at him – and nobody did, because nobody had a strong enough forum. However, television was a much more powerful forum, and Paar went after him with no holds barred and virtually cut him to pieces.

*How many game shows have you produced?*
I don't know – I would say probably forty.

*What was the toughest one to produce?*
The ones that failed. A new show called "What's Going On" – it lasted ten weeks and went off – it never made it.

*Why did that fail?*

It failed because, first of all, we were not technically ready for it. It was a show that was based on remotes before there was tape and, secondly, it was one of those concepts that sounded good in my head and just never worked, and we sold it without a pilot and it went on the air, and was an utter disaster. It's the failures that take the energy.

*What was the concept?*

The concept went like this: We had no contestants. We had three "inside" panelists who worked on our stage, and three "outside" panelists. Each of these "outside" panelists were set in different places throughout the country. Thus, we would have one panelist, for example, hanging outside the top floor of the Empire State Building, washing windows. We would project his picture on a giant screen at the back of the panel, and the panel in the studio would ask such questions as, "Where are you?" "What city are you in?" "Are you on the ground?" etc. We would put somebody on a Mississippi showboat. We would place a panelist in the Chicago stockyards "counting sheep." We would have panel members dancing with the male students in the Princeton Triangle Club. It was an enormously expensive, crazy idea for its day. It was an idea, based on "What's My Line?" plus remotes. Not what you do for a living, but what are you doing *right now* and *where* are you doing it? It sounded terrific on paper. Doesn't it sound good?

*Yes, I'll do it.*

You're free to have it. There's just no way you can make it work, for all kinds of reasons that I can't get into. It was produced by a very clever man called Alan Sherman, who has since died, and directed and staffed by top people, but it just bombed. It took all our time for ten weeks and I still wake up with flop sweat when I think about it.

*How did videotape affect your business? You have reprieve, etc., but . . .*

Videotape affected our business just the way you said. It put a safety net under the high-wire act, and in that sense it was good because we were able to take more risks. It was bad for the same reason, i.e., it took away some of the tension because you could always take back a mistake.

*Let me ask you this. How did you try out stunts on "Beat the Clock"?*

We tried them out by bringing in stand-ins and ordinary people and trying them out and seeing which stunts would work and which ones wouldn't.

*Did it ever happen that the stunt would work great during the tryout and then it wouldn't during the show?*

Absolutely.

*What sort of things?*

Well, you would try a stunt with stand-ins in the rehearsal hall before the show. They would not be able to accomplish it, so you would make it easier and easier and easier. Then, when we got into the studio with real contestants, they would knock the stunt off in three seconds, leaving us with a large supply of egg on our face.

*So there were a lot of shows that they had to stretch a little on.*

Oh, yeah, we had to stretch a lot of them.

*Imre Horvath*

DURING HIS SEVEN YEARS as a film editor for "60 Minutes" Imre Horvath edited over fifty segments for that highly regarded show. He later rose through the ranks, becoming associate producer, then producing segments for correspondents Mike Wallace, Morley Safer and Dan Rather.

Horvath received an Emmy for "Noah," a television portrait of an autistic child, and a Howard Blakeslee Award for Medical Journalism.

As producer on "60 Minutes" shoots, Horvath tells how people used to sidle up to him and say, "What is it you do exactly?" His answer was, "I worry." Since 1980 Horvath has "worried" as a successful independent producer. He is head of Rainbow Broadcasting Company, located in New York City, which specializes in magazine and long-form productions.

Since beginning Rainbow Broadcasting Company Horvath has worked on magazine projects for CBS, NBC, Omni Productions, and HBO, and wrote the cold war segment of Bill Moyers' PBS series "A Walk Through the 20th Century."

Horvath holds a B.A. from Columbia College, and an M.A. from New York University. He is a member of the Writer's Guild of America and has written for Groliers.

*What was your most dramatic moment as a producer for CBS's "60 Minutes"?*

My most dramatic moment as a producer — it's been a long time since I've made a speech on this. Well, it's the moment when someone takes your piece and ruins it, really, (laughs) but that's not colorful. There are *traumatic* moments that happen sometimes in the editing and screening areas. Somebody says, "Why don't you take that and put it over there?" And you say, "Oh gosh." It's usually somebody who's in charge. And what you have to say then is, "Well, it wouldn't work there." Your underlying message is, "I've spent eight weeks on this thing and you're just seeing it for the second time, maybe. How come you've suddenly got an insight that you think is better than the eight weeks of concentrated effort?" That's the message that goes unsaid, often, in this kind of screening-room atmosphere, because a person is either a vice-president or has a great reputation for gut feelings and their word goes, and you feel that something that you worked hard on and thought about and put a lot of effort into is kind of summarily dismissed. That was the most painful thing.

*How much should one control one's ego?*

It's an egotistical industry. If your ego is more controlled, you're probably not doing yourself a favor, because there are other people

*Photo (opposite): Imre Horvath (left) with Irv Broughton.*

whose egos are running rampant; so I think in the long run you're better off if you involve yourself in pieces so that they are a part of you.

*Okay, I suppose it depends on how we define "ego." How would you define it?*
Because that's my way of doing it. Well, you know, I don't really think of myself as wanting to do things just because it's my way of doing them, but simply because I've perhaps thought about it more – I've been close to the thing and I understand it better.

*Is there any time when you've felt you were too close to it?*
Well, you feel at some point that you're too close to the story just by being exposed to it, but that's a different kind of "close to the story."

*How do you define that "close to the story"?*
That's where you lose . . . you're unable to think of yourself as some-one coming to the story the first time, and that's when you start doing things like cutting out connectives and telescoping exposition, because, you say, "everybody knows that." Actually, you just know it because you've heard it at least forty times already and thought about it that many times, so that's the kind of thing . . . you become unable to judge what . . . the emotional impact . . . you'll always go to something new because it's new to you. Where a certain person might break down and cry in the course of the story it ceases to move you, and then after awhile you say, "Well, you know, why are we spending so much time on this?" You forget that the first time you saw it it was an adept emotional moment.

*You have a secret on how to get ahold of people. Let's tell the world.*
(laughs) People that are busy, they usually have some kind of lunch planned; their mornings are scheduled tight; their afternoons they're out at sessions at whatever they're involved in; and it's at 5:00 and 6:00 that they're back in their office and they're trying to unwind. They don't quite want to go home, often, because they don't want to inflict themselves on their spouses, and what happens is that you can usually catch them – an executive producer, or something, you're interested in . . . or the con-gressman's chief aide . . . or the ABA . . . or the Attorney General's guy . . . that you're needing to talk to – at 5:00 or 6:00 and you'll find that there's a kind of resonance or sympathy that springs up. "Oh, you're still in your office too?"

*You say they're unwinding also from the . . . having a few drinks?*
Well, they don't tend to sound that way. We don't drink in this office, or haven't in a long time. We used to have a little bar but it was all, you know, very moderate. It's just a kind of sitting around and letting that tension drain out. I think everybody who has some kind of power tends

to do this, and so that's what I say when you call at the end of the day you're going to find them sitting; probably you can picture them with their feet up on the desk.

*How about working with unions? Any tips?*
    Well, that's the standard in the industry, especially if you're working for a network. I used to be a union guy myself, so I don't know whether I have the same point of view as a lot of others. I used to be a film editor at CBS, and there are good reasons to be in a union, and there's some sense to some of the union rules. But I hate working with people whose humanity has been destroyed through a combination of the union rules and the company policies that sort of led to the union rules, or are in response to them. I'm thinking particularly of videotape editors. I don't mean ENG editing, now, I mean the big videotape machines. These are usually the hard-line union guys who will drop whatever they're doing at a quarter to the hour and say, "I'm on a twenty-minute break." In other words, they don't involve themselves in their work, as a matter of principle. Then you look around you and you can see why. You've got eight of these machines in a bank. Nobody works on cans, [headphones] — the floor is hard, the seats are hard, the atmosphere is unpleasant, and you have this eternal noise, so that it's an inhuman atmosphere and you're responding in an inhuman way. That's one thing that springs to mind when I think of unions as a problem. Otherwise, you know, camera crews are all staunch union members but they're also individuals. I mean, one guy will cheat for us all the time and another guy won't. One guy will give you a break. Instead of filling in whatever penalties he can think of, he makes some kind of trade-off that he thinks is fair. How many times do you work a crew through lunch? That happens so often. Some producers even forget to schedule lunch. They'll say, "Oh, we'll grab something on the way." You know, I think it's fair for a crew to put in a couple of hours for overtime if you've worked them through lunch and they've got to grab something. You're abusing their bodies. Don't forget that when you're a producer, or when you're a producer for a network, anyway, all you're carrying is a satchel with some papers in it. They're schlepping tons of garbage up and down stairs and whatever. They're working hard — they deserve to have some rules to protect them.

*What's the standard day for unions that you work with?*
    Well, it's an eight-hour day. You go into overtime after eight hours. It's not a standard starting time, though.

*No standard finishing time either?*
    Nope.

*What would cause you to decide to do a story for "60 Minutes"?*

When I worked with Morley Safer, for example, I had to run thirty stories past him before he'd buy one—he's so picky. It wasn't just, "Do you want to do this?" and he would respond "yes" or "no," so you're actually proposing many more stories than will eventually be done. You can't be too strong. It's sort of having a fish's attitude toward your children rather than an elephant's. If you've got only one, you're really protective, but if you have thirty or forty of them they're not that close to you to begin with. Now, they all should have the potential of being researched out to being a really top-notch story. Sometimes there is no question of it. It's a natural from the first minute you look at it. Other times you have to argue with it. I have two really good stories that would be examples of that. The story that I did on Noah Greenfield, who was . . . I guess he is called autistic, although his parents did not like that definition—it was a piece of an excerpt from a book mentioned in *Psychology Today*. In the course of the book the father mentioned that they had started a little day-care center because they didn't trust professionals very much. So I said, "Well, here's a thought that they just started the thing. Everything else is just a slice of life about the child." There was just no question I wanted to do that story, and Dan Rather, who was the correspondent on it, agreed right away. Another story took me two years to get approved. It was a story about a thyroid cancer as a consequence of childhood radiation. It was really heavy going and there were a lot of statistics in it, and then other things got in the way. For example, I proposed that first to Mike Wallace and he thought it was good, but then in Chicago he happened to see a local station do a feature on it—a hospital in Chicago had responded to this problem—and he said, "Oh, well, we've been scooped now, forget it." So I put it away for about a year. Then I saw a little item in the paper that said that they were starting up a program in Pittsburgh. Now this item in the paper, you see, was about two inches long, and unless I had been involved in trying it before, it would have never jumped to my attention the way that it did. When I got that out, then the time was right for it, and by that time I was working with Morley Safer. Now, I had to really convince Morley all over again that there was enough of a human element to this that he would shine in the area that he shines in. That was a story that took awhile—that took some argument.

*How long did that take to actually produce?*
    "60 Minutes" sometimes takes quite awhile to do things. I don't know quite the reason, but I flew down to Pittsburgh, took a look at everything to see that it looked right, interviewed a lot of doctors. Sometimes part of your scouting trip is a mutual scouting. You're looking them over, they're looking you over. I think that one still holds the record for me in that I had to sit down and have lunch at the Faculty Club, with, I think, twenty-three pillars of the Pittsburgh medical staff, all of whom wanted to know

if "60 Minutes" was going to do something bad to Pittsburgh because they had done this program. God knows they must have had some skeletons rattling in some closets, but I just straightforwardly wanted a piece that had some kind of response. So they were able to overcome their reluctance at this lunch, and come back. Then there was the question of getting a correspondent scheduled to coincide with the schedule of people that you want to film. Then an opportunity came up – after the filming schedule was set – to do a woman who was coming from New York to Pittsburgh especially for this program, and so I set up an extra couple of days to follow her; so basically, there were two scouting days and four filming days on one show and two filming days on another. So for filming and scouting days it was pretty moderate – six days of filming and two days of scouting – but this took place over five weeks of time, with the scheduling and everything else. The cutting of it was not very long. I think I did that one. Took about three or four weeks, and it sailed through fairly easily; there were no major problems in any of the screenings. So that was about a seven-week project.

*So what's the average?*

It averages about eight weeks. I think seven is what's aimed for. It depends. You can hit that kind of average if you do a lot of quickies – that is, major interviews. You go interview Ronald Reagan, let's say, it's going to take you two days, and then maybe there's some kind of a news event that ties into a book, so everybody gets involved; there is no question of approval at the screening because he [the correspondent] has been hanging out in the middle of the cutting of it, and the whole thing gets done in four or five days or six days.

*How did being a film editor help you as a background for a producer?*

Gosh, well, it helped me tremendously. It's just that you know when it's enough, sooner than other people do, in terms of banana footage – in terms of coverage and event coverage. You know how to do it; you know how much you're going to use, and you know what you need to be able to use two pieces or three pieces or four pieces, rather than thinking of everything as continuous, because a film editor can control the way the time passes in the piece. It's not much of a help in the content parts, of interviews, or anything like that – a different kind of training kicks in there.

*Some people say, "We don't want the film editor on the scene because he or she would gain some preconception." Have you ever felt that?*

Yeah, it is a good idea to have input from someone like a film editor who hasn't been there. A couple of times I have had occasion to go out and produce and direct something and then cut it myself, and I find that I start weighting things with values that are not on the film. I start saying,

"Well, shit, we waited four hours for this shot — we've gotta use it." I keep saying, "This guy was so nice we've gotta use a piece of his interview." It's more or less unconscious — you can bring it to consciousness, but you add values to things that aren't in there, just coming flat off the screen. You say, "Don't you just love this guy?" and he says, "No, you know, it really just doesn't come across." You say, "Well, gee, you should have seen how he treated his dog." "Well, you know, too bad — it's not in it." So that kind of removedness is valuable.

*Talk about communication. I produce, and sometimes find that I almost talk down to people because of the need to spell out everything.*
Okay, I kind of know what you mean. You feel somehow that they don't want to know all of this, (laughs) even though you're telling them. Well, okay, I think the subjects — depending on how sophisticated they are — don't really need to know too much about it. They need to be given some kind of idea of how much of the story is about the sequence that they're seeing. In other words, if this is the whole story, they want to know that; or if it's just part of another short story on colleges, I think it's unfair to kid people that they're going to have the whole fifteen minutes. I think that things like that are important to communicate. I think, other than that, people just tend to be overawed by the fact that they're being covered, and they're having enough trouble behaving themselves naturally, anyway, and I don't think that there is a whole lot of discussion done at the time of filming. That's another function of scouting trips: You have the discussions then, and people get to ask questions and they talk in their vein, whereas to find sometimes during the filming everybody tends to be very "show-business" and say, "That's a camera, isn't it?" and kind of show off their knowledge.

As far as talking to the camera crew, that's very important, I think. It's important that the crew know what the story is, because they have so many different ways . . . so many things are not directable . . . you're not in the cameraman's ear all the time and he's got to be using his own judgment and instincts; he may have to have different sets of them in play, depending on what kind of story you're doing. Once again, I think, it's best for the editor to tell you what the story is that he sees, and then you say, "Well, you know, what we're trying to say is — are you telling us that it's not in here?" I think it's a kind of check and balance against everybody getting carried away.

*How important is it for the producer to know when to rely on others and when to take charge himself?*
I think it's important. This is something I had to face when I became a producer from being an editor; I realize that I have to give up some of the things that I formerly had control over, because, otherwise, I demean the editor's job. Even though I'm perfectly capable of calling all the shots in

editing, I don't do it, because that's the editor's prerogative — certain rights belong to the editor, I think — and the same is true of the cameraman. If you find the cameraman has a certain style, I think you kind of have to live with it. Some men are movers and one-take kind of people, and if you know that you can use that, it's fine. I think you're better off getting a different cameraman than trying to turn the cameraman into a guy who shoots chopped up. By chopped up I mean sequence shooting where he's always . . . not necessarily cutting, but changing angles with the film editing problems in mind. I always approach the crew by saying, "Now, I like what you're doing, or I see what you're doing, now, please, just for me, do this shot, or this close-up." I tend, unless I have a real budget problem, to let 'em roll, because we never know where we'll come out.

*At "60 Minutes" did you frequently go down and interview somebody to decide if you'll do the story? What percentage of times, would you say?*
     Good interviews are a very large part of the story, and if the people don't come across, then you might want to think about a different story. There's a lot of scouting done on nearly every story.

*You literally go and interview them?*
     Yeah, you go to see them and you talk to them. Sometimes they'll fool you. For example, there's a story that's not going to get on the air, because everybody turned out to be more reserved than they were on the phone. It happened to be a story about preventive medicine. In this case, I had a guy on the phone who was knocking the fads, he was knocking jogging, he was knocking the annual physical, he was telling us that technology was not the way to do things, and that there was another, simple way of doing things. He was very good on the phone, so we decided to do the piece on the basis of this phone conversation. I think this brought up some very deep points that had to be made in narration instead, which were not very strong.

*What kind of cameraperson do you prefer to work with?*
     Myself, I am not super-aggressive, so I like that quality to be filled in by the cameraman. There's nothing more frustrating than a cameraman who is afraid to get too close, or afraid to poke his way into a situation. The cameraman that I work with — do you know Walter Dombrow?

*I know of him.*
     Yeah, well, it's unbelievable how close he gets — I don't mean always physically — how tight he gets in with his subjects. And he's never afraid to push, and he's never afraid to say, "Hey, hold on a second, we didn't get that," and get in there. Whereas if you have to sort of relay that to your cameraman, or if your cameraman first tells you kind of hesitantly that he had a problem and would kind of like it if he could get in and do a

different angle, or something like that, and then you've got to put that on his behalf to the subjects, or whatever it is, the situation will have passed you by. So I think the cameraman who is aggressive, yet not too obtrusive, is about the ideal. Also it is a matter of lighting. Some people know how to light very well, or to use whatever light there is very well, and their stuff just jumps off the screen; and other people—it will be like a passport photo.

*Do you have a rule of thumb for gauging length of time needed to edit—for budgeting purposes?*

Yeah, it's about four to five minutes a week, and the thing that you forget when you do it by rule of thumb is that you have to allow for finishing time, the mix, the transfer—all this bullshit at the end, which is enormously long. I just did an hour show; the editor worked twelve weeks. It was at least one week too short. You're probably best off not to have a rule of thumb. When I do a seat-of-the-pants budget, yes, I have a rule of thumb. And I just told you, four to five minutes a week. So that's what I had on this one: five minutes a week times twelve weeks equals sixty minutes. It was a little skimpy. Better I should have figured four minutes a week. But that's what I would guess. Three minutes a day to shoot. So you shoot a half-hour and it's ten days of shooting. Sixty minutes, that's twenty days. This is the general rule of thumb. You'll find that that's what most people will allow. The short things are tricky. Sometimes they're cheaper. Sometimes more expensive. If you're doing an hour show as opposed to a two-hour show, the second hour surely shouldn't cost as much as the first hour because you spend a lot of time editing to get down to the hour.

*Talk about how the tenacious, investigative image of "60 Minutes" has made it more difficult in recent years for the producer there.*

Sometimes you call somebody up and say, "60 Minutes," and they act as if you had just said, *National Enquirer*. They get suspicious, they think less highly of you than in the years before, and they become reluctant to do the story. As a matter of fact, in some stories that are straight stories, especially in the field of science, people become hypercautious (and that's why our guy froze up on me, the doctor I was telling you about). Balanced against that, you still have the fact that if you do mention "60 Minutes" you will more likely have the ear of just about anybody you want—they will respond, they will call back, they will talk to you. Whether they agree to do the story, now, that's where this kind of backlash comes in.

*When did that really evolve? Just recently?*

I'd say it was within the late '70s.

*What kind of mistakes might the beginning network producer make?*

Either shoot too much or shoot too little; not tell the crew what the story is; not communicate well with the crew, I would say. Fall prey to overdirective film editors; in other words, the film editor has a certain position, but you've got to maintain your own position in talking with him. Not knowing what questions to ask. I would say that these are some of the mistakes that you might make.

*You're producing on your own now. What was the hardest adjustment to make?*
I was planning to leave CBS; I was sending my cassettes around and I thought, "Oh, shit, once I leave CBS I'll have to carry things around on the subway." And then I realized, I'll have to hire a messenger service the same as CBS does. That idea was the big breakthrough. As an independent, I hire the same people, I use the same messenger services. I just pay for it myself, that's all. But on the other hand, I get the money to pay for it instead of it being handed over to a salary. That wasn't a *hardest* thing, was it? I don't have a hardest thing. I like having left CBS.

*At Rainbow Broadcasting you act as producer and you work with other producers. Is that hard sometimes?*
No, not if I'm in charge. When I left CBS I went to be a senior producer of a show called "Cover Story." It was a segmented magazine show I was doing for Al Perlmutter. And I decided right away to have a number of segments in the first hour, and that meant right away that I had nine segment producers. I made a rule. I don't want to speak to more than five producers in one day. If you're number six, you're out of luck. Because what happens is they start to be dependent, in a way. I said to Al, "Jeez, these people want you to hold their hand quite a bit, don't they?" He said, "Welcome to the world of executive producing."

*What about the freedoms of producing in different areas?*
The big difference from network is you have to get releases from everyone who is in it. Unlike the news, independent documentarians have to recognize that they are, in a sense, exploiting the person at whom they point the camera. And so they have to get permission to do it. This is a limitation. You will not find the heaviest investigative work done independently because the producer can't afford to take the kind of chances that CBS can afford to take. Like the General Westmoreland suit against CBS; like the Colonel Herbert suit against CBS. You can't afford those kinds of chances. And PBS can't afford to take those kinds of chances either. So for real investigative reporting on television, you still have to work at the network. But since I'm not essentially an investigative producer, I worry more about just getting the rights on some of the simplest things. Newspaper headlines — you've got to pay the paper; photos — at least $100 each; music — anything but the stockiest of stock

music is going to cost $200–$250 a drop, plus you have to make sure that you at least have a guarantee that they will negotiate for the ancillary rights that you might want in the future—cassettes, for example. A company that I worked for recently—I was subcontracted—the joke phrase was they wanted worldwide rights and by any media, including radar, because they wanted to have a future sale on this project. It was hard because some people, especially music people, will not deal with perpetuity rights. They'll say, "We don't know, we can't give you this kind of blanket release."

*What do you think that the film experience teaches you that video experience does not?*
    There's a basic difference between film and videotape, and my joke is that film looks good and videotape looks shitty. No, you see when you deal with film, film is a physical thing, and when you're putting it together physically, you get a sense of rhythm and tempo from just the lengths of the pieces that you're holding up in your hand. You don't get that down at your fingers in videotape. You're always asking what's the next damn number to go to.

*You seem like a hard-line film guy.*
    I think film looks a lot better. I think it's easier to work with. I think it's great material for production. Now ask me about post-production. There are nice things you can do in CMX editing sessions that are a lot of fun and they kept me interested through four magazine shows on science called "What On Earth" that I did for HBO. The studio stuff was fun to do, to chromakey in, to use the squeeze zooms, to create effects that people haven't even thought of. Now the weakness here is that we were only able to do this because it happened to be a show done for HBO, and the HBO studio let us come in one day when they weren't busy anyway. They said, "Come on down, and just play around with the equipment." I would say to the director, "What if we did this over here?" And he said, "Yeah, you know, I've never thought of this." And he'd do this and he'd say, "But you know what would be even better?" And we learned a few things. Ordinarily you're paying $300–$400 an hour for this kind of facility so you're not going to fool around—you're not going to play and you're not going to experiment because you can't justify doing it at those prices. If I can get a chance to play around with it, I love it.

*You're recognized as a high-quality producer.*
    That's by you.

*If the issue of cost comes up, what's the best way to justify a given budget?*
    Well, there's the old cliché, "You gets what you pays for." I often say

that. Sometimes people will use this argument: They'll say, "You know, you're getting paid more than any other of our producers." To which I'll say, "Yeh, that's right."

*What advice do you have for the independent producer who wants to be on PBS?*
I have produced one series, called "Cover Story," which was done through WQED in Pittsburgh, although the prime contractor was Al Perlmutter in NY. I was the senior producer, so I was a couple of lengths removed from PBS. It was therefore the toughest show I ever produced. I don't know what advice I have for a fledgling producer who wants to be on PBS. I have found that they're usually rather cliquish. Every once in awhile they open up. Some of the stations are better than others in seeking talent rather than giving it to their cousin. There's a lot of no-talent work done on PBS, by the way, so it's not like the major leagues — it's not hard to do as other things. I think you should get your work seen by the local public TV muck-mucks. But it all depends on who you are to begin with. I mean, if you're just out of film school, you're not going to make it.

*How do you think cable will impact on the independent producer? Is it a panacea?*
Yes, the more markets there are of a high quality the better off one is because we have more of a chance to sell our thing, and it becomes more competitive. It becomes more of a seller's market. We're talking about independent production jobs. Now, here I am in NY and I've done a lot of work with cable, with the networks and with PBS, but if there wasn't cable a lot of people I know wouldn't be doing interesting little projects for CBS Cable — the late lamented — but they would be doing those crappy industrials. You know, how to blow your nose, or for the army, or why you should purchase a certain kind of spark plug or how the spark plug is hot stuff.

*Would you agree that the producer is television?*
We're talking about names here. The producer as we know it — as defined on "60 Minutes" — the producer as defined in most situations is a hyphenate of some sort. I mean it's not just a money person. The hyphenate that it's usually strongest with is producer-director. There's always a creative center to everything. If you've got a creative person and he's the producer, then he's as important as the director. But when you're talking about fact films, then you're more limited than fiction. But you have to hyphenate somewhere. You have to be a producer-director or producer-writer. That's pretty standard. You used to be a cameraman, Irv. And I don't know if you still shoot. I used to be a film editor, and I know that I don't edit because I don't think that's the way the independent

should have his competitive edge. His edge is that he's not carrying some jerk in business affairs. You see, for every producing member of a big staff like CBS there's going to be three or four nonproducers somewhere. You know, the woman who orders floor wax for the goddamn building, the business affairs people, the ones who negotiate you out of your worth on the contract, you're carrying them because you're a producer, they're nothing. They're a parasite. And the other way the independent producer has an advantage is when I start a project, I have a fresh new slate and fresh new staff. I'm not stuck with good ole Joe who's been around for twenty years and is an incompetent. I don't have to carry him. We don't carry people who are incompetent. Let them get a job at the network. Independent producers theoretically are efficient. That's why I think I can do a show with the same number of people that a CBS show is done in half the time for half the money — or alternatively, I can do twice as good a show, or I can do the same show in the same time with half the people, etc.

*What's the main mistake people make in developing proposals?*
    Going too far too soon. If you go to twelve pages without having a client in mind . . . you're wasting your time unless you have two or three potential audiences and clients in mind. An idea is essentially like a flash of light. It's not in words. You put it down in words and it's the old Alfred Hitchcock chestnut about how it should have been on the back of an envelope. Put it on the back of an envelope. Now make two copies of the envelope and put one in your file under "envelopes with great ideas on them." That's the idea. Now, think who might be interested in it. Call them up. Now, you have to have this kind of relationship available or this kind of contract available, and you say, "Hey listen, are you interested in an idea about computers?" The guy says, "Yeah, maybe. What about computers?" And you go on with your one line about what you want to do. He says, "Let me see something." Now you have a client in mind. Now you pitch it in his direction. I mean HBO is interested in different things than PBS, believe me. So I think it is a mistake to develop things too much at first, to go too far. You want to know another mistake? Producers get obsessed with one proposal, as if the only production that they should make is the one they have a proposal out on. You should have — I'm looking over to see how many I have active in my tidy desk now, so that I can tell you the ideal number. Ten — something like that. Somewhere between six and twelve proposals that are hot at the moment and another ten that are a little cooler on the back burner. And you should theoretically work on two things at once; otherwise how we gonna beat the Russians, or the networks or whoever is considered dirty at the time?

*Michael Wiese*

IF, AS MICHAEL WIESE SAYS, producing is like putting together a group of musicians, Michael Wiese is himself some bandleader. Wiese has experience in a variety of producer roles—stalwart independent producer, local station segment producer and cable producer. He has also served as head of production for a large producer of political commercials.

Wiese is smart and funny, respectful of opportunities and a great believer in the value and skills of the independent film and videomaker. He says, "I used to be resentful of people who had other opportunities who were not as good as I was—or better. And I realized I just had to be successful with what I was doing and do that in an ethical manner."

He has produced some twenty-nine independent films, including *Hardware Wars* and *Dolphin*, which have been seen worldwide by millions. He has served as director of on-air promotion and production for the Movie Channel, New York, where he managed $3 million in production budgets; has supervised production of 175 political television commercials; and recently joined Vestron Video in Stamford, Conn., where he is vice-president in charge of program development.

Wiese is the author of *The Independent Film and Videomakers Guide* and *Film and Video Budgets* (a Michael Wiese Film Productions Book).

He holds an M.F.A. with honors from San Francisco Art Institute, and a degree from Rochester Institute of Technology, and has lived and travelled in Japan, Bali, Indonesia, India, Kenya, Ethiopia, Egypt, Greece, and Sudan.

*You've been a still photographer, editor, cameraman, producer. Are you ever confused as to what you are?*
Good question. Not really. They're all skills that go into producing. I'm a better producer because I know many of the different aspects—craft aspects of producing film and television. However, in the beginning it confused me because I would go out on a shoot having hired a cameraman and I would want to take the camera out of his hand and shoot it myself. I finally had to say to myself, "Hey, listen, you hired this guy because you trust his abilities; now just let him do his job."

*Your movie* Hardware Wars *has become a kind of minor classic. You even sold it to the educational market.*
When Ernie Fosselius and I originally made the film, we had no idea what to do with it. We just wanted to meet George Lucas, who had made *Star Wars*. And that would have been fine.

It turned out that our primary income came from the educational market or what's called the nontheatrical market. Pyramid Films distributes it. Somehow it caught on in schools, libraries and universities. And to help justify its use as an educational tool we prepared a study guide with a little vocabulary ("parody," "satire," etc.), a section on humor, a bibliography and class projects. And so educators look at it and say, "Yes, this is educational because it has a study guide." It has been bought for such things as Future Studies, Creative Writing and Sociology, and the strangest things. The Defense Department and IBM have bought prints of *Hardware Wars!* Although it's not educational — in the traditional sense — it's popular in the classroom. Maybe the kids blackmail the teachers and say, "Show *Hardware Wars* and we'll be good."

The home video market is really taking off. Warner Home Video distributes *Hardware Wars.* It has made as much in the last six months as in the last two and one-half years altogether.

*Did George Lucas ever see the movie?*

Yes, he saw the first print of it. He kind of gave it his unofficial blessing. A Lucasfilm spokesman said that George said it was a "cute film." I think he didn't want to say anything more because he knew we'd use it to promote the film. He did get me an appointment with Alan Ladd, Jr., who was then head of 20th Century–Fox. I had the naive notion that the studio might blow it up to 35mm and put it out with *Star Wars.* Boy, was I wrong. Anyway, I sat next to Mr. Ladd in the Darryl Zanuck screening room at 20th Century–Fox in these oversized, posh theater seats. Behind me were three lawyers who looked exactly alike in identical pinstriped suits. We screened *Hardware Wars.* Not a single person laughed. Alan Ladd, Jr., coughed once (well, it might have been a laugh). The lights went on and he said, "What do you want me to do with the film, kid?" I said, "You've done so well with *Star Wars.* Why not show *Hardware Wars* as kind of a prestige piece. You know, have some fun with it."

Needless to say, I didn't hear from Mr. Ladd.

*Tell me about making* Hardware Wars.

It's interesting that producing a funny movie is not necessarily funny — it's a lot of hard work. It's always the unexpected that I think is funnier. For example, we were very eager when we finished the film to see whether or not it was funny — because we really didn't know. We'd been working in a vacuum. So when we got our first answer print (we had our little projector in the car), Ernie Fosselius, who was the writer-director, and I went out to dinner. We were dying to show our movie to someone. We talked to the owner — we said, "Look, we just finished this movie and we really want to show it." He said fine. So we set up our projector right then and there, put a tablecloth on the wall, and screened our film while people were eating — completely inappropriate.

At first I thought the people were a little upset that their meals were so rudely interrupted by flying steamships (irons), but they applauded wildly. Later we took a tape recorder with us to a real theater and recorded the laughter so we could tell which jokes worked and which didn't. We found there were things that we needed to change — some jokes were too close together; others were too far apart.

Dolphin *was a beautiful film. How did that come about?*
     *Dolphin* came out of when I was an independent producer-director in San Francisco. It was a film that I wanted to make for ten or twelve years, ever since I met a dolphin on a beach. I was walking down the beach and saw a large group of people gathered together. As I got closer I saw that a man had pulled a dolphin out of the water. It was a sick dolphin, and apparently it couldn't get through the heavy breakers. Something drew me to that dolphin, and I pushed my way through the crowd, knelt down and began stroking its head. It looked at me and started squeaking and sending out high frequency sounds. I felt very much like it was responding to me or saying, "thanks." I was trying to give it some strength. We pulled it back into the water and watched it swim around a bit, then its dorsal fin went underneath the water and it disappeared. The crowd let up a cheer.
     Something unusual happened that day. Something I didn't really understand. I like to call these experiences "openings." I wondered if I was making it up — that the dolphin and I had communicated. Then I started thinking, what if *there were* other intelligent creatures on the planet who were at least as intelligent as we are — or more so, as we put ourselves at the top of this chain of intelligence. That idea gnawed at me for years and years. I read everything I could by Dr. John Lilly (a pioneer dolphin researcher), and it wasn't until about ten years later, when I got together with Hardy Jones, that we actually began doing it.
     One of the things about independent producing is most of my early films came out of those kinds of experiences. They were really personal quests, and the projects ran very parallel to my own interests.
     We thought we could buy a lot of stock footage of dolphins. We weren't so much interested in dolphins that were in marine parks as we were dolphins in the wild, but we found that not even oceanographer Jacques Cousteau had shot any film of wild dolphins for any sustained period of time. The film became our own quest to meet and relate to wild dolphins. The greatest problem for us was figuring out how to get the dolphin's attention and how to sustain it. Historical literature from Grecian times abounds with persons swimming with and communicating with dolphins. We took a tip from Aristotle, who said dolphins "careth for man and enjoyeth his music." In Greek times they played water harps for the dolphins, so we devised an underwater instrument — it's a Hohner melodica enclosed in a plastic case and powered with an amplifier and put out into the water by a little U.S. Navy speaker. The air from the diver's scuba tank powered this electronic harmonica, or underwater piano. It worked very well in the Bahamas, where we swam and filmed about seventy spotted dolphins.

My partner, Hardy Jones, has since gone back over the past seven years and shot more film. Each year the dolphins probably say, "Here he comes again. What will he have for us this time?" and each year Hardy comes up with something else he entertains them with. So I imagine the dolphins have a strange collection of stories about these humans who come every year about the same time and perform these bizarre rituals.

*What's the quintessential thing you learned about foreign distribution from your film* Dolphin?

One is that people worldwide love animal movies. The largest market for *Dolphin* has been foreign television — which simply requires that we strip off the English narration track and put on Swahili or Pakistani or Japanese narrations and we can play in any of those countries. It's been seen in over thirty countries so far, and now Pay TV is picking it up. The Disney Channel just licensed it.

Initially, I didn't have a foreign TV distributor for *Dolphin*, and I sold Japan, Hong Kong, New Zealand myself. The difficulty comes in knowing what to charge for it because at that time I had no experience with what the prices were, what the terms were. You don't know if you're selling it too cheaply. And of course there's a whole style of doing business that's different in every country. You don't know who the right person to talk to is, and you don't know if you'll ever see your film again, and you're communicating by telexes, and the contracts aren't clear because the language is so different.

Then I got a distributor, and that went well for two or three years; then he ran into money problems and quit sending us royalties. There's also the great problem of collecting from these foreign countries — even once the deal memo is signed and you're supposed to be paid on April 1, 1984, you may not be paid for a year or two. Then what happens is the foreign television companies wait until the dollar is at its all-time low before paying you. You may think you're going to get U.S. $5,000 from the thing, but by the time they pay, you may get U.S. $2,500.

*You produced political spots, didn't you? What was that like?*

I served more as an executive production manager, not a producer because creative control rested elsewhere. I was responsible for putting the crews together. It was a very controlled game. By that I mean in the political arena, information is power, and people who wanted to hold onto power kept the scripts and the information about the campaigns very close to themselves, which is sort of the antithesis of what I think filmmaking is, where communicating is essential. I was not privy to even the intent of what we were trying to do. It was very difficult. I was in that game for *only* nine months or so.

*Did you get burned out?*

Absolutely. It was a completely exploitative situation. I worked night after night after night, living in editing rooms and starting all over again at eight in the morning and working well into the following morning. It went on endlessly — without any regard for any other aspect of anyone's life. The same was true for crews and producers. When I hired them, I was always honest with them and told them it would be an eighteen-hour day and often it was twenty. Just burn them out and go on to the next person. I didn't really like that way of working.

*How many commercials did you work on there?*
I did one hundred seventy-five television spots and fifty radio spots in nine months, and that doesn't include revisions, which on politicals are endless. So you should probably multiply that by about three.

*Was scheduling a problem, doing so many of them?*
I was head of production and somebody else was head of politicals. I would book the crews, editors, and field producers as far in advance as possible. The field producer would schedule the politician with a farmer in the field, then in the schoolyard and then in the ghetto or whatever. At each location there are maybe twenty farmers, thirty schoolkids and forty ghetto people showing up. The producers would have prescreened and prepicked these people to look and respond and create a certain kind of ambience. What would happen often — quite frequently on the whims of the political department (who had no regard for production problems) — the schedule would be changed. We had scheduled the farmers in the morning; but instead we'd shoot in the ghetto in the morning, which would mean you'd have to move dozens or hundreds of people around. I always empathized with the field producer because he or she was the one who was always taking the heat and talking to the people, saying, "Please be in our spot, for free." He could never win because he would always be alienating fifty or one hundred people who were doing a favor for him, and the political department would continue to make totally unreasonable last-minute demands. It was very unprofessional.

*How do you like to approach things?*
I like to approach things in a very organized manner where you know what you're going to do each day and what you want to accomplish. This requires lots of pre-production and lots of planning. I don't like to function in situations where you're always winging it.

*What types of "politicals" did you like the most?*
I liked spots that were more issue-oriented and didn't involve the candidate's presence. My favorite spot — maybe it was because I had more control over it — was where we used a prop or a model in a clever way. They are called "concept spots." One was a money machine used for a

referendum in Alaska about moving the capitol. The point of the spot was don't move the capitol; it's a stupid idea; it will cost billions of dollars; what's it gonna get us? The spot showed a capitol building — a model with a crank on it, and everytime this hand turned the crank, more and more money would spew out of the capitol doors. That's a very powerful image and one people relate to and can feel something about.

So those were the spots I like — more idea spots. I mean with most politicals it's all a formula — you always see the politician late at night with his sleeves rolled up, drinking coffee at his desk, working hard. You always see him in the ghetto; you always see him in the supermarket holding babies and in the schoolyard, when in fact most of the candidates have never been in these settings until the day of the shoot.

*As a producer, have you a most embarrassing moment?*
Not a single embarrasing moment — many!! As a producer you've got to be willing to be embarrassed all the time. You've got to be willing to try things that aren't necessarily going to work, and take a lot of chances.

*You've hired many producers. What did you look for?*
I hired both men and women for the political spot production, so I have no particular biases that way. I want someone who is aggressive and yet has a winning personality — someone who can really ask for and deliver whatever without alienating anyone. There's no such thing as a shy producer. A field producer has to set up enormous numbers of people and equipment and make sure that the job gets done.

*Were you ever fooled? Did you ever miss out on hiring a George Lucas?*
Once I met a woman who came in to interview, and she was dressed very dumpily. She forgot to bring a resume. It was early in the morning and she had given up smoking a few days before, and she was shaking. She caught her purse on the handle of the chair and all the stuff from her purse fell on the floor and I said to myself, "Strike three — no way I'll hire this one." But the more I talked with her, the more I learned that she was in fact very competent. She was having a terrible day. I did end up hiring her and using her for a number of things and she was absolutely terrific. But usually I can tell if I want to hire someone in the first thirty seconds. Then I spend the rest of the interview substantiating my intuitive feeling.

*What do you feel is the greatest skill of being a producer?*
It's putting people together and having insight and good taste. You have to not only know what elements you need in terms of quality, but put a certain team together with a certain chemistry that can produce a result. Easy to say, more difficult to do.

*Can you give me an example?*

It's like putting together a band. Everyone has his part within the whole; the dynamics are what is most important. Once I worked on a shoot for a client who wanted me to hire his favorite cameraman, but this cameraman was extremely arrogant. And since he knew the client wanted him, he was the star. He had us rent a Cadillac convertible for him and get him a certain hotel room next to the pool and stock his refrigerator with health food. He got all the attention, and it created a great riff between him and the crew. He was paid ten times what they were paid, and he mistreated and abused everyone around him.

*How does one establish a relationship with a crew?*
    You obviously want to draw out the best you can in whoever works for you — whether it's a writer or editor or post-production producer. This is done by knowing enough about what you want so that you can communicate that to them and then get out of the way so they can contribute fully. I mean, you don't want to thwart any ideas they may have. At the same time, you need to be strong enough and clear enough about what you want so that they don't go astray.

*You were quoted somewhere as saying that a good relationship is better than a good idea. Can you explain that?*
    I already assume that if people are going to work together they have a good idea — so I don't every worry about that. What makes that idea real is a good working relationship among everyone involved. Good ideas are a dime a dozen. I assume if you're going to make a film or a book that there's a good idea behind it. And so what I'm more interested in is the relationship that gets that idea made: When everything is really working, people feel free to contribute everything to and improve on the idea. So you can't assume that because you have a good idea on paper that you can wave it in the air and zippo! it's real. I think it's the producer's job to set up the relationships that allow the idea to become reality in the form of a film or tape.

*You've produced a lot of break pieces at the Movie Channel. What makes a good producer of what they call "interstitial" material?*
    Let me just say what I'd look for in a good "interstitial" producer. Movies have writers and cinematographers and editors — it's all broken down. The producer of interstitial material is expected to be a writer and an acquirer — someone who can go out and research and find stock footage, find stills. So you have to write; you have to acquire the material; you have to supervise the editing, select music, mix the sound track. You have to have a graphic sense so you can put titles on it, or opening or closing logos. It's probably the closest thing to being an independent producer or independent film or videomaker because you do all these different jobs.

*Is a good producer for one field a good producer for another? What are the commonalities?*

Strangely enough, I think in the broadest sense that the qualities that make good producers would enable them to produce anything – to produce a wedding, a music show, or a backyard football game because a producer is really a procurer and organizer of people and materials. And the producer also has a vision of what the end result should be and the personality to direct the whole creative process.

It doesn't mean a producer could go and make a feature and then go and make a TV series and all that the first time out, but I think the inherent skills are transferable.

*From your experience at the Movie Channel, what's the key to doing a successful movie trailer?*

A trailer should accurately represent the gist of the film. It's real easy with horror movies to cut a trailer that from the first few frames shows what the movie is. The difficulty comes in when you have a film like *Pennies from Heaven* with comic Steve Martin. I think one reason the movie failed so badly at the box office had to do with the expectations set up by the trailer. The movie was not a Steve Martin comedy and it wasn't a '30s musical; it was closer to something like a black comedy. Yet the trailer and ad campaign promised a Steve Martin '30s comedy, which it wasn't. So when we cut the trailer for that movie we made it clear it wasn't going to be a movie for everyone, and it wasn't your standard Steve Martin fare, and it wasn't a '30s musical.

You should be able to tell by looking at a trailer if you want to see the movie or not. I think that's the function it serves, especially on a pay cable channel, where you may be running fifty, sixty, seventy movies a month. At the same time, if the audience hasn't heard of a movie or it hasn't played well at the box office, you may be trying to position it for a particular audience.

*Tell me about your time spent as a segment producer.*

I was a segment producer in San Francisco for a TV variety show that was very much like "The Buffalo Bill Show" on NBC. Sometimes I'd have as many as ten segments a week to do. I'd have to come up with an idea, pitch the idea to my executive producer and if I got it approved, I'd write it up and go out and get talent, figure how to shoot it, coach the talent, etc. The show was on live five nights a week at 7:00. I also had the job of warming up the audience. We had a live audience of 150 people so I would have to warm them up by telling jokes and announcing who was on the show as well as getting them all amp'ed up so when the host came on everyone applauded. It was hectic. At the same time I'd be juggling as many as three guests in the green room, from tot wrestlers to sexual surrogates or celebrities and bestselling authors.

*What was the hardest part of that job?*

The hardest thing for me was to adapt from being an independent producer — all my projects were very close to me — to coming up with very broad material that was pure entertainment. I was assigned all the segments having to do with "sex, food, and baby animals." My biggest problem was *not* doing my own stuff or trying to bring consciousness to the 7:00 time slot, when it wanted entertainment. I think where I got myself in trouble was trying to do serious stuff.

*Favorite traumatic moment?*

One of my jobs was to babysit the different guests when they came in, and we had a very well known actor from a major TV series on the show. Much to my surprise, this person who was on prime time television every week, was extremely nervous to be on our little San Francisco show and be interviewed.

We got the knock on the door that said three minutes to go, and as I was leading him down the backstage hallway he said, "I've got to go to the bathroom." I said, "We don't have time to do that. Your interview is in two minutes, can't you wait?" He said, "No, no, I have to go," and he ducked into the bathroom. When he came out, I saw that the front of his pants was rather wet, but that he hadn't noticed. And now we were fifteen seconds before he had to go on. I had to decide at that moment whether to tell him or try to get someone else, which was impossible because the host was already into his introduction. So, I grabbed the floor manager's headset and told the cameraman to keep all the shots "head and shoulders," and I pushed him out without telling him.

Those kinds of things were happening every day. None of the segments went as you planned. There wasn't the time to rehearse them and the cameramen didn't want to rehearse them because they didn't want to be there in the first place and all the lighting guy could do was turn on the lights and turn them off. I did a fashion show one night and I wanted to do this stylized thing with different pools of light coming on and off as these models walked through them, with the music, but the lighting guy couldn't handle it. Either the lights were on or they were off. Also, the cameramen never seemed to remember the shots you wanted and the host would not follow your cue cards, so it was usually out of control. But that was one of the things that made it fun: the excitement of live television — and the unknown.

*Any other traumatic moments you can think of?*

Yes, lots. One time we had a termite-sniffing dog on. This man had a dog who, if you want your house tested for termites, you call him up and he brings the dog and together they find the termites. So, before the show the man planted some termites in this little bowl under the host's seat, and he showed the dog where they were so nothing could go wrong.

So we are into the show, and the man talks about his dog and relates how he has hidden some termites and his dog is going to find them for the audience. So the camera's on the dog and the dog's going everywhere all around the studio except where the termites are hidden. The audience is cracking up. It ends up with the man taking the dog by the collar and forcing him under the host's seat. "Oh, here they are, good job." The reality in the studio is always different than it is on the air. I always thought about the people sitting at home saying, "What in the world is going on in this show?"

Another time we had comedian Dom DeLuise on. This was before Lady Diana married Prince Charles, and we did a little tribute to them. We told our studio audience that we had the chef of the Prince Charles wedding, the man who made their wedding cake. We said we were going to see the cake and meet the person who made it. Dom DeLuise played the chef. For the royal couple we used look-a-likes, but these people looked exactly like the royal couple, Charles and Diana. So they come out and taste the cake. Then we ask who better to taste it than the queen herself. DeLuise is like a five-year old; he just cannot behave. He's just bad. And he starts flipping whipped cream at the queen, and it's hitting her and the queen is extremely upset. (This show fortunately was one that we taped.) The queen keeps leaving the set and refusing to work with DeLuise unless he behaves himself. She took her role very seriously. Even though she wasn't the queen, she believed she was the queen. She said that her agent was going to sue. DeLuise finally had to be restrained. He would always say, "Okay, I won't do it anymore," and the minute we'd roll, he'd flip some more whipped cream at the queen or pull on her crown, or do something bad. Finally, we got a segment taped, but the queen was not very happy.

*Sometimes the producer has to be the bad guy. Are you a good or bad guy?*

When the producer is the bad guy, I think a lot of time it's because he or she wasn't clear in setting up the agreement with whoever is working for him. A good producer will try to work out very clearly with everyone who works for them what the exchange will be, how much money they'll make, how long they'll have to work, if they'll get any points, what their credits will be — these basic things are usually what the dispute is over. If something goes out of whack, I always assume it's my responsibility to make it clear. Fortunately, I really don't have too many problems in this area. I have had to fire people, but usually it's because they want to be fired or leave the show or whatever it is, and they'll do things to tip you off to this. And I say, "You don't want to be here any more, do you?" and sure enough they don't.

*You really believe in agreements, it seems?*

I've been working on a script with a writer, and we just wrote a five-page agreement. What if this happens? What if it's bought? What if it's developed? What if I have to hire another writer? So, if any of those "what-ifs" happen, we have a way of dealing with it and we can go back to this agreement even though we may have totally forgotten it. If you don't get all the what-ifs out of the way, those things are going to be in the way of the work, so I try to clear that up right away so that everyone can proceed with the work, which is what it is all really about.

*Isn't it difficult to get all the what-ifs in the contract?*
In three sentences you can get the top three and that will clear up 80 percent of the energy right there, and allow it to be applied to the work and not worrying about who gets what.

*What are the top three?*
Money, title credits, and profit points.

*How long is Michael Wiese's attention span? You're interested in a lot of things. You've done a lot of things. Has this ever been a problem for you?*
Yes, that's kind of a curse, I think, because there's not a week gone by that I don't think of some way I want to alter my life dramatically. I used to be a drummer, and my drums were stolen way back in the late '60s and it's something I never completed, so I've been fantasizing about drums lately and looking to buy a drum set and reading all the drum magazines and looking at drums. That's all I need to do right now is to buy a drum set. There are many things like that—there are many places I've traveled and want to travel again. There are things I want to study. I'm carrying around a little Indonesian language book that I read five to ten minutes at a time, teaching myself Indonesian.

What I have to learn is to focus on one thing at a time—but I thrive on having numerous projects going simultaneously. In the last two months I've finished writing two books, given five or six lectures around the country for AFI, and have begun a new job at Vestron Video, where I've reviewed more than 100 new projects in the last two weeks.

*How much of this is born in you, or comes from your environment? After all, the world of the producer is a constant search for ideas and opportunities.*
In my case I don't think I was necessarily born with it. I think I had parents who were very supportive of anything I wanted to do and validated my misconception that anything I did I would be good at. I don't think that's true—but anyway, I grew up thinking that. So whatever I wanted to do they said, "Good, go and do it." But I think that has led to some problems. As I said, I want to yank the camera out of the cameraman's hands because I had been a cameraman and now, I want to

write when there are better writers. I want to edit when there are better editors. I think I have to learn to be a producer and be less involved with the actual "doingness" of each project. The producer's job is to "be" the project in all aspects but not necessarily *"do"* any of it. The producer maintains the integrity of the project, the vision. If for one second you get involved with the detail, you lose sight of the bigger picture.

Let me give you an example: at the Movie Channel, I was responsible for a staff of fifteen and had six or seven producers working for me. They were all assigned different projects. When I first started the job, I would become very involved with the copy, with how the spots were going to cut, with the visual effects. I made the producers call me with their narration tracks and play them over the phone. I would comment on the "read," change this word, change the mix. But, at some point, I had to get off that and train my people to perform at a certain level and simply trust them to do it. We were turning out 100 pieces per month and I couldn't get involved with every one of them. Even if they didn't meet my standards every time — and I think I have very high standards — I had to let it go. My life was not at stake in each of these spots. We did the best we could within our schedule, and although few segments were masterpieces, I learned to live with them. You can't keep working on your film indefinitely; at some point you just have to say, "Okay, that's it, we're done."

*Perry Wolff*

"THERE'S GOT TO BE A PREMISE," according to Perry Wolff. "A premise consists of a subject and a verb, which has to be a transitive verb, and an object." Whatever the subject of Wolff's documentaries, the transitive verb is Wolff himself and the object is nonfiction television that tells a good story.

A graduate of the University of Wisconsin, Wolff joined CBS in 1947. Since then he has served as chief musical director of WBBM-TV, as an investigative reporter, and as director of the "CBS Morning News," and has produced more than 200 documentary hours for television, including "Air Power," the first commercial documentary series in television history.

Wolff has followed two paths in documentary—news and cultural. He produced "A Tour of the White House with Mrs. John F. Kennedy," "1945," "1968," "The Selling of the Pentagon," and a series of cultural documentaries on national characters: French, Italian, Japanese, Israeli, and Palestinian. His documentary productions are noted for their intelligence and have received every major television award—Emmys, Polks, Peabodys, Writer's Guild, the duPont-Columbia Journalism award—plus an Oscar in 1961 for "Les Seigneurs de la Foret."

First a writer (he says the great secret for writing for television is learning when *not* to write), he has also written a novel, three history books, and a volume of sonnets.

In April 1976 he was named Executive Producer for CBS News Specials, the position he currently holds.

*You were a producer back in the '50s for "Air Power." What was it like to do that show?*

Holy smokes! What was it like? I learned how to cut film. NBC had done a series which we had called "Victory at NBC" ["Victory at Sea"]. We decided we would do a similar thing with the Air Force. However, we didn't want to do just a "salute to our brave fliers." I had been in the infantry in WWII and I didn't have the wild blue yonder in my eyes, so CBS decided to do what was at the time an investigation into the success and the failure of the United States Air Force.

It was the first commercially sponsored documentary series in the history of television. There had been a considerable amount of work done before I was joined up by a guy who just wanted to do flak work for the Air Force. Sig Mickelson (then the head of CBS) fired my predecessor and then hired me.

The standards were quite different in those days.

*How were the standards different?*

Well, they weren't codified. CBS today has a book called *CBS News*

*Standards*. It tells you what it is you can do and can't do. In the '50s no one had written down the rules—it was simply to do it as fairly as you could and as honestly as you could. We were using stock footage. Stock footage often comes from propaganda films to begin with. You really did not know the provenance of the particular shot, but it didn't mean that you couldn't be fair about it.

The key story about "Air Power" is that we submitted a pilot film on a bombing raid that took place on May 1, 1943—the bombing of Ploesti. Ploesti was an oil refinery in Rumania. It was the worst defeat the United States Air Force ever suffered. In one day the bombing force lost 30% of the planes that went out. We submitted that broadcast as a pilot just to see whether the Air Force would stand still for a show about defeat. This was eleven years after World War II. In the World War II movies we always win and this was the first time in which somebody lost. They didn't like it much at the Pentagon. Nevertheless, that argument laid down the perimeters of the show. We worked out kind of an uneasy arrangement with the Air Force. The series was just the detailing of the growth of air power and what its uses were and what its limits were—its successes and its failures. It was, in one sense, prophetic because a number of episodes said you can't win wars with airplanes. It was well received. As a matter of fact, it had five network runs.

What it taught me was how to do film. I learned film language, and because I am a writer, I learned *when not to write*, which is the great secret for writing for television—documentaries, anyway—when to shut up and when to let the film play.

*Which means?*

Which means if it's perfectly obvious up on the screen, why are you talking?

*So for what purposes, then, does one use narration?*

When do you use narration? When you know something which the audience ought to know but which is not in the film itself. You use narration to point out to the audience what is happening on the film. Now that's didactic, and it's not what Grierson teaches, and it's not what you learn in colleges where the use of a narrator is forbidden, but in a communication medium, as distinguished from a theatrical medium, it is a necessity sometimes to talk.

*What is the mistake that most beginning producers make in narration?*

Well, there are two schools. It depends on where they come from. If they come out of a feature film background, their greatest error is to make a film in which there is almost never a voice-over because that's a great tradition of theater. (When I go to the movies I don't want somebody pointing things out to me.) But television is much more literal. There are times when you simply have to have narration. People who just come out of, say, the editing room, or who come out of the director's background, are adverse to narration. Then, on the other hand, you have people who come out of a totally journalistic print background, and for them the picture is often just wallpaper for people's eyes to be abused with while they listen to a totally scripted show. It's radio with pictures.

*Was there one project on which you really had ambivalence about whether to use narration or how to use it?*
    It's always the same problem, which is one's tendency to overwrite. That's one thing. The second thing, since I consider myself a journalist, is what tone shall I use — what is the proper tone to use to describe the scene?

*Can you give me an example of that from things you've done? How you've wrestled with the tone of a given piece?*
    Well, yes, I did a show recently called "The '70s: American Dream — American Nightmare," in which, for example, we went through Nixon and Watergate and all that sort of thing, and the question was how to treat Mr. Nixon. It isn't just writing; it's editing, as well as the writing. It would be very easy to find the scenes in which Richard Nixon looked like a fool, to find a scene where the cameraman has selected a lens or a position to be unflattering — to take on an unflattering tone in the script and in the editing, and, for that matter, in the music, although I don't use music much. I have a strong feeling that music doesn't belong in documentaries.

*You don't believe that? Why?*
    Well, just because music tells an audience how to feel. Music is the most emotional of the arts, I think, or at least it indicates to people . . . it tells them how to feel about a scene. It sets a tone. If you're doing a journalistic or historic account, you should get as close to objectivity as possible. Music is a great crutch, and we would rather stumble than use it.

*Let's talk about the CBS standards book. When did that come into practice?*
    I've got one in front of me right here — revised edition. It was always there in a series of memos, but the standardization of the thing that we make every employee read, even if they are an accountant here, is about 1976.

*Do you like having that in that form or do you think it just . . . ?*
    It's not the slightest bit inhibiting.

*Why?*

Because it was written by newsmen and journalists and it is not a straitjacket, by any means.

*Did you have some of your ideas reflected in there?*
Well, it grew. I mean, yes, sure, some of my ideas are there and some of it is just damned obvious. You don't pay for interviews; you don't stage interviews. It is extremely helpful. I've never heard anyone object to the CBS News standards or the publication of them. I think that NBC is about to do the same thing. You know, CBS has been run for a long time by a lawyer, Dick Salant, who is also a fine journalist, and what he's done is like Hammurabi or Solon or Blackstone or people who finally wrote down the law. He and David Klinger, who did the physical writing of it, gave you sort of what to do in the field in the sense of what's fair and what isn't fair. Now other organizations . . . *The New York Times* has one. They may not have codified it in quite the same way, but that's it—that's how you do it. If situations come up when you're in violation of what the written standard is, you simply say, "This is how these scenes were filmed," and sometimes you say it on the air. This was really triggered, I think, by "The Selling of the Pentagon." There were mistakes made in editing.

*Colonel MacNeil?*
Colonel MacNeil, probably. The answer that was given was not to the question that was asked. We had a fandango about what really happened, but the fact of the matter is that that's unfair and we sat down and said, "What's unfair? Let's lay down the things that are unfair," and the book was the result of that. "Selling the Pentagon" was '71. (I have a feeling I have a late copy of the CBS standards book.) The standards are geting more refined, but it did come out of "The Selling of the Pentagon." We stood then, and we stand now, totally behind the major thrust of the broadcast, but it's simply . . . I guess all of us who were connected with it think if something did go wrong of a minor nature, our official position is that we did nothing more than newspapers do. But, for example, if you ask the same question three times, which is something that happens in interviews, and then you make a composite answer from the same question, you should just label that as a composite answer. Things ought to be on the screen what they purport to be—that's about what it comes down to.

*Did things ever get hot for you at CBS during "The Selling of the Pentagon"?*
For me, personally, no. There ought to be a book done about "The Selling of the Pentagon," because it is a landmark broadcast. The interesting thing about it is that almost nobody saw it. It got a 15% share. Everybody pretends to have seen the broadcast but very few people did.

We weren't counting shares and ratings very closely but I just looked it up one day. I've had other episodes which were far worse than "The Selling of the Pentagon," but "The Selling of the Pentagon" — we didn't think that it would have the flap that it did. The sort of cynical but true rule of documentaries is that in the public's mind, the success of the documentary is measured by the strength of the counterattack that comes against it and where it comes from. In this case, the reason it became a landmark show was not so much what the content of the show was, but because the Congress of the United States wanted to subpoena our outtakes to see what we had done and we said — this consists of a very arcane legal thing — we said, "We're the same as the print press and you can't subpoena our outtakes."

*That was really no big decision, was it?*
     No, it was flat decision. We weren't going to do another. There are certain conditions in which they can have the outtakes. For instance, if you have a murder on camera, but it doesn't make the show — I'm not an expert on this, but if there was a crime that had been committed, we would certainly answer the subpoena. Our position is that we will decide what subpoenas we answer and which ones we do not for outtakes.

*You said you had other flaps that were worse than that. Can you give me some of your worst?*
     Well, in this area we have been subpoenaed. There was a show that I was producer of that never got on the air and we never even finished it. It was called "Project Nassau." Jay McMullen was the producer. It had to do with a force that was going to go back to Haiti — this was in the late '60s, I guess — and was going to overthrow Duvalier. We started to follow the rebels around and we realized that we had been taken. We never aired the show, but the Congress again — this was Harley Staggers — decided that we had paid for a phony invasion of Haiti, and they subpoenaed everything. That was much harder because "The Selling of the Pentagon" resulted only in Frank Stanton testifying before the Congress, but for "Project Nassau," Bill Leonard and I and Jay McMullen and other CBS officials were subjected to the House Commerce Subcommittee.

*What do you mean, "We had paid for the invasion?" You had staged it?*
     Well, they said we were paying for it. They said we were staging it and that we had somehow or other manipulated out of petty cash some money to have these poor guys go back and our cameras would be there and all that sort of thing. None of that was true. None of it was proven and nothing ever happened.

*How did you feel when you were facing Congressman Harley Staggers during the Congressional hearings?*

Oh, well, he didn't worry me as much as the committee counsel, but it's just no fun. The way it works is that they have an investigative staff, they have a lawyer and the lawyer does the questioning. To a great degree, we had been led into this, I believe thoroughly today, by the CIA. One of the men who had been giving us misinformation was a CIA man. I knew that. We had positive identification that he had gone to CIA school with a man whom I knew quite well, who identified him as such. I tried to introduce this into evidence to show that we had been duped, and Congressman John Moss of California said, "This man is not a member of the CIA. I called the CIA and they denied that he had ever been there." This is pre-Watergate. But these kinds of things, they're the dramatic movements of a newsman's life. The normal relationship between press and government certainly is not hostile, but antagonistic. That's what's expected.

*What was the toughest subject you had to deal with?*
Whatever yesterday's problem was. (laughs) It depends on what you mean. If you mean toughest in the terms of the hardest controversy, then you get into what rips you apart emotionally.

*For example?*
Well, there's an obscure show called "The Battle of East St. Louis."

*Peter Davis did that.*
That's right. And just sitting through that agony of watching the cops and the blacks vent their feelings . . . but this didn't involve me as much as "how to be fair to both sides," you know. You saw the show and it was really a wrenching show emotionally. That's one thing. If you mean hard in the sense of being fair, I think maybe the last couple of shows that I've done. I did the show on the year 1968, and I did "American Dream — American Nightmare," which was on the '70s, for which we went back into the stock footage that CBS has and tried to come to historical conclusions. That required the most reading and the most thinking and so on. But there is another way a show could be hard, and that is when the material for it that comes in from the field isn't very good and you have to see how you can make it interesting and so on. I guess I've never done a really easy program, other than live panel shows, or something like that.

*Do you like panel shows?*
Oh yes. I started in radio in 1947 and I've done it all.

*Tell me about that.*
Well, when I went to college I had been working at WHA in Wisconsin — University of Wisconsin — 1938.

*"Oldest station in the nation."*

That's right. I started there, and I always knew I wanted to do radio. I came back out of the Army and looked for a job, and just by dint of my mother making me practice the piano, I could read score; so I got hired as a music producer in Chicago. I did many of the music shows. In those days nobody wanted to do documentaries. One day somebody walked in with one of those brush tape recorders and said, "Hey, look what this stuff does." I said, "I wonder if you could cut that tape." He said, "Yeah, maybe you could cut it and put scotch tape on it and put the two sections together." So I was present at the creation, you might say. I was doing music shows, and then I was running around Chicago buying narcotics and showing how the police were being bought off and all that sort of thing; so investigative reporting in radio came to me as early as '47 or '48, and I just went on from there. It's just . . . the problems are always the same in the sense that, you know, editing is always the same, it's always the same process. The soul of non-fiction is editing. The hard shows are where you have to edit, because editing is what makes a movie great. You have to have the material to edit, but editing is when the mind starts to work. The rest of it, so much of mass communication, is . . . I just call it "plumbing"; but when you edit, you have to start making choices. The great rule of government is "to govern is to choose." So you choose.

*Did you ever feel physically threatened when you were running around buying drugs?*
Oh, sure, that was in my salad days. I was physically threatened — by the Chicago cops, who denied that there might have been anyone but a few crazy niggers who were buying dope, because Chicago was clean — and it wasn't true. And then I was threatened by the . . . at that point the narcs were all in the Treasury Department, and they said, "The fact that you can buy it means that we can bust you if you buy it." The dope scene with me started and ended before 1950.

*Did you realize these realities before you got into documentaries?*
Well, I majored in philosophy, so I knew there were many realities. There are many realities that the documentary doesn't handle.

*Such as?*
Well, the realities of a great fictional film. There are many . . . I hate to be Socratic or Platonic about it, but there are many levels of reality. There is a surface reality, there is a journalistic reality, there is a religious reality, and people are generally confused between which is which. I am not Catholic, but in the catechism — the Baltimore Catechism — it says reality is that which is closest to God, so I don't like to play the game of "real." I don't think what happens on the screen is real except in context.

*Are you cynical?*

No, not at all. I'm skeptical. There's a line between skepticism and cynicism that's somewhat like the line between ambition and pretension.

*You've also done "Conversations" over the years. How do you like the structure of conversation?*
It isn't the structuring of the conversation, it's the editing of it.

*You say, "Some of the shows that have pleased me the most have been conversations."*
Yes, I was thinking of Eric Sevareid and Eric Hoffer.

*Those were marvelous.*
There was a problem. Hoffer is an outrageous man and a brilliant man. I remember going to Dick Salant, head of CBS News, and I said, "I can make this man a hero or I can make him a shit." I had, you know, eight to nine hours of conversation. It boiled down to one hour, and I had about eight or nine weeks to edit it. That's the key point. (These conversations that they shoot on Monday and air on Wednesday infuriate me! They really don't think about their material.) I said to Salant, "What do I do?" and he looked at me blankly and said, "Well, show him fairly. If he's part devil and part angel, show it." But when you have a mass of material like that – eight to nine to ten to twelve hours . . . . The shoot was in three cameras. A good conversation, two people, isn't very well filmed unless you have three cameras, for reasons I don't want to go into now. You really have a lot of footage to go through and an awful lot of decisions. What Sevareid was getting at in the best of his shows was discussions with men who have used power, and Hoffer's power was something else. Hoffer was outrageous! In '69, I guess, when I did one of those shows, he said, for example, "If I find any of the students going through my files and my life's work, I'd kill 'em," and Sevareid said, "Oh, well, I don't think you mean you would really kill them," and Hoffer said, "Yes, I'd kill 'em." I thought, do I use it or don't I use it? I know what it was. It was an artistic explosive ejaculation of values from Eric Hoffer, which he truly didn't mean. I mean, he didn't literally mean he was going to stick a knife into somebody. Had that been on the screen it would have been another . . . it would have been a complication. Maybe I should have used it, I don't know, maybe I was wrong.

*What does a network executive producer do?*
Well, Bud Benjamin defined a network executive producer as a towel boy in a whorehouse.

*A which?*
A towel boy in a whorehouse. That is to say, everybody else is enjoying himself and you have to clean up after them. (laughs) He does a

couple of things. His job is to work between the executive and the producer, because there are two different modalities of existence. The executives see television more or less as a great river flowing. It's a flow of things: They think of program concept, they think of series, and so on. The producer sees things in a static way. He wants to make an art object – one show is an art object. Between the flow and the static quality there has to be tension, so an executive producer understands a little of what both sides are going through and tries to ameliorate. But I also act as a kind of counselor to producers, because if you compare it to an editing process in a newspaper, every good journalist wants a good editor. Every good writer wants a good editor. So that's one of the functions of the executive producer. Every good administrator wants to say to the producer, "For God's sake, take it easy. Don't get so monomaniacal," and so on, and that's what I do for the executive. So you stand between.

*So what does the producer do? The producer does the work.*
Yeah, the producer does the hard work. He gets the people together, he thinks of all the various ways that things can be done. Some producers, like Jay McMullen, he doesn't need an executive, he doesn't need an executive producer, he just goes out and he does it all and he interviews it all and so on. Producers – at least in the hour documentary – the producer in the documentary equals the director in the feature film, but we don't use the word "director," except where the unions have caused us to use it, because we don't want people to have a feeling that the subjects have been directed as to what to say or how to say it. That's why you have this peculiar title "producer."

There's another thing: Producers don't belong to unions and they don't belong to administrative staff. They're sort of like sergeants in the army, and everybody is called a producer when you look at the titles. There are assistant producers, associate producers, assistant to the associate producers, senior executive producers – they all have different functions. The general way it works is that if you just didn't use the word producer, the man who makes the show has two kinds of people working for him. He has the people who work below him – they're generally called associate producers – who present him with all the options, and he has the executive producer, who will later close down some of his options, you know, "That isn't what your story is."

*Give me an example when you, as network executive producer, had to go and really fight administration because you felt the producer was right.*
Well, let me think. It's usually done in an atmosphere of congeniality. There was a producer named Irv Drasnin, who . . .

*He did "The Guns of Autumn."*
Yeah, he did "The Guns of Autumn." I was only peripherally

connected with that because it was a show that very much interested Bill Leonard, and when the executives get terribly interested I just step aside and let them go together. There was a recent show on the unions that Irv did within the last couple of years. The executives were terribly disturbed by the show itself, and I knew that all that was wrong was a distorted scratch track. They couldn't hear the script. I said, "Just let me go back and improve the narration and change these scenes with Irv and let's see what happens." Very often, particularly in network documentaries, the first ten scenes set it up, and the story wasn't set up properly. We went back, and it looked like an entirely different picture. It wasn't, but the impetuousness of both sides calmed down a great deal.

*How do you set it up in the first ten scenes?*
Well, you ought to bring the audience in by the hand; that is, you ought to tell them what they're going to be seeing without putting up what is called "the inter-office memo." I get mad at Dick Salant and say, "Why don't you just put your damn memo on the screen, if that's what you want. Just put it up there, read the memo, and that's it." And, of course, the answer to that is that it isn't it — that there ought to be some way to bring the curtain up and at the same time, balance exposition with development of story. Every show is a little different. The way it's usually done, they put the screaming story up front and say, "This is a story of teenage rape," and you get in close and you see the girl's face, or something like that, and you say, "Now we're going to discuss rape," or something like that. Some say, "Isn't there another way? How else can you get the audience in?" But the opening to the show ought to be truthful to the close of the show. The art of telling a story well is really part of what a documentarian wrestles with. The strange paradox is that the materials he works with are so untheatrical, in a sense, that he very often becomes a better storyteller than people who do fictional films.

*A better storyteller.*
He's a better storyteller because the quality of what he has to work with is not as overwhelming as a beautiful girl or wonderful music or a great big screen, or something like that. I often go to the movies and they don't tell their story very well. They don't know what the point is. There's always one thing I tell to my people and I try to say to myself: "There's got to be a premise. A premise consists of a subject and a verb, which has to be a transitive verb, and an object."

*Give me a premise.*
Well, I did a show called "1968," and the premise was, "These are the events that got Richard Nixon elected." The value of the premise was that if I thought of including a dramatic event that wasn't related to the premise, the event had to go, no matter how glorious it was. Premises are

good, particularly in documentaries, where we shoot a different way. We shoot thirty-to-one. In a scripted, fictional show, they shoot a smaller ratio. When you just go out into the world of reality and you start shooting, you say, "Gee, that's a wonderful scene but it has nothing to do with what my show is about." It's hard to give up something that you've spent all day shooting, or trying to get at, but you have to.

*What's your definition of documentary?*
    Oh, I think when it is at its best it's just what it says. It is a document that you file with the public for the public to make a judgment on. The difference between a documentary and a propaganda film, or what did they use to call it — "films of persuasion" — is that the bias shouldn't show. You're really not selling anything. You're saying to the public, "Here's what we found, what do you think about it?" There's always that thing at the back end where Ed Murrow or a correspondent comes back and gives an opinion or an analysis of what's just been seen; but the best ones are ones in which you just say, "This is what happened, and here are the significant events, and you make up your minds on the evidence." A document has to do with evidence.

*How are those documentary units at networks organized?*
    They differ at different networks. The way we're organized here is that there is a vice-president, a senior vice-president in charge of documentaries; he and the senior members of the documentary team sit around and discuss what it is that we should do a documentary about. We have a limited budget, not as limited as the amount of air time, and there's competition on subjects.
    There are two different kinds of documentaries. There are those documentaries that explain what has happened in the news recently, and then there are the long-range documentaries where you try to get to a problem or get to an exposition or a development or something that people haven't noticed recently. The best documentaries are not necessarily news oriented. The ones that I've done, I guess, that have pleased me the most are either historical or cultural. I did many years ago a documentary with Luigi Barzini, called "The Italians," on his book, which somehow caught, I thought, the essence of the people. I did one on the Japanese. The document may be a document on culture, as well as on news events.

*How long do you like to have to do a piece?*
    Well, it depends; I would rather not discuss my own personal thing. I've done documentaries, so to speak, between 11:00 in the morning and 9:00 at night, when we had to get an explanation of something on the air, but our general run is nine months, because we find the investigation of the story takes a couple of months. We generally shoot six weeks and we

edit twenty-two, something like that. We've done hundreds of them, and that's the rule of thumb.

*Was it hard for you to learn the waiting game? Waiting to see that that "hard to get" piece would come in, that sort of thing.*
No, that's . . . I don't consider myself much of a director. I don't like it, and I don't know the agonies in the field anymore. I've done a few of them out there, but the hardest part is always in the editing room. It's waiting for those gestalts — when you think the ordinary documentary is 60,000 feet, and I've done them holding in my mind as much as 150,000 feet.

*What project was that?*
Oh, I did a show called "A Day in the Life of the United States." I had fifty camera crews running around America the day we landed on the moon, and there were forty producers in the field, and they all sent in much more than I thought they would. (I guess I went $150,000 over budget in one weekend.) But all our stuff comes in, and somehow or other it gets buried in your subconscious, and you wait for those great gestalts that tell you what piece precedes and what piece follows what, you know. The slowness of creation, I guess, is what bothers me more than that. A lot of people don't know how to do documentaries. It is a tedious, long process, and it is a form which is probably dying.

*Some people argue differently. Why do you say it's dying?*
Well, it's dying because there's not much interest in it because they don't really get very high ratings. The world has changed a great deal since the great days of the documentaries. This country right now, for reasons, I think, having to do with Watergate and Vietnam, is much more interested in the quick, fast story of the rip-off and the scam and that sort of thing. I think it's very interesting that CBS News is holding the highest rated show in broadcasting, which is "60 Minutes," and the lowest rated show in broadcasting is the documentary, and they're done by the same people, trained the same way, same kind of journalism. In a way it says something about the state of the nation, as well as the state of the art.

*Give me a typical day in the life of an executive producer.*
This executive producer is not typical, and my days are quite different from other people's. But when it's functioning right, I will be working on the one piece that interests me the most, because, as I told you before, I always produce one myself; then one of my producers will ask me to look at something that he or she has done; then another producer will come in and say, "Hey, do you think you can get this idea through management"; then management will call and say, "We've got an idea. Do you think you can find a producer that might want to do it?" Or the

budget people will call and say, "You're way over budget," and I have to look at that sort of thing, too. In the meantime, I do all the requisite reading for keeping abreast of things, and I have my own ideas.

Working for a large organization, by definition, you're in a political organization. Now, politics isn't all bad; politics is the art of the use of power, and everybody wants to use power, not only for self-aggrandizement but because you have ideas that you want to push — they're important to you.

*How about video? How has that affected the documentary?*

It has certain advantages and certain disadvantages. The advantage is that it's easier to take the picture, and the disadvantage is that it's much harder to edit. The editing of tape is nowhere near as advanced as the editing of film, so that in the projects that I just finished what I did was convert all my tape to film — edited it as if it were film and then converted it back to tape. It requires a very sophisticated computer system.

*So you do laser transfer, actually?*

Well, no, I don't use lasers. You use a computer and a time code. There are numbers on the screen . . . but what I have recently said is that with the advances that are coming, you're going to need a Rosetta stone to move between film, 3/4-inch tape, one-inch tape and 2-inch tape. What's also going on is that there is a split in the world of tape itself. There's a whole group of people who only know 2-inch. They don't know 3/4-inch. Whereas the producer used to be the one who was explained to, he, now, is explaining to the technician; he's translating between technicians. I think I figured it out once: we received last decade 110,000 hours of visual across our assignment desk. That's more hours than there were in the decade. Some were film, some were tape, some were different kinds of tape, and the ability to be able to move back and forth between these technologies is really getting overwhelming. It's getting incomprehensible now, so that very often technology swamps creativity.

*You said the film editing is more far advanced. Can you explain that a little more?*

Yes, because the editing is much more precise. You can move tracks around, you can fine-cut much better. You can take a lot of time, and you can see your picture, and you can go over it and over it again. While you can do some of that in tape, in the sense of a refinement of a story, you can't do it as well in tape.

*Can you give an example?*

I would have to show you in specific terms where I could not make the kind of fine edits that I wanted in tape that would be comparable to what I could do in film. But this group that I have right now, which is really the historic unit — we were able to do this by coming back to film, making a film of the tape. But this gets pretty arcane. There is a difference in optics; the film camera eye sees much more like the human eye than the tape does, because the focal length in tape is generally infinite. You are totally in focus all the way back. It is very rare that you see an out-of-focus shot in tape because the throw is so short, whereas the human eye is very rarely focused totally — there's always something out of focus. When you teach directing you always say, "Look at every shot and find the center of visual attention," and as a director you always arrange the camera and composition . . . you want the audience to look at the same thing that you're looking at, because that's how you arrange the shot. So that a lot of people who are in the film world find that it takes them time to get used to this change in optics. That's pretty arcane, and if your show consists of interviews, it doesn't really make much of a difference.

*Do great shots ever come off looking staged or coincidental?*
     Yeah, the basic rule of film is that things must flow. Starting at the very beginning, films never stand still. There are really twenty-four frames a second being jerked by. Your mind is creating the motion. You know there's nobody walking . . . there are twenty-four separate still pictures that make your mind think that somebody's walking by. So, once you start with that — and that's called the "phi phenomenon" in visual psychology terms — then you see that film is a series of impressions. Maybe you want something for emphasis, but if it jars the flow by calling attention to itself, you might have to throw it out. I really started many years ago . . . my first writing was in poetry, and I found that very often my best lines had to be thrown away. It's the same thing with writing a script. The little quips, the little bright or even brilliant things, don't fit, and you've got to throw them out. I said to you very early in this that the great art of writing is knowing what *not* to write, and the hardest part is when you have a great line that you have to throw out because it sticks out, and the same thing goes for the great shot. If it's pertinent, it's fine.

*What mistakes do beginning producers make?*
     They worry too much. I guess the biggest mistake, the most conventional mistake, is that they don't realize that the audience only sees it once. One's attention in television is not as rapt as in a movie house — a cinema — and you have to play fair with the audience. You cannot expect from them a degree of concentration beyond the same intensity as the producer has. Beginning producers tend to pack everything in. They simply don't tell the story well.

*What is your favorite piece that you've done over the years?*
     I don't have a favorite. Although I have only one son, if I had two, I couldn't choose. I have two cats and I don't have a favorite.

*What makes Perry Wolff run?*
What makes me run?

*Yes.*
I'm at the age where I just walk. I like what I'm doing. I think in the long run I've got the chance to meet interesting people and learn . . . God, the things that I've learned. The evolution of kidneys, for example. I didn't realize that fish didn't have kidneys. Someone said to me in 1953, "Don't you know that an amphibian has to have a kidney — you know, he's got to be able to pee on land." And I said, "My God, let's do twenty minutes on it," and we did. That's just an example of learning things. You never get tired when you're learning, and there's so much to learn.

*Speaking of learning. Where did you learn to write?*
I was in the infantry during the war, and I couldn't carry a lot of paper with me, so I used to do sonnets in my head — 140 syllables. I would really work at the sonnets and work at them and work at them. And I found out more and more, as any poet finds, the value of single words — the bluntness of good poetry where the image is no longer than it need be. I've always found a corollary in that in writing to films: You ought to say as little as possible and convey as much as you can, just for simple mechanical reasons. If you can say it well, and shortly, then the picture can play better. What I find when I try to train writers or people who don't know how to write — particularly journalists — is that they can't work tersely, and their basic writing block is not the word but the phrase. So they all overwrite.

*So poetry is really essential.*
Yes, I would love to point out to people how much they overwrite, how the ear can pick up from single words more than it can pick up from long, elaborate, complicated sentences.

*Is there anything else — any outrageous anecdote from all your years in documentaries, or taping, filming or . . .?*
Nothing I would like to see in print. (laughs) Stupidity is always outrageous, that's for sure.

*David Wolper*

TIME MAGAZINE once called David Wolper "Mr. Documentary." It is in the documentary that his influence has probably been most acute. His documentary "Hollywood: The Golden Years," one of the earliest compilation efforts, was also the first independently produced documentary on network television. Later, his "Biography of a Rookie" would pioneer the cinema verite style. He would introduce the world of bestselling nonfiction to documentary form in "The Making of the President: 1960," and brought the docudrama technique to prime time television with the "Appointment with Destiny" series.

Wolper also introduced the National Geographic specials to American television in 1965, and two years later, "The Undersea World of Jacques Cousteau." He magnified the tiny worlds all around us with early macrophotography.

Wolper proved over and over that the documentary format can have many faces and can come in many forms that are attractive to a mass audience.

History, long a staple of his productions, was the basis of one of the most popular television programs of all time: "Roots," and its sequel "Roots II." Wolper, through a chance meeting, learned of Alex Haley's remarkable novel that traced the story of Kunta Kinte, an African sold into slavery, and his successive generations. "Roots" drew over 98 million viewers in its final segment, and in each of the eight segments was in the top twenty programs in the history of television.

David Wolper started his professional show business career selling motion pictures to television stations when television was in its infancy. His early experiences on the road, which he discusses in the interview, illustrate how programming was once regarded by some in the field.

In the thirty-odd years since, Wolper has produced documentaries, feature movies for television, even network comedy series: nearly 575 different productions.

He is one of television's most honored producers. He has received the Academy Award for *Hellstrom Chronicles*, over thirty Emmys (he has been nominated for over 100), as well as awards from practically every major film festival in the world.

Wolper is taking it easier these days following a heart attack in 1966. But he is still doing what he has done so well over the years — making television.

*You started in the early days of TV, selling films to TV stations. How did the stations greet you?*

Well, at the very beginning I was attending the opening of over a hundred television stations, so in those days they were coming in with film, and looking at film was a big deal. That was in 1949. I remember

*Photo (opposite): David Wolper with "Roots" author Alex Haley, during the filming of "Roots: The Next Generations."*

going to WDAS in Kansas City—it was owned by the *Kansas City Star*—and coming in with a feature film to sell, and the president of the *Kansas City Star* actually came to the screening. They screened the whole feature film from beginning to end. It was such a new thing to see a movie in the afternoon, I guess it was a big thrill.

*How old were you?*
I was a young boy, twenty years old. We didn't really know what we were doing. We didn't know what to charge, and it was all experimenting.

*What sorts of prices did you ask? For those earliest things.*
Oh, I remember getting a feature film deal in Los Angeles, and announcing to my associates that I had just made a price for ten runs of something like $500 at KTLA, which was one of the early stations on the air.

*How many people were doing this at that point?*
A couple of companies and ourselves.

*And how did you get to thinking of television as a possible market?*
Prior to that I hadn't done anything, but I had a friend whose father had some old films that he had bought for the educational field and couldn't sell. So we asked him if we could try to sell them to the television stations. He had his own short subjects and comedies, and by three months we had them all sold out, so we asked his father to go get us some more films, which he did, and then we formed this company. He financed the films, and we went out and sold them on commission and built the company. Then we started buying feature films. I remember buying feature films— *The Adventures of Martin Eden*, and *Jack London*. I think we paid them $500 for the television rights for both pictures.

*I heard from several old-timers that people at TV stations hardly knew how to thread projectors in those days.*
Well, as I said, you walked in and they had never seen any films, so it was funny to sit there in the afternoon and show them the whole feature. They spent an hour and a half watching *The Adventures of Martin Eden* before they bought it.

*What was that movie like?*
Martin Eden was Glenn Ford, and Evelyn Keyes was quite good. It was an independently made picture by Sam Bronson, who later became big; you know, he later on made all those big epics in Spain.

*We hear a lot about the Steven Spielbergs, who have cameras at age eight. Was that you?*

No, I was more story-oriented. I loved history, and I did love to work, and I wanted to get into some phase of show business. I just had this desire to get into show business. I didn't know where I was going to fit. I was going to the University of Southern California, and I quit when this opportunity came up to sell these pictures. I had only about six months to go, but I saw an opportunity to get into business, so I grabbed it.

*Any horror stories from the early days of trying to sell?*
  I remember going around selling films. When I made my first trip, I was driving, and my associate, by the name of Jim Harris, he would drive in the other direction. In our first journey out, at the first seven stops nobody bought anything, and we were pretty miserable. And we talked on the phone, and we made another seven stops, and still nobody bought anything. We were running out of people to see because there weren't that many stations, so we met each other; he was taking the Southern route and I was taking the Northern route, and I was in Omaha and he was in Houston. And I remember the Shamrock Hotel was opening in Houston, Texas, and I was up there and we were both miserable and I said, "I'm going to fly down and rethink what the hell we're doing. We may be doing something wrong." So I flew down to Houston and sold everything I had and from then on, for some reason, we sold everything. I guess we just needed a pep talk. I do remember on that first journey the guy who ran the station in Pittsburgh — I can't remember his name now, it's been thirty years — but he got mad at me for selling this film. He started shouting at me. He said, "What are you doing here? You're a thief. You're selling film of old pictures," and I started to cry. I was all upset. It was an emotional scene. I said, "I'm not stealing your money. I own these films. If you want to buy them you've got to pay me for them." "Why should we pay you for them? We should be able to run them free. The public should know about these things. They're educational films. They should get them for free." I wasn't smart enough to answer him, but I do remember the experience. And then I went to an opening of CMQ in Havana, Cuba. The station opened in '49 or '50, I think, and sold them a lot of films.

*The producer in television is, it seems, different from the producer in movies.*
  It is true that television is a producer's and an executive's medium, not a director's medium, separating it from the motion pictures. Motion pictures . . . if I could deliver Clint Eastwood and Jane Fonda in a movie I could be a gorilla and they would name me producer, you know, as long as you have a great director. If you're Francis Ford Coppola, you can do any picture you want. The directors and the stars are the generating forces to get movies made. In television the generating force is to get shows made, and the Mary Tyler Moores, the Grant Tinkers, the Lee

Riches, the David Wolpers, the Aaron Spellings—the producing elements are key. They didn't ask me, when I came in with "Roots," who the directors were going to be and who the stars were going to be; they bought "Roots" based on me and "Roots," you see. I can't do that with a movie. With a movie, if I go in there, they want to know who the director will be and who the stars are going to be. They're not interested in what I think about it.

*You sold documentaries for National Geographic and others directly to advertisers. How was that done?*
     I would go to an advertiser and tell him that these were the shows I was planning to do, and he would buy the program, based on my reputation of being able to make them. He would buy the shows, and then I would have to get them placed on the network, and that would be the most difficult thing because the networks were not receptive to documentaries unless they came in fully sponsored. That was for a number of reasons. Number one, they had their own documentary production companies and they wanted to keep them busy, so they would rather put an in-house documentary on the air than a Wolper documentary from the outside, even though it was sponsored. Number two, sometimes they felt the documentaries didn't get the same number business as the regular programming, but in those days the fight for numbers wasn't as great, so they did take time to put them on. I flourished because, as an independent, my documentaries traditionally got higher numbers than the network's own news department's documentaries, so the programming department would always say, "Well, if we have to put a damn documentary on, let's put a Wolper's on, instead of our own news department's," and I fought with that wedge to get my shows on the air. I went right to the program department with the sponsors and with the show, a documentary that had a little more jazz, and when CBS looked at that thing they said, "Look, we'll do the National Geographic show." They would rather put that on than the "CBS Reports," because the National Geographic got numbers and the "CBS Reports" didn't.

*How did you get started doing the National Geographic Specials?*
     Well, I went to National Geographic when I heard that they were interested in a television program, and I told them I would like to do their shows. I had been successful in doing documentaries. And I made a deal with the Geographic to do them, and I did it for ten years and got them on the network. I had to fight every year to get it on, but I eventually did. Mike Dann was head programmer at CBS when I first brought the National Geographics to them.

*How did he respond to those?*
     Well, he said, "I like that stuff myself. It's probably going to die,

Wolper, but we're going to put it on." That was the first major program in prime time network shows. He said, "It's not going to equal our other programming, but I like that stuff myself," so we got it on, and it was successful and did get good ratings. From the National Geographics of course, a lot of animal and that sort of shows turned up on network television.

*You've also done a lot of reenactments in your productions. I remember one film you did that had cavemen at the beginning . . .*
    Oh, yes, I remember, that was called "Primal Man." There are three kinds of things, there's, you know — What is a documentary? We haven't defined these things yet — but I made three kinds of films. One is my documentary, which is *my* definition of a documentary, which is the creative interpretation of a reality.

*Also pioneer film documentarian John Grierson's?*
    Yes, correct. That's Grierson's, too. It isn't reality. It's the creative interpretation of it. If you just put a camera on and watch what people do, that's not a documentary to me.

*That's not.*
    No. It's just watching people do things. There's nothing to it.

*"Appointment with Destiny" predated the docudrama.*
    The first "Appointment with Destiny" was in '71. The first one was called "They Killed President Lincoln," in which I recreated the assassination of Lincoln, but I did it as though newsreel cameras were there, and I did "Dillinger" and "Crucifixion of Jesus" and then "The Plot to Murder Hitler." I used actual footage of Hitler, and I got a guy that looked exactly like Hitler, and we got actual footage and mixed it and you couldn't tell which was the real and which was recreated.

*And a reviewer was critical of that?*
    One of the critics in *The New York Times* couldn't tell the difference between the real Hitler and the actor and he felt it was unfair, and my answer was, "Well, I tried it. I told you at the beginning of the show I recreated it as though the newsreel cameras were there. You should send me an award. I did it so well you couldn't tell the real Hitler from my Hitler."

*What's been the toughest project for you to produce?*
    They're all tough, but they all have different problems. Whenever you do a new concept it's a little more difficult because you're setting the concept in form. I think the most difficulty in producing today is, and has been for many years, the pressure groups. On every show that you do,

there's somebody telling you how to do it, and they want to be involved and get a little hysterical about it. It always has been, whether it's the gays, or the blacks or the National Rifle Association. You couldn't think of a show to do that somebody isn't trying to tell you how to do it.

*What do you look for in a cameraperson?*

In a documentary? Well, a documentary cameraman, on some cases, is pretty close to being a cameraman-director. It's according to which film you're doing. Some films you're dealing in the bush with certain things, and you need certain people and certain personnel who can shoot things fast and know the creative process right away and can look through the lens and get it because he hasn't got all afternoon to shoot a certain charging rhinoceros. Some shows that you do you want a cameraman who basically has an eye for beauty, more subtle and more peaceful. We did a National Geographic special about going through Europe on canals by boat, and this was more leisurely, and I needed a cameraman who had a great eye for color and beauty. He didn't have to be one who could shoot buffalo running or giraffes attacking, or whatever. So you have to fit the cameraman to the task.

*How did "Roots" get started?*

I heard from a friend of mine about a friend of hers who was writing a book, and I tracked that down to Alex Haley. He was only half-done with the book when I bought it. I went to him and he told me who his representative was, and his representative was a lawyer that I knew. I liked the idea of the story. I like stories that I know I can sell to a network with one line, and I knew the public would go for it. Nothing like it had been done. The one line is, "It's a story of a black family, from a village in Africa to what they are today." That appealed to the network, and I made a deal with ABC.

*How did you feel when you saw "Roots"?*

I felt very good about it. I didn't expect it to be the most successful television show of all times — not only here but around the world. I feel emotional about it because it *is* one of the most successful television shows of all time. Somebody says, "Well, what happened to the guy that introduced Jacques Cousteau to the world on television, and "The Making of the President," and the whole list of shows, and they say, "You mean the man who did 'Roots'?" I don't mind it because I was glad it was the success that it was.

*Do you really feel that you end up giving a lot of yourself to a project like "Roots"? Is it pretty exhausting?*

Yes, it is. All of these projects are exhausting. I don't do as many as I used to do. I used to do eighteen, twenty to twenty-five shows a year – maybe thirty in some years. Now I try to keep myself to one or maybe a series of eight or ten a year.

*In the early days, how were you able to juggle that many shows?*
I was young and worked from 7:00 until midnight every day, including Saturday and Sunday. Almost 90 percent of it was nonfiction and a number of feature films.

*Is there any image from "Roots" that's kind of implanted firmly in your mind? There's that powerful image of holding the baby up into the moonlight in "Roots." That, to me, is unforgettable.*
I have the image of talking to Alex Haley the first time and hearing him tell me the story, which actually nearly brought tears to my eyes when he first told it. He told me the story in person, how he put it all together and everything. I remember that image of him very strongly.

*What's the key to being a good producer? What makes David Wolper a good producer?*
I think, first of all, it's the ability to know a number of audiences. You have the audience that watches the television show; that's one audience, so you have to know what pleases them. But you have another audience. You have the audience of the people who buy the show before you can get to the audience out there, so you have to know what pleases *that* audience, and it changes as management changes. As I said, I've been in business . . . I've gone through something like thirty-eight network presidents in thirty years, counting all three networks. Management changes at the networks, and you have to know not only management presidents but all sorts of people. You have to know what both these audiences want – the buyers and the final audience.

*What is your feeling about the mini-series?*
Well, what is interesting about a mini-series is that when a character is developed, you never know what's going to happen to that character. Is he going to be killed? Is he going to be alive? What's going to happen to him? So there's suspense within the character. One of my favorite shows is "Lou Grant." I know for sure when somebody locks Lou Grant up in a room that he's going to get out. Otherwise, the series would be over next week. But that's not the case in mini-series; you know, people live and die. And the mini-series give you the opportunity to explore characters in fuller range than a two-hour movie. And I think a lot more books are going to be sold to television because authors like to see their books fully exploited instead of just having one piece of it. You couldn't do "Roots" in a movie because there isn't enough time.

*What was it like producing "Roots"?*

For everyone making the film, it was like a love affair with the project. The actors in the film were mostly black actors, and the most difficult thing we wanted to do was to be sure that we had enough blacks in other jobs in "Roots" so that it was perceived as a project about blacks, in which a lot of blacks made contributions to the medium. We were fortunately able to get black soundmen, cameramen, and find those people.

*Some people said there weren't enough black writers and directors.*
We had two black directors, and as I remember, we had two black writers out of four. And Alex Haley is black. They didn't count that in, for some reason.

*(Laughs) You seem to have a special interest in minorities.*
Well, I think I'm a minority. People wouldn't say it, but I'm Jewish, and I would say that I'm a minority.

*Did you feel your Jewishness when you were a young man?*
No. I never felt that I was ever discriminated against. Maybe once or twice, but it never had any personal effect on me.

*Do you ever worry about the melting pot of America losing that quality?*
I don't consider America a melting pot. I have a different view. I think of it as a quilt. We use all the colors and sew them together. I think a quilt is more beautiful than a melting pot.

*What fundamental lesson did you learn from documentary that translated to feature TV movie production?*
Well, I like nonfiction stories, and I think that in the making of my nonfiction dramas, I have more responsibility to get things right than people who are maybe dealing in fiction most of their lives. People who deal in fiction, when they move into the docudrama field, they seem to have less of a responsibility than I do having come up through the documentary field. I make a little extra effort to be sure I'm getting it right.

*Is there anything you had to unlearn from the documentary?*
No, I think it was a good training. You can open your vision a little more. I like the docudrama. I think you can get more and do more and learn more from the docudrama than you can from the documentary. Criticism of docudrama would either be for accuracy or because of the creative adding or deducting of things that happened — you know, the chair was the wrong chair, that wasn't the chair that Jefferson sat on, and all of that thing. But one has to understand what a docudrama is. People have different views of it; and I think, again, using the same words that

you use in the documentary, it's the creative interpretation of what went on. It's your view as a creative person interpreting the events. You don't go back to a docudrama to see details; in other words, if you want to know about chairs in the 1800s, you go to a book on chairs. Most people in the world will see a film once, so what's important is to get the sense of what it was to be in that particular time in history. When you see it you don't go to a film for details. Somebody was once telling me that I did a show and the car in the background was a 1932 and the show was such-and-such a year, but I don't care. I'm not doing a film on cars. If I have the wrong car, I couldn't care less. The film is going to be seen once and what you're supposed to get out of it is the overall impact. My intent was to give you a sense of being at a certain place in history, and the feeling of what it was to be those people who experienced that moment in history.

*What do you like most about history?*
I think it's good for the best stories and a sense of reality.

*How differently do you structure your TV documentary film from another type of documentary? Do you put in commercial breaks?*
A documentary — well, all television — you do in acts, and approximately every fifteen minutes is an act's end. So you structure your films in that way, so there are four acts, sometimes five acts in an hour. You structure your stories just like you do a play on Broadway.

*What's the toughest thing about doing a compilation documentary, or a documentary using stock film?*
Well, that's tougher than most people think. I did a lot of Hollywood compilations. I started the first one, called "Hollywood — The Golden Years," done in 1960. All of the studios gave me their footage at that time.

*For free?*
Yes. (laughs) I gave a donation to the Motion Picture Home. But they learned fast after my second one and ever since. My relatives used to say, "You're doing terrific. Just cut up all that old footage and you can make a fortune." And I said, "It's not easy. It's more difficult to edit and put that film together than it is to take a script and write it and shoot it." There's words you can easily change on a script, you know; but when you have the footage and try to make something out of it, you've got to look at, maybe, thirty-to-one or forty-to-one ratio to make for one hour — sometimes you're looking at forty, fifty or sometimes one hundred hours to make the one hour. Of course, now the rights are impossible. If you want to do a subject about somebody's life, the rights are owned by thirty different people and you can go bananas.

*Thirty different people?*

Yes. Suppose you did a film on Clark Gable. He did films for MGM, for this, for that, all those studios. You've got to make a deal with all these people just to do the one film. A compilation film is hard to do because you have to deal with so many people.

*What is your view of interview?*

Well, I get bored with talking heads, to be honest with you, and I have very few on all my shows. If I wanted to have somebody say something I used to film them in action and hear what we call "inner monologue." You know what I mean? Instead of having Dr. Baker tell me how to perform an operation I'd rather have him walking through the hospital and hear his voice say, "When I come in in the morning I do this." Everything isn't right for the television form. For example, I get bored with networks doing a two-hour show on inflation and the interest rate. The form to tell that story is not television. Books are not the form to tell certain visual stories, and you don't have to waste a hour and a half to two hours of television time, which is a valuable thing, to tell us about the economy. I can get that information better by reading it.

*Let's talk about the thin line between staging and documentary.*

Well, in staging, you recreate sometimes, and I think even news people do that. They set a person up and they say, "Now wait a second," and they stage it. There are different phases in how you stage it. Sometimes animal things are recreated, and they use that line about how certain scenes are recreated as they actually are in nature. I've seen that done on all three networks.

*Networks sometimes seem to get a little nervous when the subject of staging comes up.*

The news department painted themselves into a corner by making all their own rules. As they made more rules they painted themselves into a tighter corner, and then they couldn't get out, because they convinced everybody else that what they were saying was so, including the news media. So I think the news department in the three networks made the wrong rules, and then they made them stiffer, and now they're in there and they don't know how to get out.

*So you think it's really affecting the programming?*

Sure, it affected their whole programming. They got a little hysterical about what they can and can't do. One network at one time said we shouldn't have music in documentaries. CBS said for a while, "No music in documentaries." I looked at them like they were crazy. I said, "What do you mean, 'no music'? Let's have no words, I mean, music is just another form—another adjective on the page." Music, you know, creates the emotion.

*What's the thing that rankles you most in dealing with networks?*
Oh, I have the feeling that the news department has a feeling — they're beginning to break out of it, but it took a long time — that they're the only ones that can tell stories about contemporary life. That by some magic, if you do it independently you're not clean, but if you got a check from the network all of a sudden you become holy you know, somebody sprinkled the holy water on you when you're doing CBS News. I think they're a little pompous in the news department.

*CBS or all three networks?*
Oh yeah, all three networks. I was successful in making documentaries, I think because when I came from California to New York to sell my documentaries I always had new ideas that nobody had ever heard of. The networks were talking and doing the same thing, and I would come and say, "Why don't we do an animal show?" And they said, "Gee, whoever heard of an animal show in prime time?" I wanted to see shows about undersea, and I came up with Jacques Cousteau. They were talking about the economy, and I came in with "The Incredible Machine" about the examination of the human body. Now they're starting to do it themselves. But they were always thinking that the world revolved around who was picking up the garbage in New York City and whether the Long Island Railroad was running.

*Speaking of Cousteau, how did the "Undersea World" get started?*
I did a National Geographic special on Cousteau in 1965. I met Cousteau and I thought, "Gee, this would be a terrific idea for a series." So I went to Monte Carlo and met him and said, "How about doing a television series?" And he said, "Gee, I have a wonderful idea for a fifteen-minute show for my museum," and I said, "That's a lousy idea, Jacques, I'm thinking of a tour of the world. Why don't you go on a trip around the world with your boat and we'll do a whole series of films. You do these things all over the earth and you'll be on television all over the world." He went for that idea, and I sold it to ABC.

*What did the network first think of the idea?*
What happened was I had to sell twelve hours in order to make the journey pay, and the networks all liked the idea, but they didn't know if they could swallow the twelve hours. I had the one that I had done for the National Geographic Society, which was a good film, and I had some other footage of Cousteau that I could show, and I made a presentation film. Tom Moore was then the president of ABC and a member of the Explorer's Club, and he loved all that stuff and bought it for ABC. As a matter of fact, when he bought it he asked me to ask Jacques Cousteau to come to his Explorer's Club meeting, and I said, "Tom, he's in Paris and will be here tomorrow morning."

*Did he actually come?*
He actually came and went to the meeting.

*Could you talk about the complexities of producing that series?*
Well, we had to go all over the world. Jacques had his own cameramen and we would recommend people. We had to get the footage from all over the world because he would be traveling. It would be flown to us in Hollywood and we would have to figure out what the hell he meant. He was a Frenchman, you know, and there was the translation from French to English to get the footage right, and then we would have to wait until Jacques or one of his associates or his son, who has since passed away, came to the States to sort out the material so we could edit it and then have writers write it, and Cousteau narrate what was going on. He also had to look over the script to see that what we said was accurate.

*What's the key to good documentary writing?*
I would say to be brief and clear. I'll give you the best example of all. We made "The Making of the President" in 1960. Theodore H. White, who wrote the book but had never written a documentary, came to California and was one of the best documentary writers I had ever seen. At the end of "The Making of the President" — that's the election of Kennedy vs. Nixon — we had cut the film and we needed a line to finish the show. We told Teddy, "Teddy, we need a line at the end of the show where Kennedy shakes hands with Eisenhower. That's the last scene of the show and it freezes. What are we going to say?" And he said, "How much time do I have?" I said, "You have three seconds to give this line. We don't have any more time." He went back and he came up with the line, "So power passes." That is what is known as a great documentary line. Now that's an example of what I mean by brief.

*Is there anything in documentary that you're really opposed to — canned music or anything?*
No, canned music is fine. Anything is fine if it works. I just think that the original creators of the documentary had more leeway in dealing with the subject matter than you have today because of the arbitrary rules put on to you by the network news department, who started the restrictions and convinced everybody that they are right. And now we have fewer documentaries, they're less interesting, because the more rules you have and the more stringent you make the rules, the tougher it becomes to make something interesting for television.

*How will David Wolper be remembered?*
Well, I'd like to be remembered as somebody who brought education through entertainment — that I entertained you, and quietly, sneakingly, while I was dealing with you, you were learning something.

*Bill Burrud*

BILL BURRUD BEGAN HIS CAREER in 1932 at age seven in the road show production "Music in the Air." Later he was placed under contract by 20th Century–Fox, Columbia and MGM. His education at USC was interrupted by World War II, during which he served as an officer aboard the destroyer *Coolbaugh* in both the Atlantic and Pacific theaters of war. Upon his discharge, Bill resumed his education at USC, completing a bachelor's degree in business administration.

Burrud has been producing and narrating wildlife and exotic location adventure films for twenty-nine years. His output includes fourteen half-hour family-type series; eleven two-hour features, ranging from an award-winning film on reptiles of the world to a film on lost treasure; a dozen one-hour specials and a mini-series of four syndicated exotic location–adventure films titled "The Amazing World" for the American Express Company; and his television series, including the original "Animal World" – which numbers over 800 individual episodes.

A lover of animals, Burrud produced a one-hour special in 1974, called "Where Did All the Animals Go?" The film raised over $120,000 for the Bill Burrud Anti-Poaching Fund, whose funds were used to obtain a police-type helicopter and other services for Kenya's Tsavo Park West, a prime target for elephant poachers. It has been estimated that use of the helicopter by game officials has cut the illegal slaughter of elephants by almost 50 percent.

Burrud has a new animal quiz show on "The Disney Channel" and sees promise almost everywhere. He says, "Unparalleled opportunities are now opening up for all kinds of programming due to the present electronic explosion – like Pay-TV, cable, home video, cassettes, etc. Other avenues are steadily growing for our company and others who do their homework and turn out quality productions."

*How did you get started in the industry?*

I started really as a child actor, and I got out of the business. I was under contract to Universal in the '30s, along with Jane Withers and Shirley Temple, and so I was a feature player and not a so-called "star."

*What sort of things were you in?*

Oh, I was in a good many pictures. The best one, I supposed would have been *Captains Courageous*. I had a very important part at the beginning of the picture, which was the trigger to send Bartholomew off, you know, and I was in *Magnificent Brute*, with Victor McLaughlin – a lot of Universal what they called "pot boilers," I guess. I worked with Duke Wayne in a thing called *Hell on Ice* and an ice hockey picture on the back lot – those kind of things. I took a business course at USC, and when I got out of there I wanted to get back into the picture business – but that was a tough time, after the war. I didn't want to go into acting, particularly, so I wound up in radio. I got into television in about '50. What happened was, I couldn't get a job in any television station because nobody knew what to do. So I was reading the *LA Times* one day and I saw an automobile section where people took trips in and around Los Angeles and I thought, "Well, hell, I'll go to the *Times*, they just got a station license." I sold them on the idea of taking the automobile section and transferring it to television, which you could call a local travelogue. Of course, that name has always been anathema to me because a travelogue always indicated something that the industry has never really loved. From that sprang what I call our endeavors in reality programming. That started me out, and I worked for about two or three years at KTTV just doing a local show called "The Open Road," which was relatively simple; as a matter of fact, I literally had to teach myself how to film because I didn't have a crew. I had to film, narrate, cut it and introduce the show on the air. So I became an instant packager before I knew what packaging meant.

*Were you the only one who was doing this type of show at that time?*
  It was the only show of its kind on the air. There were guys running travel pictures that other people had made, but no one was doing a sort of individual travel thing and, of course, there were no networks in those days and there was no real, what you would call, syndication. So everything was localized in the various markets. Actually, KTTV became part of CBS before they got Channel 2. They were part of the CBS network. Anyway, that was the beginning of my particular career and this company's career, and it grew from there, and we always stayed in that so-called "reality" field. We did a lot of different shows, but that in essence was the beginning, and I have pretty much stayed in that area throughout the company's career. Now we have gone into long form, but in the docudramas, where we are beginning to use actors in the features for syndication. But again with a heavy emphasis on reality.

*Some people in news and documentary have questioned the docudrama format. You apparently believe that it's a viable form.*
  Well, I think it's a viable form when it's properly used to entertain; in other words "You Are There" (CBS) was a docudrama to go back through history on television. It had actors in it but it was a recreation of an historic event. It was very successful, as I recall. As an example, the features we are doing now are involved with buried lost treasure. There are two sides to buried lost treasure. You can do a picture called "The Treasure of Jean Laffite," complete with actors, (I saw one last night and it was awful), but what we are doing now is recreating what the treasure story is about and interspersing it with reality—Did this really exist? Did so and so? Do you see what I'm saying? We've found that it can be very successful.

*What is the main difference between producing for a reality form and producing, for say, the docudrama, if you can make that distinction?*

Well, in reality – like wildlife programming, which has been our mainstay for the last twelve or fifteen years, and which was over-proliferated, as all good programming becomes – we simply told the true story, whether it was a story of the elephants in Africa or whether it was a story of the life of the wolf, or whatever. There are no actors, no nothing in it. That was strictly a reality program. In a docudrama, what you do is take a storyline and infuse it – I'll give you an example. We did a feature called "Creatures of the Amazon," which was a full-length feature film on the Amazon River Basin and wildlife. And so in order to jazz it up, what we did was explain how all the stories about the wildlife got back to the Old World from the New World through the conquistadors. We recreated sequences, which were based on fact, on known things – letters and books, etc., of that time. The vampire bat story came out of the Amazon, as an example, and we recreated a sequence where a conquistador had been bitten by a vampire bat. Now whether this was true or not I can't say. I think the distinction is that what you're doing is perhaps enhancing the reality.

*How does your organization differ in approach to TV distribution from other TV film producers? Or does it?*

Well, I don't know if we completely differ in approach. We use outside agents and we use a distribution company. But, in general, what I have tried to do through the years – and it's been much harder in the last few years – is to get a client backing and work directly with clients in the development of programming. As you know, that's kind of gone down the tube in the last six or seven years. It is coming back to a certain extent. We're negotiating now with a major client to do specials, which will, in fact, be not docudramas but true reality programming with real people experiencing things throughout the world and in the travel field – not a travelogue, but an experience of a destination, like "My Returning to Tahiti After 30 Years." So I would say that as far as distribution is concerned, we are pretty much like any other company in that we do use agents, but I think we have used more client relationship.

*Some examples?*

Well, Kal-Kan pet foods was our big breakthrough. Going back earlier in our history, when we used to do programming in Los Angeles, we would have a complete sponsor, like Nucoa Margarine. At that time – the late '50s – in L.A. we had a strip of travel shows running at 7:00 or 7:30 that were getting excellent ratings, and what happened is that it was L.A. only, so they were paying for the L.A. thing; then we would take the best of maybe four or five programs and put them together in syndication and sell them in a regular system of syndication through a distributor.

*And you would own the property?*

And we would own the property. We've always owned our property; we've never sold anything. As a matter of fact, I screened something yesterday that I want to use that's twenty-one years old, and I will take certain sections of it and use it, which is an advantage that a lot of companies don't have. But we own the property. For instance, Kal-Kan came along and bought our wildlife series on a pilot and then stayed with us for seven years. It ran on all three networks, NBC, ABC and CBS, and then went into syndication, and later when they phased it out we sold it to Procter & Gamble for three years. Now we're selling it directly ourselves to an agent, in essence, as what we call library material for stations.

*You talk about selling the programs to the networks – is that tough? What were the negotiations like, generally?*

Well, they were too full in a sense. We had convinced the Kal-Kan people, which was an independent company, now owned by Mars. It's a huge company, a private company, but at that time it was owned by a single man here in Los Angeles. Their agency was Honey, Cooper, Erik. We got together and did the show, and we were able to place it in the late '60s or early '70s on the network through the agency. They, in fact, bought the time. It was fringe time – it was like 6:00 or 6:30 on the network – and we would not run on an all-year basis; we would run it twenty weeks, like from May through October. So it was sold basically as a client sale.

*Did you work pretty closely or was it mostly in the hands of the . . .*

It was a combination of all three. It was a combination of the agency, the client and ourselves. This was true for many years in television. It is no longer very true because the costs have gotten so high on programming – on most programming – that clients can't step in and do it unless they do it on a barter basis like Sha-Na-Na and those kind of things that Procter & Gamble are doing now where they're putting it in the access period.

*What did your program cost – your network programming – a show? Do you remember?*

It's almost embarrassing to look back and quote it; but it was about $30,000 a week, which today would be considered . . . $30,000 a minute.

*What was the toughest thing to do when convincing the network to take a show?*

Well, I think the toughest thing in convincing the network was that this kind of show would pull numbers, and it did pull numbers. As a matter of fact, when we were on CBS I distinctly remember replacing "Hogan's Heroes" for twenty-two weeks when they were phased off, and during that period we were against "The Wonderful World of Disney." It's no longer the show — but we were trying and beating Disney on CBS. So we established a track record of getting numbers. Frankly, it was a semibarter deal, as I recall, where the client was paying us for the programming and buying a couple of spots and letting the network sell a couple of spots. It was a little bit like they are trying to do now with barter programming — it's generally on access time in syndication.

*What about problems of convincing the corporations to participate?*
    Well, it's much easier for their marketing people to just let their agency go out and buy spots, and it's much more difficult for them to get a program profile. There are very few companies that have any kind of program profile on television today, and that is your most difficult problem: to convince them that they need a program. Now today, if you can get into syndication, you can get in the top fifty in fair time periods, as Mobil did with "Edward the King" on independent stations. You can reach as many people for what you want as you can by buying spots from the network or by buying spots throughout the country. The hardest thing is to convince them that they need a program.

*Just pretend that I'm a potential client . . . .*
    Let's pretend you're American Express or Kal-Kan, or whatever. You've got competitors. Everybody is buying commercials, and your placement of commercials . . . unless you specifically say, "I don't want to be in any shows of violence," it's pretty hard not to be in any shows of violence, so you can't control the atmosphere in which your spot runs. You can control the program content that you're going into, and also, since now they've gone to mostly thirties and piggybacks with two thirties or four thirties, you may have the reach in frequency. But what you don't have is the image, and maybe you're better off reaching 8 million people instead of 30 million, if the 8 million people that you do reach are vitally interested in the program that you're doing. It relates not only to the company that's involved but to the fact that you are bringing the public something that that particular segment of the public may want to see. It's more of a target audience type thing. There are many, many companies who buy a spot on the network, and 70 percent of the people they reach they don't really want to reach — à la American Express. These 70 percent or 60 percent or 40 percent may not be able to use their services as such.

*What's been the toughest aspect of putting together a large package of shows?*
    Well, it's finding the right kind of people. Unlike a normal Hollywood crew that's set up in a studio with a full script . . . it's finding the right kind of cameramen and soundmen and a director that can go out with a very small crew and spend weeks trying to get — in wildlife, at

least — the story you are trying to achieve. And it has to vary with weather conditions and so on. The toughest thing is finding the right people, and we are able to find those people. They are very highly paid. They used to float between Disney and us, but they don't any more because Disney doesn't use those kinds of people any more. Now they float, say, between us and Geographic and whoever else is doing our type of thing.

*You really want wildlife type of people — everybody says it's tough to shoot wildlife.*
    Well, it's tough to shoot any type of reality show in the field, whether it's "60 Minutes" or wildlife, because you've got a lot of field problems.

*Can you give me some specific examples?*
    Well, I mean as an example you've got to go to, say, the Amazon. In the Amazon you've got a lot of problems with government restrictions and transportation, because most of the stuff that you need to shoot is in extremely hazardous and difficult areas of the world. Some of our people have been stuck for maybe six, seven or more months trying to get something done. So the cost in time . . . you sometimes will start a show and finish it in, say, a year, and you have to go back because you can't get the whole thing, and so you do an awful lot of over-shooting. We have miles of footage that we still haven't used because of the nature of our work, but you don't have the high cost of actors and other things. Your high cost goes into your key people — your photographers and your director. Usually a writer is sent because he's out here in the field and you say, "Look, we want to do a story of the ocelot or the jaguar in the Amazon jungle," and then he has to figure out how to get most of the stuff done and then to get his insert shots done by using controlled animals, which we've always done. Everybody does — because there's no way that we could get a lot of the stuff that we show.

*Controlled animals?*
    Well, Disney and all of us have access to various small companies that keep animals in compounds where we can do controlled pictures of what the animals would normally do in the wild, without endangering anybody's life. Otherwise, you are waiting forever to get a shot of an ocelot or a jaguar and its kittens.

*Have you had any trouble, for instance in Africa, with wolves or . . . ?*
    Yes, Uganda is one example. We were filming there when Idi Amin staged his coup. We were fortunate enough to finish shooting in Burchinson Falls and Queen Elizabeth Park; then we got out of the country, of course. We had the same thing happen . . . we were shooting a picture in Israel when the war started, so we switched our story

completely. We put that in syndication – "Call This Nation Israel" – and made a little money out of it.

*How did you switch the story?*
   Well, we switched it based on the fact that the war had started and we had a crew there, so we kept shooting, and the story had a different ending than we anticipated.

*A lot of it, it seems, depends on the writer; does the writer go out with an outline?*
   They go out with an outline; in other words, we sit down and say, "Okay, what we want to do is 'Return to Paradise (Tahiti).' What we're going to do is see what changes have occurred in twenty-five years." We have a lot of background on Tahiti today. We know that there are thirty-five more hotels, there's this, there's that; we do know that there are smaller islands that are building small hotels, which are like the Tahiti that I knew when I was down there thirty, thirty-five years ago. So we are able to do that kind of outline. Now, when the crew gets in the field, they may discover things that we couldn't uncover in our research department, and they may change certain aspects of the picture.

*How many people are in the research department and how long do they work per script?*
   Well, there are two people who are working constantly on research and mainly on the development of new programming, when we have new programming coming up, and they work five days a week.

*Are you ever kind of sorting through some out-takes and you say, "Huh, here's a program – maybe if I take this out-take or film and re-edit"?*
   Well, basically, I think that's what triggered our deal with American Express. We had been very successful in doing regular, normal, what you call "travelogues," saying, "Here's the Treyve Fountain," and, "Here's the Colosseum in Rome." What I had done is taken some of the older stuff I had done and tried it out and said, "Why can't we do a magazine format like a "60 Minutes," except an upbeat format, not trying to show the Marijuana Church or this problem or that problem?" We're trying to show the exhilarating experience of going to a balloon ranch and learning how to balloon, or discovering the fact that you can now take a cruise down the Amazon River, where in the old days you couldn't. That does, in fact, trigger our development in something new.

*How many feet do you figure you have in your film library?*
   We shoot at 16mm and 35mm, depending on the project – but mainly 16. But the filmstocks have narrowed the distinction between the two. It's incredible: It used to be in the old days, with the old film stock, you could

tell the difference. You could see more grain and everything. But now it's such that sometimes you can't tell the difference between 16 and 35. As a matter of fact, the blow-ups sometimes look just the same as if you had originally just gone out and shot on 35. In other words, what you're really saving on doing that is weight of equipment and cost in film and so on — weight, mainly.

*Producing wildlife films is dangerous stuff.*
Well, I think the strangest thing is the fact that you're dealing out in the field with primitive tribes and head hunters and wild animals, and we've never had any problems with that kind of thing. We've had three chartered airplane crashes, in which, fortunately, nobody was killed or badly injured, and it's a strange story to tell you because most people would think your danger would come from animals that attack.

*What is the main quality of a good producer? What makes you a good producer?*
Perseverance . . . and some creativity. (laughs) I think perseverance is 90 percent of anything in this business; it's taking any idea and getting it put down and finally getting it into the marketplace, and if you don't have perseverance it will never get there. And, I would think, the ability to deal with people and get the best out of them.

*What's the best way to sell to a TV station? We talked a little about that.*
Well, I think you really have to have a good agent when you're selling in syndication, and you've got to know what the station's needs are. Like right now what we're doing with our wildlife material is selling it on a library basis, which is an advantage to the station because they have a longer term to play off the programming. When they have a failure in a certain time period, they can put the show in, and it's a show that can play between 1:00 in the afternoon until 8:00 or 9:00 and it will get a number. After 9:00 it won't; but there's a certain area there that we've discovered when they need what we call "floating" programming. Yesterday I made a sale to the ABC-owned-and-operated stations for seventy-eight half-hours on that basis. Here in L.A. they're running it on a weekly basis and doing very well in the ratings. We changed the title from "Animal World" to "Wildlife Adventure" — not that that made a great deal of difference because people seem to be watching it, so . . . thank heaven.

*When you started "Animal World," how did you try to imprint your style on it?*
I was not an animal expert like, say, Marlin Perkins, who does "Wild Kingdom." He's a zoologist and I'm not. So what I did in most of my wildlife, I would say, "Look, I'm not an expert but I want you to meet some experts," and we would use guys in the field, like Dr. Compton, who

was a top man in crocodilian studies in the world. So I was able, in a sense, to put myself in the position of sitting in the audience as well as being on camera and just kind of leading them—a little different kind of format, plus the fact that we didn't like to do too many capture films like "Wildlife" does. We were more interested in life-cycle pictures, which are a little harder to make.

*How has the animal field changed since you started in it?*
Well, it has proliferated immensely. You know, there are only two shows that are good, or successful. The longest-running show has been "Wild Kingdom." Then they started to bring in product from England and retitling it and putting Lorne Greene on it . . . then "Survival" with John Forsythe and they had so many of them that . . . it's like news shows are like right now.

*So how did you respond to this?*
We went to long-form features and were able to sell those as features and get as much money as we would on a twenty-six- or fifty-two-week basis. We packaged six features, sold them, and then we packaged more; so we have eleven features now that are out earning money in syndication.

*These are not all animal?*
No, most of them are based on our treasure series. We did a series a number of years ago called "Treasure" about buried and lost treasure, whether it was gold, diamonds or whatever—classic treasure stories.

*Any other problems in producing for television?*
Well, I think the biggest problems that you face are the constant problems of keeping your cash coming in and keeping new programming. There are times when you get tired, and the only advantage to a production company of our size, at least—it is not true with studios that have high overhead—is that we can pull our horns in and maybe take a leave . . . just lean back and sell what we've got—reruns and what-have-you—and then we get some new ideas and start to run with them. Sometimes in the past we have tried to do too much for a small company. So now I try to do one project at a time. We don't have any desire to be a huge corporate entity as long as we can make a living and be happy in our work.

*Do you think you'll be using video in the future?*
We have been using video extensively in post-production, particularly. In other words, laying film in and then cutting in video. Ninety percent of our stuff is distributed on tape now. Now, we still have the dream of doing several of our programs in the future with lighter

equipment with total video, which, of course, is great because you can see what you've got in the can and almost edit in the field. We are not at that point, but I think we will be in the near future.

You've got to also realize that most of our stuff is filmed all over the world—that is another difference. We do handle our own foreign distribution for most of our products, and in foreign distribution we have one person who works with agents outside this country. If you shoot it all on tape, you're shooting 525 lines [of resolution] for the U.S. If you go into various other countries, you've got to go to 625, and you're up there in many other areas, so you're really limited. You can convert it, but conversion is expensive. So if you have film, you shoot on film, release it on tape in the States and other areas on 525-line tape; then you've got to eventually come up with a complete film that can be released overseas, because the conversion from 525 to 625 is so costly. There needs to be some compatibility between our system of television and those of Europe and Japan and other countries.

*What do you look for in a wildlife cameraperson?*
Well, he's got to be highly qualified—highly technically qualified. He's got to have the ability to sleep in a sleeping bag. There's maybe twenty guys that I know of—sometimes husband and wife teams like the Mallotts, who were used twenty-five or thirty years ago in Disney true-life adventure stuff. These are people that are unusual in that they are pretty much able to go on their own. That's what you look for: the kind of person who likes that kind of work. Now there's a difficulty because there's not so much work available for the people who do that kind of work.

*Was there ever a story that you went on and began to feel, "This is great stuff and we're getting what we need, but I wish I wasn't intruding on the animal."*
I think we have been very careful. One of the great problems is you want action—we wanted a lion fight. Well, you can wait for days to get one and never get one, and we needed one desperately. So I was able to find a pair of lions here in L.A., believe it or not, that wrestled, and we inserted that in a film. We were trying to show dominance of the male—there's always a dominant male in every pride. But we've never hurt any animals and we've never put them in danger in the wild or anywhere else, as far as that's concerned.

*Are you a real animal lover then?*
Oh, yeah, sure, I love animals. I used to have my own horses, and my kids grew up loving animals, too. I have a little book out now that Temple published called *Animal Quiz*, which ran in the *National Enquirer*, and people think I'm an expert, which I'm not—I can't answer

half the questions myself — but it's a fascinating field, a fascinating area of life. As civilization explodes, their world diminishes in the wild; by the year 2500, or something, we won't have to worry about it. But it's quite true that there will be little available life in the wild left in the world.

*So you sort of feel like an archivist?*

Yes, to a certain extent, and I think that all those guys who are working on it feel that way — not only our people, but "Wild Kingdom" and other guys who have done this kind of thing. In another two or three hundred years it may be the last record, you know, like Noah's Ark.

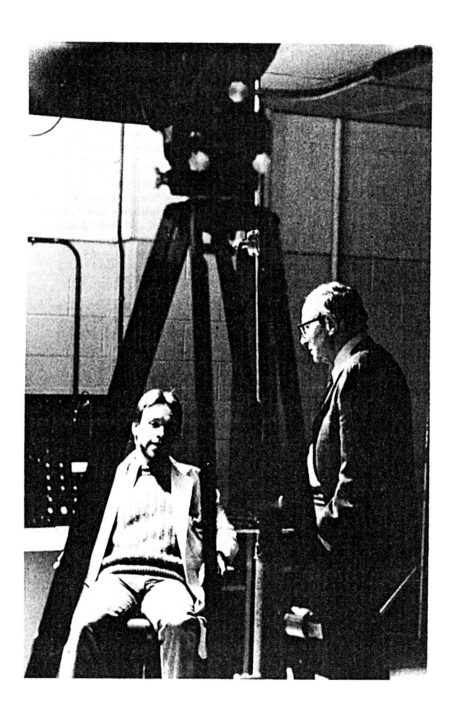

*Jay McMullen*

WHEN JAY MCMULLEN does a documentary, things happen: people are put on trial, the Senate investigates, national laws are passed. Much of his investigative work involves infiltrating dangerous segments of society. No problem for McMullen. But when President Lyndon Johnson asked McMullen to attend the signing of a new drug-control law which resulted from McMullen's investigations, McMullen went fishing in Canada instead.

Jay McMullen began his broadcast career as an Army correspondent for "NBC Army Hour." Two radio documentaries he wrote and produced provided, in his words, "the big bangs" that propelled him on his way at CBS. The documentaries were "The Galindez-Murphy Case: A Chronicle of Terror" and "Who Killed Michael Farmer?" – both narrated by Ed Murrow.

McMullen's first TV documentary, which was done for the CBS public affairs department, was "Hoffa and the Teamsters." CBS Reports was invented, and McMullen became an original member.

McMullen is probably best known for "The Biography of a Bookie Joint" (1961). The first broadcast was blacked out in Boston because the trials were still going on. For that production, McMullen says, "I spent eight months doing the show and a year testifying about it."

"The Business of Heroin" and "The Silent Spring of Rachel Carson" followed – early treatments of drug and environmental problems. In 1964 McMullen became head of CBS Fact-Finding Unit, which did investigative pieces. For one series he bought a million dollars' (on the black market) worth of drugs – legally, through a fictitious company, McMullen Export/Import. Another series focused on clinical and diagnostic labs that were not doing their work; this led to a Senate investigation.

In "The Tenement" McMullen lived over a year in a low-income tenement and really got to know the people. McMullen says of it, "From my point of view, what I set out to do and accomplish – 'The Tenement' came close. My purpose was to familiarize whites with the predicament of poor blacks living in tenements, their hopes and frustrations at a time when the two races were at a point of extreme frustration."

"Campaign American Style" was the first time anyone had examined the ad agencies that work on political campaigns, and the impact of polling. "The Mexican Connection," an examination into air smuggling from Mexico, received an Emmy. "The Selling of the F-14" was a documentary about arms sales, payoffs and politics. Recent shows include "Baby Makers," "The Toyota Invasion," and "After All Those Years."

McMullen has received four Emmy nominations, one Emmy, a George Foster Peabody Award, a Hillman Award for "The Tenement," two Writer's Guild Awards, a Sigma Delta Chi Award, an Ohio State Award, and a Gavel Award.

McMullen says of his life in documentary, "I enjoyed my work – I

*Photo (facing page): Jay McMullen (right) interviews for the CBS documentary "The Baby Makers."*

believed that what I was doing was important. My ambition was to be able to feel like I was involved in some sort of service. I ended up writing, narrating, reporting – in other words, having complete control over the broadcasts I did. For a journalist, that's great."

*You may have been TV's first investigative reporter. What do you say to that? I'm talking about "The Biography of a Bookie Joint."*
It's a hard question to answer. Because of that broadcast, I did receive a lot of publicity as an investigative reporter, and I think Fred Friendly made the statement, "This is the first investigative reporter for television." Whether that's really true or not, you know, I don't really know. In the first place, I don't watch every broadcast. I would say that if "Bookie Joint" was not the first attempt in that area for at least a one-hour documentary, if it wasn't the first, it had to be one of the first. I could make a flat statement on that.

*What was the hardest thing about doing "Bookie Joint"?*
Well, let me put it to you this way. It took eight months to do the show, and after the broadcast I was testifying about that show for over a year and going before grand juries. I would say, the post-show problems – being accused, for example, of heinous crimes by the Boston police, and having to prove that we were innocent. Accusations such as, "Those weren't real policemen walking in to that bookie joint – you used actors and dressed them up as cops. You couldn't have done certain sequences when you said they were done because we noticed that in the window there was a sign and that sign would have come later." One thing after another – little things. License plate numbers. We had to disprove every bit of that, and I had to go before the grand jury in Boston. They went over every inch of that film, and I was questioned on practically every single frame as to authenticity and so on. We had to prove by film edge numbers that the film was even shot within a certain area of time.

*How did you prove that? I don't quite understand . . .*
Well, the stock of the film; in other words, if they were saying something happened five years earlier than we said it happened, the stock numbers on the film would disprove that because the film would be of a certain date.

*How did that idea evolve?*
Let me see. I had done a broadcast on "Hoffa and the Teamsters," it was called, with Al Wasserman, and you might call that something of an investigative report. That came out before "Bookie Joint." In any case, I was invited to a meeting of independent crime commission heads. There are groups in various cities throughout the country – crime commissions, they are called. Chicago has a crime commission. New York used to have

a crime commission, independent of official bodies, and supported by outside finances. Anyway, they had a conference down in New Orleans, and I was asked to come down and show some excerpts of "Hoffa and the Teamsters." And I did, and after it was all over I invited those who were present to suggest any stories that they thought might be worthwhile doing from a standpoint of law enforcement. About a month later I received a call from Dwight Strong, who was head of the crime commission in Boston. He told me about the wide-open gambling going on in Boston and asked me if I wanted to come up and take a look at what was doing on there.

Before I even went up there, however, I had been to see Bobby Kennedy. I had gotten to know him through another program I made—oh, it was through the Teamster show—and I went in to talk to him about the possibilities of doing something in the law enforcement area. He encouraged me to move in that direction and said we ought to get into organized crime, that it was very important to do so, and so on. So there was encouragement from his end, with a promise of some kind of whatever help they could give. Then came this invitation from Dwight Strong to come to Boston to look at the bookie joint.

The other thing that fascinated me about attempting to do an exposé of that nature—that is, to try to get inside an illicit operation—was that we had to use an 8mm camera, and I had always wanted to play around with an 8mm camera to see just how far you could stretch the medium. You know, in those days, particularly, Friendly used to talk about how we carried the 10-ton pencil, as he called it, with all the equipment.

*Was that Friendly or Murrow?*

Those were Friendly's words. I could be wrong, but I'm pretty sure they were. I had come out of radio and had done some radio documentaries, where you just carried a little box around and recorded your sources and then you went back and edited the tape and did some narration and that was that. A simple thing to do compared to TV and filmmaking. So I was sort of interested in whether this could be done—whether we could, in fact, use miniaturized equipment, and thereby be able to get certain kinds of film that we would not ordinarily be able to get with the crew standing there and so forth. Those three things generated my interest in getting started on the "Bookie Joint" show.

*How hard was it to develop that 8mm? Did you have to do a lot of tests and stuff?*

Yeah, I certainly did. I tried all kinds of devices and how you hide it and how you trigger it. It would only go for three minutes at one shot. minutes of film and then you had to reload, which meant that in order to get enough film you had to keep going back and forth, back and forth in the bookie joint and you couldn't frame anything. You just had to take potluck on whether you were in focus, whether you actually had what you wanted to have in frame or not.

*Did you miss any primary things — any great things that you found were out of frame or out of focus?*
We missed some things but we were able to go back and get the thing sort of . . .

*Did you think you were going to get caught? It's a little suspicious going back with a lunchbox all the time, isn't it?*
We didn't do it every day. But the answer is yes. We were afraid of getting caught. The curious thing is that — skipping way ahead of the story here — when we turned over our material to the Attorney General, and he turned it over to the Internal Revenue Service, the IRS did their own investigation and they weren't going to tell us when or *if* they were going to raid this place. But we gave them a lot of information. Not only about that place, but about some others around there. In any case, we were filming one day and I noticed three rather official types walking up to the key shop. Then the door closed, and nothing happened. I thought, it's just a chance that those are IRS agents; so I went down and I tried the door of the key store and it was locked. I tugged at it, and all of a sudden it swung open and three guys grabbed me. I don't know if it was three for sure, but I was grabbed and taken over to a corner and searched and so on, and they kept asking me, "Why are you here?" I thought my number was up. These were pretty tough-looking fellows. I didn't recognize them to be the same three who had walked in, and I thought I had really been set up. They said, "What did you come in here for?" and I said, "To buy a key," and they said, "Ah-ah-ah, we're going to take you in the back room and beat the shit out of you," and I thought I had fallen into the wrong hands. Whereupon a man appeared on the scene, who happened to be the agent — the IRS agent — in charge of the investigation. He said to these fellows, "Let him alone. Let him go." So I left without saying anything more. I just ran out, and the next thing was we were down there with our cameras. But that kind of thing . . . fear of being caught was very much present. We had rented an apartment across the street, and we stayed there overnight. The crew didn't, but I did, and one other fellow who worked with me. We had kitchen knives and he had a revolver. It was that kind of atmosphere.

*What did the network legal department say about using the film, or did they have any concerns at the outset?*
The legal department was brought into this project right from the beginning. There were long discussions about what kind of evidence we were going to have to get in order to make this stick, and each step of the

way, problems and situations were reviewed by the legal department. There was some concern about the people who were going in making the bets, who were not technically breaking the law. The bookies were because they didn't have gambling stamps. The federal law in those days was that if you were a bookmaker you had to have a federal gambling or wagering stamp, which was also part of a tax, and that was in direct contrast to the rules and laws of some states, which forbid any kind of gambling at all; but, technically, bookies were breaking the law, and the people who were wagering with them were not breaking the law in Massachusetts, and therefore there was some concern about showing faces of the customers. That was one of the legal concerns.

*Palmer Williams did the filming, didn't he?*

Palmer Williams did not do the filming. Palmer Williams was the production manager, but he wasn't present. Filming was primarily done by a "CBS Reports" film crew. The cameraman was Bobbie Clemens, and at the time of the raid I had another crew stashed away ready to pounce if anything happened. The plan was that they would come in cars from a hotel, because I thought the coverage of the raid would require two crews, and we were pretty sure there was going to be a raid, but we weren't informed when that was going to be. It was a difficult thing to do. I guess the story will interest you because one of the things we were accused of was that we had made a deal with the IRS to stage a raid for the benefit of our cameras; but in fact, I had been told — by Bobby Kennedy himself — "Thanks a lot for the information but we can't possibly tell you when we are going to raid."

Here's how we figured it out: I did have to come in contact with the chief IRS investigator, and there was a lawyer at the Justice Department assigned to this, and these were the two key law enforcement men. One from Justice and one from the Internal Revenue Service. I was pretty sure that those two people were going to be present at the time a raid was made. So I kept calling their offices in Washington. I would telephone one fellow's office, and if I found he was out of town, I called the next office to find out if *he* was out of town. I figured that when they were both going to be in Boston, that was the danger and that was the signal. If there was going to be a raid, they would both be in Boston at the same time, and we should be ready. It turned out that it was a good idea. I remember one day going to Fred Friendly and saying, "They've had our information for a long time. We know that they've had ample time to gather a lot of information. Now here's the two top guys out of town and in Boston, and I think we had better get a crew up there because this may be the time when they're going to try a bust. But it's a big gamble." And he said, "So, go ahead and do it." So that's how we happened to be there when the bookie joint was raided. And then afterwards there was an investigation because Kennedy, the president, wanted more details on how we happened to be around when the Internal Revenue Service raided, despite the fact that we had been told that they weren't going to give us any information on the raid. Therefore, how did we know when they were going to raid? There was a small investigation on that. I told them.

*Do you think Kennedy was trying to protect the Boston police, or anything like that?*
No, but I think they would have been very happy had it been some other city and not Boston.

*Did it take a long time to get the real good stuff or was it just kind of slowly trickling in?*
In the first place, I couldn't have a camera crew there every day for eight months. Camera crews are expensive. The answer to your question is that first I got the interior material, and when I thought I had enough of that, the second step was to do filming on the outside, which would show people going in and out and the amount of traffic and all the cars double- and triple-parked and so on. And just to observe the hour-by-hour daily activities that went on that one could see from the outside. So I brought a film crew up and they were up there three or four days. During the course of the three or four days, one day we saw something like four or five police officers go in and come out again. The place was running full blast. All during the time we were there, we filmed some policemen going in and out of there, and it turned out we filmed some policemen who were in plain clothes and we didn't even know they were policemen at the time. It also turned out that we filmed some people who were in local government. We didn't know that they were in local government. We took all the license plate numbers down. We checked that, and lo and behold some turned out to be employees of the Boston government. At that point, with the inside material and with that outside material shot over a period of three or four days, we were pretty sure that we were going to have a broadcast.

*Are you a subtle or a sneaky person? I don't mean that necessarily pejoratively, but are you a person who approaches things obliquely?*
Well, my answer to that is I don't think so. I don't sneak around much. I much prefer, frankly, an eyeball-to-eyeball kind of approach where you sit down with somebody and talk things over with them. But there is no way you could do that in this kind of story. You could do that in the Teamster story. You could sit down with Jimmy Hoffa and ask him a lot of questions. You could sit down with dissident members of the union and gather information from them. This was the first time I tried anything like that on TV.

*Have you ever felt a little unnerved by a confrontation? What was your most unnerving confrontation? Other than that physical thing that you described awhile ago — the three men.*

Well, let's look at it this way. A "CBS Reports" producer wears a number of hats. He usually writes the narration. He's the director, so-called. We don't like that word because we don't really direct, we don't deal with actors — but we have to belong to the Directors Guild, so we are directors, right? Say, "Point the camera toward that bookie joint over there." That's direction, I suppose. But, in any case, we're responsible to the extent of whether a show is going to succeed or not, and if it doesn't get on the air and bombs out, there is only one person to look at, really, and that's the producer. He is the one who's in charge and probably thought up the idea and brought it in — not always.

So with that background, let me tell you this. A man named Carlos Marcello, who was called by law enforcement people the head of the Mafia in the South, found himself in Guatemala suddenly. He had gone in to report to immigration authorities, who had been after him for years. The government had been trying to deport him for years. Anyway, after reporting, he found himself in Guatemala. When he walked in to report to immigration, they put him on a plane and flew him to Guatemala and said, "Get off and stay there and don't come back." There's a long story connected with that that I'm not going to go into and wear you out, but I made arrangements with Marcello's lawyers to interview him in Guatemala. The interview, I was told, had to be out of Guatemala City. I made all kinds of elaborate arrangements — rented a villa — and we were going to pick him up early one morning and take him out there, and the camera crew would stay at the villa and we would film him there and would quietly depart. The story was not only Marcello's so-called kidnapping, but also the story of Carlos Marcello. How he got involved, his relations with Frank Costello — he and Frank were running the slot machines all over the South — and so on. And I thought I had a real live Mafia character here who was going to sing. So I told the crew, "When I bring this fellow here in the morning, you be outside under the trees and you be all ready to film. I don't want to sit around and have a long discussion with him before filming. I don't know exactly what I'm going to ask him, but I'm sure as time passes — if we have to wait for filming — that he's going to bring that up, and I don't want that brought up." Well, it turned out that for various reasons I had to pick up Marcello early in the morning, I think it was about 6:00, and drive him out to the villa. We got out there and the crew was under the trees waiting, but the cameraman said, "Jay, not enough light yet." And I said, being fairly new in the business, "Well, if there's not enough light then I guess . . . can you do any filming at all?" And he said, "I'll try, but we'll have to wait till the sun gets up a little higher." In the interim, Carlos and his lawyer began doing exactly what I anticipated they would do — asking me, you know, "What about this? Are you going to go into this? Are you going to go into that?" And I was suggesting that we get into certain areas in a certain way. But, anyway, in the end Marcello said, "Look, I'm sorry. I'm just not going to do this interview." At the moment he said that, the door flew open and the cameraman came in yelling, "Okay, let's go." (laughs) So the whole project went down the drain because the sun came up too slowly.

*So it didn't work. But you were kind of intimidated, talking with this heavyweight criminal.*
It wasn't that I was intimidated. There was too much time for him to think about it. He was very angry about being deported, and he thought he had a good case against the U.S. Government when he was deported under rush terms and so forth. On that basis he was going to talk.

*You had leeway in the old days. Rumor had it that you could disappear — McMullen, the Disappearer — for long periods of time without telling the network where you were and stuff like that.*
Well, that's not really true. Fred Friendly, who was head of "CBS Reports" at that time, always knew where I was, and I always kept in touch with him and with others. There were some shows which required a lot of traveling. I did one called "The Business of Heroin" that took me halfway across the world, but CBS always knew where I was. There were frequent calls, and it was important that they did know where I was. I never disappeared. I didn't talk much about where I was going or what I was going to do in wide circles, but in terms of the people who had to know, they did know, and there was constant communication.

*Why didn't you talk more about your projects?*
Well, because in some of the projects I just didn't think that it would be too wise to have it publicly known that I was trying to do what I was trying to do. "Bookie Joint" is an example. If I were running around Boston saying, "Hey, we're doing all this filming at this bookie joint," it wouldn't have been a very wise thing to do. It would have blown the story.

*How much of good documentary producing is, for you, instinct? Instinct about a scene, about what works, about a topic, about where people are going to be or how they're going to react.*
Well, after they've done this work for awhile, most reporters develop a certain sense of whether they're going to be able to get sources and whether those sources are going to be believable. Most every reporter develops some kind of a direction and finds out along the way whether he's going to make it or not. But you really begin in investigative reporting with some questions; you don't begin with the answers. You're not quite sure what you're going to come up with — a broadcast — until you have already expended a lot of time, effort, money. It's a chancy

thing—unless you're shooting ducks on a pond. But it's chancy if you're seriously trying to pursue something and really don't know. You've got a hunch, you've got a little bit of information, but you're not sure it's true and you're just checking it out. That's where your nose is important—whether you're really getting the straight information or whether you're being led by the nose or being deceived in one way or another.

*How do you view today's investigative reporters? A lot of people call themselves investigative reporters these days.*

I know they do. I've never called myself an investigative reporter. I like to think of myself as a good reporter. A good reporter pretty much sums up what is required in investigative reporting if it's going to be successful. The only distinction I would make between, in general, a good reporter and a good investigative reporter is that the investigative reporter usually starts in the dark and may or may not find light at the end of the tunnel; whereas, in some other kind of stories a reporter may cover, he's pretty sure that he's going to have that story. How well and how much he's going to get may be a question, but he's pretty sure he's going to get a story.

*Can you give me an example?*

The simplest example, I suppose, is a reporter is sent to cover an automobile accident—what he does, who he talks to, and what he finds out. A sloppy reporter might miss some things, which would turn it into a good story, or an inaccurate story. Let's say he's going to do an economic story of some kind, whatever it might be—a closing of a factory. Well, a factory is closing—that's the story. Now comes the question of *why* the factory is closing, and that's what he's going to be looking into. In the course of that story he might find some startling facts that he didn't know about in the beginning; but whether he does or not, he's going to have a story about that factory closing.

*One gets a feeling of a kind of relevance in your stories that sometimes goes beyond the stories.*

I do try to look for a story that—while the focus may be small—illustrates more universal truths. Sometimes by looking at the head of a pin and becoming an expert on that, you can get insight into larger problems that you ordinarily would not have gotten had you not had a small focus. On the other hand, I suppose there are disadvantages, too; your small focus could be the wrong focus. But I do look for things that I think have a relevance beyond that small focus or help to illustrate universal problems, universality in some way. I think "The Tenement" was one of those. Living and getting to know those people well and observing them every day, and finding out, for example, that most of the people who lived in the ghetto—at least in that area, and I think, generally speaking—were not the ones who were out joining the rock throwers or involved in the riots. There was a lot of that going on.

*That was in 1968.*
Yeah. The people who lived in the tenement didn't belong to militant organizations. I'm not suggesting that there's anything wrong with black dispute, with the way life was going at all. I'm not saying that. What I'm saying is that I found out that most people lived a life of quiet desperation in those buildings. They were really much more isolated than I had thought them to be—isolated from the outside world.

*What was the toughest thing about doing that film?*
Getting accepted.

*How long did that take?*
It took quite a long while. We didn't do any filming at all for maybe three months. In observing attempts by others to cover this kind of story, I kept seeing the reporters sticking a microphone suddenly into the face of somebody they had never met before—probably had had only a few words with before the cameras began rolling. Trying to do their interview that way. And it also seemed that the people they talked to were representatives of the activist groups, because the activists were the ones who were protesting and calling for reform and thereby making news. So those were the people who got talked to. I didn't want to do it that way. If you're white and are going to move into a ghetto in Chicago, you're going to attract some attention, there's no doubt about that. I had a black cameraman who moved in first with a black soundman, and they got to know the people, and they said they were trying to make a film around the neighborhood and so on. Then gradually I came in and told them CBS was involved—and now we're talking as person to person. Not interviewing them really, just, "How are you?" etc., and occasionally sitting down and talking. We found that as we got to know them, the easier it was to talk to them and the more frank they would be in what they had to say. But it took a long period of time. Then I remember one night, when I finally decided we were going to film a night scene outside. We had the cameras outside, and we became surrounded by a mob. Activists in the neighborhood surrounded us and threatened us and so on and asked questions like, "Why are you here?" The people in the building that we were in really were our protectors, in a sense, because they defended us. There were threats from some of these activists; they threatened to do us bodily harm. The police came up and wanted to know if we wanted them to arrest some of these people, and I said, "Absolutely not." (laughs)

*Have you ever been so emotionally touched by a production or by something you've been doing that you've had to stop and gather your forces?*

Well, I have had situations — I can't think of too many — I've been in interviews where I've really gotten pretty well choked up and, also, in a way, felt embarrassed that I was filming it. That would involve a very emotional thing. Somebody breaks down and cries.

*Give me an example.*

I can't think of one offhand on television, but I can think of one in radio — a radio documentary. It was called "Babies C.O.D." and it was about adoption through the black market — the baby black market. I was talking to one of the women. She had given up her baby and put it into the market, and in recounting her story she went to pieces. I guess that is the most graphic thing I can think of.

*And so how did you feel?*

Oh, I felt terrible, and I felt guilty, too, because in a way, I provoked it by asking her to tell her story.

*Was there anything that was really hard for you to get used to — any difficult transitions in coming from radio documentary to film documentary?*

Well, equipment was . . . having to work with a lot of equipment and quite a few people. In essence, having to consider things that I didn't have to consider in radio. For example, whether it was raining or snowing or a clear day, and what the lights had to be, and the impact of what happens when you bring a 10-ton pencil (of equipment) and five technicians into somebody's house. It gets in the way of what a journalist really wants to do. Ideally, you say, "Let's have everything nice and peaceful and quiet, nondisruptive, and let's sit down and talk." It's not that way in TV. You find yourself also responsible for the crew. In some situations you're possibly responsible for their lives. You're calling the shots. In radio it can be a one-man operation. It's far simpler. Words in radio . . . the writing in radio has been more important than it has become in television.

*What is your key in writing good narration? You know, everybody will say it's to be read aloud or it's to be spoken and all that, but in disseminating the information, how do you do it?*

I don't know that there's any one key. Good writing is usually clear. Clarity is certainly very important, particularly in some of the complex stories we do. Some of them have been very complex. As an example, last year I did something called "The Baby Makers." That had to do with genetics; it had to do with artificial methods of reproduction, controlling the outcome of, well, for example, whether it's going to be a boy or girl. It is difficult just in explaining the basics of a story like that. I began it by explaining what the sperm was, what the egg was, how they functioned, and tried to do that in an interesting way. It's pretty complex. How the embryo grows and that kind of thing. That requires a lot of distillation, and a little bit of poetry, and some film that's going to be of service to what you're talking about.

*You say "a little bit of poetry"?*
     Yes, a little bit of poetry, because I think science stories need it. (laughs) You know, when you're talking about life and the universe and the magic and the wonderment of this world we live in, how it functions, some sort of poetry helps, some sort of perception of this that is above just, "Well, I'll tell you what happens, you see, the sperm penetrates the egg and fertilizes the egg." Science can turn it into a kind of nuts and bolts story. Nuts and bolts are really a piece of wonderment, and somehow to put nuts and bolts in the setting of that wonderment is satisfying to me whenever I can do that, whenever I can universalize, if you will. Sometimes the poets can say things better and more concisely. I actually used some poetry in that show. It was a sort of poet's wonderment of how we all get created. I just can't recite it to you offhand.

*How much technical stuff does a good producer of documentaries at the network level need to know?*
     He has to know, or he has to have people around him who do know, quite a bit about how cameras work and what lenses to use and what he can and cannot do. He has to know a lot about editing. I sit with my editor every day. We work together in putting the films together. The producer has to know the tricks of the trade in editing. He's got to have some idea. Next, he's got to draw a budget, and he's got to make a guess in the beginning of how much it's going to cost. If he goes way over that budget he's probably going to hear from upstairs. So it helps to have that economic sense of how much the broadcast is going to cost and why it's going to cost that amount.

*What story was your biggest wild goose chase?*
     What appeared to be an honest attempt on the part of some people to invade Haiti — that was a wild goose chase. Which never came off.

*You were accused of paying for that, weren't you, too?*
     We were accused of financing it — that CBS was going to invade Haiti. There was a congressional hearing held on it, and the first or second witness that they had from the Justice Department proceeded to testify that the Justice Department had looked into the matter very carefully and there was no evidence at all that we were guilty of what we were accused of. But the committee went on to make all kinds of accusations. The end result of this was that we weren't proved guilty of anything, and we

weren't prosecuted for anything. I guess I came out as a damned fool for tackling the story in the first place.

*Tell me how that evolved. What was the toughest thing about putting it together?*
    We never put it together. It was never broadcast. It turned out that there was no serious attempt by those we thought were trying to invade Haiti actually to do so. They were collecting money and arms, but they were doing this primarily for publicity purposes. In the background was the question as to what extent the CIA may have been involved in trying to bring about a change of government in Haiti, which was what I was really looking into as much as anything else, and that's what made a congressional committee see red. "What an outrageous thing to say about our CIA." (You have to remember now, we're back in the '60s.) "What an outrageous thing. Do you think this country was going to have anything to do with undermining the government of a friendly country?" said the committee, and all this kind of stuff. Well, it turned out, of course, events later produced evidence that the CIA, in fact, had been involved, not only in the Haiti political situation, but also in Cuba and other places.

*What do you expect from your film editor? Obviously, technical competence, but what is your ideal relationship with a film editor?*
    The ideal relationship with a film editor, as far as I'm concerned, is when he really becomes a part of the team and is a contributor. He takes an interest in the story. As that story develops he reads the transcripts. (Some don't, you know.) He makes suggestions as you go along. And – purely on the technical side – he really knows and understands the matching rhythms that are required when you put narration to film. You've got the rhythm of the film and you've got the rhythm of the narration, and a really good editor, as you know, has that sense of being able to meld those two. He knows when something works and when it doesn't work. You don't have to tell him. He already knows. He'll change it himself. A lot of editing, as you know since you've done it, is trial and error. I would say those are the major things I look for in a good editor.

*The rhythm of the language. What other theories do you have about the rhythms of language in pictures?*
    When you're speaking of rhythm – talking about something of a certain rhythm going on – just in your language and your voice, there's that sound there that has a rhythm to it. Words appear at a certain time and place, and if those words don't appear in the same rhythm with the film, you're out of sync, in a sense – you've got two rhythms fighting each other. The words don't quite belong over the picture they are covering, or the picture is not a match, is not a rhythm. That can be so subtle that you can look at the sequence and say, you know, "The picture looks good.

The words sound good. The topic is good. But somehow this doesn't work. Now why is that?" It all has to do with what I'm talking about. It has to do with the timing and the rhythm.

*Have you ever had an editor cut something too short or something so you had to redo the narration?*
    That's another thing. You sit down with an editor and you say, "Yeah, well, the timing isn't working. Why don't we change the picture or change the words?" And a good editor might say, "You know, if you said something along the line of — you use this word or that word, or say the thing that you said last first, then I can leave the picture the way it is or we can change the picture around."

*It would seem to be an advantage not to be a dogmatist as a producer. One doesn't come in with this absolute notion of, "I want this picture here and I want this picture here." You come in with an open mind.*
    Yeah, I try to do that. I get into the deepest trouble when I am fixed. But on the other hand, you have to start with some sort of concept or there's no way of starting. So you have to hope that you're more or less on the right track. I've had to literally rip up films and put them back together again in a different way.

*What film did you most have to rip up?*
    I did a story on a district attorney's office in Philadelphia — a one-hour documentary called "The District Attorney." It took a look at how a district attorney's office operates and the politics there, and the problems of justice in America in terms of overloaded dockets, of people being put back on the streets because there was no place to put them — the jails were full. Also, the frustrations of the district attorney's office. That was the focus of the broadcast. I had a hell of a time, and I just got it together wrong. I showed it for our brass here, and I knew when I showed it that it wasn't working too well. In fact, I told them that before I showed it to them — and they couldn't have agreed more. (laughs)

*What did you do wrong? How did you restructure it? How did you correct it?*
    Well, I think I had to recategorize it. I think I was trying to say too much too fast and also to apply things that I thought were obvious, which apparently were not obvious. That might be a problem of a lot of writers, I don't know. What you think is obvious may not be so obvious to the next fellow.

*Is there any mistake that you might have made in your earlier productions that really haunts you? Anything that you think about now and then and think, "How in hell did I do that?"*

Well, I look at each production as starting afresh; whether experienced or not, you could make mistakes. No matter how much experience I have, I find that each show I approach I feel I've never done one before, psychologically. Each is a new thing. And so, having said that, what haunts me? I might say I may have been able to have done a better job on a broadcast than I did, but given the circumstances and my limited abilities, I did the best I could. But there was nothing like, "Gee, you made a terrible mistake. You put this thing out on the air and it just wasn't true and . . . " That never happened to me. The closest I've ever come, I think, I did a show on the arms deal. It was called "The Selling of the F-14." When I was in Iran I talked to the Shah about, you know, sort of what was going on, to some extent politically. But my focus wasn't really on Iranian politics. My focus was on how this arms deal got arranged and who was involved in it, how did it come off, and why in hell are we sending our sophisticated fighter aircraft to Iran in the first place. That was where my attention was. But within the course of the broadcast, I was talking about the Shah, and I had a background piece about him in there. It said, in effect, that he was a dictator and that his first priority was to stay in power, but, on the other hand, because of his outpouring of funds into bettering the country — building more hospitals, roads, educational programs and all of this — that most of the people appear to support him. "Most of the people appear to support him," is a line that haunts me now, because I guess they didn't. (laughs) I really didn't have the evidence to support that one line. I said they appeared to support him, but I hadn't done any surveys and I really didn't know what the hell I was talking about when I said that, other than I didn't hear all kinds of grumbles and moans and complaints when I was over there — but I guess I was traveling in the wrong places.

*Do you ever dream documentaries?*

No. I don't dream them, but I stay awake at night and often wake up in the middle of the night with an idea for something — some way of possibly improving a documentary I'm working on. The trouble with doing this kind of work is just that you can't leave it at the office. It follows you wherever you go and haunts you.

*What's the key to cutting interviews? Do you have any pet theories, pet peeves about how your on-camera interviews are edited?*

I think fairness and accuracy are the guidelines there. There have been occasions when excerpts of interviews have been presented out of context. I am not going to comment on that anymore because I don't know the specifics other than what I read in the newspapers or I hear somewhere, but it is true that you have a certain amount of power to make somebody look good or not so good. I think that is an interesting question to talk about. As a matter of fact, somebody in my class at

Columbia, where I occasionally lecture . . . I did something on a political story, and they said, "Could you have made that politician look better?" And my answer was, "Yes, I guess I could. But I'll also tell you this. I could have also made him look worse." So what we do is not totally objective. Hopefully, it's fair, but you are not an all-knowing god who can call all the shots right and be absolutely certain that he is calling them right.

*What's the weirdest interview you've ever done?*
      I would say this last show when I was in Japan. Whether this happens because the interpreter is goofing or not, I don't know, but the Japanese is asked a question and sometimes the answer that comes back does not address itself at all to the question you asked; so you stop and say to your interpreter, "Wait a minute. Are you sure you asked that question right? Let's ask it again." And the same thing happens. I had that happen to me several times in filming "The Toyota Invasion," until one day a Toyota PR man took me aside at an interview, at which I was feeling very frustrated because I was not getting the answers to the questions. He said to me, "You have to understand that there's a difference here in the cultures. We Japanese like to give answers which we think encompass enough information so that you can take what pleases you the most, and we like to be vague in our answers for that reason, because no embarrassment results from that. You're going to be happy," and so on. The person who's saying this is leaving it vague enough so I guess he isn't going to be unhappy. Another thing he said was, "You have to understand that you, in your culture, surround the truth with words, and in our culture we often try to present the truth in such a way that you may not even know you are getting the truth." (laughs)

*What are the primary technical things you look for in the interview?*
      My own personal preference is this: I look upon the reporter as someone who is there to ask questions on behalf of the audience and as a kind of intermediary—not as a central figure, not as someone who is going to be in equal focus to the person being interviewed. I think that person should always hold center stage. For that reason, I try to keep most of my questions either on the face of the interviewee or in a two-shot where the camera is over my shoulder, you know, part of my head, or something, onto the person being interviewed. That's just my personal preference. I rarely use an on-camera question where it's on my face unless I suspect that somebody's going to be really trying to evade the truth and it's going to be a real give-or-take situation. I may do some of the camera work on me, but generally speaking, I try to remain as just the representative of the public and not an actor in the drama. I'm not saying that's the best way to do it, I'm not saying that it shouldn't be done the other way, I'm saying that this is my personal preference.

*If you work on a piece for nine months, do you ever find that familiarity breeds contempt?*

I think what happens is that you begin to think that everybody knows this; you're so familiar with the subject that you begin to think that everybody else is familiar with it. You have seen at least portions of your film over and over and over again and it is no longer all that startling or interesting to you. You may have had a sequence that you thought was very funny in the beginning, and after you've seen it thirty-two times, it isn't very funny any more.

*Somebody said that a journalist can't expect to have a friend outside of the news profession. Would you agree with that?*

No. I have friends outside of the profession, but part of what he said has meaning. Journalists tend to speak the same language, be interested in a wide variety of subjects, occupations and so on; and I think journalists like to talk to each other. They enjoy the other fellow's experiences – you know, "Tell me what happened, you were in Vietnam when the helicopter crashed." They just like that. They just like to swap lies, too. (laughs)

*How has the documentary changed over the years?*

When I started, the TV documentary was a brand-new toy. Whatever we did, whatever we presented, probably had not been done or presented on TV before. I did a lot of firsts on stories.

*Give me an example.*

Well, I did the first TV story on the effects of pesticides and chemicals on the environment. It was called "The Silent Spring of Rachel Carson." Rachel Carson wrote a book that I thought was fascinating, and so the broadcast was based primarily on interviews with her about the chemical industry and on the responses of the industries. It was the first time that anybody had ever gotten into that subject on TV. How many broadcasts have been done on chemical pollution of the environment since then? God, I don't know, but hundreds at least, I would imagine. Today most subjects have been done and some overdone. As a difference, in the early days, there were topics we would be discouraged about geting into.

*Do you remember some?*

Well, I remember that I had some trouble prior to the Carson show. A friend of mine had written a book called *Chemicals in Our Food*, and I wanted to do a broadcast about that, and I got turned down – they thought on the basis of too touchy a subject. My God, you're tackling the food industry.

*What year was that?*

It was in the '50s. Middle '50s, probably. There were certain subjects (homosexuality, for example) that one probably would not have gotten into in those days. Eventually it was done, in the '60s, and we tackled a lot of subjects probably even more exciting to the audience because they had not seen anything like that before, so we had that advantage. So, coming back to your main question again, that's one of the changes. Another change is that it was discovered at a point that news could make money, and a certain amount of hyping went into it, particularly local stations. But the upshot, I would say, is that entertainment values within the general scope of the news area are more prominent today than I think they were when I began in the business.

*What's the main thing that makes you a good producer? Is there any personal trait — anything that you think is the thing that makes you a successful producer?*
   I'm not sure that I am a successful producer. (laughs) I don't mean that in a kind of false modesty. What I mean is that I never finish anything without saying to myself, "My God, you could have done that a lot better. If you just had more talent or brains or time or whatever." There are a few broadcasts that I've walked away from and said, "I did a good job there. I really accomplished what I wanted to do and I'm very proud of it." But those broadcasts are few and far between.

*Now, what makes a good producer?*
   Well, I guess his abilities to do a lot of things we've been talking about. Somehow sniff out a good story, develop it, have good judgment in covering it. Pick the right people to help him, realize that he's involved in a team effort, try to work closely with and listen to the advice of his editor, have enough sense not to think only of the audience out there and whether they're going to like it or not, but to think whether *he* likes it, because if you start thinking about the audience you're thinking about millions and millions of minds and I find that's most distracting. If I like it, that's my guideline. If I think it's fairly good, that's my guideline.

*Is there any single thing you keep coming back to — any essential ideas in your documentaries?*
   Well, my problem is that I've been around the barn so many times that I keep looking for things to do that I haven't done before. I don't want to repeat, and for that reason I think I get myself into doing stories that might stretch my abilities beyond where they will stretch, or perhaps try to tackle something that I really don't know enough about to be able to present well. In other words, it's a little bit like trying to raise the bar for the high jumper — and I don't know how high you can raise the bar after awhile. But there's a search for something new, and as I said earlier, it's hard to find something that's not been done now. You don't find those brand-new ones too often. But, basically, if there's anything I look for it is

a small focus that is going to illustrate some universal truth of some kind or other, or what I consider to be a universal truth.

*What's the main reward in doing documentaries?*
The vacation that comes after doing one. (laughs) Well, the biggest reward that you can get is the kind of reward that you get in any other kind of occupation, which is, "I think I did a good job. I'm proud of what I did. I'm happy I did it." That's the biggest reward. I have received awards for shows that I don't think were all that great, and I have not received awards for shows that I really thought were exceptional, so I don't base it on that much. It all has to do with some inner process within me. I come to some conclusion about it. I'm either happy with it or not happy with it, or somewhere in between. However, I do, in general, think that the life of a journalist is a very interesting one, in comparison to some other professions, in that you're constantly dealing with new situations, new people, new experiences – every documentary is a new experience. You get around the world and you have a lot of time to think about what makes things tick. I wish I knew the answers, but (laughs) I do a lot of thinking about it.

*Were you a member of the "Murrow Is Not God" club at CBS? Do you remember anything about that?*
No. I knew Ed Murrow, and he narrated several of my documentaries. I had immense respect for him, found him interesting to talk to and found that his judgment was usually good. I never belonged to the "Murrow Is Not God" club, but then, I never thought Murrow was a god. I thought he was a hell of a good journalist – extremely good at what he did.

*What was it like to work with him when he was doing those . . . say, on those narrations? He was a beautiful narrator. He not only had a wonderful voice, but there is so much depth of expression in how he used it.*
Well, yeah. He narrated several of my radio documentaries and I wrote the scripts. He would make a few changes here and there. But I remember the end of one of those documentaries, I had a line – it had to do with a juvenile gang killing: "Who Killed Michael Farmer?" The last line had to do with "Why do all these things happen," and the last line was, "We permit them to." Well, I didn't think that was an outstanding line, but the way he said that sent a chill right up your back.

*So he made the line work.*
He made a lot of lines work.

*Roy Huggins*

A GOOD CONCEPT is one thing, but according to Roy Huggins, "It all depends on how well it's executed." As a writer, director and producer for twenty-five years, Huggins is known for the high quality of his execution. They key, he believes, is good story-telling—and a nice touch with humor. Huggins was ahead of his time with the wry antihero in "Maverick." "Yes," he agrees, "I always try to be ahead of the times. That may be one of my problems."

His problems center not around the quality of his work, but with his working and financial relationships. He has talked publicly about his disillusionment with the Hollywood establishment. Nevertheless, he has been successful. It takes two single-spaced pages simply to *list* Huggins's published work and produced films (as writer, producer and director). One of his five novels made the journey from serialization in the *Saturday Evening Post* to film to popular television series. That was "77 Sunset Strip."

At one time Huggins had "Rockford Files," "Baretta," and "City of Angels" all running as network series—the same time he was putting together a mini-series, "Captains and the Kings." All done without getting an ulcer, which is not bad for a man who was told he didn't have the "personality of a producer." In all, Huggins has produced more than a dozen series for television.

Huggins studied political theory at UCLA both as an undergraduate and as a graduate, which he admits has not been a great deal of help. If he were heading back to school as a young man today, he claims, he would study business administration—"I would like to learn how to beat the system."

*What was the hardest thing about producing a series in the '50s?*

Ah, in the '50s. It was so easy, gosh, I can't think of anything that was difficult about producing series in the '50s. That was the time when the actors hadn't yet realized that they could take over just by saying "I won't come in." Budgets were low, but they were acceptable to the network.

*What was the typical budget back then?*

I used to make "Maverick" for $60,000 for one hour, and sometimes for less. Today it would be over ten times that.

*What's the hardest thing about producing one today?*

Well, there are so many more people involved today. The networks then really were just finding themselves, you see. Today they have found themselves, and each network has a pretty good idea of the kind of image it wants—the look it wants, the kind of audience it's looking for—and so they are now very much involved in what a producer does.

*Can you give me a couple of examples?*

*Photo (facing page): Roy Huggins (right) directs cameras.*

Sure. They will take a very strong hand in casting, script and so on. In the various factors that make up a finished show, the network is apt to have a hand in all of them, either determining who is going to be used or at least being consulted.

*How did you get started in the TV business?*
I had become a screenwriter and then a screen director, and I decided that what I really wanted to do was to be a producer, so I became a producer — all of this at Columbia. Then they decided at Columbia that, as they put it, I didn't have the "personality" of a producer. Truly, the producer is the man that makes the film — not the writer, not the director. It's the producer, because he usually is involved deeply in the writing and also in what the director is going to do, by way of casting and the selection of a director and editor. So I decided I wanted to be a producer, and they made me a producer at Columbia; then after a few months they decided I didn't have the personality.

*Did they give you any specifics?*
No, they just said, "Roy, you don't have the personality of a producer," and I said, "Okay, why don't you let me go," and Columbia fired me.

*And that's how you got into television.*
That's right.

*You've proved them wrong.*
I'll tell you how thoroughly I proved them wrong. They fired me in 1955. In 1960, when I announced I was leaving Warner Bros., Columbia called me and asked if I would come over. I met with one of their vice-presidents, a man named Arthur Cramer, at the Brown Derby, I think it was, or Luci's, and they asked me to come back as a producer, only now they were willing to pay me, I think about five times as much as I was getting then.

*How much was that?*
They offered me $100,000 in salary, an expense account, and 50 percent of the profits on anything I produced — and this was a theatrical offer, not television. At that time the television department was separate and I wouldn't have been interested, anyway. This was the theatrical department at Columbia Pictures.

*What year was that?*
1960. And I said, "No," and the reason I said, "No," was because I had come to love television and I had come to love the freedom I had in television to do what I wanted to do without interference from anybody.

*Freedom?*
   Freedom to produce what I wanted to produce, cast whom I wanted to cast, and all the rest of it. Autonomy is the key word.

*It must have taken a little soul-searching, though, to turn that offer down.*
   It was easy. I love television. I loved television as long as it remained a place where I could do anything I wanted to do. It remained that way for a long time. At that time, in 1960, to make a movie you had to get one of fifteen to twenty top stars or you couldn't get the picture made, anyway, so the whole thing was a pain. Making films then was a big pain. You couldn't make a film then like, say — oh, I can't think of a good example — well, like *Rocky*. *Rocky* was a film that was made with a new nobody. I mean, whoever had heard of Sylvester Stallone? But we are in a new era now with films, where you can make a film called *Rocky* with someone new and make a hundred million dollars.

*What's the most productions you like to handle at one time?*
   Oh, three is the absolute outside. If you're handling more than three you're in trouble. You just can't give those productions the attention they require. You can delegate a lot, but you can't delegate too much or it won't be a, you know, "Joe Smith" production.

*What can one delegate?*
   You can delegate a lot of the actual producing of the show once you have gotten the script turned out and you've got the cast and selected the director. You can leave it alone now for awhile — all you have to do is watch dailies and see if they're making any profound errors. When they finish shooting, you can go back in, and you have to give a lot of time to the editing; but you can edit more than one show at once.

*Have you ever been in a situation where you had three going at once?*
   I think at one time I had "Rockford," "Baretta" and "City of Angels" all on the air and at the same time I was also doing a mini-series.

*What was that?*
   "Captains and the Kings."

*And you don't have an ulcer or anything?*
   No.

*It must be that you don't have a "producer's personality." (laughs)*
   I think that's it.

*I've seen some of those old "Bus Stop" shows. You were executive in charge of production on some of those.*

Yeah, I was executive in charge of television at 20th when I did those. I was doing "Bus Stop" because it was an anthology show. I enjoyed it a lot. But "Bus Stop" never made it in the ratings. I think it was because it was an anthology show, except that it pretended not to be, so that it was neither one nor the other.

*Can you explain what you mean by that?*
Well, I later did a show called "Kraft Suspense Theatre," which was a pure anthology, and it was a big success; but "Bus Stop" pretended to be a series. It had leading characters and so on, but they were not the ones we used. We always told stories about people who came into the bus stop, so that it was an anthology that wasn't really an anthology; it was as limited as an anthology and didn't have the quality of a series.

*How did you get ideas for series?*
Well, I'm fairly analytical, and my approach to television has always been quite analytical. Take "The Fugitive," for example. By saying, "How can I do a show that has all the elements of a Western but in a modern setting?" I realized, when I said it, that it would be almost impossible, because the essence of a Western is the total freedom of the people involved, especially of the protagonist. In the Western you don't expect the protagonist to have a family; I mean, a Western hero with a family is absurd. A Western hero with a background isn't very important either. He doesn't need a driver's license. He has no roots. He wanders on the next day. He has his adventure and gets on his horse and rides off. I'm talking about the classic Western. And I thought, "How do you get this kind of utter irresponsibility and freedom in a contemporary setting?" And I decided that the only way you could get it was that it would have to be that the protagonist was wanted by the law — that he had to act that way. He had to be a wanderer and a man without an identity, who refused to stay in one place. That's how I wrote "The Fugitive." So I don't stumble onto things like some people. I analyze my way into them.

*It seems to me, then, that it's very important to realize the story conventions — the conventions of the Western, the war story, etc. — in order to be able to tailor them into a different form.*
Yes. I had to know all the conventions of the Western in order to break them in "Maverick."

*In "Maverick" the guy's not very good with the gun; he's not very courageous either.*
No, he wasn't at all courageous, but he also wasn't the kind of a man who went out of his way to help his fellow man, which was typical of all Westerns. In the classic Western, if someone came up to the Western hero and said, "We need help," he would give it to them. If someone came

up to Maverick and told him, "We need help," he would tell them how to find the sheriff, and then avoid them after that.

*There's a strain of humor that runs through both "Maverick" and "The Rockford Files." There's a kind of irony or a little snideness there. Of course, you used actor James Garner in both those shows.*
    The concept came first, and then I discovered that Jim Garner could play it. He was under contract to Warners at the time. I used him in a very small part in a show and I discovered that he did have a great understanding of wry humor, and I grabbed him. But the concept came first.

*Do you have a favorite wry joke from "Maverick"?*
    No, because I really think the humor came out of a character, rather than out of a line or a situation.

*That's the kind of humor you're interested in.*
    Yes, because I think it's funnier.

*Give me an example.*
    I gave you one inadvertently. The pretty woman runs up to him and says, "Oh, sir, can you help me? I'm in trouble, can you help me?" And he says, "Well, no, I can't, but right across the street there, that's the sheriff's office; there's a man in there with a gun and a star and he's paid to help people, so why don't you go over there?" That got laughs because it was so unexpected. If someone came up to Maverick in a bar and said, "Maverick, there's a guy with a gun out in front, asking if you're in here," and Maverick says, "There is? By the way, do you have a back door?" All of those are character jokes; they're not funny jokes, they're funny lines.

*Did you have any continuing gags in "Rockford Files"?*
    Well, "Rockford," you know, was one of the most popular shows in this country for the two years that I did it. College campuses closed down on Sunday night at 7:00 because every college kid in the country was watching "Rockford." Yes, any lines about, "Well, I worry about my virtue. I don't want to lose my cunning and my deceit," and that kind of thing. That was a running kind of joke that people would use. That was an attitude that developed out of "Maverick"—a respect for the guy who admits that he's lazy, cowardly, and if he's forced to resort to some kind of skills, he feels that the most effective one is cunning or deceit.

*Do producers have to be self-starters?*
    I'm not sure they have to be any more. They used to be. I think they had to be, and the best ones still are. I mean, Norman Lear is a self-starter. Norman Lear decides what he wants to do and then does it; I used to decide what I wanted to do and then did it.

*How important is it to have the same production crew throughout the series?*
Oh, it helps, especially if you've got a good one together; then you know you're going to be able to make that show in six days, or seven, or whatever your schedule is. It makes their life pleasanter to know that they're on a show that's going to be on the air for a few years. They can settle down and relax. It's good for the people involved.

*And the same director?*
If you find a good one who'll stay with you, that's great. I had two directors with me on "Maverick" and I could always be pretty sure what they could do.

*Who were they?*
Leslie Martenson and Douglas Hayes.

*I would think if you used too many directors you would run into problems.*
Oh, yeah, Bud Boetticher changed the character completely in the early days of "Maverick," and I never used him again. He was a director who took the cowardly lines away from Maverick and gave them to another guy on the grounds that heroes didn't talk like that. I never used him again, but Garner went along. Garner let the cowardly lines be picked up by somebody else.

*How often do you get ideas from the network?*
Well, I used to get ideas from the network. "The Bold Ones"—the lawyer section of "The Bold Ones" was done at the request of the network. Herb Schlosser, who is president of NBC, called me up one day and said, "Roy, we want a lawyer show on the air. Will you do it?" And I said, "Hell, yes, I'd love to do a lawyer show." So I did a pilot, and it went on the air and became one of the shows on "The Bold Ones."

*"The Bold Ones" was a pretty sophisticated thing for American television, wouldn't you say?*
I think so. We dealt with extremely interesting and intricate subjects on "The Lawyers." For example, jury nullification—the concept of jury nullification of the law. Where it's very clear the law was violated and the jury still lets the defendant go because the jury doesn't agree with the law; that's the old American concept of jury nullification. But very few people know about it, and it's something the American people should know about; in other words, the judge may tell them the law, and he can tell them what their verdict *should* be, but he can't tell them what their verdict *must* be. A jury can decide to ignore the law.

*What year was this?*

This was in the '60s. I did the same thing on "Run for Your Life."

*Does most of your stuff have some social overtones?*
A lot of it — if it's contemporary. It's very difficult to have social overtones with a Western, for example, and I never tried it because those were usually moralistic and dull. I like to make social comments that are very specific.

*Why? Why specific?*
Because then they make sense — then they may have some impact. If you want to say that the CIA mentality is totally amoral, that's a very specific thing to say, and I've said that a half-dozen times on "Run for Your Life."

*That was long before the CIA came under public attack.*
Long before they got into trouble for being amoral; but I made at least six shows on "Run for Your Life" the theme of which was the CIA is amoral. They have no morality. Their morality is winning the game.

*How do you keep from being didactic?*
Tell a good story, and keep it honest, and always be the advocate for the other side. In other words, when Paul Brian got into a quarrel with a CIA man on that subject, I would let the CIA man answer it so devastatingly that Paul Brian would have a hard time coming up with an answer — but he would. Then it's not didactic. In other words, you become didactic only when one guy is right and the other is wrong. You have a drama when there's a conflict between two people and they're both right, but one may be just a little more right than the other. Then you have something.

*You speak of being a filmmaker. That's a kind of cherished title, isn't it?*
Well, no, I don't think so. I think it's just a simple way of describing what you do, if you do what I did. I determined what that film was going to be that I put on the air. I start with the story, which is usually mine — if it isn't mine it's something that I've found — and I supervise that script and frequently write it. Then I supervise the production and always supervise the editing closely. I work with the editors over their shoulders — drive them crazy — and do all kinds of things with that film. The film that is delivered to me at the end of production never looks like the film I put on the air. There is a huge difference. If you want to write a book about how films are made, write about what you can do in editing, because that's where films can be remade — the whole story can be retold.

*Can you give me an example of a time when something had to be dramatically changed?*

Yes. I once did a show with an actor, a good actor, and the director had given him all the wrong directions. The actor wasn't good enough to know it, so he kept doing things that were inappropriate.

*Such as . . . ?*

Oh, smiling at the wrong time, or looking like he thought he was God's gift to women in a scene in which you were supposed to like him and hoped that the girl liked him. And you knew damn well, the way he was looking at the girl, that she wouldn't like him because he looked like a guy who thought he was a cocksman. What the director was allowing him to do was wrong. Now, you can fix those things. The ways you fix them are manifold. You find moments when he was not doing that, because it was a different part of the scene, and you use that close-up where he wasn't expecting to have it used; or you shoot it over, and you go down and do it yourself. I'm a member of the Director's Guild. I was a director before I was a producer.

*So that's valuable.*

Yes, it's terribly valuable to know what you can do with film, and even to be able to go and shoot it over, which I've done many, many times. That's only part of it. My gosh, you can flop film, you can blow it up, you can run it backward.

*You can actually handle the film?*

Oh, well, I don't know, I don't handle it any more. I used to handle the film, but that's not important, because there's no reason why you would handle the film, because you're right there and you can say . . . in fact, you do use the brake. You're running the film and you put the brake on and you say, "There's the frame I want." So you are, you're running the machine, and there are no restrictions on that. I don't know if there are any restrictions on your actually sitting down and doing the editing yourself and splicing it and all the rest of it. I doubt if there are any because no one would do it, anyway.

*What do you look for in a film editor?*

A good storyteller. A man or woman who knows what the story is supposed to be and who these people are supposed to be and avoids all the film that doesn't say it, or that says it wrong. A story is told three times: once by the writer, once by the actors and the director, working together on the set, and then a third time by the editor. Each time you're doing the same thing, you're telling a story, and that story gets screwed up frequently on the set and has to be fixed again and edited. A bad editor will screw it up again even worse.

*Can you give me some examples of what bad editors have done to you?*

Bad editors have just simply missed all the story points and have told the wrong story, or told a different story. In the case that I was mentioning, the first cut I saw the hero was a schmuck, he was a conceited jerk. I can't tell you his name because I liked the actor and it turned out okay, but I had to reedit everything.

*You must have to trust something to the editor.*
Oh, you have to. A good editor will give you a very good first rough cut, and a good editor will continue to help you. A good editor, if he's good enough, you don't need to do anything with it; you just let him go the way you let a good writer go. I have worked with editors where I have never changed a thing they did. They're hard to find, though.

*What are your writing habits when you're writing for a series?*
Once I decide I have to do the writing myself, I go to work on it, and I just stay with it until I finish.

*How long does it take oftentimes?*
Not as long as it should. I have rewritten scripts — one-hour scripts I have rewritten in a weekend. And I mean completely rewritten so that my name was on the screen as the writer.

*Totally in a weekend?*
In a weekend. That's a one-hour script — sixty pages. You do thirty pages a day. At the end of a weekend you've got sixty pages. Most of the good screenwriters in Hollywood write very fast once they get started. They get up their energy, and they know what they want to say, and they want to say it before they forget it.

*That's after you sort of have a treatment.*
Oh, yes, you've got to know where you're going. If you don't know where you're going it could take six months.

*What's the longest and hardest single script you've had to write?*
Oh, let's see. I don't remember. I think, oh, it was probably a thing I did called "The Profane Comedy." It was a two-hour movie that was just giving me problems and that took awhile. It was a two-hour script, and it may have taken me a month to write it.

*What was there that bothered you about it?*
I don't know. Maybe there was something inherently wrong with it and that was what was the problem. The picture turned out all right; it got some very good reviews and did very well. But I had trouble with it.

*What are the advantages and disadvantages of working in a big studio?*

Well, that has changed over the years. The main advantage is that you have everything you need, or at least it used to be this way; everything you need is there for you. Now that's becoming less true. The big, big disadvantage is that they have a bookkeeping system which is absolutely unbeatable, so you end up getting nothing out of your ownership of the material that you've done, because their bookkeeping is so metaphysical and so elaborate that in a court you just can't prove that a major studio can be making a fortune on its television department but all of the individual producers are losing money. You can't prove it. There's something wrong there.

*How do they do that?*
I really don't know because I've never contested it, but I may one of these days.

*What do you think about the old black-and-white shows coming back? Does that give you a sort of warm feeling — your own shows and others?*
Oh, yeah, you mean like "Maverick." "Maverick" is on the air, I think, every day at least once or twice and maybe twice here in Los Angeles, and I love it. In fact, every now and then I'll see one and I'll look at it for awhile, and if it's one that I did I'll sit there and wonder how it came out, because I won't remember.

*How many shows do you figure you've done over the years — different series and also maybe the actual number of shows?*
Do you know, I have no idea? I have no idea. I've done a dozen series, I guess, and each one of them went a different length of time — several years, in some cases, and only one year in others. I really don't know. I would have to sit down and figure that one out.

*How long does it take to shoot a one-hour program in the year 1980?*
You can still do them in six days if you know what you're doing.

*And then what's the process of post-production — editing?*
Well, you can get them done in a week if you've got good editors, a good composer and a good crew — a good dubbing crew.

*How many people on an average crew on an hour production?*
I don't know. That's one of the other things that I have always delegated. Once I have chosen the director and had a discussion with him about the script and have chosen the actors and talked to them about it, I don't ever go on a set. The only time I go on a set is when I'm directing it myself.

*Do you ever think you really want to get more into directing?*

Well, I've directed a feature and several television shows, always with some success, but I've never liked it. The work is just too tough for me. I have flat feet, and you can't sit down when you're directing, because you just can't get that relaxed. And I don't like to get up at 5:00 in the morning; in fact, I go to bed at 5:00 in the morning. So directing would not be something that appeals to me. It takes a certain kind of guy to direct—someone who likes to interrelate with people and has, I guess, a lot more physical stamina than I have.

*I imagine a lot of producers that you started with have kind of dropped by the wayside. How have you managed to keep going?*
I guess by continuing to do shows that work. Up until this year I've had a show on the air every year for twenty-two years. In fact, I have one on now, but that's the end of it. "Rockford" was just cancelled. So for the first time I don't have a show on the air.

*So what's the future?*
I think now I'm going to start working in films because the whole situation is reversed from 1960 when I turned down that offer from Columbia. Now you have more freedom when you make films and much less freedom when you make television.

*What was '50s TV like? It was said that in the mid '50s the networks and people started talking about adults, got interested in adult demographics. What was it like in those early days in terms of audience?*
Well, I think the networks were always concerned with the number of people who were watching the shows, but in the early days it was not as critical as it is today. I don't think in the early days it affected what they earned from their shows as critically as it does today. Today the difference of one point makes a huge difference in their profit. I don't think in the early days it was quite that rigid, nor were they so sensitive to being beat out, but maybe I'm wrong. I used never to bother asking where my shows were that week because it never occurred to me to bother. I never cared whether they were number six or number fifteen in the list of shows that were most prominent because I knew that that wasn't too important, anyway. It depends on what night you're on, what hour you're on. I mean, if you're on at 7:00 you're not going to get as big an audience as you would if you were on at 9:00, because the number of people watching television rises between 7:00 and 9:00. So I never used to feel that numbers were a terribly important thing; but after a few years in television I realized that those numbers meant everything, especially the share, and I finally became interested, because it was like a score in a football game.

*Anything else?*

No. Violence in the early days was more common than it is today, and I never did use much violence. The people at Warner Bros. used to tell me to put in more fights and I would say, "No, you don't need a fight. Audiences don't give a damn about fights. They would rather see an interesting scene." I think I was wrong. I think audiences really like fights; but I didn't think so then, so I didn't use them.

*You were able to stand off the studio?*
Oh, absolutely; that's why I stayed in television. I never did anything I didn't want to do. In all the time I've been in television, the shows I did are the shows I wanted to do and the stories I wanted to do. That's why I stayed there instead of moving over to theatrical films.

*What was the toughest lesson for you to learn as a writer for television?*
I suppose being lean and economical in your storytelling and not overwriting scenes, although I'm just guessing. I'm not sure that's true. I really don't know.

*What about writing the commercial breaks in?*
I don't do that. I may be one of the only ones who doesn't, but I don't do that because it's absolutely silly. You break it where it breaks best. I don't want to build into one of my shows restrictions on how I can edit it, so I don't do that. All of the writers in town do it, and when they work for me I have to say, "By the way, please, no breaks. Just give me a sixty-page script. We'll break it when we edit." A good story can be broken anywhere.

*That's the key to a good story?*
That's the key. You don't need these artificial "What's going to happen next" breaks.

*What's been the most frustrating moment as a producer?*
Oh, seeing the control I have over my material slowly beginning to erode. That's been a little frustrating, and it has lead, I think, to my probably leaving television.

*Can you explain that a little further?*
Well, I already told you earlier that the networks are developing a sense of identity, each network being a little different from the other networks. And the networks are taking responsibility for what they put on the air. I'm not responsible for it; they are. So as the networks developed and became multi-multi-multi-million dollar profit organizations, they tended to become overstaffed. There is probably a law having to do with this, too. Parkinson's law, or some other ironclad law of television, where they keep adding to the people representing the

network who are supposed to have control over what goes on the network. Now those people have grown in number and grown in extraordinary titles, like Executive Producer, and so on. Some of them take their jobs very seriously and have actually said to me in recent years, "No, don't do that story. I don't like that story. I don't think that's a very good story." My reaction has always been to call the top man and say, "Get rid of this fellow," because I can't work with some guy who has no credentials, has never done any writing in his life, who will tell me what story is going to work and what won't work. Up until recently I've been able to do that. I doubt very much if I could do that any more. These people have gotten more and more powerful. I don't think I could get one of those guys taken off my show.

*Have you gotten anyone fired over the years?*
     Never fired, but taken off my show.

*What do the networks do? Do they have one person who more or less supervises?*
     Yes, he is supposed to be the network liaison man on your show. Some of them would actually come in and tell you how to do the script and how to rewrite the story. My reaction has always been, "Hey, get lost. I don't need you to tell me that. You have no credentials, you're talking to someone who's had very few failures on the air, and I don't intend to listen to you." I've been a little more polite than that, although not always. That became more and more common, and I finally just gave up on it and have really not tried to get another show on the air.

*Have you got any classic examples of scripts that these guys said didn't work, that you did and won an Emmy nomination or . . . ?*
     Yeah, there are all kinds of cases like that. On "Kraft Suspense Theatre" I was told that if I wouldn't listen to them, the series wasn't going to work and it was going to be my fault and it was going to be cancelled. It became a big, big hit. The same thing with "Run for Your Life": I was told that every script that I had worked on for "Run for Your Life" was a piece of shit, and "Run for Your Life" was a very big hit.

*I've heard that if you're in good with the network there's less chance that your show will get bounced for a special; there's less chance that you'll get a bad – or less desirable – hour on prime time.*
     Yeah, I think that's true. I have never tried to achieve that kind of relationship with the network because I've always felt it was too time-consuming. You had to spend so much time going to New York and associating socially with the people at the network and being a certain kind of fellow, which I can be, but I don't want to be, and so I never have. I've always avoided doing that.

*You sound a little bit of a maverick yourself.*
Oh, not really (laughs), but I do really know what I like to do and I
know what I don't like to do.

*You're analytically minded. What other qualities have you?*
Well, apparently I have an ability to tell a story that audiences like,
because I have written practically all the stories for all the series that
I've ever done; in fact, I've written so many of them I've used
pseudonyms. I've developed about twelve pseudonyms, because
otherwise my name would have been all over the damn thing and I didn't
want that.

*Give us some pseudonyms.*
Well, the one that's most common is John Thomas James — you've
probably seen that because it's all over the air. There are others — most of
them based on my kids. Anyway, I would say that has made it possible
for me to stay as long as I have and not to get involved socially with network people. I don't dislike the network people. They're all very interesting people. I just prefer to put my time other places and do other things.

*Was there any certain year that the networks suddenly seemed to take
greater hold?*
No, it crept up very gradually, but it has now reached the point
where every producer in town is ready to do battle over it. In fact, I'm
rather cool about it. I always tell my fellow producers that in a way you
can't blame the networks, because each one of them has developed an
individual look, and they know now what they're looking for, and they
are responsible to the FCC. All you can do is expect them to be intelligent
enough to know how to deal with the people they need.

*What is the look that you strive for?*
I just strive always to tell a story that the audience will want to stay
with, and that they will enjoy seeing, and that in a contemporary setting
will have something to say, or at least some information to give them or
some insight into something very specific. Mainly I try just to entertain
them, but to entertain them in a fresh way, and not just give them
something that they saw last night.

*How does one collect producer's fees?*
Well, my deal with the studio was that I would get paid X number of
dollars per episode, and it was pay or play. If for some reason the studio
allowed me to leave a show, they still had to pay me. That was written
into the contract.

*What other things should be written into a contract with the studio?*

Well, that's one of them; and I think another one is some kind of definition of their bookkeeping that's a bit more clear than the one we get, but I don't know whether they would do that. I'm not sure they would sign a contract with someone who wanted the facts about bookkeeping clearly spelled out.

*Do you collect money for residuals as well?*
On the stories I wrote, yes, but producers don't collect residuals.

*So that's kind of tough. Has there ever been a movement to get producer's residuals?*
Yes, there is a Producer's Guild which has that in mind, but they don't have a lot of strength.

*What would you like Roy Huggins' epitaph to say?*
Oh, I think that it would have something to do with the thing I just said to you. That for twenty-five years he told interesting stories on television — interesting and worthwhile stories. I think a lot of people might disagree with that, but I would like to feel that that's what I did. It is one of my egotistical hopes, that someday — for my children's sake, I'll be dead by that time — some scholar will come along, studying this period of television — this thirty-year period when television was something that everybody looked at — and would say that there was a producer named Roy Huggins who consistently delivered a very high level of storytelling. That's what I would like to have said about me, and the reason I think it might be said — the reason that I'm willing to be that egotistical, and that hopeful — is that I had the following experiences — because, as I've said to you, this is important. I've lived in this business. I've worked in this business in which nobody thinks the quality of storytelling matters. When you talk to a network man and say, "Well, that's a good concept, but it all depends on how well it's executed," he says, "No, it doesn't — it all depends on how good the concept is." Network people put their faith in concept rather than execution because they can understand a concept, but recognizing good or bad execution requires an expertise most of them don't have. They don't want to believe in quality of execution as a key factor. They want to believe that it's cast and concept, because they can take credit for cast and concept. They can say, "We're the ones who asked for Jim Garner. We approved Jim Garner. We said 'no' to so-and-so and 'yes' to him, and we liked that concept — we saw that that concept was going to work." That's the way they like to think, and that is the way they do, indeed, think. Here is my experience with this, because I've always believed that's not true: I did "Maverick" for two years, and I wrote or cowrote (with Douglas Hayes) the original story for almost every show. That means in two years' time I had written or cowritten fifty-two stories. And when I say I wrote the original story, I'm talking about some-

thing that ran on a tape machine that I had and was transcribed; it ran as long as the script. It covered everything, every move.

*You're saying you dictated it into a tape machine?*
I dictated these stories onto tape, and then they were typed up and given to the writers and the writers would put them in script form. What I was giving them were story treatments.

*Were you giving them dialogue and all?*
Much of the dialogue was there. I was then on salary at Warner Bros., and I quit, so "Maverick," after two years, was turned over to someone else. Now, in the first year, "Maverick" was in the top twelve. In the second year I won an Emmy, and it was always in the top six — sometimes five, sometimes six — but it averaged around six. Maybe it would drop to number seven. I'm talking about all the shows on that week. Only four or five were higher than "Maverick" every week, and they were shows like "Jack Benny" or "Ed Sullivan," the big hits, and they were always shows that were on later at night when there were more people watching. I left "Maverick" and it immediately fell out of the top ten, out of the top twenty and out of the top thirty. The year after I left it, the year it was done by somebody else, it was in the low 30s, and it declined the next year into the 40s and the next year into the 50s and it was cancelled. Henry Kaiser asked me one day, "What in the devil did you do that made the difference?" I told him it was too long a story and he really didn't want to hear it.

*Henry Kaiser?*
Henry Kaiser of Kaiser Aluminum was the sponsor of "Maverick" and he saw his show go to hell and finally cancelled it.
A few years later I was asked at Universal to do "Kraft Suspense Theatre" as a fill-in, out of which Kraft hoped to get a pilot, so they could get a series on the air. It was only supposed to go one year. So I agreed to do it. It had an average rating of about a forty-five share — it was a tremendously successful show — and then I left it, because I had agreed to do it for only one year. It was so successful they turned it over to somebody else, and it failed; the next year, with much lower ratings, they cancelled it.
Now jump a few years. I put a show "The Rockford Files" on the air, and in order to get Jim Garner I had to agree to give Meta Rosenberg, his former agent, executive producer credit. I was perfectly willing to do that because I had done shows in the past without any credit at all. I know one thing, that people in the industry know who's doing it. I didn't put my name on "Kraft Suspense Theatre," for instance, except my pseudonyms. Jim Garner had just done a series called "Nichols" that flopped so badly that NBC was scared to death. "Nichols" was cradled between two big hits

and they couldn't get anyone to watch it. The president of NBC said, "Roy, we're probably out of our minds after our experience with 'Nichols,' but we're going to buy 'Rockford' and by Christ, I hope it works." I said, "It will work. This is not 'Nichols'." It went on the air and in its first year — which is usually the toughest year for a series, as you know — it was always in the top twelve. Number twelve was its average position. At the end of that very successful year, Jim Garner and I agreed that I would have nothing more to do with "Rockford Files," that it would be taken over by Jim and Meta Rosenberg and the staff that I had brought with me. I stepped off "The Rockford Files," continuing to receive all of my fees, so it was not something that was bothering me too much. "The Rockford Files," in its next year, fell to thirty-second position. The rule is that a show that succeeds in its first season will do even better in its second, because it will pick up a new audience with the summer reruns. That's how it was on "Maverick," for example. But, no, the quality of "Rockford" had changed so that it dropped and it was thirty-two, and the following year it was forty something, and the year after that fifty something. It's very unusual for a producer to have a history like that, where he does a show that is successful for a year or two and then he leaves it to someone else. I have done it three times, so I'm satisfied that quality of execution does make a difference.

*Agnes Nixon*

For over twenty years, people have been glad to "tune in tomorrow" for Agnes Nixon's soaps. Soon after she was born Aggie Eckhart in Chicago, her parents separated, so she and her mother went back to live in Tennessee. There she grew up in an Irish Catholic household with her mother, grandmother and four maiden aunts. "Now listen," she says, "that's going to make a writer out of somebody."

Nixon studied speech at Northwestern University, but after comparing herself to classmates like Charlton Heston and Patricia Neal, she decided to write, rather than act. Her father offered her a job in his business—he manufactured burial garments—but instead Nixon went to work for Irna Phillips, a pioneer of the soap opera genre. After six months with Phillips, Nixon sought her fortune in New York. Her first writing jobs were with "Studio One" and "Robert Montgomery Presents." She also worked long-distance with Phillips by mail and phone, which led to her being hired as head writer for "The Guiding Light."

Over the years Agnes Nixon has brought a fine edge to her soap opera characters by superior plotting and storytelling. She helped redesign "Another World" when it suffered in the ratings; she created "Search for Tomorrow," "One Life to Live," and "All My Children." She was a pioneer in using the soap opera genre to explore social problems such as venereal disease, child abuse, and soldiers missing in action.

She and her husband, Bob, produced "All My Children" through their own production company, Creative Horizons, and sold it to ABC in 1975. More recently, she produced "The Manions of America," a mini-series, and "Loving," a prime-time "soap."

Ms. Nixon was the first woman to receive the prestigious Trustees Award from the National Academy of Television Arts and Sciences. She is the mother of three daughters.

*How many years have you been associated with soap operas?*

Well, I've been associated with some show that was on every day, five days a week, fifty-two weeks a year, for twenty-four years.

*You would think one would burn out because it's so demanding. What's kept you fresh and going?*

One has to say, first of all, that it's an ensemble effort. The seminal ideas usually come from me, in terms of the long-term story, but after that there are writers working with me, in addition to the actors who create these characters on the air, and they, in turn, cause ideas in one's head in watching them.

*So they "write" the script, too, in a way.*

They don't write the script, but they will add a dimension or an interpretation to their character which even I didn't see was there, and that will help me to find a new avenue for that story.

*Can you give me an example of that?*

One example is in the first long-term projection of "All My Children," which was ten years old January 4th (1980). Nick Davis was to die at the end of six months, but Larry Keith brought so much to the part of Nick Davis that I couldn't possibly have killed him off. Susan Lucci, who plays Erica, is always giving me new ideas from what she does on the air.

*What sort of person makes a good soap opera actor or actress?*

I don't think it's any one sort of person, except he or she must be very professional. I think it's the hardest job in entertainment — not just in television — because it is five days a week, fifty-two weeks a year, and every day is opening night. We do 260 originals a year, an hour a day, and nighttime does twenty-three originals at the most — of any given program, I mean. So I think it requires tremendous professionalism and dedication, plus being a quick study.

*How quick is "quick"?*

A given actor is not on every day, but many are on three times a week, and they have to learn a whole hour's show. That means they do their homework, study their lines, the night before, and they come in the next morning knowing them.

*Do you have a favorite example of a catastrophe on live TV?*

There are two that are very good. One of them was on "As the World Turns." There was a scene in the Hughes's living room in which everyone was sitting around the fire and it was snowing outside — we saw snow falling outside the window — and then Grandpa Hughes had to go out for something. He went to the closet to get his coat and it was snowing in the closet. Another one was when an actor was playing a doctor and a nurse came up and said, "Doctor, the patient in 702 is very upset. She wants to see you," and he said, "I don't see why she should be upset. I just delivered her a seven-foot baby boy."

*Soap operas are moving out of the confines of the studio. That seems to be quite a change.*

Yes, we are doing a lot of location shooting now, and it's really very challenging and very exciting.

*Were you the first to do that?*

Soaps have been doing many locations for a long time, but I guess the biggest one was on "All My Children," two years ago last June, when we did a whole week's location on St. Croix. It was Erica and Tom's honeymoon, and I had written all the scenes that we were going to tape, and we incorporated those over a three-week period on the show. Last February we did location shooting in Connecticut that aired for three weeks. But we don't suddenly do some "location" story. We find some point in the story in which it will be interesting to go on location, which will enhance the story.

*You did a thing at Studio 54.*
Oh yes, we called it "Studio 45." We didn't go to Studio 54. We were at a theater, which we rented, but it *was* fun. I never knew until that moment that there were people who are professional "look-alikes." That's their profession. There is an Elizabeth Taylor "look-alike," a Barbra Streisand "look-alike," and so on. They get billed as that on the credits.

*Any unique problems that had to do with writing for an on-location soap?*
It is a unique problem (laughs) in that the little screen eats up an hour's show a day, and when we go on location, that's out of sequence, so it means that while they're doing scenes on location, they are also doing scenes in the studio, and it becomes really movie technique. When we are writing these scripts – plotting the scripts and then writing them – we have to make sure that we don't have someone in a location scene when they're supposed to be in a studio scene. It can become mind-boggling, but it all gets done.

*What kind of humor works in the soap opera? You're said to like humor.*
Well, I do. I can't speak for soap operas in general, but I do think that we have a lot of humor – of the Saroyanesque human comedy variety rather than ribald. As an example, when Tom found out that Erica had been taking birth control pills (although she told him she wanted to have a baby) and he was furious, Erica went to see his good friend, who is a priest, and said, "Well, I didn't want to get pregnant before my disco gets started. After all, when Tom started his restaurant he wouldn't have wanted to be pregnant." A line like that wouldn't be funny to an audience unless they're tuned in to the Erica character. For another example, the audience knows very well that Phoebe Tyler, who is the grande dame of main line, is being conned by Professor Langley Wallingford, who's real name is Lennie Wloseck, and that's a running gag, since the audience wants to see Phoebe get her comeuppance.

*What's the importance of recapitulation to the soap opera?*
Well, I think it gets less and less important as time goes by and competition increases. We try to do it within the context of ongoing stories. For instance, when Chuck went to a lawyer to make out a will for his son, the lawyer said, "That's very good. You're a very young man and not many young men think about making wills," and Chuck said, "Well, I probably wouldn't have thought about it, except my parents didn't expect to die so young and they were killed in a plane crash."

*How does a pilot for a soap evolve? Do you actually do pilots as such?*

No, I never have. Daytime is quite different from nighttime, and I don't think there are many pilots for daytime. Some shows, yes, but not serials.

*How does a program evolve?*

I can only tell you how I evolved. I got a job with Irna Phillips three days after I graduated from Northwestern. I wrote for her for eight months, came to New York, wrote for "The Golden Age of Television," and a year later got married. "The Golden Age" only lasted a few years, and Procter & Gamble asked me about a year later to come back and work for them, with Irna. I did "As the World Turns" and "Guiding Light"; then there was a show called "Another World," which was about to be canceled by NBC, also a P&G show, and they asked me to take it over. It became very successful, and on the basis of that track record, ABC asked me to do a show for them. That was twelve years ago, and it was "One Life to Live." A year and a half later I created "All My Children."

*How did you bring "Another World" up in the ratings? What were the things you incorporated into the format?*

Humor and some outrageous characters, plus a good ethnic mix of characters. One comic character was Lahoma Vane, a small-time beauty contestant. Once she was Miss Citrus Fruit and another time Miss Black-eyed Pea. We also had a lot of melodrama and a lot of excitement and humor, but it was also just a bit more earthy, I guess.

*How was that greeted at the time by the networks? Did they think it was going to work, or what did the industry seem to think of this?*

Since the alternative was to cancel, I was in a good position to say, "Let's try it."

*Soaps are for men as well as for women. When did it change so the male audience was a little more incorporated? Is it harder to include both men and women?*

I've never consciously tried to include men, so I can't tell you when it started. Since "Children" has been on, I've gotten an enormous amount of mail from men, and I think a lot of them are from colleges — professors who have become hooked because of their students.

*What sort of things do they write?*

Generally they are not as critical. We had a letter from a professor at MIT who said Erica was the asp he would like to have in his bosom. Then we had a letter from a man who said, "Okay, you win. I come home every day and my wife won't give me my lunch until she watches her program and I had to watch it because I had no choice." And then he said, "Now,

I'm hooked. I can't stand it. What's going to happen to so-and-so?" At the hotel in New York where I stay, the night clerk is a fan, and when I see him he says, "Oh, I can't stand it—what's going to happen?" If they're available and they're watching, men get hooked as easily as women.

*Why do you think women are a tougher audience—if that's the correct word?*
I don't think they're tougher, but if one must be at home more, with children, and is therefore a captive audience with a more isolated life, one tends to have a more proprietary attitude toward the characters. It is more than entertainment for them.

*How closely do people in the soap industry watch the competition?*
Well, I try to monitor the competition about once a week. By the competition I mean the other top shows—not every show on the air, but the ones that are getting good ratings. I don't want to do the same stories that they're doing.

*Has that ever happened to you, accidentally?*
No. It's happened that I've planned one and saw that someone else was doing it and so I changed it.

*Is there any single character in any of your soaps that has really been Agnes Nixon?*
Well, I've heard it said a writer's mind is a sieve through which experiences go and there is no person taken whole-cloth, and I agree. You start with the germ of an idea from something one has experienced oneself or one has seen someone else experience, or heard or read—as I read in *The New York Times'* magazine section about "little ladies of the night" and that story has been going on for four years now. It was about the Minnesota Strip in New York and it was, of course, about runaway girls—teenage prostitution. As I try to stay current and contemporary, we started the story of Donna Beck, who ran away from her incestuous father and came to New York and had a black pimp. Today we still have Donna Beck, completely rehabilitated. It was not till two years after that that a network finally put on a nighttime movie called *Little Ladies of the Night*.

*So is it safe to say that the daytime is really the cutting edge in terms of breaking down barriers?*
I definitely think so, because of two factors. First, the time element—we can do it faster. Nighttime is planning it a year ahead. We can plan a story and have it on the air in ten weeks. The other factor is that we have 260 episodes a year. We did an eight-month story on child abuse and, strangely enough, we were able to make the child abuser a

sympathetic character. I don't believe it could have been done as effectively at night because they have such limited time. We developed it day after day after day, saying to the audience, "These people are sick. They need help — not punitive measures." We said, in effect, "There but for the grace of God go you." Now you must understand that we didn't do just an eight-month story on nothing but child abuse. It was sandwiched in carefully with very high-intensity stories, until that child abuse story itself got to a high-intensity point. The very form and structure of the serial can be done in a fashion so that the audience can be hooked on one thing and then kind of force-fed another until it has its own momentum.

*So you really believe in a sort of social orientation — causes, etc. — in terms of the soap?*
    I feel that we have to have that or we're a rip-off.

*What was your proudest cause?*
    Child abuse. We researched it at great length with the group here in Philadelphia, which is called CAPE — Child and Parental Emergencies (on the show we called the same kind of group, COPE — Child or Parental Emergencies). I read Dr. Vincent Santana's book *Somewhere a Child Is Crying*, and the book *The Throwaway Children*. It took me a long time before I could get into this; in fact, it took me three years, because I'm hooked on kids myself and I just felt that these people were animals. We have a psychiatrist who is a consultant on our show, who is also a dear friend of ours, and she said, "You've really got to do this. You've got to face up to it." So I did, and she and I did this research with CAPE in Philadelphia, and someone had the idea that maybe we could have other cities also have these volunteer groups like CAPE to run a ribbon a number of times over a period of eight months.

*Did you say "run a ribbon"?*
    Yes, at the bottom of the screen: "If you would like to contact the volunteer group in your community, call so-and-so." The story would dramatize a volunteer group saying, "Your identity will be kept very inviolate, etc. etc." The CAPE group here called me and said, "We're overcome. We're inundated with calls." One child at home went to the group therapy session and then became a volunteer herself. This happened in many large cities. We did the same thing with drugs and with venereal disease. Kids wrote in for information about it, and then they could contact the communicable disease center in Atlanta for information about setting up their own hot lines. Those were all very successful, too, but personally, the child abuse sequence was to me the most rewarding.

*What was the touchiest or the hardest subject for you to deal with, from the standpoint of social mores?*

You would think probably that VD was, but I don't think so in terms of "touchy." In terms of difficult," child abuse was, because you had a twofold job. You had to reach the nonabusers and the abusers. You had to say clearly to the nonabusers, "These people need help, not punitive measures." Don't just say they have to be thrown into jail, which is what I used to say, because there's not enough jails to hold them. You have to say to the abusers, "Don't be afraid to admit your problem. You're going to be given help, not punitive measures," and you had to do all that within one program and also make it interesting. A tall order!

*The soap opera is in a sense your family. Do you take things personally sometimes that happen in the plot? Do you really get so wrapped up that this becomes a very personal thing?*
    I think all writers are of necessity often crazy (laughs) — schizophrenically crazy. My husband says he knows a script is good if I cry when I write it and cry when I watch it. At times I have to be both the viewer and the critic — and the creator. I have to be all those things and that is schizophrenic in a sense, but healthily so.

*Define for me, if you would, the different writing statuses in the soap opera field.*
    I don't think anyone could ever become a head writer without first being an associate writer. First, you have to be a writer. Then you have to be a writer who wants to write the spoken word and pictures; then, as an associate writer, to be able to write characters who have already been created, and write to those characters, follow an outline and realize that within that form there are still areas for creativity; but they must meet today's outline demands because tomorrow's outline has been written and some other associate writer will be doing that one.

*What transfer did you find from your creative writing field? What sort of lessons did you get? You studied under Lew Sarette.*
    Lew Sarette and Alvina Krause. Lew Sarette was a writer, and Alvina Krause taught acting, and the acting was just as helpful, if not more so, to me, because of Alvina Krause, who made one go back. I played the part, I remember, of a fifty-year-old spinster in a play called *Drama at Innish,* and I had to tell her that woman's life from the time she was born. It was very helpful in creating that whole understanding of what I now call the "subtext," which is the hidden persuader and motivator we all have.

*Did you write poetry ever?*
    No, I love poetry but I've never written it. My favorite reading is biographies and autobiographies. It's the texture of life. Our shows are from character; all the action comes from character. Characterization is

the most important thing. If you have a good character, a good solid character, then the sky is the limit. I don't mean in the terms of outlandish things, but it's just that the interaction of believable characters is life — the stuff of real drama.

*You're a Southerner. There's a whole thing in the South about Southern storytelling. Did you grow up with that?*
Yes, I did. I lived it. I didn't know at the time that I was growing up with it, of course. I think being from the South helped, and I think I have a certain outlook because of that. My outlook is also affected by the fact that my parents were separated when I was three months old and my mother went back to Tennessee — I was born in Chicago — and I grew up in an Irish Catholic household with my mother, my grandmother and four maiden aunts. Now, listen, *that's* going to make a writer out of somebody.

*Could you write a soap that you couldn't locate — a certain place or locale?*
No. I have to know where it is; I have to see it. I have to know the people, and it just has to have roots.

*Can you give me an example of how these roots affect your writing?*
Well, I'm very Irish as well as being Southern. I think that I am more Irish, even, than Southern. I think being Southern was an overlay. I came from a very, very Irish family, in terms of roots, and being Catholic in the South, we were extremely discriminated against in that time. In fact, it was so much that I didn't even know I was discriminated against because the church and everyone just sort of gathered round us. It wasn't until I was in high school — I went to a parochial school — that I realized this thing. In the meantime, I had been exposed to the entire oral tradition of the Irish, and it was a wonderful thing. My mother was the youngest of twelve children who spanned a twenty-four-year period. My grandmother married at sixteen a man twenty years older and she had a child every two years for twenty-four years. She was a very old lady and she remembered when Lincoln was shot. I sat on a footstool and listened to her stories.

*What is the thing that makes you exceptional?*
I don't know that I am exceptional, but I do enjoy my work. It's a lot of hard work, but when I know I've done a good story, it's thrilling. I'm not setting myself up to be Kay Boyle or Joyce Carol Oates, but it's a rewarding thing when I get letters from people saying, "You made me go home," "I was on drugs and I got off them," or from someone who was made to go to her doctor for a pap smear test and found that she had uterine cancer and said, "You saved my life." That's a reward in terms of

social service, I think. But I also, all by myself, writing a script, I get a charge out of it when I feel that it's good.

*Do network bureaus of standards and practices work closely with soaps, or do they let you go pretty much your own way?*
    Well, they have somebody on every day, watching every show — reading every script. But we have very little interference. I mean, we know what we can do, and I would hope that before someone would have to tell us that we were in bad taste that we would know it ourselves.

*So they never affect things?*
    Oh yes, there have been questions — in advance. The big thing is they never want the bad guys to be rewarded. That's understandable. We have little kids watching. I was concerned about this when I decided to do the teenage prostitution thing, and I knew from research that 95 percent of the pimps in New York City were black. I wanted to do it truthfully but I was concerned, not about the black viewers objecting to this, but any young black boy in the ghetto who would say, "Hey man, that's what I want to do when I grow up." We are a totally integrated show, and one of the stars on the show is John Danelle, who is black, and who plays Frank Grant. I called him at the time and said, "What do you think about this? Do you think this black pimp will become a hero figure?" And he said, "Well, not if you let me beat him up in the end. I've got my black belt in karate," and that was indeed what we did. Now we got a lot of letters in protest from Southern ladies, who said when we had the young white girls in bed with a black pimp they didn't like that a lot, and we had some black viewers who were furious. "There you go again — always making the black person the bad guy." But if you're going to have 10 or 11 million people viewing a day, ten letters like that is about par for the course, and I think it came out pretty well with Dr. Frank Grant, who is black, at the end having the black pimp groveling. That is what Standards and Practices is concerned about.

*How many people does the average soap employ?*
    There are half-hours and hours. For an hour show we have about thirty-six guaranteed performers — probably two hundred people, including the larger behind-the-scenes number.

*What are the costs of an hour of soap opera running these days? Soaps tend to be cheaper than other programs, particularly prime time.*
    I honestly don't know, because my husband and I produced the show for five years and then we sold it to ABC. It's been five years since then, and it's gone to an hour. One of the reasons we sold it was so we wouldn't have to be worried about all of those aspects of it. I just know that it's very profitable for the networks. Of course, now with all the locations

we're doing it's costing a great deal more suddenly, but still, nothing compared to nighttime. The networks will certainly readily say that we support a lot of the nighttime.

*What was the hardest lesson for you to learn about soaps when you were a fledgling?*
    I think I learned it so young that it wasn't hard. I came right out of college and I really don't have any memories of that, honestly. It's always hard — I'm not saying it's easy — but the hardest lesson, I guess, is self-discipline.

*Let's talk about your writing schedule. How long does it take you to write something, and how far in advance do you work?*
    Well, I work in various areas. I just finished a year story projection, which is like a novelette of everything that's going to happen in nine different plots — stories. Then we do the daily outlines of what's going to happen in each episode, and that goes out to the associate writers. I also write some of the episodes. From the associate writers the script comes back and that is edited; so you see we are in many time frames simultaneously. A year for a long-term outline; eight weeks ahead in an outline — daily outline; the script comes back about two to three weeks later; we keep production three weeks ahead of the script; and then we're a week on tape.

*What other techniques do you use to keep people coming back?*
    Well, it's just a sort of "tune in tomorrow" syndrome. You try to make them laugh, make them cry and make them wait. There's no particular technique; you try to tell an interesting story and try to take it to a point each day that will be suspenseful.

*Soaps have a lot of plots going at once.*
    We have nine plots going, five major and four minor. This is necessitated in an hour's show. We have about thirty guaranteed players, and it gets difficult at vacation time, since each gets two weeks vacation and most get three or four. That means there's not a week goes by that somebody is not on vacation, so we have to juggle things.

*Do you ever worry about running out of contemporary subjects?*
    No, not really. I'm not a cockeyed optimist about it, and I know that it could happen, but as long as there are people — and people are interesting, people are stranger than anybody — I just think that there will always be something new. Actually, if you're interested in people and interested in their lives, you'll find that there'll always be something. There's nothing really new under the sun; it's just a new person involved in a situation which gives it a little different twist.

*Do people feel defensive around you — for fear you might be using them for material?*
Just the opposite. "Have I got a story for you!" (laughs)

*Give me an example.*
Oh, that's all — just, "I've got a story for you. Just hear my story and write it up." They think if they give me this wonderful idea of theirs, it would be duck soup for me for the rest of the way.

*One final question: What was the hardest thing about producing "The Manions"?*
Coming from daytime as I did, I guess it was having to tell a story in just six hours. The storytelling is different; it has an end; it is a totally different form. Then too, the filming technique was so different, with daily "rushes" — one scene, ten different angles. That's quite different from videotape, where you take a look at it and if it isn't right, you do it over. The film process is so much slower. I found that a little hard. Daytime does 260 series a year, so I'm used to a more prolific pace.

*How did "The Manions" get started?*
I gave the network a twelve-page synopsis of the idea and they said just do it. I could have produced it myself, but as a professional I didn't understand film that much. I think the true mark of a professional is to know one's experience and lack thereof.

*"The Manions" was, it seems, your "roots."*
I had grown up hearing stories from my grandmother. She was the next to youngest. My great-grandparents came over at the time of the great potato famine and were storytellers, and it was always an interest. I had an affinity and it was my roots. I read and did research for five years before the story crystallized in my eyes.

*Earl Hamner, Jr.*

EARL HAMNER HAS MADE GOOD USE OF his experiences growing up in Schulyer, Virginia. First, he wrote *Spencer's Mountain*, a novel which became a movie starring Henry Fonda. Then, "The Home-coming: A Christmas Story" brought to American television the rich interrelationships that were continued on television in "The Waltons." Getting that program accepted on the network was not easy, but through the intervention of CBS executive William S. Paley, it became a long-running, popular series.

However, Hamner didn't break into television with "The Waltons." He began by writing for Rod Serling's "Twilight Zone." And curiously enough, Serling used to hold the very same position at WLWT in Cincinnati that Hamner had held before going to New York to write *Spencer's Mountain*.

Hamner is now producing "Falcon Crest," which is listed as one of the top ten shows of 1984. He is eager to continue to write and pro-duce for the successful series he has created; that way, he says, "You can protect your creation."

*You created "The Waltons." What does "create" mean, exactly?*

It was a term that was devised by the Writer's Guild of America to describe the person who thought up the concept of the show. "Created by" means that you came to the network with a concept, characters, time period, a locale, a situation and a challenging kind of overall concept. It also means that you are entitled to certain royalties.

*In some series we don't see the term "creator" — that's because it's a group effort?*

It may have been that it was a group effort, or it may have been that the idea was so bad that the creator didn't want his name on it.

*What rights do you, as creator, reserve over production?*

It varies. It depends on what kind of contract you can get with the production company or the network. I think it varies with almost every television show, but usually it's to the production's advantage if the person who created it remains with it. I have done this with "The Waltons" for these eight years. Usually the person who creates a series has the best kind of fix on the characters: where you want the show to go, how you want the people to grow, the direction that you want to carry it in.

*It was an uphill battle, I understand, to get "The Waltons" on the air at first.*

Well, there were some problems. In the first place, the network wasn't sure that there were enough stories about the people. Freddie Silverman was head of CBS at that time, and he asked me to write some sample story ideas. I did and I was able to assure him that we had a wealth of story material. At that time we were opposite "Flip Wilson" and

"Mod Squad," both of which were very highly rated shows, and in the beginning I think we were near the bottom of the Nielsen ratings – very, very, very low, but the chairman of the board, Mr. Paley, liked the series. He said, "We've been taking from the bottom of the barrel too long. It's time we put something back." He recognized the quality of what we were trying to say and the values that we had in the show. Consequently, instead of being yanked like so many shows are, without even being given a fair shake, we stayed on for the entire first season. Ordinarily a show that is rated that low is cancelled, but the network took an ad which said: "This show is too beautiful to last," or words to that effect. Also, the television critics saw what we were trying to do – that it was a unique kind of thing. The television press got behind it, and then gradually the audience learned about the show by word of mouth. They warmed to it, and by the end of the first season we were number one in the ratings.

*"The Waltons" has a certain serial quality. What sorts of added complexities are there – there must be a lot of them – in dealing with a program that has that kind of continuity?*
     I think of the series as a novel. Each of the episodes is a chapter in a continuing novel. I've been with the show for the full run, so I'm sort of the repository of the history of what has gone on in the past, the growth of the characters. That keeps the events from repeating. But, also inherent is growth and change, so the characters are constantly changing as time goes by. We are given new challenges by their growth. For instance, when we started, the show was in 1933, and John-Boy was an aspiring writer. We followed his career through his graduation from high school to his going to college, to his being drafted, to the publication of his first book. At about that point Richard Thomas left the show, so we were left with no actor, but we did have the John-Boy character. We kept John-Boy alive offscreen for a couple of years – the sixth season and the seventh season – and in our eighth season we recast the character of John-Boy. He comes back, having been shot down when he was observing in a bomber as a member of *Stars and Stripes*.

*Was there much deliberation on your part whether to bring him back or not?*
     Well, that came about because Michael Learned, who played Olivia, the mother, was only with us for ten episodes and we had to explain her absence. Because of the kind of character she is, we felt the only reason she would leave the family would be if someone else in the family needed her. So we created the situation where John-Boy had been shot down and was in a hospital in Washington. When Olivia left it was supposedly to take care of John-Boy and to stay with him.

*What's the hardest part about writing a program like "The Waltons"?*

I would say for a professional writer it's catching up on all the past history. Most of the writers who have done the best shows have stayed with us. We use a small group of writers, mostly people who have been with us all along. They know what happened in the past and how it affects the particular episode they are writing. Most professional writers can grasp the basic situation in the usual television show, but there are special problems with this one. We deal in human relationships — people relating to each other, people sacrificing for each other — and there is a great deal of character development. It's most important that the writer grasp the real character of that person, and also that he manage to write the character the way he exists at this very moment — not five years ago — because of the changes time has brought.

*One of the things that would seem to me to be hard to do is to keep it sensitive without becoming overly sentimental.*

What we attempted to do was to create full-blooded, full-bodied people. None of them is a perfect character. Olivia was extreme in her views of the Baptist Church. Grandma is almost a bigot. John, as opposed to the father in "Father Knows Best," never really knows best. He feels his way along and he does what he thinks is best. Sometimes it isn't the right thing. The problem for the writer who doesn't know the show that well is that he feels that the people have got to be good all the time. The danger is that these people are already *so* good that if you write them nice, then they come off boring and saccharine. The secret then is to toughen them up, to go away from what is expected.

As an example, we once did a show where a book salesman came to town, and instead of sending the money he got back to the book company he was putting it in his pocket. The reason he was doing it was to buy a Christmas present, which was a doll, like one that Elizabeth had. There was a scene at the end of the show where Elizabeth stands holding the doll and the man departs without the money for the Christmas present for his daughter. Someone who didn't know the show might say, "Oh, that sweet little girl — she's going to give him the doll for his own child," but she didn't do it. That was an example of pulling away from the expected to keep the characters tough.

Also, in language we can cut down on the niceness, which keeps them believable. We had Olivia say one time — this was during the Depression — "Damn this depression." This is a startling thing for a devout woman to say, but it just happened that it came at a time when the Depression had pretty much defeated them.

Another way to keep the people in touch is to confront them with a tough situation. The villain in "The Waltons" was the Depression itself. People with sort of frontier values were trying to survive at a time that was most difficult, so they had a formidable adversary. Then they went from the Depression directly into the threat of World War II. Now in this eighth season we are in the year 1944, and the last show this year will deal with D-Day. I just saw an episode this morning that had to do with the extermination of Jews in Germany. We were able to dramatize that by bringing the young Jewish soldier to Walton's Mountain, where he gets news that his grandfather has been murdered. What we try to do is to reflect — the way "Upstairs, Downstairs" did, the way a mirror reflects — some social change that's taking place at that time. We were doing it before "Upstairs, Downstairs." I think that's one of the things that's kept "The Waltons" alive and meaningful. We are always forty years behind the times, and from that point of view we can go back and examine an historical event. We did the Hindenberg, we did book burning. Recently, we did an episode on rape.

*I have a question on that. I've followed the show some over the years, and I was a little surprised that Mrs. Walton took on the sheriff the way she did in that episode. She's changed a lot.*

Well, yes, she's changed. She has become more modern in her attitude. There was a time when she would have said, "Well, I'm just a housewife and I'll let my husband take care of it," but over the years she's moved out of the housewife role to become a more liberated woman. I think her husband wants her liberated, and also I think that having seen the children grow up and having graduated from high school, in a sense, she has become more schooled and exposed to more ideas. That particular scene with the sheriff last night — we did it to let her be the spokesperson for every woman who has been threatened by a rapist to express the point of view that women often don't have a chance to say.

*That gets us into sort of social action. Do you think the Waltons have turned more toward social action?*

Our aim is still to entertain, but whenever we have an opportunity to make a comment on some social situation we certainly do. I think it was in the fourth season, we did a show about a young musician who died and how one might accept death, and that episode was requested by many people representing organizations who deal with the dying — to help people face death. There was one episode we did on drugs. After that episode we had some letters from young people who were into drugs, who said the show had helped them get a hold of their lives and they had gone back to the family they had run away from. I don't think our intent is to give a message, but if there is a statement that we can make and it's not out of character to the people, then we make that statement as best we can.

*It has to have a context rather than just kind of hit you over the head.*

That's exactly it. We don't get all together and say, "Let's do a show about old people — the meaning of elderly people in society." We get together and say, "Let's do a show about Grandma or Grandpa or an older person — wouldn't it be fun if . . ." But because of the values that these people have, a message does somehow come through, even though it may be as basic as, "Elderly people can contribute to our society — elderly people should not be shunted off into rest homes."

*"The Waltons" grew out of "The Homecoming." What was the biggest change from "The Homecoming" to the series?*
    Not that much, really. "The Homecoming" was a two-hour show, and for a series we brought it down to one hour. We made some cast changes. Edgar Bergen played the grandfather in "The Homecoming," Will Geer played him in the series. Patricia Neal played the mother in "The Homecoming" and Michael Learned played her in the series. We also recast the two old ladies who make "the recipe." These were New York actresses, and we needed someone who lived in California. We shot "The Homecoming" on location in Jackson Hole, Wyoming, and it passed very well for Virginia in the winter. We didn't shoot toward the Grand Tetons. We shot toward the lower, less impressive mountains, which are more like the Blue Ridge. We filmed "The Homecoming" on location, but we do the series on the back lot here at the Burbank Studios. Basically, the format remains the same. That's my voice in the beginning. We retained that, and we retained the basic structures of the special, then my doing the closing narration and then going back to the longshot of the house at night with the voices saying "goodnight." Basically, the changes were not that great. It was more of an accommodation to episodic television.

*Of course, characters come and go.*
    I would say the main change has been a constant maturing. When we started, Elizabeth, the youngest girl, was six years old, and now she's fourteen, so the stories we tell about Elizabeth naturally have grown more mature. We have stories this year which show her problem when she gets all A's on her report card — the problem of being a girl and being smart. In our society we only expect the boys to be smart. Also, this year Elizabeth will have her first date. As another example, Jason got a harmonica for a Christmas present in "The Homecoming." Later on we saw him going to a music school and conducting his own orchestra. Jason's career went from getting a harmonica at Christmas to an interest in music and then getting his own band, then going to music school and finally being drafted into the Army, where he is now. His interest in music remains, even though he is a sergeant in an Army camp.

*When Grandpa actually died and you integrated it into the show itself, did this become almost unbearable, or was it almost cathartic in a way, in a sense that you put him to rest?*
    Whenever something as tragic as losing Will happens, we have felt

that rather than simply ignoring it on the program, if we can integrate it, as you say, it becomes a catharsis both to those of us who loved Will, as well as to the audience who loved him. Our opening show two years ago was a tribute to Will because it was a kind of letting go of him on our part. We designed it that way, thinking it would comfort the audience as well. When Ellen Corby had her stroke, we wanted Ellen to come back, and Ellen wanted to come back. What we did was to say that Grandma had a stroke, and then, thankfully, when Ellen was well enough to come back, she did. Her appearance showed the effects of her stroke. I think she was an inspiration to a great many people who had to overcome some kind of physical handicap.

*Was that really a tough script to write for Will?*
I did not write it. It was written by Rod Peterson, our producer, and his wife, Claire Whitaker, our story editor. I'm sure it was hard for them to write it. It was hard for all of us who were associated with Will, but, as I say, it was comforting.

*You were the story editor for a time, weren't you?*
I still have a title, which is Executive Story Consultant. That means that I go to all the script conferences and meet with the writers. I discuss stories with them, and then I read all the scripts and make suggestions for revisions, and before the script is copied, I go over it for one final polish.

*What's the toughest part of being a story editor?*
I think keeping the material fresh, finding writers who understand the show, being careful not to repeat.

*Did it fit your writing to be a story editor? Did you become more conscious of anything or . . . ?*
Yes, I think for awhile I tended to have a kind of editorial viewpoint when I did my own writing, but after awhile I learned to change gears, stop being the editor and be the writer. There is a danger, that in being a story editor you try to enrich the script, or you're looking for words that will express something stronger, or you are trimming so you can frame the script down to its right size, or you're adding so you can have the proper length to your script. Your mind is set in kind of an editorial way. But if you can then change gears and stop being the editor and turn to being the writer, then you're okay. The danger is becoming the editor and forgetting how to write.

*What was the toughest mistake that outside writers — writers that weren't in your organization, freelancers — would tend to make?*
Well, that happens rarely because we are careful to be sure that a writer is right for the show before he starts.

*How do you assure that?*

We look at scripts that he has written for other shows. We talk with people he's worked with, and you can sometimes just get a feeling from the writer at the meeting with him, or her. I find that writers who have had some stage background or have written books usually have a deeper understanding of character. Some writers have grown simply in television and, therefore, have seen character in a sort of one-dimensional way; I like to work with writers who see fully dimensional characters. A couple of times we have gone wrong and a writer has turned in scripts that were totally off target. If they'll listen to what we need, then we'll work with them, but sometimes a writer will simply close his mind and do what he wants to do rather than what we need. In that case, if the script is retrievable, we might rewrite it here in the office. If it is beyond retrieval, then we have to abandon it, which is costly.

*How closely did your family resemble the Waltons?*

There are corresponding members of my family for every member of the show. When we started out the characters were very close to the real people, but over the years they have grown and I would say the differences have become great. But there is a character for each of them. I did model Olivia very much after my mother, and John Walton is very much my father, and John-Boy almost completely modeled after me.

*Did it bother you if, for example, you felt John-Boy should do something but maybe you weren't being true to your own life?*

I had to think of the television series. I did have to make John-Boy a better writer at an earlier age than I was. John-Boy published his first novel, I think, when he was 22. I didn't get my first novel published until I was 27. I do compress time and feel free to change things around for the series. For instance, Jim-Bob, when he was about thirteen, brought home a peacock. That really happened, but it happened differently. My brother, James, when he was about thirty, drove up in the yard with a peacock. He had found the peacock on the road and brought it home. I changed the time there so that it happened to him at an earlier age than it did in real life.

*When you've had to really dig through your past, have you learned a lot about yourself?*

Yes, I guess I've learned to appreciate what fine people I came from, and it's kept alive a respect for those values in a day when those values don't apply all that much any more. I see the Walton children going to church, doing chores around the house, respecting their mother and father, and then I look on Hollywood Boulevard and see the same age children as runaways and on drugs and I think, "My God, what a schism between real life and what seems to be going on today where the family seems to be in great trouble." At least on the series we have retained a respect for those values. I think those values are still useful, and we have discarded them in today's society without having found anything to take their place.

*How did you communicate dialogue to the actors — that old Virginia twang?*

It's almost impossible to do because Virginia speech is very distinctive. It tends to be very slow, and there are some unique sounds in Virginia speech that are hard for an actor to duplicate. It's not genteel; it's just friendly, because Virginians tend to be friendly and open — gracious. So it was almost impossible to reproduce Virginia speech, especially for actors that come from such different backgrounds. Michael Learned came from England, and a lot of the children came from local California communities and each had a special speech pattern. What we did was simply to try to write country cadences, and whenever possible I would drop in a phrase, or examine the speeches for a kind of cadence that was countrified as opposed to the more staccato speech of city people. Sometimes the actors would drop in an attempt at a Southern accent. I would discourage it if it sounded actorish. Usually it was better to just kind of use a rural speech rather than to try to capture Virginia speech. Virginia speech took over 200 years to learn, and I don't think actors in television should be expected to perfect it overnight.

*Your voice is a trademark on the show. Could you comment on that?*

I think it gives some verisimilitude to the show. My voice is not really a trained voice, but I try to do that narration to talk right to the viewer as if we were in the living room together and not to dramatize it the way the trained narrator would. When we did "The Homecoming," we auditioned many professional actors for that job, but the director of "The Homecoming," Fielder Cook, said, "What we need is somebody to sound as rough as Earl." Then he said, "Why don't you read it?" I said, "I'd better rehearse it once," and Fielder said, "Rehearse it, hell, you wrote it." So I got in front of the microphone and read the narration and he said, "That's it," and suddenly I found myself an actor. I even had to join the Screen Actors Guild.

*Have you ever been too close to a script? I've talked to poets and writers who've said that sometimes a plot or an idea just hurts a lot.*

Well, "The Homecoming" was that way. My father had only been dead about a year, and it was very painful because it reminded me so much of him and the type of man he was. A lot of material in "The Homecoming" was very autobiographical.

*You worked with Lee Rich. Was it hard selling him on the concept?*

I didn't do it. A friend of mine who had been an agent, and who had joined Lee's company, showed the script to Lee. Lee called me and said, "I like this book a whole lot. May I show it to CBS?" And I said, "Of course." So Lee bought the concept and I didn't have to do any selling at all.

*What are the advantages and disadvantages of the team writing approach?*
   Well, I think you get the benefit of a committee's ideas; you get a richness that comes from many people contributing. It becomes the one writer's job to do the actual writing, but you do get input from a good many people. That is typical television: It's a group effort. As such, you share the glory or the defeats.

*How does that work?*
   We have a show coming up this year called "The Spirit," which is a Christmas show, done by a marvelously talented writer named Kathleen Hite. Kathleen lives in Arizona, but we talked on the phone. We've had a notion that we ought to do a story that had to do with a German prisoner of war, and we mentioned that to Kathleen and she said, "That might be a good idea for the Christmas show." So we said, "Why don't you think about it and call us back?" So Kathleen called us back and had a plot which had to do with this person showing up on the mountain, but hiding out most of the time. Then one of the younger Waltons meets him and becomes a friend and smuggles food to him, leading to the discovery of the fact that this man has escaped from a prisoner-of-war camp in North Carolina, and he's hiding out there on the mountain. Kathy wrote first an outline, which we then submitted to CBS. CBS made some comments, and we read it and thought it was marvelous and gave her the go-ahead. She finished the Christmas show; as a matter of fact, it's been filmed. But around here it's kind of a casual getting together and then thrashing out ideas and trying to be helpful to the writer.

*Does the network have approval over every script or just the Christmas specials and the like?*
   I wouldn't say it's approval so much as a consultation. They will contribute ideas that hopefully will hype the rating. If we agree with the ideas, we will accept them. If we do not agree with them, we will reject them.

*Can you give me an example of an idea from the network?*
   Yes. We had a show called "The Remembrance," in which an eighty-four-year-old distant relative of the Waltons comes there to look the Waltons over to see if they are suitable custodians for an old fiddle which is in his possession. He wants to pass it on to whoever might be proper custodians – whichever branch of the family might respect this old

heirloom. In the original script the old man talks about somebody in the nearby university town who is going to give him an honorary degree, and we think maybe this old man is crazy. But what the network suggested is that we actually see the old man go to the nearby town, and again we think that he's interfering with university business, when actually, as it turns out in the very end, he's there on perfectly legitimate business and he's going to donate his apple farm to the agricultural students. It was the network's notion that instead of talking about his having been seen in the nearby town, we actually show him there. That necessitated a small rewrite, but it was a good contribution to the show.

*You can say yes or no to the network then. Can most series do that?*
    I think the longer you're on and the stronger your ratings are, the more independence you can have. Certainly I don't knock the networks because they pay our way and without them we wouldn't be there. It's a marriage and you try to compromise.

*When you get to screening, as a writer, how many changes can be made?*
    You can make a lot of changes. The editors are really geniuses. I remember one show that we did. We had a character named Yancy Tucker, and he and his wife were on the verge of divorce. Elizabeth was involved with these people, and she said, "I think you would be happier apart." In fact, she was urging them to get a divorce. When we got it on film and looked at it we said, "That's not the function that Elizabeth should serve. She shouldn't be urging older people to divorce. The Waltons really stand for trying to make a marriage work." So, even after we had gotten this on film, through the most clever editing I've ever seen, the editors made it appear that Elizabeth's attitude changed totally and that she was against this divorce. This was an extreme case.

*This was without reshooting?*
    Without reshooting. It was possible through cutting and substituting words, dubbing in new words, that her attitude totally changed. Often, in editing, what you do is trim down to size, take out scenes or parts of scenes that don't work, and sometimes when the whole thing is assembled it has a totally different emphasis than you wanted when you saw the dailies; so you adjust, and shave, and improve.

*How far ahead do you work? You know John-Boy is going to do this . . . how many years ahead do you plan?*
    Usually when we start filming one season we start thinking about what we can do next.

*And so before you start filming for the next season, do you have outlined what the show is going to be about?*

Not in detail, but we have a certain time period and certain highlights of that time of year. When we introduce a new character that gets married, they might have a baby; or when we introduce a character that is going to get married, then we know how long the courtship will last. Any of that type of thing that you can foresee.

*What does it take to be a successful television writer?*

Talent. Perseverance. Good health. A sense of humor and a drive to succeed, I think, and a confidence that what you want to tell is interesting to you and it will be interesting to an audience. You have to be fascinated by the material, whatever your subject; you have to have a passion about it, and if you have a passion for it, then that passion will get communicated in the writing.

*Is there any show that epitomizes the Waltons to you? Any single show other than "The Homecoming"?*

I think each one is a small epitome.

*Pat Weaver*

Few people have played so large a part in shaping American television as Sylvester "Pat" Weaver has. He began in radio, where he developed the "I Was There" concept and where he produced the great wartime radio show "Command Performance." He produced radio shows for Young and Rubicam during the days when ad agencies produced shows rather than sponsored them.

Weaver was quick to realize the importance of television. In 1949 he accepted the job of heading all of NBC's television activities. Weaver felt the network should become a programming company that sold advertising, and began to develop one hit show after another for NBC, bringing the best of Broadway and vaudeville to the tiny screen: "Broadway Open House," "Saturday Night Revue," "Your Show of Shows," "The Colgate Comedy Hour," "The All Star Revue," "The Kate Smith Hour," "Producers' Showcase," "Ding Dong School," "The Home Show," and the still-going-strong "Today Show" and "Tonight."

Weaver left NBC during the 1956–57 season over a disagreement with General Sarnoff. At the time he was chairman of the board. Since then he has been consultant to Kaiser Industries, has run Governor Rockefeller's election campaign, has been chairman and chief executive officer of McCann, Erickson, and has been Disney's television consultant for EPCOT Center.

Always a visionary, Weaver joined Subscription Television, Inc. (STV) in 1963. Though this pioneer cable effort met with success from subscribers, legal problems caused STV to suspend operations and go to court. STV won the court battles up to and including the Supreme Court, but Weaver's partners quit. He took the company through Chapter 11, but finally STV was taken over by a new group.

Weaver graduated from Dartmouth College, magna cum laude, Phi Beta Kappa, majoring in philosophy and classical civilizations. He is married to the English actress Elizabeth Inglis. They have two children: Trajan, an advertising executive, and Sigourney, an actress.

*What was so unusual about the "Today Show" format?*

"Today" started in '51. We postponed the actual start till January 14, '52, but it was laid out to start in about November of '51. I had wanted to start a TV service in early morning time to get more revenue. In those days we were running short of money. There had been so many big success stories in radio in the morning—Captain Dobsie in San Francisco, "Don McNeill and the Breakfast Club" in Chicago—and I did a couple of shows on the coast that were very successful. When I was running the CBS station in San Francisco, Tom Brenaman did a show for me in the afternoon, but then he went down and did "Breakfast at Sardis" in the morning out of Hollywood, a big success. So I thought, originally, we would do that sort of show in the morning. Then I realized that if you looked down the road we would not have the terrible problems we were having with the news coverage. We had marvelous radio news and we had lousy television news because it took so long to develop the film and get it on the air.

*How long did it take to develop the film?*
Oh, I can't remember, but in any event you couldn't compete with radio. We did really cover the world; in other words, your radio reporters would come in and say, "This is London, and the major story today in the United Kingdom is blah-blah-blah," and the next guy would pick it up and say, "This Rome and here in the Mediterranean the big talk is about blah-blah-blah," you know, and then, "Here's Tokyo," and so on, and you had a feeling of world coverage. Actually, I liked the news better than I do now. It's so silly watching people talking. You don't have to see them. There's too much time spent at the desk, you might say, or standing in front of the White House, or something.

Anyway, we had started to do other coverage programs. The "Wisdom" series was a talk show that started about that time with Bertrand Russell and major intellects. Of course, we knew that when we got lighter equipment, when we would be able to use less light and so on, we would be able to do a real job of world coverage. The more I thought about that in terms of conceptual design for the future, the more I thought that the morning show, while it should have a certain amount of buoyancy, of lightness to it, and should not be a news show in the sense of giving you the bulletin headlines or covering the police blotter, should be a coverage show. It should tell you what has happened since you went to bed the night before, bring you an update, not only on the world events and national events, but on major stories that would cover anything new, whether it was a new book or a new scientific development or a new something in Washington, or even getting over into coverage of the new play – and in those days we still had nightclubs, so new openings of all kinds. And we did movies and plays and books, of course, so a coverage show made a lot of sense the more I thought about it. I knew it should get better as we got a better feel for the world.

Also, in the morning we would be able to have photographic essays that we could put together when we knew where the stories were coming from. We could bring the stories in by radio so we could get in some of that coverage. "In London the story is . . . ," and what you're looking at for thirty seconds while they give you the headlines from London is basically the Thames and the houses of Parliament.

*Can you remember any anecdotes about outrageous photos that you propped up against the audio?*

No. You would have to ask the guys who did the show about that sort of thing.

I gave NBC, for the "Today" Twenty-Fifth Anniversary, the presentation I made of the show. NBC used a little bit of it with Churchill and Eisenhower, but it was basically the pitch I made to the stations. "Today" would be considered, in the long-term future, to be as important an event in the coverage world, the broad press world, as anything else that had ever happened, I said. In time we would be there whenever anything happened of importance, and we would pick it up and give people an in-depth coverage of the major event, as well as structure a show that would be full of information for the people as they left home to go to work – not much of things like weather reports or the modern kind of interview for "how to" stuff, and that sort of thing. "Today" was all timely. Anything that could have been put on some other day was really wrong for the show. That's the reason why it's suffering now.

*Two hours of live programming, that must have been one of the major . . .*
Three hours. It started at 7:00 and it ran until 10:00 because we didn't have tape, and therefore in Chicago it was too early; so we ran it the extra hour so it would be two hours logged in New York and two hours logged in Chicago.

*Did people think that was a crazy idea, to try to mount that kind of effort?*
Yes, naturally. Everybody always thinks it's a crazy idea to do anything different, but it was a success quite early – a tremendous success with the population. We couldn't really get ratings because it was too early to call people up, but we got such terrific, fabulous mail. Because we couldn't get ratings it was harder to sell, but it moved along rapidly and it wasn't that expensive because – well, it's relative.

*Roughly, how expensive was it?*
I don't remember that either, but I do remember one thing, because I'm reading it off the wall now. *Billboard,* August 14, 1954, reported that – the headline was – " 'Today' is the biggest one-year grosser of show business," and the story goes on to tell about how even "Gone with the Wind" hadn't made that much money in a single year, and this would be '53–'54, I guess they would be talking about. However, the point is that there was a myth that it took years for the show to get going, which is really not true. The show was a great success. The hard part was to get the stations to open up in the morning and spend that money as early as '52, you know. They only did it because they could understand that its potential was so fabulous, as indeed it turned out to be.

It doesn't make as much money as "The Tonight Show," which, when I laid it out, was to cover more the entertainment end, as well as be a good show. We did it on Broadway, just off Broadway. We opened on Times Square with "The Tonight Show," and we usually would have anybody that opened in a new movie or a new play or in the nightclubs on, if not right away, very shortly, mainly because they wanted to promote what they were doing. But it gave timely coverage that "Today" didn't do until morning. Even in the original planning we were going to do some news coverage. I don't think we ever did. I think we dropped that in the run-throughs because Steve and his Allen's Alley of comics was strong enough that we didn't need that.

*How did the news department group greet "The Today Show"?*
At the beginning they were all very keen about it, but then they began to give me so much trouble that finally, I had a choice of firing Davidson Taylor, who had been news head at CBS, and Bill McAndrew, who had just been made head of news under Dave Taylor. Dave was really in charge of all coverage, which meant that I could avoid the trouble of the provincial parochialism of the newsmen, which I was already finding and which I really knew about from radio. They really have a very low view of what coverage is and what it should be, and they're always talking about impartial stories and so forth when there aren't any. They gave me a lot of trouble, so I finally had to set up "Today" without NBC news itself. The principle news objection was mixing up a show that had both coverage of news with news people and of the world in general with people who were not wholly news. Dave Garroway had had some news training and so did Hugh Downs, but the fact is the news people don't consider them news people.

*Did you say newsmen were "inkstained wretches?"*
The "inkstained wretch" is an old cliché about people who are trained to set the type up, to know the whole newspaper business. What happens with them is, I mean for television, instead of giving you real coverage, they're either doing police blotter or, in effect, what they're doing is what I used to do when I did the CBS news in San Francisco — reading the AP dispatches. You might as well read them as write them yourself. How many different guys do you need out covering a story? What you need is a story. And the stories, most of them, are not really investigative reporting — they're just stories. Anyway, we had enough trouble so that I insisted that we use someone like Jack Lescouli, who was doing sports, and he was kind of our clown on the show to keep it light because Dave was kind of low key and soft, and then Jim Fleming was our newsman. The news people thought that was awful, and so finally we set up a separate news bureau, even with its own union, called the Today's News Bureau, or something like that. It ran for eleven years, and the news department had nothing to do with "Today." When they did take over the show it almost dropped out of sight.

*Can you explain that?*

Well, Dave Garroway left and they put John Chancellor on, and I like John very much, but he's not a good host for a show that is aimed at coverage with a light touch. He's dedicated to news, and there's always a danger when you put on a newsman in a job that requires him to think more about the audience and less about the story that he'll do a bad job.

*The critics panned "The Today Show" in the beginning. What did you think about that?*

I didn't pay much attention to the critics, particularly the negative critics. I had so many things going on, you know, new things, that had been raved about by the critics, that I didn't really kick too much if they took some things out and panned them.

*It was said that in the beginning of the show it was a little heavy on gadgetry.*

One of the things that we did drop that I made them do — one that we should not have dropped, in my opinion, but it was just too much trouble to fight — was that we had all of the major papers, *The Guardian* and *The Times* of London, *The Observer* on a rack so that Dave, in talking about a story, could actually pull out the *New York Times* or the *L.A. Times* or the *Denver Post* and show the headlines. That would give the feeling of coverage, you know, that we knew what was going on in the whole world. That was cumbersome, they felt, so we finally let that go. I imagine the one that was technically the most guilty of gadgetry — I don't know how long we used this — was running the headlines across the bottom of the screen all the time. People would be getting up and going in and out of the show during the three hours, and there would be stretches without the news, and we wanted to hold people and we didn't want them to turn on the radio to get the news. You know, a lot of people, by inclination and custom, would get up and turn on the radio just to see what was cooking. Remember this was the early '50s and we were still not sure whether we were going to have peace with Russia and we had Korea already started, or just about to start. There was no sound, but there was a headline, just like you would see in a newspaper, with the major story of the day, so everybody would know whether there was war or peace. That bothered too many people, so we finally eliminated it. The other thing, where they were totally wrong, was that in the show Dave was presented at his desk, which was in front of a series of monitors that showed different pictures of different pick-ups that we had. This has come back, of course, in more recent years as a major good thing. I've always felt that it was their inability to comprehend what we were doing that made them not understand why we would want to have a series of monitors on a show that was, in effect, reaching out and bringing in pictures from all over the world. The obvious way you do that is you have all the pictures live and then you pick the one that you're going to bring in next. You go to that monitor and then dissolve through to the action, and it worked very well, but it was criticized.

*You did an actual pilot for "The Today Show."*
   I did a presentation to get the stations to carry it. It was all about world affairs, how we would be there in the future when anything happened, and the stations could realize that when they opened up in the morning that the major event that would be skimpily covered by the press because of their time lag, would be electronically covered on "Today," like magic. We would all be at the scene at the great event that was taking place and get an in-depth coverage of it, and when there was nothing important going on they would still have a show full of invaluable information for people before they left home. And it was also pleasant and diverting.

*Where did you play that?*
   I played it at the affiliates meeting at the end of '51 to get them to pledge that they would open up — I guess it was the fall of '51. It was mainly equipment. It showed teleprinters and it showed ultrafax, RCA's transmission equipment where you could transmit all of *Gone with the Wind* in ninety seconds, and it showed our various interconnection capabilities and monitors and the way you would change covering the world from some goon sitting at a desk into more of a massive thing. It was very effective and we got our network.

*What did you tell them about videotape? What did you know?*
   I wanted it developed and talked to RCA about it, and they were experimenting. But it was too early to discuss it as a practical matter. If you could take audio and convert it into electronic signals that would make a machine take the signals and then duplicate the audio, which is what you do with an audio tape recorder, then all you needed was the wider, bigger tape and more signals and you could also do the picture. If you look at it simply like I did, not being an engineer, I just said, "Look, if you can do this much information, you can move up to 100 times that much information. It's just a matter of working on the hardware," and they did. It was a few years after that, really, that RCA started. They had a "run for your life" room, where in order to get the information they had to have a huge reel. If the tape should break, it was going so fast, the whole room filled with broken tapes in about thirty seconds, so they had thirty seconds to get out of the room.

*What about using J. Fred Muggs, the chimpanzee, on air? That must have been a little bit of daring.*
   No, I thought that was marvelous. You've got to remember that the

physical location, on 49th Street, was all windows on one side, and you set the studio up, really, so that people walking by could see what you were doing, and the studio was full of people. All the workers on camera, writers and what not, were there, and Muggs was just an extra unusual attraction that would not only get people to stop and look in the window, but also keep everybody amused on the location while they were doing the show. Keep them awake, you know, they were there at 4:00 in the morning to start rehearsing, everything being live. So I don't think Muggs was much of a challenge. Also, you know, what the hell, you put something on a show like that — you throw it off if it doesn't work.

*Did Muggs ever eat any scripts or anything?*
   No, he bit Dave a couple of times. That was the most trouble he gave.

*What makes Pat Weaver a good programmer?*
   You know, when I left Y & R, I had half a dozen top radio shows and half the top ten television shows at Young and Rubicam, and there was one at NBC, Milton Berle. So I did what I had been doing for my clients, but now all America was my client. I laid out the kind of structure that we should have, that would give enough entertainment to get people to buy sets and to tune in, but then to use the entertainment, also, to give them a better product and more excellence in quality and to try to make better people out of them because of what they saw.

*What was the toughest thing about translating these things to television?*
   Well, the hardest thing that I ever had to do for about four years, I guess, was to make the television special, the spectacular, the event program, the single program, a regular part of the schedule, because nobody would agree to it. The stations didn't like it. They were all for "meat and potatoes," you know, the same show every week like they had in radio. The advertisers didn't like it, the agencies hated it, and, in fact, nobody liked it except me. I was determined we were going to do it and, as a matter of fact, for years I was not even sure when I left that they might not drop the form. Earlier, companies like the American Tobacco — my own company, where I had been ad manager — wouldn't sign contracts that gave us at the network the right to preempt their time, as they looked at it. Earlier in the radio business, it was not NBC's time that Jack Benny was on at 7:00 Sundays for twenty-five years; it was General Foods' time first, then American Tobacco's time second. So to be able to get one-shots dropped into the schedule for shows like "Producers' Showcase" in '54, when I couldn't get anywhere with the clients, I finally withheld from sale every fourth week the whole year. I would only sell P & G three weeks out of four, and made them pretty angry. The fourth week we had a show that somebody else sponsored. "Producers' Showcase" was Ford Motors

and RCA. Another series was Oldsmobile's on Saturday night, produced by Max Liebman, seen live every fourth week. I couldn't preempt; therefore, I withheld from sale, and that's the way we broke the back of the whole problem, and after a few years the problem disappeared. Of course, this was during transition, anyway, where the agencies were falling back and not doing the shows, and we were doing more and more of the shows and selling them. The network was really a program company, the way I had devised it, and all of our big hits virtually were controlled by the network. As a matter of fact, they also were sold by me in what we called the magazine concept, which was usually in minutes. "Show of Shows," for instance, started February 1950, and for the first time ever was sold in minutes. This was considered heresy, because the conventional wisdom, which was true but not exclusively true, was that advertising was successful because it had continuity and frequency. Radio advertising and television program advertising also had sponsor identification. It had the gratitude factor, where people bought your product because they liked what you gave them for nothing on the show — things like that. That was all true, but it was also true that if you put advertising on the station or a network, it would sell. We knew that from spot radio, but it was not accepted by the business that you could run network minute campaigns and be successful. We quickly proved that belief was completely idiotic, but later the network idiots went totally the other way. By now it's all done in half-minutes, and they've lost all the major advertisers who used to do so many good things in my time, you know, the Golden Age.

*In the '50s, was there a big difference in program philosophies between the various networks?*
Well, there was because my philosophy was the dominant one and we were the most popular network and made the most money and over a period of years had the most popular shows. And it was geared to kind of a master plan. The other networks were really just radio networks that were also getting into television and doing things, but we did most of the pioneering at NBC, and then the other people picked that up. For instance, one that you hear the most about is "Playhouse 90." I had left NBC before it had even started on CBS, but we had been doing ninety-minute shows — "Show of Shows" was ninety minutes — since 1950, and we had been doing dramas in the ninety-minute and two-hour form from the beginning. I had eleven live dramas of an hour or longer on NBC every week when I left. So what I'm saying is I think both ABC and CBS, but particularly CBS — which was important, ABC wasn't — were much more kind of pragmatic and slow to change with the new world which was coming; hanging back a bit, partly, I guess, because their radio network was still very popular. I just think that, basically, most of the guys who were running the network were friends of mine, and I knew them, but I

don't think that they ever had a basic philosophy the way we did at NBC. Out of that came the things that we did that were different, and the ones that worked, like the TV special, were finally adopted. In fact, some advertisers, like Hallmark, for instance, even went to that form and are still doing it.

*How were ad agencies set up to do TV programs in the '50s?*
There was still the radio-TV department. No radio program was ever done by the network in those days, and all the good programming was done by the agencies. They were set up to run the shows. At first there was no difference between radio and television. One is blind and one isn't. But the agencies produced the shows until TV started building.

*Take a program idea for television and tell me how you went through the process.*
There would be different approaches. One very obvious one was that you were always trying to find a new star, so that when somebody would come along, the agency would build a show around him or her. We were more sophisticated when I went to NBC. We had a comedy development plan and we had a writer development plan. We went out and found comics Jonathan Winters and George Gobel, and we spent a lot of money giving them the best writers. Then we put them on the air to see if they would hit. I mentioned a couple that did work; there were a lot that didn't, and in the agency business we did less of that. For instance, when Bob Hope was hitting on Broadway, we tried to get Bob as the Jack Benny summer replacement. In those days, the star worked thirty-nine weeks and there was a thirteen-week summer show. We never did get Bob, although Bob was at Y&R with me, later with Lever Brothers. But you would take a new personality and you would try to build a show around him, get writers and try to create a structure that would make the show work. Some worked right away. The classic that took a long time to develop into a hit was "Fibber McGee and Molly." It took five or six years before it became a great success. Some shows would hit quickly and die, but in general their success was very, very long. Now, occasionally in the early television days and the late radio days, the networks did do some packaging. I bought Arthur Godfrey as a CBS package. I had known Arthur for a long time, but we were his first radio clients, and he made a big hit with "The Talent Scouts" for Lipton Tea as a radio show. We merely brought the cameras in and showed the radio show on television later. It was right in the top ten because the show was a great show, radio or not. Many of the good radio shows — great situation comedies like "Life of Riley," "The Aldrich Family," and "The Goldbergs" — were easy to switch to TV. In some cases you really didn't have to do very much to convert them into television shows, because the strength of the half-hour form and the people who did the show and all that, was such that you

really had a modest problem. What the agencies did in most cases was hire the producer as an employee of the agency and put the writers and the cast on the show budget. There were variations, of course. Fred Allen would do most of the writing himself, although he did have writers who would bring stuff in, and I would be the one who had to put everything together and run all the rehearsals and that sort of thing. It was certainly not like buying something from Warner Bros. The show was assembled, it was cast, it was directed, etc., by the agency personnel. That's why when I went to NBC I got the heads of eight radio-television departments and hired them. We knew all the customers. We knew all the different forms for our planning about what would be better television.

*Let's talk about some of the shows you watched over or were involved with. What about "Colgate Comedy Hour"?*

That show was originally co-sponsored by General Motors and Colgate. Bob Hope did seven or eight shows, Mike Todd had six or seven productions, starring Bobby Clarke, another part of the series. Martin & Lewis, Fred Allen and Eddie Cantor were the others, and the comedians each had once-a-month presentation, so they had four weeks to get their show ready. It was a way to get a much better show on, and a formula where I had full control. I lost control over the years to Colgate because General Motors dropped out and Colgate took over all four weeks and wouldn't let us experiment. Mr. Little, the president of Colgate, would take strong positions. Even though Jackie Gleason was a smash when he did a one-shot for us and I was trying to get him into the company, Mr. Little just said, "I won't have him on for us again." I don't know why he didn't like Jackie. You know, what did he know! We had others: Phil Silvers and Jack Paar. Looking back at the thing now, I should have put my foot down and thrown Colgate off and done it my way, in which case the show would still be running, because there are always new comics coming in. Now this formula means seven or eight shows a year for a star to do, so basically, you need two or three strong ones like we had with Martin & Lewis, reasonably good ones like Eddie Cantor (Fred got sick and we replaced him), and some other strong ones like Donald O'Connor, who for two or three years did some beautiful shows for us. Now, in that case, it was the structure that I set up — these artists and these deals; I had to do that. But I didn't go and tell Norman Lear and Ed Simmons how to write the Martin & Lewis show. They were the writers, young writers, and Jerry and Dean were young performers who had just failed on radio; in fact, everybody on the "Comedy Hour" except Bob Hope had been fired on radio, and yet the show was a runaway hit, a smash — 99 percent cumulative Nielsen. That means that over four weeks there was nobody who wasn't watching at least one show. It was probably the strongest show we ever had. In spite of the fact that we knew everything about scheduling from running a radio schedule, totally, that is, the networks had nothing to say about the radio schedule. The agencies did. We knew that a comedy show after a comedy show, or a drama after a drama would hold the audience. So the obvious thing, once we had a runaway hit, was to put, say, Red Skelton, whom we also had, on at 9:00, or put him on at 7:30. We put him on at 10:00 because we wanted "Television Playhouse," which was our best drama, to get the inheritance of this huge top five "Comedy Hour" audience with the enticement of Red Skelton to come after the drama, and maybe they would sit through the drama when normally they wouldn't. We were able to keep the ratings high on "Television Playhouse" — higher than they would have been if we hadn't scheduled it that way. Of course, it gave Red a little problem. We moved him to 7:30 the next year, and I've forgotten what happened the third year. He did quit and make a deal at CBS. I can't remember that. It was a great loss, but you win some and you lose some.

*Tell me about a few of the other shows — Paul Winchell . . .*
Paul Winchell and Jerry Mahoney — I had them at Y&R. One of my best ideas for Bigelow Carpets. Paul Winchell and Jerry Mahoney did a very entertaining show, particularly for children, because it's a dummy, you know. I mean, Jerry is a little wooden creature. Charlie McCarthy had been a big success in radio, so I put Winchell on with Dunninger, the famous seer and mind reader, doing all that kind of mysterious stuff that he did — he did a great vaudeville act. We would have Dunninger and Mahoney and Winchell, and with the two acts then I would have no orchestra; I had no sets; I had no stagehands; so I had no cost of that kind. I had two acts. One act came on for a short thing at the beginning, and then Dunninger did a major spot, and then Jerry Mahoney came on for his second piece; then Dunninger finished with his biggest act. So you had a show with all the money up front for the talent. It was absolutely ideal and it got in the top ten. It was a great show. I put Winchell & Mahoney on in our NBC lineup. They did well enough to hold the 8:00 time for a period; I've forgotten how long. We had all comedy at 8:00 on NBC as a matter of format. It was after the news and we would go then to comedy and at 9:00, we would usually go to drama, although not always.

*Was there an option time concept back then?*
Yes, there was. At the time, network option time was 7:30 to 10:30.

*So what did that mean exactly?*
Well, it meant that the news was in network time, as against where it is now — the national news is now out of network time. And it meant that theoretically the stations didn't have to carry your programming before 7:30 and they could get the time back at 10:30; in other words, you had to persuade them to take clearances for, like "The Tonight Show," because it was not in network time. Neither was "The Today Show," of course.

*You pioneered again with a show called "Home." Could you talk about that?*

It should still be running. That's the first thing I'll say about it. "Home" was Arlene Francis, and with Hugh Downs as her co-host, and had a very simple premise. I mean, after all, I was in the agency business. Besides being a writer-producer, I had gone into the agency business, and I knew a lot about advertising and I knew the power of the women's books. There was nothing like it on television. The service show never quite worked in radio, but we had a beautiful basic concept in a tremendous set and a way of doing that show in segments. Arlene would move from the cooking set to the beauty set to the this and that subject, in physical form. I agreed to do the show, to gamble the money to do the "Home" show, once I saw the designer's drawing from what I had asked for—a mobile of different segments, each segment having its own little housing, you might say, so that you would cover the same thing the women's books covered. With Arlene you had a most articulate, gracious, witty hostess, and Hugh is still showing how good he is, and the show was a great success. I think in the second year we were up over $5,000,000. As a professional, I always figured, first, how much does the show cost? Then, how much does the interconnection cost? Then, how much does the station compensation cost? And what was left was the gross amount of money that you had from that attraction. On that basis it was a very successful show, and, as I say, it should have run forever, and the idiots took it off. All of the advertising money immediately went back to the women's books. None of it stayed in television. It was a show built for the women who were not watching soaps, game shows, daytime stuff, and we knew already from radio and television research that almost half of all the women in the country do not watch or listen to that stuff. So this was a show for them, and we got good ratings.

*Why was it dropped? The audience got upset at the time.*

It was dropped as part of the remaking of NBC. They tried to make everybody forget that I'd been there. They dropped "Home"; they dropped the specials and the TV spectaculars; "The Today Show" was renamed "The Dave Garroway Show"; and, actually, "The Tonight Show" was renamed "Broadway After Dark." It was such a flop that they went right back to "The Tonight Show," but they purposely tried to drop all of my shows. They did drop "The Comedy Hour"; they did drop "Home," and "Matinee," and "Wide, Wide World."

*Why was that? Why did they want to get rid of them?*

Well, that's because General Sarnoff, you know, a man who was not admirable in any way in my view, was trying to persuade Bobby, his son, to get rid of my remaining influence over the service. Not only did they drop my shows, but they dropped all of the programs. They fired everybody who was any good and became a facility again, as they are today. It just happened that they could not drop "Today" and "Tonight" because they were making so much money, although as I say, they did try to. Then the agencies forced all the networks to keep the TV special in as a major part of the service. That's because they're much smarter than the networks, you see, with the combined brains of the advertising business — a lot more brains than the combined brains of the networks. It was a purely childish, stupid, idiotic thing and a reprehensible act.

*What year did this happen?*
It would have been through '57, '58, through those two or three years there.

*What was the summer schedule like in those early days?*
We had summer shows. Some of them weren't so bad, and we could experiment with new talent in some of them, but it was not our best time. We weren't really worried that much about it. We were thinking ahead.

*Do you remember the worst thing you ever saw in the summer?*
No, I didn't watch much of it, to be honest with you. I never did watch TV, though, as far as that goes. I've never been the one who watches the tube and pays a lot of attention, really, to reading the scripts and all that stuff. I look for the basic concept, the star, the evaluation of what it will mean to the public, who is likely to like it and what they're likely to get out of it, that kind of conceptual thing; then you run it, and then you see whether you're right about the public acceptance. If you are, then you don't have to look at it at all, unless it's something you, personally, like.

*What about "The Texaco Star Theater"? Did you introduce that in '47?*
No, I was at Y&R then. I had Milton Berle on an option, but my client wouldn't buy him, even after he hit with "The Texaco Star Theater."

*Who was your client?*
Well, it was a drug client, who said, "I don't want anybody on my program who'll be more important than the product. I don't want a star who will overshadow the product." So I could see that there was no use talking to him. Anyway, Milton was a big hit on that show, and as I say, that was the one show in the top ten that was there when I got there. The rest of them had already gone to CBS, I think. Anyway, we were in bad shape when I went over to NBC.

*What things did you like to write the most?*
Of course, once you get into management, the discipline of writing gets away from you, because it is the hardest thing in the world. I am

finding that out. I've been trying to write my book for a dozen years, or maybe twenty. It's just too difficult. Anything that happens, like someone calling up, so I can flee from the typewriter, I'll do it. Basically, my work at the typewriter, even in the agency business and at American Tobacco, was taking ideas and trying to develop in writing a picture of what that idea would mean: why you would do it, why it would be good, etc.; in other words, a memorandum of a concept and why it should be done. I use that as a very valuable tool, but actually, that was what I wrote. I didn't write any programming material.

*But you wrote earlier, though?*

Oh yes, I wrote a lot of things. The last regular writing that I did, I think, was the basic — what we call "continuity," where you introduce each hunk of the show to come up — of "The Fred Allen Show," which was an hour show, every Wednesday from 9:00 to 10:00, repeated live at midnight. I would write the continuities and put the hunks in that Fred would write, and he would go over my continuity and punch it up or change it, or not. But I had to write that every week for Fred, and I loved to do it, I might add. Writing jokes for him, too. He didn't use too many.

*Do you remember any of those? Do you have a favorite thing you wrote — a favorite joke?*

I think my favorite joke that I wrote was a good early sick joke back when I was at CBS in Los Angeles, and was writing more there because I was the manager by the time I got to San Francisco — head of programming. This was a sketch. These were big shows in the times — I'm talking about '33, say. Raymond Paige and a big orchestra and a lot of people who had come from the vaudeville business — they were very, very popular shows. This particular one was called "The Merrymakers," every Sunday night at, I think, 8:00. In this sketch, a take-off on *Uncle Tom's Cabin*, Simon Legree rides up on his horse, and you can hear the sound effects, you know, "Simon Legree is coming," and then the horse gallops, gallops, and then he jumps off the horse and he begins to beat the horse with his stick. The horse whinnies and whinnies and Simon Legree says, "That will teach you to get blood on my spurs." That was my favorite joke.

*You seem a little bit the dreamer.*

Well, I wouldn't say that. Some of my dreams happen, you know. I'm somebody who is accused of being ahead of his time, but the actual fact is that the people who are behind are the managements of the different entities that can block you from doing something new. In other words, everything that I've said that people will accept has virtually turned out to be true. For instance, running the subscription television business here in California in '63 and '64, we were put out of business by referendum in the '64 election. We lost that election because the broadcasters wouldn't sell us time on the air—you know, we had a terrible time in the campaign. Also, we were short of money because the *Wall Street Journal* had ads where the theater owners said that they were going to put us out of business, which scared a lot of people who had committed to buy stock in us. So we didn't have as much money, anyway, and that part is a long story. The important part of the story is that in the 100,000 homes we were passing with our cables in two cities 500 miles apart, L.A. and San Francisco, 25 percent of the people sent their deposits in to get the service when they read our material about what they would get in the telecommunications sense above television on their own sets for modest amounts of money. And when the salesman called, another 25 percent. In other words, half of the people in the below-median-income homes were ready in '64 to get my kind of service, which was far better then than Home Box Office. That is the kind of service they are now buying and will buy by the millions, because they've been ready for it for fifteen years, at least. So it's not that I'm ahead of the people. I'm with the people. We are all ahead of the people who are able to block change and innovation and progress because they're afraid it will hurt them. They want things to stay as they are, status quo. I got Jack Webb to do "Dragnet" on TV. I knew Jack from radio, and as a matter of fact, we had an old show called "Calling All Cars" that I wrote occasionally, and that Bill Robson had done at CBS in Hollywood way back. Anyway, I said to Jack, "Don't listen to these idiots. They are going to tell you to make this show more visual. What you've got is a good strong structure with good characterization that works. Put it on the air like you've been doing it on radio, except remember now that you're not blind. You've got cameras, so you can see the pictures of what you did, but don't change it too much." Jack's first fifty-two shows were his radio scripts, and the show was a runaway hit and got in the top ten.

*What about the action line idea—you know, TV programmers like Fred Silverman talk about the importance of keeping a hard action line in a series. Was that a consideration back then?*
    No. But remember we didn't have money to do really good suspense stories back then. We knew that we would have. We knew that we would be going to pictures for the things that the movies did the best, like suspense stories, like mysteries or Westerns, that we would be able to do that by the late '50s, but by then I'd gone.

*You originated "Wide Wide World." That was a pioneering effort, wasn't it?*
    It was the first time that we took people out to different and beautiful locations and did a wide range of literate, quality presentations. I remember in San Francisco in the Japanese gardens in Golden Gate Park,

Gower Champion and Marge did a beautiful ten-minute ballet. We had the first coverage of surfing, the first coverage of downhill ski racing. We had the first coverage of some of the outdoor events, you know, the Hollywood Bowl, the Festivals. And then we would invent things. I remember Kate Smith with the orchestra, all up in Yosemite, where we shot Kate singing "America the Beautiful," and behind it was El Capitan across Yosemite. You showed everybody what people with privilege, people with taste and intelligence and the ability to go places and see the very best things saw. We let everybody see them in segments every Sunday, and the show, of course, was aimed at the future where we would be able to go all over the world. Even on the first show we went to Mexico, where we had Cantinflas, who was in *Around the World in 80 Days*. He did his comedy bullfight in Tijuana. We went to Havana and picked up something there for our first show, and we went to Canada. So we did have an international field for "Wide Wide World," but of course, the show was originally planned for AT&T, and I was hoping that the first satellite interconnection and things like that, that we all knew were on their way, would be for "Wide Wide World." That was about '53 when we were planning it on the air in 1954.

*What did you look for in a producer when you hired one?*
   I wanted guys who would do what I told them up to a point, and then if they absolutely insisted on some extra something because of their own creative qualities, I would let them do that, particularly after they had been successful with some things. But, you know, we had the best producers. We had Tony Minor and Fred Coe in drama. When you look at the people who have moved on up, I think they all, practically, worked for me back in those days—Norman Lear and Ed Simmons, then, Woody Allen and Doc Simon and Mel Tolken, and Mel Brooks and Larry Gelbart. Those last ones were all with Sid Caesar, of course, and Carl Reiner, on both "Your Show of Shows" and later "The Sid Caesar Show."

*Any programs that you were really for that you knew probably wouldn't make it, but you wanted to try?*
   Well, I knew that a show like "Producers' Showcase" would be difficult to sell. Our producers on that series really were the most illustrious list you can think of, from an Otto Preminger on one side to a Jerry Robbins. They really were, you know, the top Broadway-Hollywood people. One reason the spectacular-special concept would work was that the artists would take a single job in television, because it would be over quickly and they could go make money somewhere else (because they wouldn't get it from us). But when we laid out a lot of those shows I wanted, and we got—coverage of the performing arts, really great theater and the opera show *Night at the Met* and the Royal Ballet dancing the *Sleeping Beauty* for ninety minutes—things like that were

very difficult to get big audiences for. If you let the clients have what they wanted, naturally they would all want Mary Martin's *Peter Pan*, and they would all want Humphrey Bogart and Henry Fonda in *Petrified Forest* and *Mayerling* with Audrey Hepburn and Mel Ferrer. They would want the hot stuff. We did those theater shows and got tremendous audiences for some, and for some we didn't get such good ones. It was a problem to hold together the concept that the advertiser has very little to say as to what he's going to put on the air. This was very difficult to do, but we were able to do it. Naturally, they'd never do anything like that now.

*You said the network was really poor when you started. Can you give me an example about how poor you were?*

I didn't want to go ask for money because I didn't want to set up a formula under which I would get hurt by having somebody else second-guess me on what was valuable, so I got permission to go ahead with "The Saturday Night Revue" and "Show of Shows" in 1950. The minute that show hit and became a success we sold it for thirty-nine weeks, noncancellable, through the next year to minute advertisers, although there were some alternate half-hours. Anyway, we sold it thirty-nine weeks firm. Now, the minute that was done, I took the amount of money that was represented, which was substantial, and went right out with "The Comedy Hour" and started signing up the talent and selling the show to the two clients. As soon as I had that sold, which took me a couple of months, I did "The All-Star Revue," which was the same show exactly — comics rotating through: Jimmy Durante, Danny Thomas, Jack Carson, and Ed Wynn — and I sold that to three clients. Once that was sold thirty-nine weeks firm I took the same amount of money and invested it in "The Kate Smith Show," which was a five-day-a-week daytime show, and by then the season had started. But what I'm saying is, if I had had to go out and get permission and the budget for those difficult entities I could never have done it. As it happened, I was able to sell the first one and had time to think up and sell the second one in time to think up and sell the third one and the fourth one, all with the same money that I got for the first show. I just never went back; if the show was sold and that money was now safe, I just reinvested it without asking anybody.

*You must feel that a program is really one person's vision.*

Well, it depends on what kind of a show you're talking about. If you're talking about a major entry — like "The Today Show" or "The Tonight Show" — obviously there will be input from all kinds of people. "The Tonight Show" would not have been the same if Steve hadn't done it; it would have had a different structure. Steve was already doing a local show where he showed how good he was, and he had done several successful shows with his particular style. Within a more structured form with a group of comics, he would be almost as good as Fred Allen — not really, but he was very good. So there would be input from Steve and the writers and Bill Harback, who was the producer. All the comics probably had an input, too — Louis Nye, Bill Dana, Tom Poston, Don Knotts. A going operation of a big, continuing series will have all kinds of input. But the thing that you're referring to really is where a single show is going to be done by somebody. There are a lot of Hollywood people who believe in the single vision. First of all, they usually exaggerate the importance of a single part of the whole team, like the director or the star, if he can get away with it, and there are a lot of producers in Hollywood who have that classic feeling that, "If I personally like it, enough people will like it to make it a success." That's totally foreign from my view of show business, because I like very few things, so it wouldn't work with me. I like the concept of usefulness for the public, that's what I like, and there are a whole lot of parts to that, and I want people to do the different parts in intelligent ways. The creative process is really reordering the pattern, you know, as I've said often enough.

*You seem to be in tune with the public.*
I understand the total public — and the moviegoing public — from the Y&R research that we did through the years at the agency, because we had clients from Castoria to Serutan and we had to reach everybody; we learned about all people. Dr. George Gallup, our research director in the early days, would give us the demographics by age group, by locality, by rural-urban, by everything you can think of. We had marketing problems across all segments. Once you work in that field you begin to get feelings about people. You get a feeling of how you can put together a kind of a Gallup pattern of the whole country and how they might interact with certain things, and what would be valuable to them. Then you begin to fulfill what you see as their needs, or at least, usefulness patterns.

*How would you be remembered?*
God knows. I hope I'll be remembered by what I do next.

*Steve Allen*

QUESTION: WHO IS RECOGNIZED as an actor, poet, philosopher, nightclub performer, lyricist, scholar, and, last but not least, a television producer?
Answer: Of course, it's Steverino! He is all of the above and more — a "one-man creative conglomerate," as one observer put it.

Allen dropped out during his sophomore year at Arizona State Teachers College and had only three years of piano lessons as a child; yet he has created and hosted some of the finest hours of television and radio comedy on such shows as "The Tonight Show," "The Steve Allen Show," and "I've Got a Secret," and he is listed in the 1984 edition of *The Guinness Book of World Records* as the most prolific composer of modern times.

In January 1977, PBS presented Allen's 18-year dream — the ultimate talk show, "Meeting of Minds." Created, written, and hosted by Allen, the show features great minds and personalities of the ages, exchanging ideas in the talk-show format. If you have ever wondered what Attila the Hun might have to say to Emily Dickinson, watch this show. "Meeting of Minds" has earned the respect of scholars for its intelligent renderings of great thinkers and doers. It has received a Peabody, three Emmy nominations, and a TV Critic's Circle Award, and the Encyclopedia Brittanica Award.

*Tell me about starting "Meeting of Minds."*
It's been a long process. It took me eighteen years to get the thing on the air. I originally thought of the idea back in 1958. At the time I was doing a Sunday night comedy variety hour show, and occasionally, we would have someone come on like Charles Laughton — not doing comedy, but just to change the pace a bit. So I thought it would be interesting to take about twenty-five minutes of our show some night and have five or six important people from history discussing some significant subject.

I recognized from the start that I couldn't have them discuss freedom of the press, or something, or most of our audience would go to sleep, except for a few bright people. So I knew I had to select a subject matter which in itself would be sensational and controversial. I made an obvious choice: crime and punishment. Everybody is interested in murder and electric chairs and prisons and all that; and, of course, almost all the important philosophers have delivered opinions on that subject. So Nat Hentoff and I put a script together and we started rehearsing it. An argument was going on with the network during this part of the process. They didn't want it on and we did; and since it was their network, they won the argument.

There was great public embarrassment for the network at the time because publicity on the show had already gone out. Norman Cousins had become so concerned about the idea he made it a cover story in *Saturday Review*, and there were quite a few references in TV columns around the country: "Be sure and watch 'The Steve Allen Show' this week. Something very exciting is coming up." It took about another eighteen years before I could get the thing on in the proper way. It never would have happened if they didn't have a PBS network.

*Can you tell me about how the format evolved from your first show?*
Yes, there were differences. We have now settled, as you know, on just three or four guests at a time. They appear twice on consecutive one-hour shows, a total of two hours. The programs are really plays disguised to look like talk shows. We no longer restrict ourselves to a discussion of one issue, such as peace, freedom, disarmament or whatever. We let the conversation flow more naturally, although we might give quite extended discussion to one important point or another. But a mistake I had made in the early stage, because of excitement I had about the idea itself – I had too many people at the party. I think in the first script we had six participants and that was at least two too many. I later realized that twenty-two minutes, or whatever the first script ran, wasn't long enough to do justice to any important question.

*Were there any "minds" you wanted to have met intellectually but you found later, when you were writing it, that you just couldn't or shouldn't?*
That hasn't happened yet, although there are some people I've floated close to and somehow just haven't been able to get myself to the writing stage yet – oh, John Locke, David Hume, Maimonides – but we'll probably get to them eventually.

Some can be written up easier than others. We've had very good sessions with Aquinas, Augustine, Socrates and Aristotle, although the philosophers are tough to write. It's much easier to deal with a general, a president or a king, or someone who has been connected with one issue, such as Susan B. Anthony or Frederick Douglass. But a philosopher deals with everything, and we only have two hours and each participant gets only 25 percent of that. So, obviously, it's ridiculous to try to compress the role of, say, Plato, into a half-hour. It can't be done properly. Therefore, we sometimes just scratch the surface.

Another difficult factor is that many of the things you are dealing with are abstract matters. There is the technical problem of keeping your listeners awake while instructing them, and it takes a little more trouble on my part.

*What about your writing habits? Do you have to brush your teeth before you sit down? (laughs)*
No, fortunately, much of my work is automatic and compulsive. I say "fortunately," because I am by nature, at least so I perceive myself, a somewhat lazy person. I tend to put off fixing a doorknob, or something. As a matter of fact, I'm not even competent; I'm lazy in that sense.

Therefore, it's just fortunate that I am driven to think and it all happens up in my head in a sort of automatic way. I talk practically all of it into a tape recorder. I have it with me, literally, at all times, and that gives me a number of advantages. I don't have to go to a typewriter. That means I can dictate for hours in an airplane, in the bathtub, a barber chair, out by the pool, at the beach or in the car. Every day I get more hours work in than the average man can, because of that factor.

*Do you find that you can handle dialogue even better when you talk it out?*

Yes, but dialogue has always been the easiest thing for me in writing fiction. I don't know why that is, but I guess writers vary as regards that question. I'm not totally incompetent at the other details of writing. I've had two novels published and quite a number of short stories.

*Don't forget to admit that you're a poet.*

(laughs) Okay. But dialogue, as I say, comes easier than the plot construction. Plot construction seems more mechanical; and therefore, I have a bit more trouble with that before I can finally wrestle things into shape.

The poetry, too, always comes fast. I don't know why, but everything I write comes fast. I've read statements by writers, some of them great writers and some not so good, referring to the agony and pain and physical labor of writing. I can't make any sense out of that at all. To me it's all very easy.

Unfortunately, the ease of it has no connection with the quality of it. There are good writers who struggle and good writers who write fast, and bad writers in both categories.

An important breakthrough for me came one night about six or seven years ago when in the middle of the night I got an idea for a novel. I couldn't get back to sleep and got up, intending to go to the typewriter and get it out of my system, and on the way upstairs I just began talking into the tape recorder. The ideas were coming so fast that I never started typing. I just sat there for what turned out to be hours, until noon the next day. I filled up seven or eight sixty- and ninety-minute cassettes. When it was transcribed a few days later it added up to about seventy-five pages.

While I was waiting for all that to be typed I kept thinking, "God, it would be terrible if I've produced seventy-five pages of mostly garbage." I thought on the other hand maybe it would be better than what I usually do. It turned out that it was neither better nor worse. It was just the same as what I produce at the typewriter, which was fortunate.

Once I made that discovery, of course, I never went back to the typewriter because I can speak faster than I can type, although I type fast.

*Are you kind of awed by the idea of creativity?*

Well, I have enormous respect for it. Not my own, because I'm well aware that the quality-level of what I turn out is not, by any means, Olympian. But the process itself, in anyone, does fascinate me. I think the best book on the subject is Arthur Koestler's *The Act of Creation*. I've written a few pieces at the request of people specializing in the study of it. I've written a couple of things for *The Journal of Creative Behavior*. There's another magazine called *Creative Living*, and at their request I wrote something.

One of the reasons it's a mysterious process is that — well, this is a circular statement — it hasn't been explained. Nobody really knows *how* it occurs. We know a few things about it, but nothing we know adds up to an adequate explanation. Obviously, if we could program it, there would be a hell of a lot more poetry and music and everything creative in the world. When you realize that fact you begin to perceive the mysteriousness of it all. In my own experience there are factors which dramatize the mystery. For example, my most successful song, *This Could Be the Start of Something Big*, I dreamed. Fortunately, I retained it when I awakened, perhaps a few seconds or minutes later. But that shows the involuntary, automatic nature of the process.

*Do you find when you're creating you have a kind of absolute focus?*

Sort of, yeah, but it's a bit like the driving-your-car pattern. After the first few days you learn to drive you never pay *attention* to the act of driving again. You just go from Point A to Point B and can talk to your wife all the way. Or you can listen to music on the radio, work out your income tax in your head, or whatever. What you're consciously thinking of is what's in your head. You're not thinking, "I'll place my left hand on this part of the wheel and I will tighten my bicep and turn the car," and all that. It's all automatic. So in that sense, as I've already said, there's an automatic easiness to everything I do.

*Do you think we can inspire creativity in children?*

We can nurture such creative gifts as are already there. It's very difficult to say, and I would be inclined to doubt, that we can teach people how to *be* creative. I think it's more a matter of squeezing out such creativity as the accidents of genetic nature may have provided.

It's probable that a lot of creativity is cut off early because teachers say, "Stop that nonsense and get back to your books," or mother says, "Tommy, don't think such silly thoughts." But I think people who are geniuses survive such discouragements. There may even be evidence that a certain amount of discouragement, short of such extreme things such as chopping fingers off, may even prod them on to more achievement.

I have been conscious, on rare occasions, of feeling an emotion, which had it been expressed in words, might have gone like this, "Oh, yeah? I'll show *you* folks." I think the case may be encountered in athletics or politics; it could be any area of human achievement. The matter of being challenged, or not appreciated, can somehow set you into action in a reactive way.

*Novelist George Garrett talks about these kinds of ineffable experiences. George is about as good a wordsmith as I know, and he feels that sometimes there are things that we almost can't express in words.*

I know that feeling. I once participated – this has been a good many years ago – in one of the earliest experiments with the drug LSD. I happen to be an anti-drug type, for whatever weight that fact may carry, but one of the early researchers, Dr. Sidney Cohen – he's still involved in the field at UCLA – was administrating a program in which the drug was given to people actively creative in one field or another, to see what effect, if any, the drug would have on their creativity.

Apparently the answer was "Not a hell of a lot." It made it different, but I doubt if it improved it in any remarkable way.

But I was one of the subjects with whom he conducted an experiment; therefore, I have a little more insight than anyone could have that had never taken any such drug. People who are drug types – apparently it's pretty much a commonplace – often have the feeling that they are just on the edge of some profound wisdom. And yet later in the afternoon when somebody says, "Now, what *was* it?" they can't say. I suspect it's because it wasn't really there.

In some cases you *can* tell them, but it turns out to be only a moderately interesting thought and not always totally original. Generally it has to do with the unity of life forms, the sense of brotherhood – not only with humanity, but even grass or animals or plants – things of that sort.

*What keeps Steve Allen down to earth? What keeps him down on the farm?*

I don't know. I still feel – it sounds like a dumb way to put it – I still feel like just *me*. I don't feel like a star or a bigshot. There are certain ways in which fame can spoil you, but I'm not talking about the cliché way. I'm talking about the little ways. If you're in television, for example, you're met at the airport with limousines, and people open doors for you and pick up checks in restaurants and give you a good table and that sort of thing. That can spoil you, because occasionally you'll get off an airplane in another town and stand there in the rain looking for a cab. Ordinarily, that would simply be the way life is, but if it's the first time it's happened to you in three years, suddenly your lower lip can go out and you'll say, "Where's my limousine?" (laughs)

But those are small ways in which fame can spoil you. For the most part I don't feel any different than I did when I was twelve years old. One of my old school friends from Chicago days is Richard Kiley, the actor, and we used to compare notes on that point. We both enjoyed early success and when we would get together we would realize that I still felt like just old Steve and he felt like just old Dick, regardless of how the world regarded us.

*What was the primary difference between producing for commercial television and producing for public television? Was it hard for you to go to public television where there isn't quite the money?*

Oh no, I enjoyed that. My PBS work is a labor of love. There isn't enough money there to do anything the way you want to, although they do have to pay union scale. And if I write six shows, I get $36,000 for that. There is some money for me, but I'm really losing money in terms of how much time I put into it. I could stop doing "Meeting of Minds" and just play nightclubs and concerts and make a heck of a lot more. But money has nothing to do with the reason I do this. I would do it if I didn't get paid at all, literally, because it's something I'm doing for the world, not for myself. This program can make an important contribution socially. It's the only socially important thing, in fact, that I've ever done. The rest of it is all fun. It's nice to have people enjoy your music and laugh at your jokes. But the old shows may never be watched again. And if you die, for a couple of days in the media they say nice things about you, and then it's all just old newspapers blowing down an alley. But the tapes of these "Minds" shows can be seen with profit, and I rather think they will, a thousand years from now.

As I said to somebody the other day, they won't know who the tall guy with the glasses is, but they'll still know who Einstein was, they'll still know who Freud was, they'll still know who Aristotle was.

*Commercial TV is often painted by critics as the land of the mindless. You're clearly an intellectual, and yet you're willing and able to work in it.*

Well, I'm not responsible for all of television. I'm lucky if I have full responsibility for my own production. Sometimes you have to share a lot of that, but I don't feel that I've copped out or — what is that cliché word — "sold" out. Television permits a certain minimum amount of excellence, and it's up to those of us who can contribute toward that little to do what little we can.

The premier telecast of NBC's "The Big Show," for example, — I'm not talking about only my portions of it as head writer and co-host, but the whole show — was two hours of excellence. There *are* little things, obviously, of which television can be proud. The Henry Fonda drama that was on last night, and there are certain other shows. Even many television situation-comedy shows are very well done. They're better done, in fact, than they were in the 1950s, by and large. But I deplore the Chuck Barris sort of attitude toward television. But that's his problem and the viewer's problem and there's nothing I can do about it.

*What was the hardest thing about the transition from radio to TV for you?*

The hardest thing was something that troubled all radio comedians who made the transition in the 1950s. Fred Allen once commented on it. He referred to the "bloody commotion" that goes on in television studios. People who came from nightclubs were not so conscious of it because a nightclub is sometimes a noisy place, even while you are performing. There are waiters walking around taking orders, delivering drinks, there may be two or three drunken hecklers, you can hear automobile horns from the street. There's always this background noise in a nightclub, whereas in radio, *silence* was an absolute law. There were signs that said, "Quiet, please," "On the Air," and that sort of thing, and they had rugs on the floors of the studios so that the actors would not make sounds with their feet as they approached microphones, and people would make signals if you were so forgetful as to make a little noise. People at home didn't want to hear anything but the program, and if they suddenly heard somebody talking over in the corner, that would have confused them.

So this was the background, as I say, that all of us who did radio comedy carried with us when we moved into television. But television studios in those days, when everything was live, couldn't possibly be quiet, because while you were doing your, say, five-minute monologue, there was somebody else over to one side of the stage getting ready to do a live commercial. Behind him there could have been four or five stagehands carrying a ladder and a door they were putting up some place. There would be maybe five or six chorus girls moving around, getting into position for their next dance number, and there could be all sorts of people moving about, maybe not speaking at full volume, but there was this low, annoying hum of conversation and motion.

You might think, well, if you're being paid for your services, why should that bother you so much? The answer was that if you were a singer, it didn't bother you at all, because the orchestra and your own voice drowned out such sounds. But a comedian, for a living, makes people laugh, and if there were 300 people in the studio audience, instead of looking at you and listening to your jokes, they would be lollygagging around looking at the chorus girls or the stagehands or the men moving the camera and microphone booms. And it was suddenly certainly much harder for comedians to get laughs than it had been in our previous experience.

*Did you have a thin skin at all? Suppose you had a heckler in the audience, did that heckler ever bother you?*

That never happened in my radio-television experience, I guess for a number of reasons. For one thing they don't have drunks in such audiences as they do in nightclubs, and generally people come to see radio or TV shows because they already have heard the show and they like it.

Or they're just in town from the country, looking for a free show, so they're always very respectful and attentive. But in nightclubs you do have hecklers occasionally. Sometimes you can actually use them — at least those of us who can ad-lib — to turn the moment to your advantage. But with certain kinds of routines, hecklers are just death. For example, a Bob Newhart routine, which is very meticulously put together word-for-word, and cannot be deviated from, or a Bill Cosby story about how his father used to take him out for a stroll on Sunday afternoon, something of that sort, is really loused up if some dummy begins to yell lines from the back of the room.

On the other hand, a Don Rickles, Shecky Green, or somebody who works a little like me, sometimes can use that, but it's always annoying.

*What were remotes like in those early days? You did some of the earliest remotes on the old "Tonight Show."*

Yes, though I can't take any credit for the technical part of that. I had the easy part, just up in front of the cameras doing the talking on the stage. The remarkable achievement was that of the technical people, the director, and our production staff, because it was a little like organizing the Normandy invasion. It would suddenly throw all of us into Cleveland at a certain specified time, or Dallas, or Fort Worth, or Miami, or wherever.

*What year were you doing some of those early remotes?*

I did the late night show for three years — that would be '54, '55, '56 — and so it was during the last two years (because the first year the show was just seen in the New York, New Jersey, Connecticut area) and the next two years it was on the full network. It was during those two years that we occasionally went out of town. Then in '56 NBC also had me doing an early evening comedy show, which I did for the next four years, and on that show, too, we would occasionally go out of town. We did an interesting show from Havana once, for example, and on another occasion from Miami.

*What was the hardest thing about doing that remote, for you?*

Again, for me it was easy. There were a lot of funny moments, but perhaps I should put whatever points I can recall into a philosophical context. We never simply went to these places and did our regular show, because that would not have been very creative. We always built a show around the locale, which, if I do say so myself, was quite creative.

*Such as the Luxor baths.*

Yeah, the Luxor baths around the corner from our studio in New York. When we were in Miami one time, for example — all the shows then were live — the show started with what appeared to be an invasion. We had gotten a landing craft from the Army, and we had a bunch of guys in soldier garb, and just before we came on the air at 11:30 I waded out up to my neck. Actually the waves were up over my head, and I don't float too well when I'm wearing Army boots. I also had a rifle, so I had to be helped up over the side of the damn thing. And then at a signal, the theme music started and Gene Rayburn made his announcement, "From Miami, it's 'The Tonight Show'" — and then somebody flashed a signal light at us and we attacked the beach!

Somebody turned on the engine and we roared in and put the front of the thing down, and the troops rushed off, and I rushed off with them and stepped on a plank with a nail, which went right through my boot. I was wounded in action in the first moment of the invasion.

It didn't go into my foot very far, just enough to cut the skin a little bit, and hurt. But later there were complaints because there had been actual gun fire — they were blanks, of course. We just thought it would be a funny thing to do, and it was. But later we found out that some people in the area panicked because there were rumors that Castro was taking over in Cuba at the time, and it was the first of that stupid talk about "Remember, it's only ninety miles from our shore." Some local people who didn't think very well thought tiny Cuba was invading the enormous United States.

Another funny moment comes back to my mind, on one of the other shows, and this was again from Miami. I opened the show by coming up out of the water, gradually walked to shore, and did my opening monologue in trunks there on the beach against the water. I had some lines about the beautiful scenery in this part of the world and at that point a pretty girl with a lovely figure was supposed to just walk behind me — it wasn't a big joke, just a reference to the local beauties. But when we rehearsed the routine just before we came on the air, somebody had said, "Just walk behind Mr. Allen," so the young lady did literally that. She walked into the picture and *stood* right behind me.

Somebody said, "No, wait a minute," and they went over and they said, "Sweetheart, when we said to walk behind Mr. Allen we didn't mean to walk and *stay* there behind him. Just *stroll past* in the background, and then keep going."

She said, "Oh, okay." So a couple of minutes later we were on the air live and I came up out of the water and did my opening jokes and gradually, as I turned my head from side to side, I could see that the girl — who was wearing a two-piece leopard-skin bathing suit — had indeed followed her instructions and had strolled past me. I forgot about her and went on with the joke. Six or seven minutes later I said, "We'll be right back," and at that point I just happened to look to my left. The poor girl was now about four miles down the beach, following orders strictly. She'd been told to keep walking and if somebody hadn't run down and whistled at her I guess she would have walked to North Carolina.

*What was censorship like for you in those early days with "The Tonight Show" and the early shows?*

There was hardly any because the shows were almost all ad-lib and what was there to censor? Nobody said anything wrong. We didn't do a great deal of scripted stuff, though occasionally we would, and we gave NBC no trouble anyway. Dirty jokes, we wouldn't do them on the show. Occasionally, there was an innocent dirty laugh. Someone would say something that nobody had intended to be off-color and you just laughed.

*Can you remember any of those? Anything in particular?*

Oh, let's see what comes to my mind. One night when I came to the theater I saw that there was on my desk a doll house — one of those two-story $50.00-looking doll houses, the kind you see in store windows at Christmas, but don't actually see in people's homes. And crawling in and out of all the doors and windows of it were about fifteen cats — kittens and grown cats. For some reason the phrase "cat house" immediately crossed my mind. So I went over to Gene Rayburn and Steve and Edie and everybody standing around and said, "By the way, be sure that none of us refers to this thing as a 'cat house.'" And they laughed and said, "Of course, nobody should do that." So, about forty minutes later we were on the air. I can't remember if they brought the woman out immediately. She was the first guest. The little house was on top of my desk, and I said, "Our next guest is Mrs. So-and-So." She came out and I said, "What *is* this thing here?" And she said, "It's a cat house."

I laughed louder than anybody. It was one of those things where everybody was having a good laugh but nobody was to blame for it.

*What is your all-time favorite "boo-boo"? Tell one on yourself.*

Well, the most terrifying moment, about which there is nothing whatever funny, happened one night when I had my own radio show. After the "Smile Time" show went off I then went over to KNX, the CBS station here in Los Angeles, and did a late night one-man show for three years, during which I evolved a lot of the ideas which I later applied to television. One evening I had gone to see Sammy Davis opening here in a club in town. I noticed there were three or four men sitting at a table down in front who did not applaud for him all night long, even though he put on a terrific show, and that has always annoyed me. First of all, the rudeness, the insensitivity of it, I find annoying. I may be more sensitive to it because I grew up in and around theaters. Perhaps when I was three years old I got annoyed because somebody didn't applaud for my mother. But whatever the reason, I'm sensitive to that. Oddly enough, it has nothing to do with me as a performer, because when you're on stage you can't see who is applauding you, or isn't, and if 99 percent of the audience is it sounds the same as if 100 percent is, so there is no personal problem; but it's still rude.

So I happened, on the next night on the air, to think of this, and did a little speech, mentioning the various points I've mentioned to you here. And I said, "Well, so much for that. And now here's our next guest, singer Miss Peggy Lee," and Peggy walks out and she gets a big welcoming hand. I suddenly looked down in the front row and there's a guy just sitting there not applauding. So I thought, "What's going on in this dummy's head?" I had just finished mentioning the very point. Here is the talented and very attractive Peggy Lee and this guy's not applauding. When the applause subsided I said, "Peggy, make yourself comfortable here; I'll be right back." I jumped down off the stage with my hand mike. I wasn't going to attack the man, I just wanted to say, "You're entitled to your opinion, if you have some other viewpoint on this. Maybe you think the performer has to be great before he deserves your applause." I just wanted to see why he had done that. I walked up to him with the hand mike and just as I got to him I saw that he had no hands. He had two hooks. Part of my brain turned into oatmeal at that moment. I was on the air live. The fellow handled the situation perfectly. He knew exactly what was going on in my mind and he just kind of smiled at me as if to say, "Now you understand." So I talked to the woman *next* to him and said, "I've been noticing this hat you're wearing. Do you mind if . . . ," you know, I went into this dumb conversation about a woman's hat and what she had in her handbag, and only the man with no hands and I knew what had really happened. It was a horrifying experience and there was nothing funny about it.

*If Steve Allen was to come back as someone throughout history, some great figure, who would that be?*
    That's a fascinating question. I don't know. I've always hated to make choices when presented with questions of that sort, whether they dealt with music, philosophers, presidents, or whatever. My mental computer quickly enough suggests possibilities, but I can't settle on one. It just keeps clicking out more and more names and, as I say, I feel uncomfortable if somebody says, "There's a gun at your head. Give me one name and that will be the end of it."

*Give me five names.*
    (Laughs) Well, any of the important philosophers. It would be great to hang around and see how Aristotle did what he did. Or it would be fun to hang around Jefferson; it would be fun to hang around Thomas Paine, or Ben Franklin. But there again, I could mention 400 names. That's part of the answer, I guess. I hate to be pinned down. There's too much greatness. How can you rule out Shakespeare or Leonardo da Vinci, Beethoven, Mendelssohn?

*What things can you ad-lib on TV and what things need to be scripted?*

Well, you can't ad-lib a sketch. You can ad-lib *within* a sketch. In fact, I invariably do. But you just can't say, "Okay, gang, we're going to do a cowboy sketch. Now get your hats and go out there and ad-lib."

I used to ad-lib courtroom sketches on one of the shows I did a few years ago, but we would set up certain rules of the game. We would get eight or ten people out of the audience and I'd say, "You sit up there. You're the jury." Then I would get some comic who could ad-lib, like Louie Nye or John Byner or Jack Carter, or whoever was on the show, and make them the judge. One guest would be the prosecuting attorney and I would be the defense attorney, and we would get somebody out of the audience — somebody who had been given a ticket for speeding recently — and we would ad-lib. But that's the only case that I have ever heard of an actual full, strong sketch being totally ad-libbed. Obviously, that's why sketches are written.

On the other hand, I can ad-lib my way through a conversation easily and get laughs, *if* there's an audience. For some reason I'm rarely funny on the phone or in a one-to-one situation. But if there were 400 people listening to us right now I would be different. I would say something funny about every fourteen seconds, on the average. I don't know why it works that way but it does.

*You worked with Don Knotts, Tim Conway and Pat Harrington, Jr., and a lot of writers who are really coming into their own in recent years. Does that give you a feeling of satisfaction?*

It gives me a feeling of satisfaction for them, because they're all friends of mine, as well as coworkers. They've always deserved success and it's just terrific that the world finally wised up. I knew they were that funny when I saw them. Sometimes it takes many years for the world to understand what I meant when I first introduced these people, and that's just great, knowing that simple justice sometimes takes place.

*What do you think of shows like "Real People" and "Laugh-In," etc.? You were pioneering in some of that type of humor back in the '50s.*

I have not as yet seen "Real People," so I don't know about that. I did see "Laugh-In" once, and I must say that (producer) George Schlatter and (comedy hosts) Dan Rowan and Dick Martin were all very generous. Whenever they would get interviewed they would invariably cite my show, and (comedian) Ernie Kovacs' early shows, as sources from which they drew a lot of their ideas. They never beat about the bush about that at all. It would be nice if everybody who borrowed your material was so honest about it. But they were personal friends, and I always was pleased by their success, and I appeared on their shows as a guest a few times.

*Is there any fundamental thing you keep expressing in your work?*

There is, more or less. It's not reflected in my humor and perhaps rarely, if at all, reflected in my music, but it is consciously part of my writing, part of my speaking and part of my television work. I'm concerned about the relative inability to *reason* in modern society. There seems to be a massive, herd-like rush into irrationality in the present part of the century. I don't mean it started last Tuesday, nor do I mean it's ever been totally absent from human experience, but the line on the chart at the moment is very high. And that deeply concerns me. "Meeting of Minds" grows out of that concern. So does a table game I created, "Strange Bedfellows," the point of which is to encourage people to respond to statements on the basis of their meaning and merits and not on the basis of their source. A professional educator and games theorist, Robert Allen, got in touch with me after he noticed something in a couple of my books, in which I did something like this: I said to the reader, "Let me give you here a couple of instances of blatant Communist propaganda," and then I quoted a couple of paragraphs that did indeed sound like that. Later I revealed that the author of the first paragraph was Abraham Lincoln, and the author of the second was Pope Pius XII.

Robert Allen said that something important was done here, and we got together and made a game out of it.

The third thing that has grown out of my concern about the irrationality of the world is a record album for children, called "How to Think." I've made a proposal to PBS to try to interest them in a large television project dealing with the process of thought, the process of reasoning, the history of it, the function of it, the relationship of it to brain function, etc.

"Meeting of Minds" is pretty much a one-man operation, but the next thing I'm envisioning could not possibly be a one-man operation, and even if it could be, I'm not the man, I'm not that competent. But I know it ought to exist. I could help to produce it, help to write it, perhaps host it. So in answer to your question, yes, there is that theme that seems to run through much of my work.

*Give me a typical day, if there is such a thing, in the life of Steve Allen. How do you keep all these projects floating?*

I'll have to give you a sort of averaged-out day, because, as you perceive, there isn't any day that's really typical, but an averaged-out day would go something like this: I get up maybe about 8:30, make sure that the tapes that I have dictated the previous evening are at the front door, along with any papers I might have produced, or letters I might have opened and answered. Somebody comes around 9:00 and takes the tapes and the papers to the office and starts transcribing. I get to the office around 11:00 and get on the papers immediately and at that point, function as editor, and then give the papers back to our office staff, and they are typed and put into the proper categories.

There might be a few pages of a novel I'm working on, a page and a half of jokes, three or four memos about some ongoing project, some letters to the world—a senator, or a philosopher. Maybe I'm speaking to an author whose book I've just read. I produce an enormous volume of correspondence, for better or worse. And, as I say, all of this gets moved out into the proper categories. That's how all the books and scripts get written, and all the musicals get written. The poems, of course, don't work exactly that way, although some of the song lyrics do.

I am a musical illiterate. I don't read or write music. When I write a song I put it onto a tape recorder and wait until I have maybe 10 or 14 melodies on that tape. Then we send it out to someone to transcribe. That's usually someone who can't compose a note but can handle that sort of secretarial assignment.

*You said something to the effect that when you're composing music you're a composer, when you're writing you're a writer, when you're mowing the lawn you're a lawn mower (laughs). Do you find people really want to pigeonhole you?*

I think it's the case with some people. There are many, of course, that don't care (laughs). And there is a second category who realize that I do about fourteen things for a living, and they can accommodate that. But very often when I'm interviewed, about every fourth interviewer seems to have about two and a half minutes of trouble with that one point and they try somehow to get me to describe myself essentially as a comedian who does a few other things on the side. Sometimes it has to do with their interests. Sometimes they'll say, "To tell you the truth, I'm not knocking your comedy, but I see you chiefly as a composer." And the question can take different forms. But it's always a dumb question no matter what form it takes. I'm simply a man who does a number of things professionally.

*James Joyce, I think it was, felt that at a certain point he could do just about anything and it was tough deciding what direction to go. Have you felt that?*

No, I've always felt lucky in that there were a number (I've never really counted the number of things that I do. I'll say eight—just to arbitrarily grab a number). I've gone all eight ways. There's nothing wrong with that. It's nice to be permitted to do all those things, and for the world to permit me to become professional at them and reward me in those various categories. I don't know any way to compare the rewards either. It's obviously a very pleasant moment when I'm riding in my car and just happen to turn on the radio and hear Bing Crosby singing one of my songs, and it's also very pleasant if I'm walking down Fifth Avenue in New York and I look in a bookstore window and there's one of my books, but how do you compare those two moments?

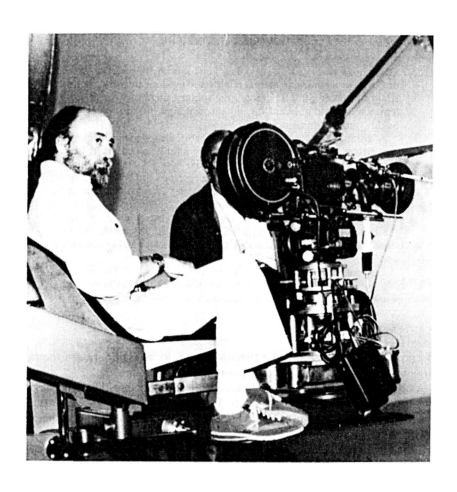

*Len Levy*

FOR OVER TWENTY-FIVE YEARS Len Levy has been producing some
of the most memorable commercials on television: the slow-motion
spray of a juicy Sunkist orange; the solitary Olympic torchbearer;
a marching band in Evanston, Illinois, singing, "Pucker Power"; the
Schlitz "gusto" commercials.

A graduate of Roosevelt University in Chicago, Levy began in
that city as production manager of Kling Film Productions in 1954.
He started producing commercials in 1959. After reading a list of his
clients one wonders, "Who's left?" Some agencies and companies he's
produced for include Foote, Cone & Belding (Zenith, Armour and
Co., First National Bank, Ovaltine); J. Walter Thompson (Quaker
Oats, Seven-Up, First Federal Savings); Leo Burnett Co. (United
Airlines, Schlitz Beer, Allstate, Nestle, Procter & Gamble, Mem-
orex, Kellogg, Mazda, Suzuki, ARCO, Winchell's, Hughes Airwest,
and U.S. Forest Service).

Currently, Levy is VP and Executive Producer at Oglivy and
Mather in San Francisco where his accounts include Blitz-Weinhard,
California First Bank, Gallo, Oakland A's, Southern Pacific, and
Swanson's.


*In producing commercials the functions seem to be split between the in-
house and the out-house — if you'll pardon the expression.*
You really do have two different roles. You have the advertising
agency people who are writers, art directors, producers, etc. And then
you have what I refer to as a line producer at the studio, which is
essentially a function of budgeting, organizing and, occasionally,
research and pre-production. So they're really different functions. One's
an advertising function where you have to know film, and the other is
essentially a film function where it's necessary to know advertising.

*Take me through the preliminary steps you go through in producing a
commercial.*
Well, in our agency the producer or the production group, which is
the company I head up, is part of the creative department, so I'm involved
in commercials from the very beginning. When a campaign is
required — or new commercials for a new campaign are required — there
are meetings. We have a lot of meetings at ad agencies.

*Are you a good "meeting"?*
No, I have a short attention span. I tend to get bored easily, so I
generally tend to be a little late to meetings and let them get some of the
dull stuff out of the way first. When the project starts there is an art
director, a writer and maybe a creative director involved, as well as the
producer. The producer is involved with a production from its very
inception to the moment it's ready to be sent out to a television station or
released to be duplicated. I feel a producer wears two hats. I liken it, one,

to a very attractive tweed hat, a little natty, certainly creative, and two, to a green eyeshade, which is very much the accountant, the business, the administrative side. You have to have both.

*What mistakes would the beginning agency producer make?*
The primary mistake, I think, that any person makes in life is assuming they know everything. I don't know everything; but within an hour I can have the answer to anything because I have a telephone on my desk and I know who to call. It's as simple as that. I think admitting what you know, and what you don't know, is terribly important. If you're an agency producer you need to have taste, which is required in any area, and tact because you're dealing with, on the one hand, creative people, and on the other with what we refer to jokingly in ad agencies as "the empty suit." That's the account executive. Also, you're dealing with clients, and in recent years, with research people who take your ideas and try to find out if they are any good. So you need a lot of tact; you need a lot of taste. Some producers come from being in film crews; some come from television stations—anywhere. There are no entrance exams and few, if any, training programs.

*Have you ever been intimidated by an important client?*
No. Intimidated might be a stronger word than I would use. For one thing, bigness doesn't turn people into ogres. Usually the big ones who are spending millions and millions and millions of dollars putting commercials on the air are not worried about whether you spend $5000 or $10,000 for part of a commercial because they're spending $100,000 to run it once, and if they're going to run it often, such as major clients do, they're spending millions of dollars. So they're usually intelligent enough to know the value of the dollar and how it should be best spent. Clients can be difficult to deal with, but that doesn't necessarily make them intimidating. Sometimes you have to work a little harder to spell out certain things because we can't assume that everybody that we deal with knows what we know. Why should it cost so many dollars for this particular kind of commercial when it doesn't appear on the surface or in the storyboard to have necessarily a lot of expensive scenes? Well, it may have a lot of expensive opticals, or it may require a lot of talent, or any one of those other factors. So we're always prepared to take our client through a budget and show them, as our studios are prepared to do with us, what the dollars are like. We do advanced estimates on every piece of work before it even goes out for bids. We know what it's going to cost, and I think that's the key to success with clients.

*Are you saying that the agency producer can go over budget with relative ease?*
No, you never go over budget with relative ease. We prepare a

budget, and the budget usually has a contingency factor that permits me as producer to spend a certain amount of extra dollars without getting approvals. It's merely there; it acknowledges that I'm an expert at what I do and that I have a certain latitude in which to work. We don't always use the contingency, and the client is only billed for what we spend, plus agency commissions.

Our estimates to clients go through a lot of elements. There's the studio bid; then there's post-production, which is usually bid separately; there's music and there's talent and negative preparation, etc. The studio bid is usually about one-half of what the client pays for the commercial, so we take generally 10 percent of the studio bid. Let's say the studio bid for a one-day shoot is $30,000. We'll put in a contingency of $3000. Other commercials, particularly those with a lot of exterior shooting, may require a little bigger contingency because of the possibility of needing it for weather.

*Have you ever said, "I can't possibly give you a budget on this commercial! There are just too many variables"?*

You have to give a general indication of what it's going to cost. I have said to people at the agency, when I learn we're only going to have the commercial run for two weeks in only one market as a promotion, "We cannot do this commercial for what I think the client is prepared to spend. This one has to go back to the drawing board." Or, we've also told clients when we got into something that had a tremendous number of variables that we had to give them a bracket between here and there. The brackets aren't usually very wide, maybe 15 percent. But we tried to make the client part of the decision-making process so that we're not saying, "Well, you'll just have to give me a blank check on this one." On the other hand, we are saying, "There are an awful lot of variables in this and we really prefer to tell you what we think it's going to cost, get you to approve that figure, and we'll give you a complete accounting when we get back."

When I was traveling around the world doing the Schlitz stuff, we gave the client a fairly good estimate of what the spots were going to cost. But the client and one representative of the client with us knew that if we got somewhere and decided we were going to film something additional, as we did in Africa, that it would cost extra. In this case we decided we needed to do some night filming in addition to day, which meant getting lights. There are no lights in Kenya — at least there weren't any about fourteen years ago; so we had to bring in lights from London and a couple of people. So there were some additional expenses. The client was right there, and we said this was going to cost additional. He said, "Let's go." If the idea's a good idea and the advertising campaign has been working and is successful, you'll generally find not a lot of objection — provided you have not abused that confidence. I believe we have the confidence of all our clients. I worked very hard, as do all my producers, not to abuse that confidence. They know that we're looking out for their interest. Our charge is to produce the best possible advertising, most efficiently.

Most efficiently means on time and on budget. Now, an efficient budget may be very small for a certain kind of spot and very large for another kind of spot, and my contention is that the cost of the commercial is part of the commercial the moment the piece of paper comes out of the typewriter. If the commercial calls for helicopter photography in Grand Canyon, then it calls for a helicopter in Grand Canyon. No way around it.

*What about the role of happy accidents in production?*

Well, happy accidents happen all the time. You cannot plan a commercial down to every frame, or every piece of movement, or every possible thing that will happen. We deal with film, but we don't deal with it as often as our directors and editors do. We go out to these people on the outside, who are experts, and we really want their help. We don't want them to merely execute what we have written. We want them to improve upon it. That's true of the director and the cameraman, and the editor and the music composer and everybody. So you always like to prepare as well as you can, but leave room for modifications or accidents — whatever works. And I haven't done any television commercials that I can recall offhand that didn't have something different that wasn't planned.

*What was the greatest thing that happened of that variety?*

I did a Schlitz spot in Australia, and it was a happy accident to get those two actors who worked so well together and were such a part of making it a better spot. And it was a happy accident to get a lot of improvisational things to work when we were shooting. I don't think I could pinpoint one. There are maybe little ones that happen that don't even look like an accident. An editor comes up with a suggestion. "What if I do a flutter cut or what if I go to black and come back up from black instead of doing a dissolve?" I say let's try it. In music we get those things happening all the time, where the music arranger/composer who wasn't involved in the shooting and wasn't involved in the editing comes in and sees the edit and starts to work it out, and all of a sudden finds some things in the film that we have been looking at for so long we haven't seen, and he says, "You got something happening there. Let me do a certain thing there musically, kind of a hook" — as arrangers call it — and he adds a whole other dimension we hadn't planned on.

*Any other examples?*

We shot underwater for about three hours a day for two days off the Great Barrier Reef and, in addition to filming of rock formations, we also did some filming of eels and fish, etc., to intercut as flavoring. In one particular sequence, we were filming this guy supposedly filming a sea turtle. Ron Taylor, who was the cameraman and who also shot the live shark footage in *Jaws*, and *Blue Water, White Death*, was focused on a ray covered with sand, and the ray just kind of rose out of the bottom, obviously bothered by all the people that were there. It kind of glided away, and Ron stayed with it. That was a happy accident. Furthermore, when we looked at the footage we found other takes where we were chasing the sea turtle, and there was that ray in evidence.

*What's the most difficulty you've had as far as foreign shooting was concerned?*

Knowing the customs of the people and not insulting them.

*Have you ever insulted people?*

We came close. We hadn't been able to do as much research as possible, and we had some stuff planned, and we got in a particular country and started discussing it with local people we were working with and they were saying "Oh, we don't do those things here," or, "We don't depict the people that way." They were open enough with us to tell us, so it was a matter of rewriting.

*What specifically are you talking about?*

We were in Australia, and we had Aborigines in the commercial. We had it written so that they were literally dancing around a fire like American Indians. And the Australian people we were working with said, "We are not proud of how we treat the Aborigines — just as Americans are not proud of how they treat the Indians; and therefore we would not run film depicting the Aborigines in what they might think of as an insulting manner. They work and have good jobs and are just like any other minority. So," they said, "we'd appreciate it if you don't do anything like that." We had a very young writer with us who thought that every word he wrote was hammered into bronze, and he didn't want to change it. So I suggested that he better change or we would stop the production then and there, get an airplane and go back to Chicago. A threat that I wasn't exactly crazy about carrying out, but it got his attention. Ultimately, it was changed.

*Is the writer always on the scene in your level of production?*

Almost always. Some spots are more visual spots, and let's say the writer who wrote it might be busy on something else — then you might just have an art director with you. Other kinds of spots, primarily aerial photography, I do alone.

*Talk about the early United Airlines spots you did. You pioneered some things.*

Some of the people I work with have pioneered. I kind of merely urged them to pioneer. We went out and looked at this Lear jet, and the pilot said that some one individual had wanted to do some filming and they had modified the entrance to it, but the camera could only take a certain type of magazine and a certain lens, etc. The particular cameraman I was working with then and still work with today, Ron Dexter — you don't tell him things like that because he'll go home in his garage and build it. He won't build a new Lear jet, but he will build a new base plate for his Arriflex. (One of the spots we shot for a cigarette client in Arizona. Ron said, "Let's build a bridge," so he built a bridge out of tubular aluminum — aluminum I-beams. So we carried it in a helicopter to Lake Powell and installed it. It was 52 feet long and about ten feet wide. Then when the shoot was over, we took the bridge apart and put it back in the truck.) In the case of aerial photography, Ron developed pieces and parts for the Arriflex that allowed us to use a bigger magazine and any one of several lenses. So we weren't pioneering so much as we were adapting and modifying because we knew what we needed to do — the speed we had to accomplish and the kinds of moves we had to make — and then we figured out how to do it.

*When was that?*
    1969.

*What speed did you have to accomplish?*
    Fortunately, United Airlines always gave us the airplane because they were the client, the advertiser. It was usually an empty plane. It required very good communications, very good briefing between the two pilots before they left, and you obviously hope for good weather. Then you take the time to do what you need to do. Usually we had three to four hours of early light. Sometimes we'd work one airplane in the morning . . . a DC-10 in the morning and a 747 in the afternoon. It wasn't terribly difficult once you got the equipment thing out of the way. Because once you're up there, the one advantage of the Lear jet is that it is so fast and so maneuverable that it is never out of position. You can change position and be ready to shoot literally in seconds, whereas with any other form of aerial photography you back out and reposition and get ready and move back in again, and it can be minutes.

*How close were you to the other plane?*
    As close as you need to be, depending upon the lens. We did some stuff with the 747 where we wanted the 747 to fly out from under us. We were shooting forward, and the cameraman had the cameras through the floorboards. The only way to create that shot is to shoot it in reverse, climb up over the airplane, then reverse the film. (Fortunately, we were high enough above the terrain that there were no cars moving

backwards.) I was wearing a headset and standing between the pilot and the copilot talking to the cameraman, and all of a sudden I noticed that our wing came up. The pilot got a little too close to the tail of the other airplane, so he just lifted his wing. Sometimes you get pretty close.

We use Continental mounts in helicopters. In the Lear we use Astrovision, which is like a snorkel, a periscope. Ron has used a rig in a fixed-wing aircraft where the camera's inside the airplane. It's built on a hinged mount that swings over the outside of the airplane, and then down, and shoots back. It shoots aft. We shot Grand Canyon and Hoover Dam and Bryce Canyon and other things like that.

*We're talking technology, but there's no substitute for a good idea.*

Nowadays it's easy to get caught up in the technology. You try to avoid that at all cost. As a matter of fact, one of the things in teaching that I never or almost never discuss is equipment. Someone says, "Did you use a Titan Crane in that shot?" I say, "What difference does it make?" I wanted the camera in a certain position. I could put the camera in that position by building a platform or by putting it on a crane on top of the truck. You name it. But the only thing that's important is deciding on the shot you want. Then go get it. Don't get all caught up in "Boy, you can be the first guy on your block to use such-and-such piece of equipment," because what ends up happening is the equipment dictates the shot instead of you dictating the shot. And that's a mistake.

It's true of equipment or it's true of people. It's the responsibility of the production company to decide as a subcontractor who are the right people, the right crafts, and what is the right equipment. We will discuss it, and if I have any ideas, I'll make them known. But if I say to the production company, "I think you should use so-and-so as a cameraman," that's assuming certain liability that I'm not prepared to assume, legally. Because if the cameraman comes in and shoots the job badly, I'm at fault, the studio's not. So I may ask the studio who is cameraman because I am curious; but I will never dictate those things. It's like saying to a music arranger, "Well, I wanted to use so-and-so as a singer." No way.

*What's the toughest thing for the beginner to understand about unions?*

I don't think there's anything that's terribly difficult once you are able to get briefed on what unions you are involved with and some of the rules and regulations of those unions. Read the Screen Actors Guild Code and read the Musicians Code and talk to the studios about the time, overtime and golden time — things like that.

We find that most of the production companies we work with — they're all union, but they don't necessarily hew strictly to the union contract. I mean I've run camera on location if we want to set up a second camera, third camera. I'm a terrible cameraman, but if they set it up and they point it and all they ask me is to turn it on or turn it off, I can usually handle that. Or I'll pick up equipment and move it from one place to another, move lights, etc. I don't mean to say that I do those to deny employment to someone. But what I'm saying is that we are all out there to get a job done, and if I pick up something we may be able to make the next shot a minute or five minutes or ten minutes sooner. That's all. Just a matter of "we're all here together."

*Do you have all the logistics, all the itineraries mapped out?*
No, usually that's handled by the studio. The production company will generally handle all transportation arrangements except for arrangements for people within the agency.

*How long did it take you to learn the producing of film commercials?*
I'm still learning. That's a question that I must say I don't recall ever being asked before, but I don't think there's an answer.

*To the point that you were comfortable?*
Probably ten years. And I think that depends to a certain extent on the kind of projects you're doing and the people you're working with. Because in some cases you could work on things and work with people who didn't exactly give you confidence or give you reasons to be confident. And then in other cases you walk away from a job feeling really terrific about the job and knowing that you really made a contribution. Now a lot of times people say to me, "What did you do in that commercial?" I say in some cases I did very little – there was a very good script, and I was smart enough to hire the very best director, and it was all there. I was physically present, and not without responsibility, but it was all there. People say, "What did you do?" Did I frame that shot? No. Did I decide what edit to make there? No. Did I write it? No. Sometimes the contribution a producer makes can be very minimal in terms of something you can put your finger on, and other times, depending on the type of job and the problems that occur on the job, it can be quite a large contribution.

*What are some of the things that you really remember?*
The first commercial introducing Adorn Hairspray – there were dogs and balloons and girls in pretty hairstyles. One outrageous thing of about 120 people marching down a street in the Midwest singing "Pucker Power" for Lavoris. We closed a street in Evanston, Illinois, and had a marching band – outrageous. Fourteen or fifteen years ago. I think the Schlitz stuff I did which ran from 1971-1973, the gusto man at sea stuff and the stuff at the 1972 Olympics, has probably been seen by more people, won more awards, and was more gratifying and attractive to me because I had a chance to travel around the world and meet people and visit parts of those countries that even the people who lived there hadn't seen.

*I remember the Schlitz stuff with the runners in the snow forest, preparing for the Olympic games. That was beautiful stuff.*

The commercial called for three runners – it called for a Kenyan runner, an American runner and a Swedish runner. We were in Africa and we did the Kenyan runner. We found an American there and shot him on the sand dunes in Africa. You're there – why go back to California to do it? We went to Northern Sweden and did the Swedish runner. One interesting thing about those spots: If you take any of those commercials and stop it at fifty-five seconds, most people could not tell you who the advertiser was. The word Schlitz is not mentioned; there's no visible reference to beer or shots of labels until the last four seconds. As a matter of fact, I've done it as an exercise in class. I've passed out the script and I chop off the last two lines, so that all you're talking about in the script is trying and failing and getting up and trying again, and failing again and getting up and finally doing it. Then I play the spot for them, cutting it off at a certain point, and then finally play them the finished commercial. It's a series of revelations to see that you don't have to keep telling the name of the product every third word, that there is a way of creating an impression, creating a mood and an emotion without having to do that. We did another with a big fellow who threw the discus, and the whole activity was to show how he gets himself psyched up. He doesn't throw the discus until the last two or three seconds. He's angry and he's snorting and he's doing things within himself. It was very, very difficult because we were working with amateurs, in the sense that they weren't really actors. They were athletes. The director had to insult him and do all sorts of things to get him angry.

*So producers end up changing their approach to the material sometimes to make it work?*

Yes. I did a spot in Greece for the Olympics that was really a marvelous spot. We started the runner in Greece at Olympus with a torch, and we had the torch changed several times. We took the runner across Europe and picked him up. We didn't take him across the entire route. We picked him up in Bavaria, etc., and then took him into a tunnel – the theory being that this would be the entrance to the Olympic stadium in Munich. Well, the stadium in Munich hadn't been completed when we were shooting it, so we found another tunnel, and instead of having him come out of the tunnel we just brought the logo up.

We were originally going to score it musically, and we got to looking at the footage, and the particular editor who cut the spot worked with a click track – made a little loop of a tempo to cut by – with the rhythm being the same thing as his running pace. And we got the thing cut, and I decided we really didn't want to use the music. So we just used a drum – a single drum and then applause. There again, we had planned to go a certain way, but as the film edit started to develop the approach changed.

*Have you ever been in a shoot where you felt you were really sticking your tail in the air — taking a chance?*

I would say probably two-thirds of what you do, if you do your job the way I believe a producer should, you are on the line. I don't think you have adversary situations, but sometimes you have so many unknowns that there is a risk factor involved. Almost any kind of commercial that you do where you really haven't done it before is that way. Now I can go in and shoot a Winchell's commercial with doughnuts on a table top, and there really isn't a hell of a lot of risk involved because I've produced probably twenty of them. I could do a Sunkist commercial probably without waking up because I've probably done forty of those. In both cases I'm smart enough to hire the best tabletop shooter in the world, and usually we give him a shot list and sit down and I do the crossword puzzle. It isn't really that simple, but the number of variables has been reduced. But when you're going out somewhere to do some activity — the logging in Idaho or the aerial photography around the top of the bank building to show off their sign — there are an awful lot of variables.

I prefer to work with people I've worked with before. You start reducing the number of variables that way. I'm a very bad gambler. If somebody handed me a sealed envelope and told me to get on a plane and fly to Salt Lake City and shoot this commercial tomorrow, and I couldn't open the envelope so I don't know what kind of commercial it is, I don't know what I'd do. I think you reduce the risk factor by being able to control as many of the elements as possible. So in that regard I think I'm probably a little more conservative than some of my compatriots in the business. There are some people who with every job will try a new director or a new cameraman, a new something else, and I won't. My clients don't look at the name on the film; my clients look at the film that's on the screen.

*What makes you a good producer?*

I've outlived most of the bad ones. I am a good one, I think. I said earlier I think I'm honest about what I know and what I don't know. I think I approach the business as a job, as a profession, as a business, and not necessarily as show business. I try to do my homework. I think homework is terribly important, whether it's research or just sitting and staring at something, rereading the words over and over and over. Before we go to a shoot I'll have the voice track, and I'll listen to it maybe twenty times, and things stick. I'll make notes and I'll keep making notes. I'll make the same notes a half-dozen times and finally I've got the notes to where they're up here in my head. But it's a hard question to answer; some answers will come off being very, very egotistical.

*What was it like working with Rod Serling?*

Like working with Jose Ferrer or Vicki Carr or Joe Campanella or any person of some status. It is probably one of the great pleasures of the business. Whether they are the top cameraman like Bill Fraker or a top writer like Rod Serling or a top actor like Jose Ferrer, it's a pleasure because they are true professionals. They have already done the climbing and, if you will, they have already reached a certain status; and so therefore most of them feel that they don't have to prove anything. It is those people who are somewhere in between and who are still climbing — and usually climbing over other people's bodies — who are difficult to get along with and are on ego trips and aren't particularly pleasant and aren't particularly talented. Working with Rod Serling was one of the pleasures of my life — a tremendous, tremendous talent and one of the nicest people in the world.

We signed Rod Serling to be a spokesperson for Mazda, and he did a certain number of commercials on camera and a lot of voice tracks. In the summer he resided in Ithaca, New York, where he taught college. He never considered himself an actor; he considered himself a writer.

Jose Ferrer was the voice, before Paul Stewart, of Schlitz. Wherever he was performing in *Man of La Mancha*, I would fly there and record him and have dinner. I think I saw *Man of La Mancha* five times.

I must tell you, there have been certain periods of my career when I have been somewhat embarrassed to accept the money — even though I don't turn it back. But I consider that I have a hell of a lot of fun, and I think if the time ever arrives when I'm not having any fun, I'll probably get on a boat and go sailing off into the sunset. It's great fun. It's fun to work on good ideas, and not every idea is a good one. It's tremendous fun to work with such talented people, and not all of them are that talented. But hell, if you get fun 51 percent of the time, you are certainly ahead of the rest of the world.

*Pamela Hill*

In 1964, THE MAJOR BROADCAST TELEVISION NETWORKS produced a total of 121 documentaries. Twenty years later they were producing less than half that number annually. Along comes an optimist who actually believes that documentary as a form can compete with other program genres. The optimist, Pamela Hill, has gone some way toward providing evidence for the thesis since she joined ABC News in 1973. Ms. Hill is the head of ABC's landmark "Close-Up" series, featuring hard-hitting documentaries. Her documentary "Sex for Sale: The Urban Battleground," described by the *Christian Science Monitor* as "tough, terse, and mercilessly honest," received the highest rating in the history of ABC's hard-news documentaries. "Fire," another of her productions, ranks third in popularity on the all-time list.

Hill brought a flexible approach to the nonfiction form. She opened the bastion of network documentary to the outside producer. Her acquisition of "The Police Tapes," the compelling work of filmmakers Alan and Susan Raymond, was remarkable both because the filmmakers were not "network" and because the image quality inherent in 8mm film could have been rejected automatically on technical grounds. But Hill stood her ground, and "The Police Tapes" drew a large audience. Believing that pictures must tell the story, she put movement in the network documentary with cinematic storytelling techniques, freeing it from its traditional burden of too many words.

*You were in politics before you joined ABC. Specifically, how does the political background help the documentary field?*

I was in the issue side of politics. I was foreign affairs analyst for the Rockefeller presidential campaign, and my work there was almost entirely academic. It had to do with government policies and whatnot in the field of foreign affairs. So I suppose in terms of familiarizing myself with the way the government works and generating a certain sophistication about our foreign policy issues, that was very helpful to me when I made the transition.

*Was there anything you had to unlearn from the world of research to the values of the documentary?*

Not really. I mean, as I say, most of what I learned there on the issues side was very helpful. When you come into journalism you're covering a wide range of stories that have to do with more public issues and so, as a journalist, you bring a sense of analytical frame of mind to bear on an issue. I had that same frame of mind in the Rockefeller campaign, because my job there in a way involved analyzing — compiling and analyzing — government actions. Now, that job was in the service of a political candidate, but I had nothing to do with the way that material was used, really; I mean, I wasn't really involved in writing position papers. Occasionally we might do a draft or something, but basically I provided summaries of specific issues, and I had various possibilities for NATO and arms control and nuclear testing and the Common Market and things like that.

*You started as a researcher at the network. What about that experience? Was that valuable?*
Well, yeah, I started at the bottom of the ladder and worked my way up. I came in on the three and one-half-hour foreign policy show that NBC was doing from 1945 to 1965, and it wasn't a difficult transition. I was doing a lot of the same kind of work that I had been doing over in the political campaign; that is, I was compiling information at the research level and analyzing it.

*Exactly what does a network researcher do? Is it searching out interview subjects or information in the library?*
I was primarily in the library, though I think it's both — I mean, I think the researchers here today, and the production associates, do a lot of getting together of a lot of the book work, and they do a certain amount of compiling material and analyzing it. They also are responsible for certain recommendations about who to interview.

*What about the tendency to emphasize research in network documentaries?*
Some people criticize documentaries for being too academic or didactic. I believe that the tone of the documentary has not to do with the amount of research, but with the manner in which that research is put together and the skill with which a given producer uses his material. My school of thought is that you can't research something too much. I think the more you know about a given subject, the more you are a genuine authority on it. When you're taking an hour of national time to tell fifteen million people about an issue, I just don't think you can know too much about it. That applies to the pure research sense of familiarizing yourself with all the written work in the field and also to the intensity with which you pursue your journalistic efforts.

*I suppose it depends on how you define research. You could spend a lot of time researching in the traditional sense or you might have found out the same things by getting out and starting the film and interviewing people involved. That's research, too.*
Of course it is. I always assume that my people here do both. I assume that they know totally what the reference books say, and also what the people on location say, on a given issue, and that they are also around talking to the key authorities in the field.

*Are you a taskmaster?*

I think that the people who work here would probably say so. I hope I'm fair, too.

*What sort of things are you particularly on the lookout for?*
I think that we have high standards here, both in terms of the quality of an hour that we expect — emphasis on new material, new insights into a given problem — in terms of the craft by which the documentaries are put together. I can push people pretty hard, but I hope they think I'm fair about that.

*How long did it take you really to understand film, tape, and the language of visuals?*
Not an incredibly long time, but, of course, that's one of the reasons I wanted to go into television: because it was a visual medium. I started out before and ended up on the purely cerebral side of things. I started out wanting to be a painter, and so I always had that visual interest. I had a lot of interest in still photography, even at the time that I went over to the networks, and of course, I came up partially that route. I came up from being associate producer — I was a director for three years for the NBC "White Paper" series — and then, of course, I was doing a lot on the visual side of it.

*What does a director do?*
Well, in the sense that we use them in "Close-Up," we have two full-time directors here. They are responsible for the look of the dramatic structure of a documentary, and they work real closely with the producer and the investigative reporter on a show.

*What was your most difficult story to research?*
Oh, that's an easy one. The hardest show to research was a story I did around 1975, on the world food problems and on U.S. agricultural and economic policies. It got me deeply into agriculture and economics, a very complex area and one with which I was not at all familiar. I think I spent about six months on the research, but by the time I was finished I could talk with anybody in the government about those issues.

*Has a project you have been producing ever gotten away from you to where you had to sort of rein it in?*
I think that has happened to everybody at some time or another. I did a sort of quasi-magazine show for "Close-Up" at one point, and with some incredible sense of my own — with an exaggerated sense of what I was able to do — I tried to do all four segments of it in the same period in which we might do a documentary. It was impossible. We ended up getting somebody else to do one of the segments, but it wasn't very good and I wasn't particularly proud of it. There's only a certain amount of

time that you've got, and to do four different stories at one time is to make oneself crazy.

*What is the period of time that you normally work in?*
I think a good period for a documentary is eight or nine months. You can do them faster, but any kind of an investigative documentary takes that long.

*How does that break down in terms of research, shooting and post-production?*
Well, it takes a month to shoot a show. On an easy schedule it should take two months to edit it, so there's three months right away. Then there's a period of time prior to shooting it — well, let me start again. I think that on a complicated story, and particularly a complicated investigative story, you want three months, four months, to really research it and know all the material. After knowing the book material, you get out in the field and get to know all the experts and talk to your sources and things like that. Then there's a period in which you're writing proposals and things like that, and that might take you into six months. As I say, they can be done in less. They're back-breakers to do in less time. I did one called "Fire" in four and one-half months, and your life totally stops on a schedule like that. That is punishing because, as I say, you've got to have a month to shoot it and you've got to have at least five weeks to edit it.

*How many film crews do you have going on, say, a month's shoot?*
One. A producer will only have one crew, except occasionally he'll bring a second crew for a specific situation.

*In what stages do you try to check up on your progress or lack of progress on a given thing?*
I check it about four different times during the course of the making of the program, and in different degrees and intensity. We always have an initial conversation, obviously, about what direction I'm giving the producer on a go-in or show ideas and whatnot, and that's usually fairly brief; then we agree on a show idea and we talk a little bit about that. Once we've agreed on the idea, we talk about the concept, and if I've got strong instincts or if they've got strong instincts about a given story, we talk about those. Then there's a stage at which I ask for a quite complete written proposal — an act-by-act, written proposal — that bears on not only the journalistic material that they have and the organization of the program, intellectually, but also on how they're going to visualize that program.

*How long is that, usually?*

Well, it can vary. Some people like to do it in four pages, but that doesn't make me terribly happy; others like to do it in thirty, which makes me a little bit more happy. It's just that I know more about what they're thinking about. Most people have a kind of pride in giving me a very solid and complete proposal. Then Dick Richter, who is senior producer and who is as crucial to this operation as I am, is particularly in touch with people on the road. When they're out on the road filming and they're having problems or on a sort of journalistic basis, he's in touch with them all of the time. When they come back into the editing room, then I really get involved at a certain point. They show me a rough cut, really, and then we talk about it, and there are various screenings and organizational things, and then we go in for a screening at a later point with the executive, Susan Montacablo.

*How does that usually work?*

I guess Roone Arledge and Dick Wald and David Burr are the three people who screen these shows. They usually come as a group, or ideally they come as a group, and there's usually just one screening for them; then they make whatever comments they have.

*For what types of things do you like to use video, and for what types of things do you like to use film?*

Oh, I generally prefer film, at this stage of the game. "Close-Up" is still in film and, I think, will be. There are some projects that we're going to go to video on, but with two exceptions, we haven't done that yet. I think film generally has more subtlety at this point for the kinds of things we're doing. In "The Shooting of Big Man" we bought the raw tape and edited it in a special arrangement with Harvard, who shot it. We're also doing a tape piece on television in the campaign right now, because of all the material that we're using is on tape and it was obviously easier to go with tape. But tape facilities are pretty tied up right now; the network is still in the process of converting. The news department, of course, has converted totally to tape, but tape facilities aren't so available at this point that they just log them off.

*You did what was really kind of a pioneering thing in using "The Police Tapes."*

When Roone Arledge brought me aboard, we had a series of conversations about where the documentary ought to go and what its problems were, why everybody was writing that it was dead or dying. We came up with this group of goals, and one of those goals was that we wouldn't take the attitude that the networks were the only place that intelligence and expertise resided. There was obviously talent out there, in terms of nonfiction filmmakers, and we were going to be open to that kind of talent. At the same time, we would be very insistent that they should match our own people in terms of technical sophistication and sophistication on the issues. I very much support the work of the independents. I don't have as many hours as I like to buy something from the outside, but I support what they're doing. I do think that there's a danger that a news operation could get themselves involved with someone that's not experienced about the issues that they're covering, you know, where there's a lot of good intent. Obviously, that was not true with "The Police Tapes" and certainly was not true with "The Shooting of Big Man" either.

*What about the need to put the journalistic structure on things? I've heard some critics say that journalism is really the kind of vocation that's constantly trying to be a profession.*

There is an interesting question about where journalism and the creativity to make a documentary intersect. I'm not exactly answering the question you asked, but I'm answering a question that I think is important. One of the hardest things to find in one person is someone who is a very strong journalist, someone you can trust to inform fifteen million people; someone who will never forget that responsibility, and at the same time, who has this creative sense to structure things in a way that pays maximum tribute to the story and whatnot. Independent documentarians Susan and Alan Raymond are very interesting examples of persons who probably can do both. They have a very cold and somewhat objective detachment about the stories they're covering, and yet they are filmmakers at the same time, with a talent for structure and for putting their material together. I think that one is always trying to find the way that these forces of very solid journalism and the best analytical intelligence combine in some way with the structure so that it properly tells the story in the filmmaking sense — that it properly tells the story that any given producer might have. You either find it in one person or sometimes find it in combination with a journalist and a director, or something like that. I don't think you can be too concerned with the quality of your work and the integrity of your people, because you're going to fifteen million people. It's an incredible responsibility.

*I think it was Emperor Constantine who said "I beseech thee that in the wars of Christ ye may be wrong."*

Oh, well, of course, I don't think people around here think of conducting wars of Christ. I think, I hope, that any people I have been working with here approach any given program without any set of ideas about it, without any set of conditions about it — that they simply come with an inquisitive mind, and compile the information, and out of that information are able to draw certain conclusions. I would be incredibly uncomfortable with, and I don't think that I would have working here, anybody that I thought was an ideologue, who came to a given problem with a set of preconceived ideas.

*Have you ever gotten into a situation where you were doing a piece and it seemed logical to assume such-and-such, and then the rug was pulled out from under you by the next interview or by a turn in research?*

I haven't had that experience, but certainly that's always possible. I guess I *have* had that happen, because we started out thinking, on one or two stories, that they were investigative stories, and it just didn't pan out. Of course, that's one of the things about investigative reporting, and even the newspapers do it. It is an incredibly expensive undertaking. You take somebody who spent a lot of time building up an extraordinary familiarity with the story, and it may not take you where you think it's going to take you. It's one of those dicey things in committing a lot of time and money to it the way we do, and you just never quite know when you're on the scent of a story exactly how it's going to pan out.

*What was the one . . . you just gave an example, but can you be specific?*

Yeah, we did a show on the supernatural, and we started out assuming that if we really looked into it with that sort of tactile sense that one has about an investigation that we would find a number of operators who were sort of enriching themselves at the expense of some innocent people, or who were caught in the swirl of value changes, where church and family weren't quite what they once were, and who were turning to the supernatural for answers. We didn't really find that. The story turned out differently. It turned out that there were a lot of people — a lot of sort of innocent people who, indeed, were searching for answers, and they were creating a market, and the supernaturalists weren't taking much money off them and believed they were helping the people. It was a funny situation.

*How long did that take? How long was that evolution?*

Well, several months. We finally did the show. I would say seven months, or something like that. When you're on an investigative story and the story doesn't pan out quite that way, then you're faced with the decision as to whether or not to go ahead. That's always a difficult decision because you're already several months down the line and you're committed to it.

*"Police Tapes" wasn't slick. What sort of problems by network technical standards did that present, and were there any problems when you were trying to sell the network on the idea?*

No, there were not. Everybody thought it was a powerful piece of work, and nobody really questioned it. Interestingly enough, the black-and-white didn't seem to make any difference at all in terms of people viewing it. We didn't have much response about the black-and-white, and I thought it was interesting and it certainly didn't affect the ratings. The ratings were extremely good.

*You did a piece on homosexuals, you've done a number of things where you've had to deal with certain vocal minorities. What have you learned about reasoning with minorities?*

Well, look, almost every group who's organized in some way has an axe to grind or they wouldn't be organized in that way. I think what I've learned is that over a long period of time—not just the short time I've been executive producer here, but the period I've been in the news business—you maintain a skeptical stance, and you try to assemble as much information as you can from as many views and draw your conclusions based on that. You can't allow yourself to be buffeted by storms; I mean, you understand, going into certain controversial stories, that there's going to be some sort of storm, and you understand that certain people may or may not like the way that the story turns out, and you just go ahead. You maintain the most dispassionate sense possible, the most objective approach possible in dealing with the material.

*Has that ever been hard for you?*

No. I almost feel that that's a turn of mind. I increasingly feel that sense of dispassionate approach, a neutral approach to issues. I almost feel that it's something that you're born with. I look at the people working for me now, and in one sense or another they all have it, and we have a lot of different talents here working under the same roof. You can tell from the shows—"Close-Up"—from the hard investigative shows to the shows like "Homosexuals," which has a more forensic component to it.

*You're from Middle America. What do you bring with you from Middle America? What traits? What values?*

That's an interesting question. Nobody ever asked me that question before. A lot of baggage, I suppose. On the positive side, a certain sort of strength, I suppose, that comes from growing up in a community, a very homogeneous community where certain values were stressed that had to do with a sort of decency and integrity and order. I mention the homogeneous community because it's important when you come from a small town, as I did. When you're a very close-knit family that goes back for generations, there are a lot of connections between the different families, and there is a sense of family and of the ongoing qualities of life. On the negative side, a certain amount of insecurity that comes from having grown up "out there" and not having all the experiences that one might have had growing up closer to the center of things. Though I'm not sure that's a negative, by the way.

*Of course, the news has been criticized over the years for drawing too heavily from the cities.*

I think the centralization issue does create certain problems. I think the news department has really tried to overcome it and I think, in a sense, they are overcoming it. I think it is less of a problem now that it was a decade ago, because a lot of it has to do with instant communication. People can be any place at any given time, and if you're a professional journalist you can be all over the world, you can move through any chaos. I think that that criticism of the news department as being Eastern and liberal and highly centralized is becoming less valid every day. I don't think any news department thinks that news is in big cities any more. We're moving into an era now in the '80s — well, from the mid '70s into the '80s — where foreign news is dominating after a decade and a half of domestic news dominating.

*How do you respond to the criticism that network documentaries are oriented too heavily to politics?*
Network documentaries have not covered politics for a period of time because they are always fearful of that morass of equal time and whatnot. We've got a piece coming up on politics, which is the first one I remember in a long, long time, on the political process, and it's going to bear on the role of television in the political campaign — in the presidential campaign.

*Do you feel a frustration in doing subjects that aren't visual? You touched on economics earlier. How do you do a documentary on liberty?*
I've always felt there are certain ideas and certain things you ought to do just because they're important enough to do them, even if fewer people watch them or they're hard to visualize. You just ought to do those things from time to time. We did a show recently called "The Iranian Factor." It was quite visual, but there were parts that were very complicated to illustrate. That's often true with investigative stories. Economics is a difficult subject, but economics is the most important issue in our life right now. We're talking about a lot of economics stories right now, but we're still at the talking stage. They're very difficult, but they ought to be done, and I feel sort of perplexed with it. Dan Cordtz did a sensational job the day that ABC sort of took a day with the economy. Dan was on at noon, and then on a series with the evening news, and then on late night as well.

*Who decides if a sponsor should be dropped from a documentary? How is that handled?*
Well, that rarely happens.

*It happened in "Terror in the Promised Land."*
Well, that was an instance where some sponsors dropped out, and there was a decision there for them not to jeopardize the others by making them feel awkward, so then they were all pulled. That's a corporate decision. That's not a news decision. Other times sponsors just dropped out. If it's a controversial show, then they might say, "We don't want

anything to do with it." That's not unusual with controversial shows. Again, that's part of our charge. Our charter is to inform the public on a wide range of issues, and if sponsors drop out, I think that's part of the public service obligation of the network.

*Do sponsors ever ask to be in on the rough cut, or anything?*
No, that's a widespread misconception about the role that sponsors play in television, and I think . . . I don't know anything about the entertainment side of the role that they play, but that misconception must stem from the entertainment side because in news, sponsors are never involved. Occasionally, if you have a controversial show, they will be given the courtesy of screening it to see if they want to drop out, but that's it.

*How is the documentary department looked upon at the network in terms of, say, the news department and maybe the entertainment side?*
Well, documentaries are . . . their prominence at any given time has to do with the needs of the network and the network news department for prestige. They are high-prestige items, they are public service obligations, they lose money, and when you've got a building news department, like we've got now, an extremely competitive news department, they become quite important because they contribute to the prestige of the news department. I think they're viewed extremely favorably by the news department and with respect and understanding by the corporate side. But I don't think the corporate side loves the fact that they don't rate like other shows.

*You've said that the independent documentary and the network documentary have some of the same problems. Do you really believe that?*
I guess that I think that they do in the sense that in each one, you're trying to organize your material with lucidity and you're trying to get the story and present it clearly and powerfully. While the independents say that the networks aren't showering money on them—because they're a money-losing proposition—the networks aren't showering the news departments with extra hours and things like that either.

*You're proud of your documentary accomplishment today. What are you most proud of?*
Well, I think, rather than citing a single documentary, I'm proud of the staff that I've built here. Network news departments can get very entrenched and they can become bureaucratic so that change becomes difficult. I was extremely fortunate in coming in under Roone Arledge, because he had a commitment from the corporation and he's kind of a visionary guy himself—he's a big dreamer. He just sort of gave me this

charter; he said, you know, "Build the best department that you can," and at that moment there was some money available to do it and the commitment behind us, and we brought a lot of new people into broadcasting. I think they are going to be heard from for years and years to come — young people who really care a lot and who are extremely bright and extremely talented. I think that to the extent that "Close-Up" is doing well, it is doing so because of the quality of the people who are here, from the producer level right down to the research level.

*What makes a network documentary different from the independent work that you see?*
      That's a difficult question. Well, first of all, with the issues we cover, most independents aren't really doing hard-news issues. A lot of them are doing softer things that have to do with families or personal problems and things like that. The second thing is, I think, that the network standards are higher in terms of craft. Other than that, I don't know. In terms of standards in terms of journalism, it just varies a lot; I mean, some of the independents are quite sophisticated and others are less sophisticated, less knowledgeable about the issues.

*Describe in a handful of words what a Pam Hill documentary should do or be.*
      I hope it would be a sophisticated level of analysis of the problem. I would hope that there would be a premium in it on good reporting and new material. I would hope that the best possible craft would be employed — both in the writing and the filming, and then the editing. Beyond that I can't say.

*Edwin T. Vane*

Edwin T. Vane began his career in the broadcasting industry at
NBC-TV as a page. He worked in the network's advertising and promotion department until 1961, when he became Manager of Daytime Programs, East Coast, for NBC-TV. In that position, he
developed such long-time successes as "Concentration" and "Jeop-
ardy." He went on to serve in a variety of executive positions for
both NBC and ABC, supervising or developing programs of every
type: "Good Morning America," "Family Feud," "The Dating Game,"
"Dark Shadows," and "The ABC Weekend Specials."

Mr. Vane is perhaps best recognized for the ABC Theater presentations. Among them were "Missiles of October," "Eleanor and
Franklin: The White House Years," "Pueblo," "Mary White," and
"The Gathering," winning a total of thirty-five Emmy Awards and
six George Foster Peabody Awards.

He is currently President and Chief Executive Officer of Group W
Productions and also heads Filmmation, an animation company,
and Group W Cable Productions.

Mr. Vane is a graduate of Fordham University and holds an
M.B.A. from New York University. He and his wife, Claire, are the
parents of four sons: Christopher, Richard, Timothy and Brendan.

*You've been in broadcasting for thirty years. Did you realize "back when"*
*that it was going to last this long?*

Well, I began in the industry in 1945 as a page boy at NBC, and have
been in the broadcast field ever since: eighteen years with NBC in various
capacities, and then fifteen years with ABC, and the last four years with
Group W Productions.

*What was it like being a page boy? We hear all these myths about people*
*starting as page boys. Was it glamorous, or was it boring?*

It was not boring. It was a lot of fun and page boys had an opportunity to meet the great and near-great. I found it very exciting and very
informative.

*Did you have trouble getting access to any famous people, or did you*
*really feel like you could get close to them?*

Most of them were very accessible just to say "hello" and have social
types of conversation. Perry Como, for example, and his supper club
radio show — my, that goes back a long way, doesn't it? He was a very
nice, informal fellow, and he remembered all of the pages at Christmas
time. Most of the stars made themselves available.

*So you moved over to television when it came in?*

Yeah, an interesting thing about that. In 1948 I graduated from
college. I had been going to college in the daytime and was serving as a
page boy in the evening. When I graduated from college, I quit being a

page and went to the advertising and promotion department. At that time, each of the departments was doing dual work. As a promotion writer I would be doing the basic promotion material for a radio show, but every so often a television program would come by and we would have to do material on that. The interesting part was that then the television was seen as the "pain in the neck" thing – you know, "Oh, my gosh, I've got to do another one of those." Radio was the big and glamorous medium, and anybody who went into television was seen as a poor unfortunate. This was in 1948–1949, even as late as 1950. Then most of us recognized that the future really was going to be in television, and it was a plum to get a television assignment after that.

*What were your early promotions like?*

Well, we were preparing the promotion kits, and it really hasn't changed an awful lot in thirty years; that is, the materials have gotten better, but the form of promotion was the same then as it is now. Slides, film promos, biographies, suggested press releases, suggested on-the-air promos – all of those that would be done in 1950 are exactly what's in a promotion kit today.

*Did that promotion experience help when you finally got into network program development?*

Oh, yeah, I think that promotion experience was very valuable in a number of ways. For one, when we were producing on-the-air announcements, they were, in effect, mini-shows. But, secondly, to do a good promo, you really have to understand the essence of the show – what is it in the program that will appeal to the audience – and then extract that to make the effective promotion spot. Well, training like that helps you make the program itself; that is, you realize what is the essence of the show. What is the basic appeal? Once you understand that, then the making of the program is a lot easier. Then when I had the Fred Silverman experience – I worked daily with Fred for three years – the sense of the importance of promotion was reinforced. The one thing that Fred always stressed in programming is that making the program is only half the battle. The other half is to promote it and publicize it and get the audience intrigued by it. He would spend almost as much time in the development of the promotion of a series as he did on the series itself. I agreed with that and found that my promotional background was very helpful.

*We hear a lot about Fred Silverman. He is kind of an extraordinary programmer. Is it hard to argue with Fred Silverman, assuming a certain amount of equal status?*

Well, Fred might listen to a point of view about a program, but he was generally convinced that his view was more right than somebody else's. However, if you made a point that had escaped him and he agreed, he would be flexible enough to change.

*You started the "Good Morning, America" show. What was your role in that?*
    There was a show that preceded "Good Morning, America," which was called "A.M. America." I did not have any involvement with that program. That sounds like I'm copping out, but it happens to be a fact. That program went on the air, and in a very few months it was clear that it was not going to be effective. The problem with it was that it really was the same as "The Today Show"; there was no distinctiveness. We were doing "The Today Show," but without the twenty-five year headstart "The Today Show" had. The result was that there was no motivation for the viewer to watch the imitation. It got very low ratings, and it was evident that we had to make a change. Fred Silverman came in 1975 and said that there was no way that "A.M. America" was going to work. He gave Bob Shanks and myself the assignment to come up with a new early-morning program that would have an informational base but would be much zestier than "Today." The show should have a style and a character of its own that would offer a viewer an alternative to "The Today Show." So Bob and I worked on the development of the format, the approach and the whole philosophy of "Good Morning, America," and then we submitted this proposal to Fred. He made some modifications and the program went on the air in October of that year.

*What was the hardest thing about getting that show on the air?*
    Well, the hardest thing was to find a host. We came, if I recollect, within six weeks of our announced premier date without having a host under contract. We had a list of 150 or 200 names, all of whom for one reason or another were either unavailable or not appropriate for the assignment. I forget exactly how David Hartman's name came to be mentioned, but when it surfaced we all said that it was very promising. He was the right kind of host for the program that we had designed. Fortunately, he was available, and fortunately, he was interested, and we made the contract with him. It could not have been more than a month or so in advance of the premier date. As things turned out, he certainly was the right choice.

*Can one plan on making a complex new show perfect the first time, or do you plan on doing some adapting?*
    Well, I think we are all experienced enough to know that programs do go through an evolutionary process. You plan them the way you think will have them come out right, but, always, once you get in the studios, you discover that some things will work better than you anticipated and others are not going to work, and so you have to adapt. I think that

"Good Morning, America" was one of the less evolutionary programs in that a couple of years after the premier, that program was pretty much the same structure. What had happened, of course, was that the various personalities involved all got better at their jobs. Some of them didn't quite work out and were replaced. The show got smoother and more comfortable when everybody improved, but the basic design of "Good Morning, America" at the end of the first year, was, I would say, 90 percent of what it was the day it premiered.

*What is the most evolutionary show you've ever worked on?*
    Well, a lot of the daytime serials do that. I think "General Hospital" underwent an age of transition over a period of six months or a year. The ratings had come down to a very low level, and a whole new group of characters was introduced; some of the players who had been on for a long time were put into positions of secondary importance; and it really was a totally new show within a year. It is now the number one program in daytime. So I think serials are very evolutionary. And in prime time, I would say "Happy Days" was an example. The program was originally developed as a family showcase, with the Cunningham family, and the Fonz was a secondary character who was there just for flavor. After a year or so, everyone felt that Fonz was going to be the strength of the program, and so two-thirds of the shows in the series became "Fonzie oriented" and only one-third were Cunninghams. Of course, once that change was made, it went from a kind of marginal program in the twenty-eight or thirty share level to forty-five.

*Tell me about daytime TV. Is there any time of day that's especially pivotal?*
    We have always felt that the most important part of the day was the early afternoon. The reason for that was, going back a few years, CBS and NBC did not program 1:00 to 1:30. That was local time and a lot of stations had local news in there. 1:30 was really the gateway to the afternoon, and failure at 1:30 could have jeopardized the entire afternoon schedule. Sets in use are higher in the afternoon than they are in the morning, so from a commercial point of view, it was essential that the afternoon be successful. The best way to protect that success would be to have a powerful program at 1:30. We were fortunate at ABC in that "All My Children," which for many years was the strongest serial in the daytime, was placed at 1:30, and that protected our interest.

*What's the toughest thing about doing daytime programs, in your experience?*
    Well, the toughest thing is to get serials that are effective. If you look at the afternoon schedules you'll see virtually all serials, and the audience is quick to see which of the shows have good storylines and characters,

and which ones are weakening. There must be daily vigilance to be sure that the serials don't falter.

*Is daytime tougher to keep an eye on than prime time?*
Well, no, I wouldn't think more so than prime time, but certainly not less so. There is a tendency, I think, on the part of those outside the industry, to say, "Oh, once you get a good serial you just wind it up and it runs for twenty years on its own," which is not the case. Steady viewers of daytime serials, as I mentioned before, very quickly perceive when the storyline is softening and when characters are weakening, and so people in the daytime program department at the network have to be very analytical about this and be sure that the long-range storylines are always strong. That's a tough job.

*How has daytime programming been structured in terms of the programming department in the network?*
Well, there's a vice-president in charge of daytime programming, and then, normally, a support person in development, and several others who are in charge of making sure that the program can stay strong.

*Coming from the network, what did you have to unlearn when you went to work for a group organization?*
I didn't have anything to unlearn. I had a lot of things to learn. I was pleased to discover that the elements of program making in first-run syndication are the same as at the network. The people you work with, the agents, the lawyers, the representatives and so on, are pretty much the same. Selling programs is not that much of a novelty. When you're at a network, even though the industry considers you a buyer, you spend as much time selling to stations, to advertisers, to your own management, as you do in the buying process. What I had to do was learn some of the more sophisticated procedures in syndication.

*For example?*
Well, how to price the market, how our sales staff goes about getting clearances for various programs, the whole experience where stations come and buy your product and how that negotiation process works. That had been foreign to me as a network programmer, but I find it fascinating and I think, if I have not mastered it, I've learned the rudiments by now.

The toughest thing is to accept the fact that it has to be a market-by-market procedure. In the network, when you decide to put on a certain program, one of the least concerns is station clearance. You just assume the station lineup will cover 98 percent of the country. In syndication you don't get any such guarantees. You have to go out with the sales staff and do it market by market, and then there's a certain point at which you say,

"We have enough clearance now to justify production." There was nothing like that in the network field.

*What sort of controls does Westinghouse have on its various owned and operated stations in terms of programming?*
We work closely with the stations. The stations do not have a mandate to carry every program that we produce, nor are we mandated to make available every one of our programs to the five owned stations. We would prefer to have the stations carry our programs and we would prefer to have them on our stations, simply because there is a family feeling.

*You handled "The Mike Douglas Show," which was successful for many years. Are there any particular problems one runs into with that type of show?*
Well, the major thing in a program that's been on the air eighteen years is to keep it fresh, to maintain a sense of creativity, excitement and enthusiasm. On any long-running show there might be a tendency for people to get complacent and not throw themselves into the creative side with the same vigor and imagination that you do when a program is brand-new. I must say that the staff on the Douglas show fought that spirit of complacency and right up to the very end was resourceful and energetic in keeping the show fresh.

*What's the relationship, normally, in terms of ownership, between somebody like Mike Douglas and Group W, for example.*
The ownership is entirely in the production company. Mike is a salaried employee.

*Would that be true with most such operations like "The Merv Griffin Show"?*
Well, Merv is different. He has his own production company that owns the show and produces it. I don't know what his specific arrangement is, but I'm sure it's his ownership. But in the case of Mike and the "Hour Magazine" program, starring Gary Collins, Group W Productions owns the programs, and we just have contractual arrangements with each one of them.

*Are you a stern taskmaster?*
I would say, demanding. I don't like mediocrity or any kind of slipshod work. I prefer to do things by enthusiasm rather than hollering.

*How does one handle broadcasters with large egos? Any tips on that?*
Well, you have to be sensitive to them. While, privately, you may bemoan the fact that an artist has an ego that makes his position some-

what unrealistic at times, he or she is, nevertheless, the star, and the ego must be dealt with as a reality. It calls for some patience and some lip-biting and understanding, but to resist the star's ego is probably to jeopardize the project.

*Any anecdote in dealing with egos?*
(laughs) I think I'll sidestep that one.

*You did "Eleanor and Franklin: The White House Years" about President and Mrs. Roosevelt. Can you talk about how that project got started?*
Well, it got started with the purchase of the rights to the book by ABC. When the first script came in it was not, well, up to standards. The second draft was not effective either. A year after ABC had bought the book we were close to a half-million dollars invested and didn't have a single usable word. It was not a pleasant experience. But David Susskind, the producer, said, "Let us use James Costigan. I think he will have a feel for it." So we said, "Yes, let's go ahead." Costigan wrote a perfectly beautiful script. The IBM people read the script and shared the same high regard for it, so they became the single sponsor. The production then got underway, with Susskind as executive producer, and of course, what came in was one of the finest programs in the history of the medium. It was born out of desperate circumstances. I'll tell you, it's an awful feeling to be a year into a project with a half-million dollars invested, and nothing useful to show for it.

*What do you feel most proud of in terms of what you contributed to "Eleanor and Franklin"?*
Well, one of my contributions was to approve Edward Hermann to play the role of FDR. There was never any question about Jane Alexander. I have been a great admirer of hers for many years, and when David came in and said, "We want to make her Eleanor," that was an automatic approval. But Hermann was a lot different. He was a relative unknown, and to give him a major role in a multimillion dollar project was very chancy. Susskind said, "Well, look, why don't you meet him," so we set a date for him to come up to my office. The day he arrived, we shook hands, and then I had to step out of the office for a minute. When I came back, there was Hermann, sitting in the chair, holding a cigarette in a holder in that jaunty manner that FDR had. He was wearing a white sort of fishing hat, and as I stepped in the door and saw that, I said, "Never was there any man more right for a role than Edward is for FDR." I applauded Ed and David for the showmanly way in which they made a point.

*How do you keep track of the budding actors and actresses, and do you have any tips or anything on that?*

Well, at ABC there is a huge talent department of very experienced people, and when a casting situation comes up they always have deep resources. It was not necessary for every program person to keep a private file of possible performers, although we all kind of did that informally by watching a lot of television plays and movies and filing things in the back of our minds for future use.

*What mistakes does a novice make – a novice programmer – in going into a screening room?*
Well, I think a lot of them have difficulty in looking at a rough cut and envisioning what the final picture will look like. There is a tendency on the part of inexperienced programmers to just look at what's on the screen and make a judgement on that basis rather than being able to look ahead at how the show will intercut and what the final product will be.

*What about the challenges of a job like yours?*
The biggest challenge is to find new ideas that will be commercially successful. There were plenty of new ideas that would come to a network person, but they were either inappropriate for television or simply wouldn't work. The difficulty is to get a program that has qualities that you can be proud of, and which, at the same time, will achieve a commercially successful audience level.

*Give me a composite day. I know there is probably no average, but could you just give me a day in the life of Ed Vane?*
(laughs) It might start off with a staff meeting from 9:30 to 10:30, followed by individual get-togethers with the producer or the production staffs of the various programs. We then have a meeting with the promotion person to make sure that the ad campaigns are being worked on successfully. Then I have certain management responsibilities. We have a duplication center in Pittsburgh, which requires some attention. We are new to the field of programming for cable, and I might read a script or some program idea which involves cable possibilities. I get together with the research person to make sure that, if it's favorable news that's coming through, all the right people have that information. And of course, there are daily conversations with our management in New York. It's a day that goes by rather quickly.

*Are you a good "meeting," as the slang goes?*
I really don't have much patience for meetings that drift off into other matters, where we're not getting done what the meeting is supposed to achieve. I like to keep them on target.

*What personal trait do you think is most important to your successful functioning as a broadcast manager?*

Enthusiasm. It's not just a job, and we don't do it in a routine manner. When I become involved in a project that I believe in, I really become a cheerleader and become very active and energetic and enthusiastic. I think that that gives a good impression to those I'm working with and might possibly stimulate them.

*Can you give me a specific example of your cheerleading?*
Oh, I would say "Missiles of October" was a very good example of that. That was not an idea that everybody immediately took to. They thought it might be risky; that it wouldn't get a big audience; that it might have political ramifications; that casting would be impossible. But I was totally convinced that it would be a worthy project. I just kept my enthusiasm going and tried to sweep people along with it.

*Can you talk about that program?*
The key to "Missiles" was to put together Herb Brodkin and Buzz Berger with Viacom. I knew it was going to be a very difficult show to produce and that it really needed the fine hand of one of the best in the field. I think that Herb and Buzz are among the very, very few at the top of the ladder. Once that union took place I was confident we would be in pretty good shape. After that, I think the hardest part was the casting, particularly JFK. We agonized for a long, long time about that, but Herb and Buzz said, "We are convinced that Bill DeVane can do it." I had originally thought of Bill DeVane as Bobby Kennedy, because he had played that role in an off-Broadway show. But we had a chance to get Martin Sheen, who could play Bobby very well, but who certainly was not right for John Kennedy. So I agreed with them that it should be Bill DeVane, and he turned in a magnificent performance.

*Do you think you'll ever be bored with this business?*
No. Heavens, no. How could one get bored in this business?

*If they're writing an epitaph for Ed Vane, what are they going to say?*
(Laughs) First of all, I don't want any epitaphs. I would hope that they would make some comment that I had made some contribution to the industry. That I was an honorable man to do business with and I made it all fun and enjoyable, as well as productive.

*How can Group W stations compete with the network in terms of programming? How can anybody compete?*
Well, it would be very difficult for groups to compete in network time. That's the arrangement that the networks have with the affiliates. It makes it very difficult for any syndicator to break in. But we must bear in mind that there are many hours in the broadcast day that the network does not fill. These are open for the producers of syndicated programs.

*Do you believe in the "least-objectionable program" theory?*

Oh, I think that was a kind of a flashy and whimsical phrase. I think it was a colorful way to say a thing, rather than to be really accurate about it. I really think people go for the program that gives them the most pleasure. I don't think they take the negative point of view, and say, "Well, that's the least rotten of the three shows that I have to choose from." I think more often than not there is quality in a certain time period and that quality will win out.

*Tell me another thing about the young person coming into the field as a programmer, say, at the network. How important is it to have courage? We hear a lot about how everybody is running scared at the network.*

I do think that courage is an important quality. There are times when somebody has to just ram a program idea through. We were talking about enthusiasm. Somebody who really has convictions about a program must take risks in order to get it through. The stakes are very high at networks, and a single half-hour in prime time involves many millions of dollars, so you want to be sure that it's as successful as you can possibly make it. In the case of "Mork & Mindy," that was a courageous move on the part of Marcie Carsy and Steve Gentry, who just absolutely convinced the management that a program starring Robin Williams would be successful. There was some skepticism in the building about such a show, but they were so convincing that a chance was taken. Of course, that one turned out well. Similarly, there have been occasions when people were absolutely convinced a thing would be a hit, the management went along and the show bombed. You have too many like that and then you leave the industry.

*What is your view of the artistic control clause in regard to series production?*

Well, I think the networks have to exercise some control, because, after all, they are the ones who have the legal vulnerability. The stations that the networks represent are the ones that have to go to the government for license renewal, and if anything that is untoward is said on a program, it is not the production company that bears the heat, it is the network. I think that if the network is going to have the vulnerability, they must have the right to protect themselves. Now I don't think that that should be unreasonably maintained. But for a network to say to a production company, "Give us twenty-two hour episodes this season," and then never supervise it, is to leave the network extremely vulnerable. I don't think that they have to be in that position.

*What do you look for in a production company when you're selecting one?*

I would meet the people that they are going to put on the

project – the producer, the director, the story editors, all of the principals who will be making up the show. First of all, you have to buy the idea that the basic concept of the program is good. Then, once you have that, the next important thing is to examine the staff of people who are going to work on that concept.

*Let's talk about the pressures of the job.*
    I can tell you that the toughest thing I ever went through was the whole "Soap" experience. The negative reaction to that, the criticism, the pressure groups, the lobbyists, all of those people who did everything humanly possible to prevent that program from ever getting on the air. That was a daily torment to everybody at the network. I think ABC really had no choice but to go forward with it, because giving in to the pressure would have meant tolerating prior restraint. But I tell you, that was a long, hot summer.

*What really got to you of all that criticism?*
    Well, what got to me was that it was so ill-founded. Here were groups trying to prevent a program from getting on the air when those groups had not only never seen a foot of film, but had never even read a script, never read an outline, had no idea who the cast of characters were. The whole pressure was built around the rumor that certain dreadful things were going to happen if "Soap" came on the air. And it was more than just a letter-writing campaign. The pressure that was brought on the ABC network at that time was unimaginable, and it was just amazing that the program went on the air and achieved a nice rating. The morals of the nation were not corrupted, and people still go to church, even though "Soap" is on the air. It was "All in the Family" all over again. Remember the dreadful predictions of what would happen to the moral fiber of the country if that program were permitted to appear week after week? Seven years later it won a Peabody Award.

*Were you really on the hot seat?*
    I was in charge of the ongoing production of it, and therefore absorbed a fair amount of the attack. But it was not just me, it was everybody at the network, from Leonard Goldenson on down, and there was incredible pressure.

*What lesson stands out as being quintessential in the programming field?*
    That one for me is easy. That is, to put it in slang, "Go with your gut feelings."

*Jon Epstein*

Jon Epstein was born and raised in New York City, where as a youth he came under the spell of radio. Upon graduation from Lehigh University in 1947 at the age of eighteen, he got a job with the Ziv Corporation, which was heavily involved in electrical transcriptions and recorded drama.

He spent several years as an office boy and mimeograph operator, but by age twenty-one he was directing soap operas for Ziv. In 1950 he was drafted and sent to Division H headquarters in Yongdongpo, Korea, where he worked as a mimeograph operator. Later, when his division was ordered to Japan, he spent the remainder of his tour producing and directing shows for the Special Services.

Epstein returned to the United States late in 1952 to resume his career in radio, directing stars such as Tyrone Power and Walter Huston. In 1953 he moved to California with the Ziv Corporation and entered the world of syndicated television and series production. In 1961 he left Ziv and produced his first network television assignment, "Arrest and Trial" for Universal.

Over the years Epstein has concentrated on producing for Hollywood's best-known companies: Screen Gems, Filmways, Banner Productions, Mirisch-Rich, and Universal. Some shows he has produced include "McMillan and Wife," "The Flying Nun," "Rat Patrol," "Tarzan," "Kraft Suspense Theater" and "Rich Man, Poor Man," one of the most successful programs in American television.

*You were the producer of "Rich Man, Poor Man"?*
Right.

*This was the first mini-series to be done for American television?*
In my opinion, that's correct, but there are those who would argue with that; I've heard it already. "Vanished," which was done here at the studio, had preceded us as a two-partner with two hours on consecutive nights, or some such thing, and "The Blue Knight" was done as four consecutive hours, I believe, over at Columbia; but as we know it, in terms of the novel for television, certainly "Rich Man, Poor Man" was the original. There are just a few insiders that would question that.

*What was the main obstacle in getting the mini-series concept off the blocks?*
You probably need to be talking to a couple of other people, but when it was originally brought to Universal by ABC's Barry Diller, who was then head of programming at ABC, now chairman of the board at Paramount, it sat for a number of years. It was given to Harve Bennett to develop, and Harve developed it and put it aside, and everyone was afraid of it because they didn't know whether or not the concept would work for television. It was something new and it was something different, and as you and I both know, sometimes television moguls are afraid of difference.

*Did you ever feel like you had your neck out?*

Well, I did to this extent: When they came to me and asked me to make the series, it had already been in some development for a couple of years. They were announcing, "We are going to make this thing," and there was no question about it. I was told by both Universal and ABC that if this worked, it was going to be the granddaddy of them all and there would be others coming, and if it didn't work, the concept was going to probably die quietly. Now Universal's main concern, and one of the reasons I was chosen, was that they felt that from my record I was one of the responsible people on this lot. There are some who are not concerned about, you know, budgets and runaway production costs. So their concern was to get a guy whose track record showed that he could stay on top of the series, because if it ever started to run away from them it could get gigantically expensive, because you're tying people up for months and bringing them back later. The very nature of it was so unique in television—four and one-half months or five months on a series unnerved them. ABC executive Brandon Stoddard told me personally, "I have about eight hours that haven't been finished—I have about eight hours of a project that I'm very excited about in script form. It's called 'Roots.' If 'Rich Man, Poor Man' makes it on television, we will make 'Roots' and if 'Rich Man, Poor Man' doesn't make it on television, I will have to abandon the script." So he had a great interest in it, and I had a great concern about wanting to do it. I told him at the time—I said that I thought it was his job to see that it was *sold* to the audience. I thought we would do our job in terms of bringing them something worthwhile, but he better damn well let the nation know that something special was coming. I must say that one of the greatest jobs in the whole project, in my opinion, was the publicity, under Stoddard's direction—he was the top guy in all the areas to do a job of promotion—with full-page ads, such as "Biggest Motion Picture in the History of Television," or in the history of anything, and suddenly it was a twelve-hour movie, and they'd never had anything like that before. It was so big, and I think the proof is that we came on against two very established hits. On CBS at the time was "Kojak," and on NBC, "Columbo." We came on that Sunday night and we did very respectably against them. We got like a thirty-four or thirty-five share, something like that, and we built from there and went off the air with a fifty-four, so we were starting against gigantic odds. We were very respectable and built from there, so obviously they liked what they saw.

*Did you have any input on the promotion?*

No, not really, other than the fact that I was obviously deeply involved with the casting of the people. What they were looking for was a promotable cast, and we realized that we were aging three principals from roughly seventeen years of age to thirty-seven years. The story went from about 1945 to about 1965, and we had to get people that were somewhat in between — close enough in age to the seventeen-year-old to play it legitimately, yet not so young and so close to seventeen that when you aged them to become thirty-seven they would look ridiculous. That meant we had to find people in their late twenties or early thirties to kind of compromise that, so that we play them young and mature them. We realized that if we found people like that, we were not going to find unknowns, because there are no unknowns at thirty-two. They've either tried it and failed or they've made it. We couldn't do it with people who had made it, because that would have sent us right out of the ballpark in terms of cost; trying to tie up major stars for five months of television would have been prohibitive. So we got people who we felt were *about* to make it — who had been around the block, done some guest shots, done some hourly TV here or there and were on the rise — and that's how we ended up with the three people we did. We were concerned that no one was going to tune in to see Nick Nolte, Susan Blakely and Peter Strauss, whom they had never heard of, so we surrounded them with established stars. It's a long answer to a simple question, but to that extent I feel that we made a major contribution to ABC's promotional thoughts and activities. Everything they did do they sent across our desk and we nodded in approval because, frankly, I thought they did a great job.

*The character of Falconnetti was really evil incarnate in the series. He was a key.*
    He certainly was one of those, and we thought he was so useful, as you probably know, that we kept him around for the second year. He was one of the characters that we still hadn't used up at all, because it was a clash between good and evil and he certainly represented that.

*Did you have any trouble staying within budget?*
    Amazingly not. I would say certainly we went over — everything goes over — but we went over lightly.

*What do you mean by "lightly"?*
    Well, I can't give you exact figures because frankly I don't remember them. Otherwise I would be happy to. But we had something like eight days per hour so, say, give or take ninety-six days, I don't remember exactly. So we went probably 101 — maybe 100. The point is we went just slightly over. If the budget on it was five and a half million, I imagine we probably spent six million, but it could have been twelve million. Once those things start to get away from you it's like a rolling stone. It just gathers and gathers and gets worse and worse.

*What's a sign something is getting away from you? Is is always obvious, or are there some subtle signs?*
    It's probably a combination of both. I think sometimes you start to

slip a couple of pages. You've got a schedule — a number of pages to shoot per day — and you find that you're dropping a few hours' work, which is not so terrible. But if you do that three days in a row, suddenly you're a full day behind, and you see that you're only going to get worse instead of better because maybe you've got some of the toughest stuff coming up. You try not to start with the toughest stuff, but you don't want to start with the easiest stuff either or you'll be lulled into a sense of false security. Also, the availability of certain actors that you wanted for certain parts determines to some extent the scheduling of the show. Ed Asner was a very important factor — he played in the first three hours or so, and we had to be sure to schedule our shooting before "The Mary Tyler Moore Show" went back into production. I would say that, generally speaking, there are no subtle signs. You can usually tell if you're going along smoothly, making the schedule, and the weather is breaking well for you. That was one area we were very lucky with, and I suppose a lot of it had to do with just the general scheduling. When you shoot from May to September, as we did, you have less likelihood of weather problems than if you shoot from November to February, which I have also done, with projects that require a lot of exterior shooting. You're sure to borrow weather problems in Southern California.

*Any major mistakes that you made, or that anybody made, in "Rich Man, Poor Man" that you would have corrected if you were going to do it again?*

I tell you — I'm not going to give you a glib answer on that — not that I know of. We were fortunate in that all of the elements seemed to fall into place rather neatly. Some of it was good planning, some of it I would like to think was talent, but a lot of it was luck. It just seemed to work. Who would have known when we hired Peter Strauss that he was going to be every bit as good as we had hoped he would be? The casting of Bill Smith as Falconetti, I think, was just a stroke — he's been around a long time — but we kind of felt that he would be right for it and it worked. David Greene was probably a very fortunate stroke. Harve and I had seen very little of his work. He had been recommended to us by friends of ours.* He had done a two-hour "Ellery Queen," and he had hardly emerged as an important director, but we saw something we felt that would make him right for this project. We hired him, and I think that the results of David's work are obvious. He won an Emmy for that — all as the result of our hiring him. So I would say the mistakes were minimal and the good strokes of fortune were maximal. It received something like twenty-six Emmy nominations, of which we are very proud.

*Was it very tough overlapping the sequences in terms of writing or*

---

*Dick Levinson and Bill Link.

*producing — in other words, when to cut off a given show and how to overlap?*

Harve worked more closely with Dean Reisner than I, but in an article written in the *Los Angeles Times*, I said the one person that really deserved to win an Emmy more than anybody was Dean Reisner, because he juggled that so deftly. The tough thing was to reprise enough (remember we're in a new form) for the people that hadn't seen an episode, or missed it, and still not bore the people that had — to build it in to the body of the project so you're not doing just a two-minute flashback of "In case you missed last week, here's what happened." The goal was to be able to have certain characters consistently restate, without letting the audience feel that they were restating. That was what was handled so deftly by Dean by weaving into the present what had taken place in the past without stopping the show.

*You worked with a lot of directors, didn't you, on that?*

We only had two directors on it. The first four hours were directed by David Greene, the middle four hours by Boris Sagal, and the last four hours we came back to David Greene. We had intended to go with three directors — four, four, and four — and after seeing the early stages of David's work, we were so excited about what he did that we went back to him for the last four hours. You see, we started the first four hours before the last four hours were finished, so he couldn't have done all of it, because it wasn't ready, and you need to prepare the material ahead of time; so while David was shooting his first four hours, Boris was preparing his second four hours, and then when Boris was shooting his middle four hours, David was preparing the last four hours.

*How long does it take you to prepare for a given show?*

It varies, but I can only tell you that, in my opinion, the key to quality television is in the preparation period. Of course, you have to have talented people, but under the gun, problems of television are so common; half the problems of mediocre television are because we don't have enough time. The best example I can give you is that Dean spent close to fourteen *months* in writing the twelve hours, and Michael Gleason, who was involved as executive producer in the second year, had fourteen *weeks* to get it ready. There's no question it suffers because you don't have the time to take the care that you need. Sometimes it gets a little costly to take time up front; you don't have the luxury of time for many reasons. Usually the network orders the program suddenly and you've got to go. They have air dates to meet, and we all understand that; but if we ever had the luxury of time, even though it costs a little more money, it would save money in the long run, because a well-prepared picture will come closer to budget and will be better because it has all the care up front.

*What are the primary mistakes that a newcomer, or relative newcomer, in your particular area would tend to make?*

Well, the thing that I have learned more than anything else, and I don't mean to sound pompous — I truly don't mean it as such — but I think, experience. I thought I was a good producer twelve years ago. I was a much better producer six years later because I had six more years of things and I had gotten better at it. You just learn the short cuts, you learn the nuances and all of the shadings that come into decision making. It becomes easier for you to make the right decisions if you've been there before. It is just *doing.* Some very bright guys out there, as they develop, get better. You don't have to be a genius to be a good producer. You have to have a little good taste, some inherent talent, and then you've got to build on it and *experience.* It wasn't genius that caused Frank Price to come to me — it was track record. The networks find that out all the time, and they'll come to Norman Lear with a one-line idea and say, "Go make a series out of it," and they'll know what they're going to get because Norman has a track record. That doesn't mean that there aren't opportunities for the young people. There are plenty of opportunities all the time, as long as they understand that they are in a learning phase, and during these developing years if they can absorb all that they'll just be better off for it four or five years later.

*What was the hardest thing to learn as a producer? Was there one lesson that was tougher to learn than others?*

Well, I've never had that question posed to me. I would say again that it is the acquisition of knowledge, in general. The more you work with things the easier they seem to come; I mean, you just get better at it. I suppose it's like wanting to play tournament tennis and getting out on the court, and if you play every day you're just going to get sharper. Some people reach the level of their ability and that's as high as they go. There's nothing the matter with that. But there are others who just keep absorbing more and more and getting better at it. It isn't any single tough thing that came to me except my realization that the script was all-important. I also think surrounding yourself with talented people is, of course, one of the greatest things a producer can contribute — not only how to guide a writer, but picking the right guy; not only knowing how to get the best out of a director, but who is that guy? — and surrounding yourself with talented people in all departments and letting them function and being able to step in and knowing when they're not doing it. I guess I'm telling you the function of a producer. The best function a producer can serve is to pick his best people and then lay back and only deal when something goes wrong.

*What about personalities? You must sometimes get into a situation of "Can we work with this person?"*

In a prehiring situation sometimes that affects your thinking – no question about it. I believe a couple of things. One, that you really want to get the best guy for the job, but if he's impossible, sometimes it's just not worth it. Sometimes you're going to say to yourself, "Not only is my stomach going to suffer, but the product is going to suffer, because this guy is just too damn difficult." There are people like that out there – actors, directors, writers, and I suppose there are producers who are so impossible that it just isn't worth it. It's tough enough to make pictures without having to deal with gigantic personality clashes and egos. So you try to find talented people who are good to work with. I'm not saying you should find untalented people just because they can do it without problems, but certainly you can get a combination of the two. Ed Asner, as I mentioned before, is not only a big talent, he's a sweetheart – intelligent, sensitive, and he gets in there and he does his job like a complete professional. There are plenty of others, too, I might add. Once in a while you run across someone who is just more trouble than he's worth and you say, "Okay, I've learned from that experience, I'm not going to come back to him – let someone else do that."

*Blacklisting is the wrong term, but these reputations must catch up with people who are impossible to work with.*

I suppose if somebody is totally impossible, word sort of gets around – the actors themselves carry it, you know. Ten actresses are on the set when that person has an hysterical fit, and that story gets around town pretty fast. But by and large, I would say there aren't too many of them. Sometimes you have to learn for yourself, and I might add that I have found a couple of cases – personal situations with actors I know – who were impossible and who learned because they started to get cold. They realized . . . in a sense, they found religion and they said, "I've been a bastard all these years and I'm making a lot of people miserable and I am ready to change." In one case, a guy that I worked with twenty-five years ago when I first started in the business was really impossible. Then he had a very difficult operation – I believe it was either a brain operation or it was something to do with the head, and he thought he was going to die. He told me, personally, during that experience he realized what a bastard he had been and he said, "If I get out of this, I swear to God I am going to change." And he changed, and he became a pussycat, and everyone loves him. He works all the time. He's a character actor today.

*What would he do? Did he blow up on the set?*

Absolute hysterical fits on the set – screaming, hollering, walking off the set, arguing on every point. You know, it was partly insecurity, fear – that's what causes it more than anything, and it doesn't belong only to actors. It's just that they're more obvious because they're known, so they make more interesting copy (and I put "copy" in quotes). If word gets around about a director, it's not really as interesting as hearing it about actors that you know.

*Let's talk about confidence — that's a pretty important virtue, isn't it?*
   That's right. I believe that I know what I'm doing, and you don't have to be egotistical to believe in yourself. I think it's the same in any field. You get out there and you do the best you can. If you know you're doing the best you can, you know you're going to be right because if you're pretty good, you're going to be right 85 percent of the time. Producers have to make quick judgments. I can't just sit around and say, "I'll think about it." There are people like that, and nothing gets done because there's money wasted and everything. I have found that if I really agonize over it and make a judgment that's instinctive, then I'll also be right 85 percent of the time. So you do it, and you have to suffer the consequences, and if you blew it, you blew it. It's not the most important thing in life. You just do the best you can, and you acquire confidence from doing and from having been there before, and again, from that word "experience."

*I've heard that the story editor is the one to really belly-up to in Hollywood. A writer told me that. Do you think that's true?*
   I think it's sometimes true in certain situations. For example, depending on the series, if you've got a producer with a strong story mind, who is able to make it and is a major contributor, then your story editor becomes an arm of that guy; you function probably in tandem and he is, in a sense, agreeing with you, not because he's in that position, but because you think alike. Sometimes the producer is not a strong story person and counts more on his story editor because the story editor has more muscle in a given situation. But I think, generally speaking, your better producers are very strong in the areas of the story, or they're former writers. Now, the fact that they're former writers does not necessarily make them good producers. Some of the studios have found — and it's not something I subscribe to — that they make their writers into producers and just let them write. The play's really the thing. If they get a writer to do the writing, the rest of it will take care of itself. Now I happen to feel very strongly that there's a lot more to producing than just the scripts; on the other hand, I do feel that the scripts are *the* most important thing. But smart writers who become producers acquire the knowledge in other areas. There are a lot of contributions that can be made to casting and choosing personnel and working in the cutting room and working with the composer — all those little touches that go to make the difference between a good picture and a fine picture. Why should a writer just be made a producer because he's a good writer? The ideal is to get a producer who is not a writer, in my opinion, but who has a good story mind and who's worked with writers over the years.

*What was it like working for the Ziv organization?*

Well, that company was the hottest company in the business in the syndication field, and we made everything cheaper than anyone else. I gotta tell you, plenty of people went by the wayside, but other people used that as a learning experience. When you're given no money, you can't buy the best writers in town or the best directors in town, and you have to hang in there on your ingenuity and your own abilities — you know, when they're not giving you all the tools and they're giving you less tools than the next guy, you're either going to collapse under the effort or you're going to acquire more abilities because you're forced to. I would like to think in my case that's what happened. I really learned from the ground up with not a lot of help. I mean, they said, "Here it is. This is all we've got. Now go make it." I was with them for a number of years. I started doing my first producing with them, but I had gone through being a story editor and I ran the story department, supervised all the scripts at the studio. Eventually, as they started to phase out of the business, television grew, and the Ziv Company just kind of went in the other direction. Before Ziv went out of business I got out of there in time. I was a loyal guy, and I liked being there; there was a very happy family relationship and we all had a wonderful time. It was a great learning experience. But it was time to move on, and I came to Universal for a couple of years. I did my first real serious network producing here for a couple of years. Then I went on to "Trials of O'Brien" for a year and then did "Rat Patrol" for a couple of years. Then three years at Screen Gems, producing other things, and then back here, and I'm now completing nine more years with Universal. I started in business very young. I'm fifty-one now, but I started when I was nineteen in the mailroom back East, so I've had a lot of experience and I've been around a long time, even though I do not yet consider myself an old sod.

*What about working with unions?*

Strangely enough, when you are under the umbrella of a studio, as I am and generally have been, I don't find that all that difficult; we have so many buffer zones that we are protected from that. The studio says, "You're the artist. Make the picture. We'll worry about the other things." They provide you with a terrific physical plant here and they provide you with some wonderful production people who really know their business. To that effect, there was a book written that might interest you. It is called *The Making of Rich Man, Poor Man*, and it was a paperback book — company owned. I don't know what unit of our company it was, but it was out there a couple of years ago. I don't know how easily obtainable it is now. It really described in great detail and very accurately, in my opinion, everyone involved in that particular show and how it got to be made. One of the things I said in it was that the real hero in the piece, besides the writer, was a guy named Benny Bishop. He was our production manager, and he really handled the physical making of the picture, so that I could address myself to the decisions that had to be made, the decisions that he would bring to me. He was the guy that a good production manager can be — that you can really rely on.

The studios also have labor relations departments and that kind of thing — law departments — so that I, as a producer not in the independent field but under the umbrella of the major, don't have too many of those concerns.

*What do you look for in a production manager?*

I hate to use that word again — well, experience, to begin with, but if you're no good, even twenty years of experience isn't going to mean anything. I think partly enthusiasm, in addition to experience. If he attacks the project and feels about it as if it were his baby, and he approaches it as if it were his money and has the excitement about the project that we like to think we have — not just doing a physical job. Somebody who has the understanding of the creative problems involved and is not just looking to do the one thing that he has to do and must do — cost controls, etc. — because that's one of the things he must be concerned over. He's got to understand that when the director wants a different place to shoot, even though it's a little more expensive, it might make the picture better; so he has to understand those needs and still protect the budget, among other things.

*Was author Irwin Shaw involved with "Rich Man"?*

No. At one point he was involved, long before I, in some way. I do not know how that was, but I know the creating of the script and the development of it all was done without Irwin. Universal had the rights to it and that was that. As a matter of fact, the quote that I have used so often, "Irwin doesn't know what hit him." He was so pleased when he came back from Switzerland one time and found that his old book had become a gigantic success and had made him quite rich, because he had, obviously, retained his royalties to the book, and the book sold an extra five million or so. He had really put it away and gone on to other things because it was 1970 when it was a hit — a semi-hit, I should say, and yet not one of his great achievements in terms of the reviews and everything. When he came back, he was astounded at what had happened. It was after the picture had been shot and, I think, aired, that he ran the film — all twelve hours of it — here at the studio on two successive days, came to my office after the screening and said to me, "I want you to know that I have never been happy with material of mine that has been translated to the screen, but this is an exception. You have done the book proud." That pleased me, of course, because you like to have a guy whose work you respect and have adapted. That makes a difference — feeling good about it.

*Was there a conventional knowledge in the business of "Well, you can't do 'Rich Man, Poor Man, Number Two' — that's overkill, or . . . "?*

Well, I think there was some hesitancy about it, but the greater hesitancy was, "How do you go off the air with a fifty-four share and not cash in on the success?" So they decided to do an original and continue with the story of the people. Fred Silverman, who headed programming, was one of the driving forces behind that. He, at that time, had come into ABC after "Rich Man" had been filmed, but before it had been aired, and he was probably one of the guys, if not the key guy, involved in how to put it on the air and how to program and when. He had himself a hit on his hands and said, "It's ridiculous, let's continue." And it did well, by the way. It didn't have the impact nor the quality nor the time of the original. It was a series, it was a television *series*, instead of a special event. It was a good television series — something that we're not at all ashamed of — but because of the nature of the beast and the short time we had to prepare it and the fact that we were not working from original Irwin Shaw material, and had no time to really create a novel of our own, we had a story to tell that we had to conceive from the very first moment in the spring and it had to be on the air in the fall. We started with nothing. Michael Gleason was the driving force behind that; he served in much the same capacity as Harve Bennett served on the first book and under circumstances that were not nearly as terrific because he didn't have any time. I thought he did an amazing job. Peter Strauss has been quoted as saying how disappointed he was in the second year. Well, Peter Strauss is right, but he is also not practical, and he must understand that he signed on for a television series and not a twelve-hour special that had a lot of time and money in it, and the real world greeted him and he wasn't thrilled with it. I've got to tell you, under the circumstances the quality of the program held up remarkably well — much better than average television fare. I'm not saying it was brilliant, at all, but it certainly was better than average.

*What portion of you is dreamer and what portion of you is pragmatist?*

I am all pragmatist except in one area: The dream in me is to make the definitive film some day. When I work on a project I am a total pragmatist. When I think about projects that I would like to develop and have tried to develop, that's when I do my dreaming. One of the things that I'm doing now started, if not with a dream, at least with the germ of a dream and an excitement about a project that I really wanted to go forward with — a movie for television called "The Gossip Columnist." It took me over a year to get everybody together to get somebody to say, "Yeah, go make it." And I'm finally in the middle of making it. But once I get down to it I know what I have to do. I know the business I'm in, I don't kid myself that it's going to be something that it isn't. I really believe that I try to do the best job within the confines of what I've got. If somebody says to me, "Here's two million dollars, go make the picture," I believe in my case at least, that I have enough integrity to say, "Okay, I've got two million dollars and that's all they've given me and I'm going to do the best I can with the two million dollars." It's easy to let it slop over and do it at two and a half million and maybe it will be better, but that's not fair, that's not what I agreed that I was going to do. I have the responsibility, and I try to exercise it.

*Talk about "above- and below-the-line" costs and how they break out, say, with "Rich Man, Poor Man" and with your average show.*

It's a tremendous variance. I'm really not . . . it's not that I'm not at liberty to say, but I don't think that I can give you an intelligent answer to that. There is so much difference between the two. Let me try to tell you . . . I'm looking at something of mine right now that has above-the-line of $450,000 and below-the-line of $770,000. Now you put direct cost on top of that, which is a 20 percent surcharge, you get the budget of a project, but I don't know how much of a relationship there would always be – it varies greatly. I could dig out another budget. Here's the budget of an episode: total above-the-line $300,000; total below-the-line $400,000.

*What episode was that?*

It's an episode of "The Contender," which is a mini-series that I just completed for CBS about a boxer. It will go on the air in January, and they like it enough to now want to change it from a five and a half-hour mini-series to a series. They want to start already adding on to it. Since it's an original to begin with, there's no bounds. Again, it's another variation of the same form.

*What consists of above-the-line costs?*

Above-the-line is the writing and the producing and the directing and the talent, basically. Below-the-line is the making of the picture.

*What do you look for in a property to convert into a mini-series?*

I'm ashamed to tell you that I think I would look for something that I think I could sell to the network. You know, it doesn't do you much good – going back to that dreamer question – it doesn't do you much good to think, "Wouldn't this make a marvelous mini-series," if I were convinced that if I were the guy sitting over at CBS, or wherever, that I would say, "Yes, it's a swell idea but you would get an audience of twelve." So I need, from a practical point of view, what I think is an audience-getter. That's what I look for in a mini-series as much as anything else, and how you make it is up to you. You can always make it good or you can make it not so good; it's a matter of injecting it with your quality. If everything falls into place you get lucky. Some of the casting on the original "Rich Man" was pure good fortune. We had hoped we were going to get what we were going to get, but, you know, I didn't know that Bill Bixby was going to turn out to be as wonderful as he turned out to be.

*As a director?*

No. He directed for me later — he directed in the second year. I mean, as an actor. He played Julie's first husband — he fathered Billy. He was wonderful. I always knew Bill was good, but he had never had an opportunity — not that there was anything to be embarrassed about or to apologize for in the previous work he had done, but he had never done anything of really dimensional stuff, because he had never had the opportunity. When we presented the material to him, he wanted to do it. Harve and I felt that he was more than up to it and we were right. You're not always right. As I said, I think we might have gotten lucky.

*Do you believe in treatments — story treatments?*

I certainly believe to this extent — like I talked to you about preparation, earlier, as being so vitally important. That is the writer's preparation. Yes, if a writer can write, all you need to do is give me good dialogue, once the treatment is conceived and approved and finalized. That's where all the work is, in my opinion: You write a script from a treatment, that's the easy part, the fun part, and all you need to do is write good people after that. But to conceive it and to know how to line a story is the hard work.

That's what I feel is out of kilter in the Writers' Guild contract with the producers — with the producing company. I think the back-breaking work is in the storyline, and the rest of it is easy, comparatively; yet the big money is in the script and the little money is in the treatment or the storyline or whatever you want to call it. It seems to me for any good writer, once you've got a good treatment, you're home free.

*How long is an average treatment that you do?*

It depends on the length, usually, of the show. I would say, for an hour, anywhere between ten and fifteen pages — for a two-hour I need anywhere between twenty and forty pages.

*What do you look for in a good treatment? Is a good treatment the same as a good story?*

Yeah, that's all it is — it's a good story, it's a good yarn, and you've got to remember what you're making it for. You have got to get off to a pretty fast start if you're in television. If you have an audience sitting in a motion picture theater, they're not about to walk out on you, but in television you'd better grab them fast. So I look for something that will do that, hopefully, and will build, and just like any good yarn, it will hold the attention. It's instinct, I guess, and experience, again, as much as anything else.

*I understand that local TV salespeople weren't used to selling the type of program that "Rich Man" was. This is particularly true because of the way that it was run on air. Was that a great problem?*

I'm sure it was, to the point where — this is not in my purview — but to the point where they finally resold it. They were breaking it up into all kinds of lengths. Their concern was, of course, — it was the concern originally of the show — will the audience sit still for it? What happens if an audience doesn't see the first two parts and suddenly along comes the third part and an audience is ready to look at it but says, "Yeah, but I didn't see the first two parts so I'm not going to start now"? They go to another channel. When you have an established piece of material that's been done on the tube and it's been sold to syndication reruns, it has a reputation that precedes it and people either commit to it or they don't. In the hands of a network they have found they're able, on a short-term basis, to look at it week after week, if it's programmed carefully and it's quality. "Dallas" is on every week and it's a continuing story. "The Contender" is going to be on once a week; it's going to be a continued story. What you look for, though, is self-contained programs; in other words, you've got to be able to fulfill an audience if they tune in Episode Three so they don't feel cheated — they should understand what's going on, even if they've missed one or two. It's a little tricky; you use reprises, and you use trailers and all that sort of thing. But, my gosh, soap operas have been doing that for twenty-five years in television and forty years in radio. The thing is though, soap operas move so slowly that you can afford to miss a couple of shows each week and still know what's going on, whereas in a series of our kind you can't do that. So it's risky — let me give you an example. In "Rich Man, Poor Man, Book Two," we had a thirty-one share when we came on the air. We stayed, incredibly at that level; it rarely fluctuated by more than a point. Even "Charlie's Angels" will fluctuate five or six points from one given week to another, but our audience, once they stayed with us, seemed to stay with us. By the same token, we never seemed to acquire a new audience. Now I can't tell you that they were the same people all the time, but I would say the nucleus was pretty much the same.

*Where is the mini-series going in the future?*

I think if it is not overkilled like anything else that it will continue to have a very strong life of its own. I think NBC made somewhat of a mistake in turning out mini-series upon mini-series a couple of years ago and calling it "Best Sellers." There are just too many of them. Some of the hot ones do very, very well, and I think if you present the audience with quality and subject matter that they're interested in seeing — your guess is as good as anyone's as to what that is — that they will come and look at it. "Washington Behind Closed Doors" intrigued them; they watched it. A couple of others in the past couple of years. I think "Scruples" will probably work, and if it's good, it will continue to work. The real key is, if you get them to tune in, give them something worthwhile so they want to come back.

*In "Rich Man" you hired a lot of people from off the lot and . . .*

Only actors — actors and extras — but they're all the free-lance people that you get all the time, and there's nothing peculiar about mini-series. You're provided, generally, with studio personnel, and they're the same people that go from one show to another — the sound people, etc., and the physical production people. By and large, your key people are all studio personnel, with the exception of the director, whom you buy for the job, and the actors that you buy by the piece.

*What motivates Jon Epstein?*

I guess I can answer that very simply: I love what I do, and I'm not anxious to be Number One. I don't have that ego drive and that illness that says I've got to drive everyone crazy, including myself, and reach the top. I would be very content, say, with 200 guys in the business who do what I do, to be Number Nine. That doesn't mean I'm going to settle for Number Eighty-nine, and it doesn't mean that I won't aspire to the top, but the drive that I have I would like to think is tempered with other things, and it's a healthy kind of drive — it's like an ego. People have said to me over the years, "Ego is necessary. Too much ego is unhealthy." I think if I find the right balance of wanting to enjoy my football games and my other activities, whatever hobbies I have, and the balance of life that's out there — just getting out in the fresh air once in a while and saying, "To hell with it. I'm not going to read a script today" — it seems that I come back with the continued vigor of the previous week. I try not to bust my ass working on weekends so that I can come back refreshed — just having gotten away from it — and really hot to trot on things. But I love what I do, in answer to your question, and I think that is it probably more than anything else. It's hard not to be excited about this business.

*Al Masini*

AL MASINI IS LISTED by *Broadcasting Magazine* as one of the top fifty industry leaders of the 1970s. And Masini did indeed make a mark on broadcasting during those years, as he continues to do today.

Masini began his career with CBS in the late 1950s. For twelve years he worked for Edward Petry, where he developed, among other innovations, spot-by-spot pricing. Then Masini founded Tele-Rep, which is now the third largest rep company in revenue and represented stations.

In 1976 Masini and Tele-Rep organized a group of stations under the name Operation Prime Time (OPT) and began to chip away at the networks' control of prime time. Their first mini-series, "Testimony of Two Men," was an unqualified success. Since then, Operation Prime Time has produced dozens of mini-series and television specials and has proven that local stations can produce hit programs with the audience appeal and quality of the best of network fare.

The OPT mini-series have gathered an impressive share of ratings and awards: three Emmys for "A Woman Called Golda," a Peabody and ten nominations from the British Academy of Film and Television for "Smiley's People." Masini has developed three weekly series as well: "Solid Gold," "Entertainment Tonight," and "Star Search."

Masini has been active in industry organizations, including the National Sales Committee, the National Committee of the Stations Representatives Association, and the TVB National Sales Advisory and SRA Executive committees.

*How did Operation Prime Time get started?*

In 1976, in Los Angeles, there was a meeting at the INTV (Independent Television Association). They have a convention each year, and I was the speaker at that time. They asked me to speak about independents as I know them and what I thought should be done in the future. The gist of my speech was that independents in recent years have made great strides by programming reruns of syndicated products, and they were able to get twenty-five and thirty shares in those particular areas. You know, like putting sitcoms against the news and so on. But the area that was not touched and was not really successful was prime time. If independents as a whole got a ten share in prime time, they were doing enormously well, and yet prime time, from 7:00 to 11:00, is where the heavy viewing is—fifty or sixty percent of the audience is watching. And many independents were only getting a five share. So I said, "Why aren't we making it in that area?" Well, the answer is obvious. In that area the networks are putting on their best shows—they're all eighteen to forty-nine [age] viewing, and they're first runs with heavy budgets. And what are the independents putting on at that particular time? They're putting on reruns of old network shows that had hit their peak and had really outlived their lives. Everything that the syndicators were putting into syndication had run on the networks at least twice and then had run in another daytime slot on the networks. For instance, the networks were taking "Happy Days," "Laverne & Shirley" and those things and running them twice at prime time and then putting them on in the daytime and running them twice more, and they were taking the hour shows, like they're doing now, and putting them on at 11:30 at night, so that by the time they got into syndication, they had at least four or five runs on them. And then you put them on the affiliates — on the independents — at prime time and you're then putting them against a first-run product on the network. That's the reason you're not getting the big ratings.

So what happened, we actually developed our own first runs equivalent to what the network was putting on, because strangely enough, in the history of television, in twenty-five or thirty years or more, no one had ever produced programs of network quality available to the stations for purchase. The only way you could get those things was after the network produced them, and when they were through with them in their runs, you could buy them as reruns. The syndications, which are basically put-together shows, are really game shows or low-budget shows that never went into the high-budget area. So I suggested that the independents get together and form an association sometime and try to finance something of that scope. They tried to do it, but it was very hard because nobody agreed on anything. So it was not successful. But they said they would bring it up again at the next convention in the industry, which would be NATPE, the National Association of Television Program Executives, in San Francisco, in February of that year.

*That was 1977.*

Yes. At that particular time they took it up again, and they still couldn't agree on anything and the friction was too much. So they decided that even though the idea may have had some merit, they had to abandon it because of the impracticality of trying to implement it. I was catching a plane from the NATPE and I met Shelley Cooper, who was the manager of WGM in Chicago. Shelley said, "Gee, it was too bad about your idea — somebody really should do something about that," and I said, "Shelley, somebody is us, because, you know, you're general manager of one of the larger independents in the country, and I'm president of a rep company, and who's going to do it if *we* don't do it?" So we had a lot of time on the plane to speculate — if we were able to do it, what would we really do? And we decided on the plane that we really couldn't do regular programs because, first of all, you want to do it sporadically, as a special. And you want to see things that would really have enormous impact and publicity value so you could get somebody's attention because it's not a recurrent thing — it doesn't have the habit pattern. And one of the things that was coming on the scene at that time was "Rich Man, Poor Man," which was a novel for television. We said, "That has lots of possibilities." We didn't know it was going to catch on, but we said, "Certainly, you have the name, author, and a lot of people are familiar with the book and if you cast it right it certainly would work."

I said that if we were going to do it, what we really ought to do is have about twelve stars and have a good studio do it, and we could publicize something like that and really make it go. It certainly would be worth a shot. So I said that when I got back I would try to look into the possibility. We finally decided that we ought to look into Universal, because Universal was doing "Rich Man, Poor Man," and of the studios, it was certainly one of the bigger ones, and not knowing too much of what we were doing, we would be safer to go to somebody who was established than to an independent producer.

So I came back and I met with Lou Friedland, who is head of MCA distribution here, and he was very enthusiastic about the idea. We did some early computations and tried to figure out, if we took the independent universe, how much money we could raise. It was very enlightening in looking at the independent universe, because a lot of people don't know this: At that time there were fifty VHF independent markets in the country covering 33 percent of the United States, and there were eighteen independent UHF markets covering 23 percent of the United States, making a total coverage of independents in the United States of 56 percent. So, if we did a project for independent television, we would only have half the potential that the network has when they produce a show and put it on their affiliates, and it wasn't practical financially to try to do something like that. We learned that any project of this type would not be an independent project; it would really have to be a project designed for both affiliates and independents. The affiliates have the same need as the independents. They really had no opportunity to program something for themselves on which they could put their own local commercials. If a local bank or a local department store wanted to put commercials within a show, they couldn't do it because if you're carrying the network in prime time, all you have is the preceding spot and the following spot. You have nothing within. So a station, even an affiliate, would like to have a special into which they could put national spots as well as local spots.

The net result was, I thought we could sell them. I knew a lot of affiliates that I represented, and I knew what they were doing, and I said, "Let's try to look at the budget and see what we can do." We were looking at the budget for hour shows, and they were running at that time around $300,000 an hour on the network. But the novels for television were running over $400,000, more like $500,000, an hour. I looked at how much the stations normally pay for top syndication. At that time in history they had paid about $200,000 an hour for distribution of something like "Six Million Dollar Man" or "FBI." On the basis of that, you might say that if we got them to pay twice as much as they've ever paid before for an hour, we would just about be getting into the range of what was needed to produce the kind of thing we're talking about. And that was a pretty stiff order because most people weren't accustomed to spending that kind of money. Since then, I must say, even in syndication it has gone up; now "Laverne & Shirley" and "Three's Company" would range between $500,000 and $600,00 an hour in syndication after being exposed on the network. At any rate, I said we would try to form a committee to look into the matter and see if we could clear it.

One of the things, most obviously: We must have New York, San Francisco, Chicago, L.A. That's why the networks are capable of putting together a network – they had operating stations in the key markets. Just to give you a "for instance": While New York represents over 8 percent of the U.S. in population, it represents over 11 percent of the dollars of the syndicated product. L.A. represents about 11 percent of the syndicated product, so just New York and L.A. alone represent 22 percent of the money you need to do any kind of thing like this.

So, Shelley Cooper was the man on the plane with me from WGM in Chicago; Rich Frank, who was at that time general manager of KCOP in Los Angeles and later went on to become president of Paramount Distribution, as a result of all this, and Evan Thompson replaced him; Bill Schwartz at KTVU in San Francisco; and then we added Gaylord Broadcasting with Crawford Rice and Taft Broadcasting with Don Chapin, and we filled in some of the medium-sized markets right below that. As a result, we, as a steering committee, could get about 45 to 50 percent of the dollars we needed going in and I only had to sell the rest of the country to make it work.

I asked them to meet with me in Chicago at the NAB. It was funny because here were all these high-powered executives and they didn't have a meeting place at the McCormick Place, so we sat on the steps. We had our first meeting, and we all agreed that we would put our own money up in this experiment venture because nobody had ever tried it before. We thought we would do something in the programming area. We didn't think we would set the world on fire, but we thought we would try to do something new. We said we would meet with all the producers in Hollywood in May. In the meantime, I put together a presentation to stations as to why they should join this thing, because as I pointed out, any other business would spend a lot of money on research and development. I thought that even if this thing did not produce a profit, they should go into it just as research and development. Having done that, we tested it on a few stations and they seemed to be interested. We went out there and we listened to all the producers for three days, and finally we went back to Universal and had a meeting with Sid Steinberg of Universal Studios. Frank Price was head of Universal Television, and we met with him in New York. We stayed at that meeting, I guess, for about five hours and came out agreeing that if we could raise $400,000 an hour, they would give us about a $500,000-an-hour project. Now, they were counting on getting a 10 percent reduction in cost through the guild because this was a new area. This didn't work. Then they came back to us and said the $400,000 had to be $440,000, so I had to go back to all the stations and ask them to raise a little bit more money. Then we got it all together and made it work. It was a very close call. It was very tough to have sold them on $400,000 and then have to go back and tell them they would have to come up with 10 percent more on top of that.

At any rate, we looked at about fifty or sixty different projects and finally picked "Testimony of Two Men." We were going to do an eight-hour book but finally, because of the timing, ended up doing six hours, and we barely got the thing together in time. We put it on in May 1977 on a lineup of 100 stations, covering 90 percent of the country, and we got ratings that were equal to the average network ratings in May. We were very pleased, as this was the first time it had ever happened. In addition, we made a test of other areas and even sold a minute on a network basis to General Foods and Bristol-Meyers, and that was a first. So we proved we could do it, and everybody who got into it just on research/development actually made a lot of money, and everybody was very enthusiastic about it. We did three more projects the following year. We did John Jakes's series *The Bastard* — that was the first of the John Jakes series — in May; that did a twenty-three rating and it outpolled every network show on in the month of May, I think except for six or seven shows. We also did *Evening in Byzantium*, an Irwin Shaw book, in the middle of the summer when the networks were doing reruns, and it got an eighteen rating, and that outpolled all the networks. Then we did *The Immigrants* in the fall. We told the stations to run it any time they wanted to but not to pick the same day and time because we had a combination on that first go-around of about twenty-two independents and about seventy-eight affiliates. So we had a predominance of affiliates, ironically enough; you have to have that, you know, or it doesn't come out. They all did very well. We asked them to run it approximately the same time — the same week or a week-or-two span so we could coordinate national publicity.

*How did you publicize it?*

Well, we had an on-the-set publicist who issued pictures and slides and stories to the papers around the country, and Universal also arranged the publicity things we put in magazines, and we got coverage here and there — even *TV Guide* picked us up and gave us a plug. It was basically working pretty well, considering there was no organization and I was running a $230,000,000 rep with about 240 people and only did this in my spare time. My secretary, Mary Jane, was my only help, and we were doing the calling and the clearing and all the coordinating and publicity and everything else. At any rate, we managed to keep on going and put on five more projects over two years.

Everything up to that point had been with Universal, and we were almost to the point where we were doing what *they* wanted more than what we could see was available around. We thought we should open it up to other people. So the next ones, we said, would be whoever came in with the best products. We did listen to them all, and we finally ended up doing for 1979 the next two books in the John Jakes series — *The Rebels* in May, *The Seekers* in November, and then we did three more projects for 1980. They're all four hours. The first one is "Top of the Hill," an original written by Irwin Shaw for OPT that would be produced by Paramount. From that a book was developed, and Irwin Shaw came out with a hardcover just this month and it's set to come out in January and February. The project for May is to Columbia with Harold Robbins' *The Dream Merchants*, and that's four hours. Then we have a four-hour book, a John McDonald book, *Condominium*, which will be in November, 1980.

One of the limiting factors of all this is that while the independents can take a lot of this, the affiliates are limited to how much they can preempt. When they preempt they're clearing a lot of CBS and NBC stations, and the networks get kind of upset. They are not going to preempt probably more than one of these a quarter, because otherwise they are going to have trouble holding their affiliation, and realistically, that's one of the reasons why people term this "the fourth network." But you can't have the fourth network because you have to have some affiliates with the independent stations. So we decided we would try to come up with another thing called "the next step." "The next step" is six projects for 1980 in what we call the dual form — that means two-hour specials. The specials will be available in a two-hour block, done vertically in prime time by the independents, or five half-hours horizontally in access time for the affiliated stations. So they won't have to preempt the network. For the first time it marries the need of prime time, the greatest need for the independents, and the access area, which is the greatest need for the affiliates.

Another thing, we wanted the six projects to be potential series, because each one of them you're looking at as a pilot. If they do well they might go on as a two-week basis in the future. OPT has been made into a nonprofit legal entity; its sole purpose is to try to keep this thing going and basically produce different programming. Tele-Rep, which I head up, is actually the contracting agent because, basically, right now, we do the work. In the beginning I contributed all of the advertising, promotional sales brochures and all that — I guess it ran us $150,000 or more per year for a couple of years to make it go.

*Was it hard for independent stations to come up with the bucks, and how long did it take to raise the money?*
What we did, we had to design it to resemble syndication. The network puts a third up when they commission a thing, a third up when

they get the final script and the final third when they get the actual program. We didn't have that kind of money – no cash whatsoever – to work with. In syndication there are arrangements that are payments over a twelve or twenty-four-month period. So what I did was call the stations, and I said, "Will you give your commitment to me so I can take your commitment to a studio?" So I took all the commitments and brought them to a studio. The studio signed a residual contract with each of the stations on the basis of the commitments to me, and the contract was set up so the station had six runs over a four-year period and they're actually paying for it on twelve equal monthly installments. We set up all the payment schedules and we do all the coordination of the publicity, etc., even arrange for the stars to use the station and everything else.

*How did you decide how much each station contributed?*

In syndication, 85 percent of your money comes from the top fifty markets, so you have to have your weight there, and you have an even heavier weight in the top ten markets. The rule, basically, was historical performance in the syndication business in the past – what did they actually pay for a product before? A breakdown – taking them all, averaging them together, going out in the marketplace and seeing if it was right.

*What type of information did the stations have on the different shows? Were they concerned about input?*

Well, the input was through the steering committee. The steering committee was a seven-man committee. Gaylor had seven stations; Taft had six; some had five stations; I represent twenty-two stations. Obviously, you can't do it with ninety-five or 100 stations, having each one vote on it. It's almost too difficult to do with a seven-man steering committee, because we are reading scripts all the time and I have my couch just filled with submissions and scripts and all kinds of things. What we usually do is to fly into the Chicago airport, or someplace like that, and we meet right at the airport and then fly back. If we need to do something that's visual and we need to have people there in person, we have usually, weekly, a telephone conference to discuss all outstanding matters and we just connect everybody and discuss what's up. If they've read the scripts or whatever it is then we can vote on them.

*Did the word "bastard" in the John Jakes title throw anybody?*

We had a hard time, I must say, on "The Bastard." I suggested Jakes's series because I thought it was a good one and I thought "The Bastard" was an attention-getter if we needed one. There were eight stations who did not want to run "The Bastard." We issued it under both ways – you could run it as "Kent Family Chronicles" or you could run it as "The Bastard." Only eight stations elected to use "The Kent Family Chronicles."

*It seems that there's been an emphasis on spectacular programs based on literary work by bestselling authors. That was a conscious decision, wasn't it?*

Oh, yes, very definitely, we purposely selected bestselling authors, bestselling novels, because we thought that would give us the best attention. We also insisted, if you look at our shows, that about twelve people be known stars. They may have been older stars, but they were people who were very recognizable and promotable. We thought this formula would help them to get attention. We've gone from that to the things we're doing in 1980, which are not bestsellers. It's going to be curious to see how they work.

*How supportive were the authors — Caldwell and Fast and all those people?*

Taylor Caldwell at the beginning did not express an opinion. John Jakes was very supportive. He came out to the set and was willing to do anything necessary. He played a bit part as a secret agent (he's the guy that gets stabbed accidentally by George Hamilton), and so he was very helpful — even did promotional clips and everything else. Howard Fast was actually not very complimentary; in fact, he said he thought it was terrible. They quoted him in *TV Guide* just the week before and, of course, the *TV Guide* said if he was willing to sell the rights, he shouldn't complain. Irwin Shaw was not happy because they screwed up his *Rich Man, Poor Man* in the reruns, but he wasn't so unhappy that he wouldn't write a script for us and issue a new book on the basis of that. It's almost axiomatic that once you put them on the air as we did, they pop up on the bestseller list. But the only one that I would say really cooperated intensely was Jakes.

*Do you have any ideas about working with authors or contracts, or anything that you would do differently?*

No, the only thing that I've learned now is that I think the best idea, when you go from a book to a script, would be to have a treatment, have script approval and cast approval in these things and a final approval of what goes on the air. Have a show with everything laid out so you know what's going to happen in every scene ahead of time, and even go into the details of the dialogue. Otherwise, you get the whole thing structured to the dialogue and it really isn't the story told in the way you want to tell it. I think, for instance, "The Rebels" didn't lay out well and I didn't think that was a good TV structure. We did have a step outline in "The Bastard"; in "The Rebels," we didn't and they changed the book enormously. "The Seekers" is very close to the book. If you take those three books you can see, if you watched the shows, that "The Bastard" was very faithful to the book and I think it was very well executed. "The Rebels" really was distorted and I don't think came out well.

*But you don't always have to stick terribly closely to the book?*
I think you can modify. I only say you should step out of line to see how you are changing it and see if the result you are trying to accomplish is going to be satisfactory when you see it in the total.

*Do you actually sell time to national advertisers, and what were the big obstacles? What were their objections? Were they afraid of the networks?*
What happened on the first one, we sold the first time to General Foods and Bristol-Myers and there were a lot more that would have bought it. The only thing is that the demand was so great, strangely enough, and there was also such a demand by local advertisers that most stations felt that they could make more money selling it individually rather than selling it on a network basis. As a result, we have never sold another one in that particular fashion. That doesn't mean it couldn't be done. I would think, though, that in the future what we will experiment with is along the lines of Mobil. Mobil has done this with "Edward the King" — in fact, we turned that one down. They take a show and they fully sponsor it. Mobil has it in about forty-six of the top fifty markets, and they actually buy the time and put it on the station as a fully sponsored network. The only thing is, the economics of that are a little bit different. It's hard to come out with the kind of budget that we use to do that. They're paying more like $100,000 to $150,000 per program on something like that. We figured that we could maybe go up to $300 and some thousand on a fully sponsored basis. That doesn't say we can't go further, but to get an easily sponsored program you could do that. We're spending, as you know, some $500,000 to $1,000,000 per program, so we're going to have to figure out a different way to do that if we proceed and try to marry the sponsor with an up-front, but we would certainly try to explore that in the future.

*Was there ever a time when maybe you thought OPT was a lot to pull off — maybe too much to pull off?*
Every day. Let me put it this way. I think more than anything else it's a matter of sheer determination. The only reason it worked is that we just were very determined to make it happen. Having started it, I wanted to finish it, and if we failed we would fail gloriously. It was an idea that was good and would only be executed by putting in abnormal effort. I think that is true any time you try to change an existing structure. It takes enormous input — no great financial reward.

*Have you had any network execs whispering to you in a bar, "You're causing us trouble!"*
No. Nobody ever talked to me. I know they put pressure on the stations not to clear it, but beyond that, nobody came around and said, "Don't do this," or "Don't do that." I think at first they didn't think we

would succeed. Then we got on the air with "The Bastard," and we were heads up against "The Dain Curse," which was CBS's first venture into the novels for television, and we beat them. After that I think they knew we were there, and I think they're concerned about keeping the thing under control. The only thing I can say at this point is that I certainly don't have the time to be upset by the network, that's for sure, and, realistically, we can't clear that much time on the affiliate stations. If we do go to dual forms, we're in an access and we're not hurting. So I think there's a reasonable balance. I think there is certainly a need for three or four of these a year, and we will continue to do some form or another in the future. We are getting many better submissions than we got in the beginning.

*In what format did you distribute the programs?*
　　We started as an hour format or building blocks giving us two hours. Universal — I have to compliment them as pioneers for having the guts to do it. They had to send out about ninety-five prints — usually they bicycle these things around — but it cost them, you know, a couple of hundred thousand bucks, I am sure, to get it to the stations on time when we first went on the air, and that's not easy. Now, of course, we're working with much more time and we know what we're doing, but at that time it was not easy. In fact, it was so tied up that David Birney, who started it, was running from one set to another and if he caught cold, we would have never made the date. We have always done them in two-hour segments — that's been the easiest way to work, we feel, from the scheduling point of view. We've also charged the stations to do them on consecutive days rather than from week to week. It doesn't matter — some will run them on Monday of this week and Monday of next week and it still comes out all right, so there's no real absolute rule on how to run them. We've asked the independents to double-expose them, to give them the additional reach. They had six runs and we said, "Why don't you double-run it at different kinds of time in the same week? That way, if you run it prime time one night and somebody is not home that night, you run it maybe late night or on a different night or maybe on a weekend and a guy has an opportunity to catch it." And that's worked very well.

*That's basically what independents tend to do, anyway, isn't it?*
　　They do it, but they haven't done it in quite this format, you know, a prime time kind of thing. They have done it in some of their movies. It's certainly something that's not foreign to an independent.

*What was the most difficult OPT production to date, and why?*
　　I would say the first one was obviously the hardest because we were trying to convince everybody to do a new idea. Once it works it's amazing how quickly people jump on the bandwagon. The hardest thing

was to get them to do it in the first place, and the next hard thing was to convince them to do the dual form, which again is changing the ground rule. Once you convince somebody it works a certain way and you keep doing it that way, it's no problem. Another thing that was hard was to break away from where everything was handled by one studio and to have to deal with a multiplicity of studios.

*What was Hollywood's first view of this? They are used to working with the networks.*
     I don't think anybody understood what we were talking about. For a long time I don't even think they understood what "spot" is and how you can get it on stations. And, quite honestly, I think you probably know more than a lot of people at this point of how it occurred and what it means. There are people who think we have a whole building full of people here and they keep sending stuff in and say, "Will you please bring this before your organization?" or, "Why don't you have your production department take a look at this?" There really isn't anybody here. We don't have all those things. I think people who think in terms of network, think in terms of another structure like a network, and they think these stations are our affiliates and they're really not. They're just a loose assortment of stations that we line up. Now, I would say that about 85 percent of the stations you have stay with you, but there is still some turnover from year to year and you get different stations in the mix.

*Have you got any gray hairs to show for this?*
     (Laughs) I lost my hair. Let me put it this way—it's been a fun experience. I like to do things that are different. I consider the challenge and excitement of accomplishment probably more than the money. It's a lot of work. It absorbs an enormous amount of time and I had to do it in my spare time, but I think there is a good feeling of accomplishment. I guess the thing that worries you most, as it grows, is, can you stay with it and spend enough time to guide it properly, or will it get out of control?

# Index

Names of interview subjects and the pages
on which their interviews appear are in
boldface.

## A

The Admiral Broadway Revue 2, 4, 7,
8, 12
"The Adventures of Martin Eden" 118
"Air Power" 101
"The Aldrich Family" 212
Alexander, Jane 268
Alice in Wonderland 44
"All in the Family" 14, 272
"All My Children" 181, 183, 265
"All-Star Review" 220
Allen, Fred 10, 213, 217, 220, 228
Allen, Robert 235
**Allen, Steve 220, 223–236**
Allen, Woody 42, 45, 219
"A.M. America" 264
Amin, Idi 135
"Animal World" 137
animated characters 38–39
"Another World" 183
Anthony, Susan B. 224
"Appointment with Destiny" 121
Aristotle 90, 224, 228, 233
Arledge, Roone 254, 259
Around the World in 80 Days 219
"As the World Turns" 181, 183
Asner, Ed 277, 280
Augustine, Saint 224

## B

"Babies C.O.D." 152
"The Baby Makers" 152
Bacall, Lauren 19

Ball, Lucille 11
"Baretta" 164
Barker, Bob 63
"Barney Miller" 32
Barris, Chuck 228
Barzini, Luigi 111
"The Bastard" 294, 296, 297, 299
"Bat Masterson" 18, 22
"The Battle of East St. Louis" 106
"A Bear for Punishment" 41
"Beat the Clock" 72
Beethoven, Ludwig van 233
Benchley, Robert 42
Benjamin, Bud 108
Bennett, Harve 274, 284
Benny, Jack 210, 212
Bergen, Edgar 196
Berger, Buzz 270
Berle, Milton 3, 11, 216
"Best Sellers" 287
"The Big Show" 228
Billboard magazine 14, 206
"A Biography of a Bookie Joint" 143,
149
Birney, David 299
Bishop, Benny 282
Bixby, Bill 286
Blake, Amanda 29
Blakely, Susan 276
"The Blue Knight" 274
Boetticher, Bud 167
Bogart, Humphrey 19, 220
"The Bold Ones" 167
Boone, Richard 32
Boyle, Kay 187
"Branded" 61
"Breakfast at Sardi's" 205

301

Brian, Paul 168
Bridges, Lloyd 20
broadcasting, early color 41
"Broadway After Dark" 215
Brodkin, Herb 270
Bronson, Sam 118
Brooks, Mel 2, 5, 219
Brown Derby Restaurant 163
"The Buffalo Bill Show" 95
Bugs Bunny 39, 43
Burnett, Carol 11, 14
Burr, David 254
**Burrud, Bill 130–140**
"Bus Stop" 164, 165
"The Business of Heroin" 149
Buttons, Red 11
Byner, John 234

# C

Caesar, Sid 2, 9, 11, 219
Caldwell, Taylor 297
"Call This Nation Israel" 136
"Calling All Cars" 218
Campanella, Joe 247
Cantinflas 219
Cantor, Eddie 213
"Captain Dobsie" 204
"Captains and the Kings" 164
"Captains Courageous" 130
"Card Sharks" 69
Carey, Josey 51, 52
Carr, Vicki 247
Carson, Jack 220
Carson, Rachel 158
Carsy, Marcie 271
Carter, Jack 234
cartoonists 40
"CBS Reports" 120
Champion, Marge and Gower 2
Chancellor, John 208
Chapin, Don 293
Chaplin, Charles 5, 42, 43
character animation 39, 40
Charles, Prince of Wales 97
"Charlie's Angels" 287
chase scenes 21
"Chemicals in Our Food" 158
"Children's Corner" 51, 52
"The Cisco Kid" 18, 19, 20
"City of Angels" 164

Clarke, Bobby 213
Clemens, Bobby 146
"Close-Up" 252, 254, 257, 260
Coca, Imogene 2, 5, 9, 11, 13
Coe, Fred 219
Cohen, Dr. Sidney 227
Coleman, Ronald 19
"The Colgate Comedy Hour" 213, 214, 215
Collins, Gary 267
Collyer, Bud 63
Columbia Pictures 163
"Columbo" 275
"The Comedy Hour" 220
Como, Perry 262
"Condominium" 295
Conrad, Bill 25
"The Contender" 285, 287
"Conversations" 108
Conway, Tim 234
Cook, Fielder 199
Coombs, Ernie 51
Cooper, Shelly 291, 293
Coppola, Francis Ford 119
Corby, Ellen 197
Cordtz, Dan 258
Cosby, Bill 230
Costello, Frank 148
Costigan, James 268
Cousins, Norman 223
Cousteau, Jacques 90, 122, 127
"Cover Story" 83, 85
Cowan, Lou 66
Cramer, Arthur 163
Crawford, Broderick 20
"The Cricket in Times Square" 41
Crosby, Bing 236
Crosby, John 9
"Crucifixion of Jesus" 121
Cullen, Bill 63
Curtiss, Ken 26

# D

Daffy Duck 42
"The Dain Curse" 297
"Dallas" 287
Daly, John 63
Dana, Bill 221
Daniel Tiger 52
Dann, Mike 120

"The Dave Garroway Show" 215
Davis, Peter 106
Davis, Sammy, Jr. 232
Dawson, Richard 63
"A Day in the Life of the United States" 112
"Death Valley Days" 26, 28, 32, 33
DeLuise, Dom 97
Devane, Bill 270
Dexter, Ron 243
Diana, Lady 97
Diller, Barney 274
"Dillinger" 121
Dillon, Matt 25
The Disney Channel 91
"The District Attorney" 155
"Dolphin" 90, 91 (documentary)
Dombrow, Walter 81
"Don McNeill and the Breakfast Club" 204
Douglass, Frederick 224
Downs, Hugh 207, 215
"Dragnet" 218
*Drama at Innish* 186
Drasnin, Irv 109, 110
"The Dream Merchants" 295
Dunninger 214
Durante, Jimmy 220

"FBI" 292
Federal Communications Act 65
Ferrer, Jose 247, 248
Ferrer, Mel 220
"Fibber McGee and Molly" 212
film 84
film editing 79, 80
"Fire" 253
flash act 6
Fleming, Jim 207
"Flip Wilson" 193
Fonda, Henry 220, 228
Fonda, Jane 119
The Fonz 265
Ford, Glenn 118
*Foreign Correspondent* 38
Forsythe, John 138
Fosselius, Ernie 88, 89
Fox, Freddie 3
Fraker, Bill 248
Francis, Arlene 215
Frank, Rich 293
Franklin, Ben 233
"The Fred Allen Show" 217
Freud, Sigmund 228
Friedland, Lou 292
Friendly, Fred 143, 144, 149
"The Fugitive" 21, 165

# E

Eastwood, Clint 119
"Edward the King" 134, 298
8mm film, used in documentary 144
"Ein, Zwei, Drei" 52
Einstein, Albert 228
"Eleanor and Franklin: The White House Years" 268
"Ellery Queen" 277
Epstein, Jon 274–288
"Evening in Byzantium" 294
"Everybody's Fancy" 57
Explorer's Club 127

# F

"Family Feud" 63, 68
Fast, Howard 297
"Father Knows Best" 194

# G

"The Gabby Hayes Show" 49
Gable, Clark 126
Gallup, Dr. George 221
Garner, James 166, 167, 176, 177, 178
Garrett, George 227
Garroway, Dave 207, 208
Geer, Will 196, 197
Gelbart, Larry 219
"General Hospital" 265
Gentry, Steve 271
Gleason, Jackie 213
Gleason, Michael 278, 284
Gobel, George 33, 212
Godfrey, Arthur 212
"The Goldbergs" 212
"The Golden Age of Television" 183
Goldenson, Leonard 272
"Good Morning America" 264, 265
Goodson, Mark 61–73
*Gone with the Wind* 206, 209

Gordon, Herb 20
Green, Shecky 230
Greene, David 277, 278
Greene, Lorne 138
Greenfield, Noah 78
Grierson, John 121
Group W Productions 267
"Guiding Light" 183
Guinness, Sir Alec 38
"Gunsmoke" 24, 25, 26, 32, 34, 35
"The Guns of Autumn" 109
Gwenn, Edmund 38

H

Haley, Alex 122, 123, 124
Hamilton, George 297
Hamner, Earl, Jr. 192–202
"Happy Days" 265, 291
Harback, Bill 221
Hardware Wars 88, 89
Harrington, Pat, Jr. 234
Harris, Jim 119
Harris, Ken 39, 41, 43
Harrison, Rex 8
Hartmann, David 264
"Have Gun Will Travel" 24, 26, 32
Hayes, Bill 113
Hayes, Douglas 167
Hell on Ice 130
Heine, Sonia 40
Hentoff, Nat 223
Hepburn, Audrey 220
Herblock 40
Hermann, Edward 268
"The Hickenlopers" 11
"Highway Patrol" 20, 21, 22
Hill, Pamela 250–260
Hite, Kathleen 200
"The Hit Parade" 50
Hitler 121
Hoffa, Jimmy 147
"Hoffa and the Teamsters" 143, 144
Hoffer, Eric 108
"Hogan's Heroes" 133
"Hollywood Showcase" 31
"Hollywood – The Golden Years" 125
"Home" 215
Home Box Office 218
"The Homecoming" 196, 199, 202
"Hopalong Cassidy" 24, 25, 35

Hope, Bob 212, 213
Horvath, Imre 75–86
"Hour Magazine" 267
"How the Grinch Stole Christmas" 41, 42
"How to Think" 235
"Huckleberry Finn" 34
Huggins, Roy 162–178
Hume, David 224

I

"I Led Three Lives" 21
"The Immigrants" 294
"The Incredible Machine" 127
International Theatre 13
"The Iranian Factor" 258
"The Italians" 111

J

Jack London 118
Jakes, John 294, 295, 296, 297
James, John Thomas (Roy Huggins) 175
Jones, Chuck 38–47
Jones, Hardy 90, 91

K

Kaël, Pauline 41
Kaiser, Henry 177
Kallen, Lucille 5, 14
Kanab, Utah 34
"The Kate Smith Hour" 50, 61
Kaye, Danny 2, 7, 10
Keaton, Buster 42, 43
Keith-Ablee Circuit 181
Kennedy, John F. 146
Kennedy, Robert 144, 146
"Kent Family Chronicles" 296
Keyes, Evelyn 118
Kiley, Richard 227
Kilgallen, Dorothy 71
Klinger, David 104
Knotts, Don 221, 234
Koestler, Arthur 226
"Kojak" 275
Kovacs, Ernie 234

"Kraft Suspense Theatre" 165, 174, 177
Krause, Alvina 186

## L

Ladd, Alan, Jr. 89
"Laugh-In" 234
Laughton, Charles 223
Laurel and Hardy 43
"Laverne and Shirley" 291, 293
Lawrence, Gertrude 8
Lawsuits 83
"The Lawyers" 167
Lear, Norman 166, 213, 219, 279
Learned, Michael 193, 196, 199
Lee, Peggy 233
Leonard, Bill 105, 110
Leonardo da Vinci 233
Lescouli, Jack 207
**Levy, Len 238-248**
Lewis, Jerry 11
**Liebman, Max 2-15**
"Life of Riley" 212
Lilly, Dr. John 90
Lincoln, Abraham 41, 235
*Little Ladies of the Night* 184
Locke, John 224
Loew Circuit 6
"Lou Grant" 123
Lowe, Herbert 40
Lucas, George 88, 89, 93
Lucasfilm 89
Lucci, Susan 181

## M

McAndrew, Bill 207
McCarthy, Charlie 214
MacDonnell, Norman 25
McFarland, Dr. Margaret 58
McLaughlin, Victor 130
**McMullen, Jay 143-160**
MacMurray, Fred 19
MacNeil, Colonel 104
"Magnificent Brute" 130
Mahoney, Jerry 214
Maimonides 224
"The Making of the President" 122, 128
"The Manions" 190

Marceau, Marcel 40
Marcello, Carlos 148, 149
Martenson, Leslie 167
Martin, Dick 234
Martin, Mary 220
Martin, Quinn 21
Martin, Steve 95
Martin and Lewis 213
Marx, Groucho 31
"The Mary Tyler Moore Show" 14, 277
**Masini, Al 290-300**
"Matinee" 215
"Maverick" 162, 165, 166, 167, 171, 176, 177, 178
"Max Liebman Presents" 4
"Meet the Press" 64
"Meeting of Minds" 223, 228, 235
Mendelssohn, Felix 233
Menjou, Adolph 19
Meredith, Burgess 8
Merrill, Robert 8
"The Merrymakers" 217
"The Merv Griffin Show" 267
Meston, John 25
Mickelson, Sig 101
Mickey Mouse 39, 43
"The Mike Douglas Show" 267
"The Milton Berle Show" 3, 210
Minor, Tony 219
*Miracle on 34th Street* 38
"Missiles of October" 270
"Mr. Dress-Up" 52
"Mister Rogers' Neighborhood" 51
"Mod Squad" 193
Montacalbo, Susan 254
Moore, Gary 63
Moore, Mary Tyler 119
Moore, Tom 127
"Mork and Mindy" 271
Morris, Howard 9, 11
The Movie Channel 94, 95, 99
Muggs, J. Fred 209, 210
Murrow, Edward R. 111, 160
The Murrow Is Not God Club 160
"My Mother the Car" 69

## N

*National Enquirer* 82
National Geographic 120, 122, 127

National Rifle Association  122
Natwick, Grim  39
Neal, Patricia  196
*The New York Times*  104, 121
Newell, David  54
Newhart, Bob  230
"Nichols"  177, 178
"1986"  110
**Nixon, Agnes  180–190**
Nixon, Richard  103, 110
Nolte, Nick  276
Nye, Louis  221, 234

# O

Oates, Joyce Carol  187
O'Connor, Donald  213
O'Hara, Betty  29
Oldenberg, Claës  40
Olivier, Sir Laurence  38
Olson, Johnny  64
"One Life to Live"  183
"The Open Road"  131

# P

Paar, Jack  71, 213
Paige, Raymond  217
Paine, Thomas  233
parlor games  71
"Password"  62, 65, 68
*Pennies from Heaven*  95
Perkins, Marlin  137
Perlmutter, Al  83, 85
"Perry Mason"  14
Peterson, Rod  197
Phillips, Irna  183
Phillips Petroleum  20
Piazza, Marguerite  13
Plato  224
"Playhouse 90"  27, 211
"The Plot to Murder Hitler"  121
"The Police Tapes"  254, 255, 256
Poston, Tom  221
Power, Tyrone  19
Preminger, Otto  219
Price, Frank  279
"The Price Is Right"  63, 67, 69
"Primal Man"  121
"Producers' Showcase"  210, 219

"The Profane Comedy"  170
programming, early telelvision  2
"Project Nassau"  105
*Psychology Today*  78
Pyramid Films  88

# Q

"The Quiz Kids"  66

# R

Rainbow Broadcasting  83
Rainsberry, Fred  51
"Rat Patrol"  282
Rather, Dan  78
Rayburn, Gene  231, 232
Raymond, Alan  255
Raymond, Susan  255
Reagan, Ronald  33, 79
"Real People"  234
"The Rebel"  61
"The Rebels"  295, 297
Reiner, Carl  9, 219
Reisner, Dean  278
"The Remembrance"  200
Reynolds, Burt  26
Rice, Crawford  293
Rich, Lee  120, 199
"Rich Man, Poor Man"  274, 275, 277,
   283, 284, 285, 287, 288, 291, 292,
   297
"Richard Boone Repertory Theatre"
   61
Richter, Dick  254
Rickles, Don  230
"Rikki Tikki Tavi"  44
The Roadrunner  43
Robbins, Harold  295
Robbins, Jerome  2, 7, 219
"Rockford Files"  164, 166, 172, 177, 178
*Rocky*  164
**Rogers, Fred  49–59**
Roosevelt, Eleanor  268
Roosevelt, Franklin  268
"Roots"  120, 122, 123, 275
Rosenberg, Meta  177, 178
Rowan, Dan  234
"Run for Your Life"  168, 174
Russell, Bertrand  205

## S

Safer, Morley 78
Sagal, Boris 278
Salant, Dick 104, 108, 110
Sanner dolly 12
Santana, Dr. Vincent 185
Sarette, Lou 186
Sarnoff, Bobby 215
Sarnoff, General David 215
"Saturday Night Revue" 220
*Saturday Review* 223
Schlatter, George 234
Schlosser, Herb 167
Schwartz, Bill 293
"Scruples" 287
"Sea Hunt" 17, 20, 21, 22
"The Seekers" 295, 297
Sellers, Peter 38
"The Selling of the F-14" 156
"The Selling of the Pentagon" 104, 105
Serling, Rod 247, 248
Sevareid, Eric 108
"'70s:American Dream – American Nightmare 103, 106
Shakespeare, William 233
Shanks, Bob 264
Shaw, Irwin 283, 284, 294, 297
Sheen, Martin 270
Sherman, Alan 72
"The Shooting of Big Man" 254
"The Sid Caesar Show" 219
"The Silent Spring of Rachel Carson" 158
Silverman, Fred 192, 218, 263, 264, 284
Silvers, Phil 213
Simmons, Ed 213, 219
Simon, Doc 219
Simon, Neil 2, 5
"Six Million Dollar Man" 292
"60 Minutes" 75, 81, 82, 112, 135
"The $64,000 Question" 65, 66
Skelton, Red 11, 214
"Smile Time" 232
Smith, Bill 277
Smith, Kate 219
"Soap" 272
Socrates 224
*Somewhere a Child Is Crying* 185
"Spectaculars" 4

"The Spirit" 200
Sponsors: Adorn Hairspray 245; American Express 134; American Tobacco 210, 217; AT&T 219; Bigelow Carpets 214; Colgate 213; early television 20; Ford Motors 210; General Foods 210; General Motors 213; Hallmark 212; Kal-Kan 134; Lavoris 245; Lever Brothers 212; Lipton Tea 212; Mobil 134; Nucoa Margarine 132; Oldsmobile 211; Procter & Gamble 20, 133, 183; RCA 211; Schlitz 240, 241, 245, 246; Sunkist 247; United Airlines 242; U.S. Borax 26; Winchell's 247
**Stabler, Bob 24–36**
Staggers, Harley 105
Stallone Sylvester 164
Stanton, Frank 105
"Star Trek" 14
*Star Wars* 88, 89
Steinberg, Sid 293
"The Steve Allen Show" 224
Stewart, Paul 248
Stoddard, Brandon 275
"Stop the Music" 66
"Strange Bedfellows" 235
Strauss, Peter 276, 277, 284
*Straw Hat Revue* 8
Strong, Dwight 144
Studio 54 182
Sullivan, Ed 177
Susskind, David 268
"Survival" 138

## T

"The Talent Scouts" 212
Tamiment 2, 7, 8, 10
Taylor, Davidson 207
Taylor, Ron 242
television, golden age of 11; production time of shows 17; rates 21
"Television Playhouse" 24
Temple, Shirley 130
"The Tenement" 150
"Terror in the Promised Land" 258
"Testimony of Two Men" 294
"Texaco Star Theatre" 216
"They Killed President Lincoln" 121

"This Could Be the Start of Something Big" 226
Thomas, Danny 220
Thomas Aquinas, Saint 224
Thompson, Evan 293
"Three's Company" 293
*The Throwaway Children* 185
Tinker, Grant 119
"To Tell the Truth" 62, 63, 65, 68, 69
"The Today Show" 204, 206, 207, 208, 209, 214, 215, 216, 220, 264
Todd, Mike 213
Todman, Bill 66
Tolken, Mel 5, 14, 219
"Tombstone Territory" 18
"The Tonight Show" 206, 207, 214, 215, 216, 220, 230, 231, 232
"The Toyota Invasion" 157
"Trials of O'Brien" 282
Twain, Mark 45
20th Century–Fox 89
"21" 65

# U

"The Undersea World of Jacques Cousteau" 127
United States Air Force 101
"Upstairs, Downstairs" 195

# V

Vane, Edwin T. 262–272
"Vanished" 274
vaudeville, on TV 9; definition of 10
Vestron Video 98
"Victory at NBC" (Victory at Sea) 101
Vietnam 112

# W

Wald, Dick 254
Walker, Nancy 11
Wallace, Mike 78
The Waltons 192, 193, 194, 195, 196, 198, 202
Warhol, Andy 40
Warner Bros. 163, 173, 177, 213
Warner Home Video 89

Warren, Charles Marquis 26
"Washington Behind Closed Doors" 287
Wasserman, Al 143
Watergate 103, 106, 112
Wayne, John 130
Weaver, Dennis 26
Weaver, (Sylvester) Pat 12, 21, 204–221
Webb, Jack 218
"West Point" 18
"What on Earth" 84
"What's Going On?" 71
"What's My Line?" 61, 62, 63, 65, 72
"What's Opera, Doc" 39, 41
Whitaker, Claire 197
White, Theodore H. 128
"White Paper" 252
"Who Killed Michael Farmer?" 160
"Wide, Wide World" 215, 218, 219
Wiese, Michael 88–99
"Wild Kingdom" 137, 138, 140
"Wildlife Adventure" 137
William Morris Agency 25
Williams, Palmer 146
Williams, Robin 271
Winchell, Paul 214
Winchell, Walter 71
"Winner Take All" 61
Winters, Jonathan 212
"Wisdom" 205
Withers, Jane 130
Wolff, Perry 101–115
Wolper, David 117–128
"The Wonderful World of Disney" 133
Wood, Gene 64
Wynn, Ed 39, 220

# Y

"You Bet Your Life" 31
Young and Rubicam (Y & R) 210, 214, 216, 221
"Your Show of Shows" 4, 5, 7, 8, 211, 219, 220

# Z

Ziv, Frederick W. 17–22